NORTH ATLANTIC COAST FISHERIES ARBITRATION AT THE HAGUE

ARGUMENT ON BEHALF OF THE UNITED STATES

BY

ELIHU ROOT

EDITED BY

ROBERT BACON

AND

JAMES BROWN SCOTT

CAMBRIDGE
HARVARD UNIVERSITY PRESS
LONDON: HUMPHREY MILFORD
OXFORD UNIVERSITY PRESS
1917

CONTENTS

INTRODUCTORY NOTE

The collected addresses and state papers of Elihu Root, of which this is one of several volumes, cover the period of his service as Secretary of War, as Secretary of State, and as Senator of the United States, during which time, to use his own expression, his only client was his country.

The many formal and occasional addresses and speeches, which will be found to be of a remarkably wide range, are followed by his state papers, such as the instructions to the American delegates to the Second Hague Peace Conference and other diplomatic notes and documents, prepared by him as Secretary of State in the performance of his duties as an executive officer of the United States. Although the official documents have been kept separate from the other papers, this plan has been slightly modified in the volume devoted to the military and colonial policy of the United States, which includes those portions of his official reports as Secretary of War throwing light upon his public addresses and his general military policy.

The addresses and speeches selected for publication are not arranged chronologically, but are classified in such a way that each volume contains addresses and speeches relating to a general subject and a common purpose. The addresses as president of the American Society of International Law show his treatment of international questions from the theoretical standpoint, and in the light of his experience as Secretary of War and as Secretary of State, unrestrained and uncontrolled by the limitations of official position, whereas his addresses on foreign affairs, delivered while Secretary of State or as United States Senator, discuss these questions under the reserve of official responsibility.

Mr. Root's addresses on government, citizenship, and legal procedure are a masterly exposition of the principles of the Constitution and of the government established by it; of the duty of the citizen to understand the Constitution and to conform his conduct to its requirements; and of the right of the people to reform or to amend the Constitution in order to make representative government more effective and responsive to their present and future needs. The addresses on law and its administration state how legal procedure should be modified and simplified in the interest of justice rather than in the supposed interest of the legal profession.

The addresses delivered during the trip to South America and Mexico in 1906, and in the United States after his return, with their message of good will, proclaim a new doctrine — the Root doctrine — of kindly consideration and of honorable obligation, and make clear the destiny common to the peoples of the Western World.

The addresses and the reports on military and colonial policy made by Mr. Root as Secretary of War explain the reorganization of the army after the Spanish-American War, the creation of the General Staff, and the establishment of the Army War College. They trace the origin of and give the reason for the policy of this country in Cuba, the Philippines, and Porto Rico, devised and inaugurated by him. It is not generally known that the so-called Platt Amendment, defining our relations to Cuba, was drafted by Mr. Root, and that the Organic Act of the Philippines was likewise the work of Mr. Root as Secretary of War.

The argument before The Hague Tribunal in the North Atlantic Fisheries Case is a rare if not the only instance of a statesman appearing as chief counsel in an international arbitration, which, as Secretary of State, he had prepared and submitted.

The miscellaneous addresses, including educational, historical, and commemorative addresses, the political speeches in days of peace, and the stirring and prophetic utterances in anticipation of and during our war with Germany, delivered at home and on special mission in Russia, should make known to future generations the literary, artistic, and emotional side of this broad-minded and far-seeing statesman of our time.

The publication of these collected addresses and state papers will, it is believed, enable the American people better to understand the generation in which Mr. Root has been a commanding figure, and better to appreciate during his lifetime the services which he has rendered to his country.

Robert Bacon.
James Brown Scott.

September 16, 1917.

THE NORTH ATLANTIC COAST FISHERIES ARBITRATION

FOREWORD

On the 4th day of July, 1776, the British colonies of North America, with the exception of Canada and Newfoundland, proclaimed their independence of Great Britain under the name and title of the United States of America, and by the treaty of September 3, 1783, Great Britain recognized the independence of its former colonies as of the date of July 4, 1776. As colonists, the citizens of the new republic had fished off Canada and Newfoundland as they were minded, for they were British subjects and they claimed the rights and privileges of subjects. But when they ceased to be British subjects they naturally lost the rights of British subjects, except in so far as those rights inured to them under international law or were secured to them by treaty.

Notwithstanding the claims of Great Britain to jurisdiction beyond three miles from low water mark — claims forced upon France and Spain and accepted by them in the Treaty of Paris of February 10, 1763 — the Americans refused to consider themselves excluded from the fishing grounds beyond the three mile line recognized, as they maintained, by international law in the absence of an agreement to the contrary. They were, however, unwilling to content themselves with the extreme rights and privileges under the law of nations, as understood by them. They insisted upon the right to fish in the territorial waters to the north of them after as before the Declaration of Independence, and as the result of persistence they secured the acceptance of their contention in Article 3 of the treaty of peace in the following terms:

> It is agreed that the people of the United States shall continue to enjoy unmolested the right to take fish of every kind on the Grand Bank, and on all the other banks of Newfoundland; also in the gulph of St. Lawrence, and at all other places in the sea, where the inhabitants of both countries used at any time heretofore to fish; and also that the inhabitants of the United States shall have liberty to take fish of every kind on such part of the coast of Newfoundland as British fishermen shall use (but not to dry or cure the same on that island); and also on the coasts, bays and creeks of all other of his Britannic Majesty's dominions in America; and that the American fishermen shall have liberty to dry and cure fish in any of the unsettled bays, harbours and creeks of Nova Scotia, Magdalen islands, and Labrador, so long as the same shall remain unsettled;

> but so soon as the same or either of them shall be settled, it shall not be lawful for the said fishermen to dry or cure fish at such settlement, without a previous agreement for that purpose with the inhabitants, proprietors or possessors of the ground.[1]

It will be observed that the negotiators of this treaty obtained the recognition of their claim to continue to enjoy unmolested the right to fish in the neighborhood of British possessions to the north of them beyond the three mile limit, and that, in accordance with their conception of their rights under international law. They claimed it as a right, they called it a right, and it was conceded to them as a right. It will be observed also that they secured the liberty to take fish elsewhere in such places as British fishermen had hitherto used, which to them meant the right to fish within British jurisdiction, and which by international law might be denied them in the absence of a special agreement to that effect. Furthermore, it will not escape notice that American fishermen were not only to have liberty to take fish within the territorial waters of British North America which British fishermen had used, but that they were to have the liberty to dry and cure fish on dry land, as specified in the treaty, as long as it remained unsettled, and thereafter in accordance with agreement had and obtained from the owners and possessors of the ground.

It is proper to add before leaving the treaty of 1783 that the American negotiators, while understanding the distinction between right and liberty, thought that the word liberty was used in the sense of right, and, if John Adams is to be trusted, they were justified in so believing. For the word liberty in the second part of the treaty of 1783 was used because the British negotiators felt that it would be less objectionable than the word right might be to their fellow-countrymen. They said, John Adams informs us, "it [liberty] amounted to the same thing, for liberty was right and privilege was right; but the word *right* might be more unpleasing to the people of England than *liberty*, and we did not think it necessary to contend for a word."[1]

So matters stood at the outbreak of the War of 1812 and so they stood, according to the American view, after the conclusion of that war. The British view was opposed and irreconcilable and hence the fisheries dispute.

The Americans maintained, or at least John Quincy Adams maintained for them, that the treaty of 1783 was in the nature of a partition of empire, establishing the boundaries between Great Britain on the one hand and the United States on the other: that as the outbreak of war does not change

[1] U. S. Statutes at Large, vol. VIII, p. 80; Malloy, *Treaties, Conventions, International Acts, Protocols and Agreements between the United States of America and other Powers, 1776–1909*, vol. I, p. 588.

boundaries it would not affect the fisheries article, for this, like boundaries, could only be changed by conquest or by an agreement of the parties.

Great Britain, on the other hand, stoutly denied all of these contentions, in so far as they were meant to apply to the fisheries article, which it regarded as in the nature of a commercial grant or a concession revoked by the outbreak of war, not merely suspended in exercise during the continuance of war, and which reverted of itself with the conclusion of peace. As Lord Bathurst, speaking for the British Government, said in a note to John Quincy Adams, then American minister to Great Britain: " She [Great Britain] knows of no exception to the rule, that all treaties are put an end to by a subsequent war." [1]

These views were irreconcilable. The acceptance of one necessarily involved the rejection of the other, and the achievements of the United States in the War of 1812 were not of a kind to force the arm that had overthrown Napoleon. The question of fisheries was indeed discussed, although no agreement was reached, in the negotiations leading up to the Treaty of Ghent of December 24, 1814, which put an end to the war, and which fortunately has been unbroken for more than a hundred years. But with the return of peace the New Englanders bethought them of taking, drying and curing fish, as secured to them by the treaty of September 3, 1783. The British were minded to prevent the taking, drying and curing of fish by the New Englanders in accordance with a defunct treaty. Seizures of American vessels occurred and further seizures were likely to continue as long as American fishermen fished according to the provisions of a treaty which they believed to be in force but which the British denied to be binding. The United Kingdom, fortunately for itself but unfortunately for American fishermen, was in a position to make its contentions good.

The atmosphere was cleared, as it were, by a treaty, known as the Rush-Bagot agreement, concluded after the war, and whose observance has been, it would seem, the cause of the hundred years of peace between the two nations, a peace which not even the fisheries disputes and the Civil War succeeded in breaking. This modest document was signed at Washington, April 28, 1817, and by its terms the two countries agreed to dismantle their war vessels upon the Great Lakes, pledging themselves to keep not more than one vessel of 100 tons or under, and armed with one 18-pound cannon on Lake Ontario, two vessels of like armament upon the upper lakes, and one vessel of the same kind upon Lake Champlain, and that " all other armed vessels on these lakes shall be forthwith dismantled, and no other vessels of war shall be there built or armed." [2] The absence

[1] *American State Papers, Foreign Relations,* vol. IV, p. 354.

[2] U. S. Statutes at Large, vol. VIII, p. 231.

of armament upon the water has justified the lack of armament upon the land, and from this period the two countries have been able to discuss and to settle their disputes without the constant fear of a frontier incident. A year later an agreement was reached upon the fisheries, which, if a military term be permissible, was rather in the nature of an armistice than a treaty of peace.

The negotiators on the part of the United States were Albert Gallatin, formerly secretary of the treasury and at the time minister to France, and Richard Rush, formerly attorney-general, negotiator of the Rush-Bagot agreement, and later to be secretary of the treasury in the administration of John Quincy Adams, and who at the time was minister to Great Britain. The negotiators on the part of Great Britain were Frederick John Robinson, later prime minister as Lord Goderich, and Henry Goulburn, later chancellor of the exchequer. It is thus seen that the American negotiators were already men of great distinction and that the British negotiators were destined to become such, although at the time of the agreement they held minor posts in the Government. On October 20, 1818, the negotiators put their hands and seals to a convention, of which the first article, dealing with the fisheries, is as follows:

> Whereas differences have arisen respecting the liberty claimed by the United States, for the inhabitants thereof, to take, dry, and cure, fish, on certain coasts, bays, harbours, and creeks, of his Britannic Majesty's dominions in America, it is agreed between the high contracting parties, that the inhabitants of the said United States shall have, forever, in common with the subjects of his Britannic Majesty, the liberty to take fish of every kind on that part of the southern coast of Newfoundland, which extends from Cape Ray to the Rameau Islands, on the western and northern coast of Newdoundland, from the said Cape Ray to the Quirpon Islands, on the shores of the Magdalen Islands, and also on the coasts, bays, harbours, and creeks, from Mount Joly, on the southern coast of Labrador, to and through the Streights of Belleisle, and thence northwardly indefinitely along the coast, without prejudice, however, to any of the exclusive rights of the Hudson Bay Company: And that the American fisherman shall also have liberty, forever, to dry and cure fish in any of the unsettled bays, harbours, and creeks, of the southern part of the coast of Newfoundland, hereabove described, and of the coast of Labrador; but so soon as the same, or any portion thereof, shall be settled, it shall not be lawful for the said fishermen to dry or cure fish at such portion so settled, without previous agreement for such purpose, with the inhabitants, proprietors, or possessors, of the ground. And the United States hereby renounce, forever, any liberty heretofore enjoyed or claimed by the inhabitants thereof, to take, dry, or cure fish,

> on or within three marine miles of any of the coasts, bays, creeks, or harbours, of his Britannic Majesty's dominions in America, not included within the above mentioned limits: Provided, however, that the American fishermen shall be admitted to enter such bays or harbors, for the purpose of shelter and of repairing damages therein, of purchasing wood, and of obtaining water, and for no other purpose whatever. But they shall be under such restrictions as may be necessary to prevent their taking, drying, or curing fish therein, or in any other manner whatever abusing the privileges hereby reserved to them.[1]

It will be observed, in the first place, that the differences, to remove which the treaty was negotiated, deal not with the right as stated in the treaty of 1783, but with the exercise of the liberty, which, if John Adams is to be believed, was understood by the negotiators of the treaty of 1783 to mean the same thing. The right to fish in the high seas was unquestioned and was not referred to in the treaty as causing the differences. It will be further observed that a distinction is drawn between the territorial waters of British North America, as in certain specified regions American inhabitants are to have forever the liberty to fish within three miles of the coast, that is to say, within the territorial waters of Great Britain. In other territorial waters they are not to fish, although beyond the three miles of the coasts, bays, creeks or harbors of the specified portions they may still fish. We are here in the presence of a compromise, as American inhabitants are to be allowed to fish within some territorial waters, thus accepting part of the American contention, whereas they are excluded from other territorial waters, thus admitting part of the British contention.

It was recognized, however, that American fishermen should, under certain circumstances, be allowed to enter the bays or harbors in which they were forbidden to fish. This was a very special permission, and limited to what might be called the necessities of the case, for they were to enter only for shelter and to repair damages, to purchase wood and to obtain water. To prevent the abuse of the privilege of entering the bays or harbors, Great Britain secured the clause in the treaty, from abundance of caution, it would seem, that American fishermen entering these waters should be subjected to such restrictions as might be necessary to prevent the abuse of the privileges.

As in the treaty of 1783 so in the convention of 1818, American fishermen are to have the liberty forever of drying and curing their fish in certain unsettled bays and harbors and creeks duly specified, and to dry their

[1] U. S. Statutes at Large, vol. VIII, p. 248; Malloy, *Treaties, Conventions, International Acts, Protocols and Agreements between the United States of America and other Powers, 1776–1909*, vol. I, p. 631.

catch on certain portions of the coast which had not been settled, and if or when settled, with the consent of the inhabitants, proprietors or possessors of the ground.

There are some general observations of a non-controversial kind to be made upon the article before proceeding to a discussion of the differences of interpretation which caused much friction between the two countries, and which led to the submission of those differences to arbitration in the year 1910.

In the first place, it will not have escaped notice that in some parts of the article the word liberty is used, whereas, in the latter and concluding portion, the expression privilege is preferred. Again, it will be seen that the first part of the article in which the term liberty is used deals with the right to take fish and another part with the right to dry and cure fish in certain places, including specified portions of unsettled country; and that in the last part dealing with privileges American fishermen are permitted to enter for four specified purposes the bays and harbors in which the United States renounces the right to fish and from which American fishermen are therefore excluded.

We do not need to consider the liberty of American fishermen to dry their catch upon British territory, because this question was not submitted to arbitration. There are two matters, however, that require to be considered, as they are the source of the differences submitted to arbitration in 1910.

In the latter part of the article there is conceded to American fishermen a privilege to enter certain waters for purposes which may be termed humanitarian. In the first portion of the article American inhabitants are to have forever the fishing liberty "in common with the subjects of His Britannic Majesty," without an express reservation or statement on behalf of Great Britain to regulate the exercise of the fishing liberty; whereas, in the case of the privilege, there is a reservation or a right stated on the part of Great Britain to frame such restrictions as may be necessary to prevent the abuse of the privilege. This distinction is important, because the Americans contended that the expression "in common" meant that American inhabitants should possess the liberty "in common," in the sense that it was not to be claimed as an exclusive liberty on their part to the exclusion of British subjects, as claimed by France in regard to the liberty granted to French fishermen. In the French grant of 1783, in the treaty of even date with that of 1783 between Great Britain and the United States the word liberty is used, which the French interpreted to be a liberty excluding British subjects from fishing in the granted portions. The Americans insisted that the phrase "in common," inserted in the treaty of 1818, was therefore employed to prevent a claim on their part to exclude British competition within the waters where the Americans possess the fishing liberty, not that the words " in common " meant the subjection of American fishermen to any restrictions which Great Britain might care to impose upon its subjects in the exercise of their fishing rights, which might be wholly withdrawn from British subjects but which could not be withdrawn from American fishermen, because of the treaty. The French likewise claimed that their fishing liberty in Newfoundland waters was not subject to regulation by Great Britain or the Newfoundland authorities and French statesmen made good the claim which was contested and denied to the Americans, although the grant was in identical terms. The British contended, on the contrary, that the expression " in common " referred to the enjoyment of the liberty under such restrictions as the British Government might care to impose upon British fishermen plying their calling within British jurisdiction. The liberty of the Americans was to be equal to the right of the British, and each was to be subordinated in its exercise to territorial sovereignty.

The Americans placed great stress upon the fact that the last sentence of the treaty, relating to the privilege to enter waters in which they were forbidden to fish, stated, on behalf of Great Britain, the right to impose restrictions in a case where the right to impose them appeared to be self-evident; that the right to impose restrictions was not general in its nature but was couched in special terms; that it referred, solely and exclusively, to the privilege to enter bays and harbors from which the American fishermen were specifically excluded; that it did not refer to the liberty, from which it is grammatically as well as logically separated; and that if the exercise of the liberty was to be regulated in so far as American fishermen were concerned the British negotiators would have stated and retained the right so to do, as they did in the case of a mere privilege, if the right to regulate was to be claimed in the case of the liberty.

The second point to which attention should be called is the so-called renunciatory clause, by virtue whereof the United States gave up for its inhabitants the liberty to fish " within three miles of any of the coasts, bays, creeks or harbors of His Britannic Majesty's dominions in America not included within the above mentioned limits." It is clear that American fishermen were not to fish within three miles of the renounced region; but the point is not stated or suggested from which the three miles should be drawn. It was, however, necessary to draw the line, as, without an agreement upon the points from which and to which the line was to be drawn, disputes were inevitable between the fishermen and therefore between the contracting countries. Without arguing the matter, it has been thought advisable to mention in this connection the differences of opinion on these points.

The Americans believed, and therefore insisted upon stating, that they renounced something, which something was, in their opinion, the liberty to fish within three miles of low water mark of His Majesty's dominions in North America, as granted in Article 3 of the treaty of September 3, 1783. The British contended, on the contrary, that the Americans had nothing to renounce, because the War of 1812 had put an end to Article 3 of the treaty, and that therefore they could not very well renounce a liberty which they did not possess. As a result of prolonged discussion, the American negotiators prevailed in "renouncing" the liberty which the British contended was "non-existent."

This may seem to be a small matter, but it was regarded as a very important one by the American negotiators, because, according to their view, the treaty of 1818 was not a new grant but the recognition of an existing grant, which they retained in so far as it was not modified or renounced. According to this contention, the three miles would be measured from the point where Americans had the liberty to fish by the treaty of 1783, that is to say, three miles from low water mark on every portion of the coast, following its contour; American fishermen could enter any bay of British North America more than six miles wide at its mouth, and they could not be prevented from entering its waters whenever and wherever the bay in question was broader than six miles. Great Britain maintained, however, that the fishing liberty in its entirety was a grant of the year 1818, that it had nothing to do with a defunct liberty, and that the new grant was to be interpreted solely with reference to itself, not with reference to a preëxisting grant. To the British commissioners the renunciatory clause was meaningless.

It is not the purpose of this introduction to argue the matter, as this has been done once and for all by Mr. Root. The purpose of the present introduction is to state the differences which arose concerning the meaning and application of the convention of 1818, to describe the negotiations leading up to and resulting in the agreement to submit these differences to arbitration, to state and to analyze the terms of the submission and to explain generally the award of the tribunal of arbitration on each matter submitted to its determination.

On July 7, 1905, Mr. Root became Secretary of State, and shortly after coming to Washington to assume the duties of his office the whole question of the rights and duties of American fishermen, under the convention of 1818, was raised by the alleged seizure in British waters of an American vessel, contrary to the terms of the treaty. Although the seizure in this particular case was denied by the British Government, Mr. Root availed himself of the incident to express the views of the American Government regarding other incidents which were called to the attention of the Department of State, and he added that if Great Britain concurred in the views which he had expressed an understanding of the two Governments would be reached and the difficulties of the kind specified, and indeed of other kinds, would be prevented.

It was reported in October, 1905, that the Newfoundland Ministry of Marine and Fishery had "forbidden all vessels of American register to fish on the Treaty coast where they now are, and where they have fished unmolested since 1818." The charge contained in the quotation seems to have been without justification. Several American vessels had been ordered by the Newfoundland authorities not to fish in Bonne Bay, situated within that portion of the Newfoundland coast in which the right of American fishermen to ply their calling was recognized by the convention of 1818, and Mr. Root felt it advisable to take up the question of American rights in what may be called the treaty waters of British North America, as defined by the convention of 1818, and to reach an agreement, if possible, upon this subject. He believed that the time was propitious, because at that time a very friendly feeling existed between Great Britain and the United States, and Mr. Root's experience in the settlement of the Alaskan boundary question showed how desirable it was to settle even a small question between the two countries when they were well disposed, without allowing the question, through delay and mismanagement, to assume an importance which it did not and which it should not possess.

The views of the two Governments upon the fishing question proved to be divergent, as will be seen from two paragraphs, one from Mr. Root's note of June 30, 1906, and one from Sir Edward Grey, His Majesty's principal secretary of state for foreign affairs, dated June 20, 1907, stating the views of their respective Governments.

Thus, Mr. Root said that the United States:

> is willing and ready now, as it has always been, to join with the Government of Great Britain in agreeing upon all reasonable and suitable regulations for the due control of the fishermen of both countries in the exercise of their rights, but this Government cannot permit the exercise of these rights to be subject to the will of the Colony of Newfoundland. The Government of the United States cannot recognize the authority of Great Britain or of its Colony to determine whether American citizens shall fish on Sunday. The Government of Newfoundland cannot be permitted to make entry and clearance at a Newfoundland custom-house, and the payment of a tax for the support of Newfoundland lighthouses conditions to the exercise of the American right of fishing. If it be shown that these things are reasonable the Government of the United States will agree to them, but it cannot submit to have them imposed upon it without its consent.[1]

[1] North Atlantic Coast Fisheries. Proceedings in the North Atlantic Coast Fisheries Arbitration before the Permanent Court of Arbitration at The Hague under the provisions of the General Treaty of Arbitration of April 4, 1908, and the Special Agreement of January 27, 1909, between the United States of America and Great Britain, vol. III, part II, p. 984. (Washington, 1912.)

Sir Edward Grey said:

> The main question at issue is, however, that of the application of the Newfoundland regulations to American fishermen. In this connection the United States Government admit the justice of the view that all regulations and limitations upon the exercise of the right of fishing upon the Newfoundland Coast, which were in existence at the time of the Convention of 1818, would now be binding upon American fishermen. Although Mr. Root considers that to be the extreme view which His Majesty's Government could logically assert, and states that it is the utmost to which the United States Government could agree, His Majesty's Government feel that they cannot admit any such contention, as it would involve a complete departure from the position which they have always been advised to adopt as to the real intention and scope of the treaties upon which the American fishing rights depend. On this vital point of principle there does not seem to be any immediate prospect of agreement with United States views, and it would, therefore, seem better to endeavour to find some temporary solution of the difficulty as to the regulations under which the Americans are to fish.[1]

The result was the negotiation of a temporary agreement, called a *modus vivendi*, and the negotiation of an agreement between Great Britain and the United States to submit the fisheries question to arbitration, in order that the rights of both countries under the convention of 1818 might be impartially determined.

As a result of negotiations between Mr. Root, on the one hand, representing the United States, and Mr. Bryce, on the other, then British ambassador and representing the British Government, an agreement was reached on January 27, 1909, not only to submit certain specified questions to arbitration, but to settle any future disputes concerning fisheries that might arise between the United States and Great Britain by a method devised by Mr. Root and acceptable to both countries without a resort to arms, and without embittering the friendly relations of the two countries. It was natural, indeed it was inevitable, that the present dispute should be submitted to arbitration, because there was an existing treaty of arbitration of April 4, 1908, concluded by Messrs. Root and Bryce on behalf of their respective countries, and ratified by each, providing that " differences

[1] North Atlantic Coast Fisheries. Proceedings in the North Atlantic Coast Fisheries Arbitration before the Permanent Court of Arbitration at The Hague under the provisions of the General Treaty of Arbitration of April 4, 1908, and the Special Agreement of January 27, 1909, between the United States of America and Great Britain, vol. III, part II, p. 1005. (Washington, 1912.)

which may arise of a legal nature or relating to the interpretation of treaties existing between the two Contracting Parties and which it may not have been possible to settle by diplomacy, shall be referred to the Permanent Court of Arbitration established at The Hague by the Convention of the 29th of July, 1899."

The questions involved in the fisheries dispute were legal; they also related to the interpretation of an existing treaty between the two contracting parties, namely, the convention of October 20, 1818, and both countries had declared it to be impossible to settle them by diplomacy. There were two questions, however, that the countries did not submit, the question of the liberty to dry the catch upon specified portions of British territory, which has already been mentioned, and a further question concerning the Bay of Fundy " considered as a whole apart from its bays and creeks," and also the question of " innocent passage through the Gut of Canso." While excluding these questions from arbitration, the contracting parties stated, in respect to them, that " their respective views or contentions . . . shall be in no wise prejudiced by anything in the present arbitration." [1]

The questions actually submitted were seven in number, and they went to the root of the controversy:

> *Question 1.* To what extent are the following contentions or either of them justified?
>
> It is contended on the part of Great Britain that the exercise of the liberty to take fish referred to in the said Article, which the inhabitants of the United States have forever in common with the subjects of His Britannic Majesty, is subject, without the consent of the United States, to reasonable regulation by Great Britain, Canada, or Newfoundland in the form of municipal laws, ordinances, or rules, as, for example, to regulations in respect of (1) the hours, days, or seasons when fish may be taken on the treaty coasts; (2) the method, means, and implements to be used in the taking of fish or in the carrying on of fishing operations on such coasts; (3) any other matters of a similar character relating to fishing; such regulations being reasonable, as being, for instance —
>
> (*a*) Appropriate or necessary for the protection and preservation of such fisheries and the exercise of the rights of British subjects therein and of the liberty which by the said Article 1 the inhabitants of the United States have therein in common with British subjects;
>
> (*b*) Desirable on grounds of public order and morals;

[1] Malloy, *Treaties, Conventions, International Acts, Protocols and Agreements between the United States of America and other Powers, 1776–1909*, vol. I, p. 841.

(*c*) Equitable and fair as between local fishermen and the inhabitants of the United States exercising the said treaty liberty and not so framed as to give unfairly an advantage to the former over the latter class.

It is contended on the part of the United States that the exercise of such liberty is not subject to limitations or restraints by Great Britain, Canada, or Newfoundland in the form of municipal laws, ordinances, or regulations in respect of (1) the hours, days, or seasons when the inhabitants of the United States may take fish on the treaty coasts, or (2) the method, means, and implements used by them in taking fish or in carrying on fishing operations on such coasts, or (3) any other limitations or restraints of similar character —

(*a*) Unless they are appropriate and necessary for the protection and preservation of the common rights in such fisheries and the exercise thereof; and

(*b*) Unless they are reasonable in themselves and fair as between local fishermen and fishermen coming from the United States, and not so framed as to give an advantage to the former over the latter class; and

(*c*) Unless their appropriateness, necessity, reasonableness, and fairness be determined by the United States and Great Britain by common accord and the United States concurs in their enforcement.

Question 2. Have the inhabitants of the United States, while exercising the liberties referred to in said Article, a right to employ as members of the fishing crews of their vessels persons not inhabitants of the United States ?

Question 3. Can the exercise by the inhabitants of the United States of the liberties referred to in the said Article be subjected, without the consent of the United States, to the requirements of entry or report at custom-houses or the payment of light or harbor or other dues, or to any other similar requirement or condition or exaction ?

Question 4. Under the provision of the said Article that the American fishermen shall be admitted to enter certain bays or harbors for shelter, repairs, wood, or water, and for no other purpose whatever, but that they shall be under such restrictions as may be necessary to prevent their taking, drying, or curing fish therein or in any other manner whatever abusing the privileges thereby reserved to them, is it permissible to impose restrictions making the exercise of such privileges conditional upon the payment of light or harbor or other dues, or entering or reporting at custom-houses or any similar conditions ?

Question 5. From where must be measured the " three marine miles of any of the coasts, bays, creeks, or harbors " referred to in the said Article ?

Question 6. Have the inhabitants of the United States the liberty under the said Article or otherwise, to take fish in the bays, harbors, and creeks on that part of the southern coast of Newfoundland which extends from Cape Ray to Rameau Islands, or on the western and northern coasts of Newfoundland from Cape Ray to Quirpon Islands, or on the Magdalen Islands?

Question 7. Are the inhabitants of the United States whose vessels resort to the treaty coasts for the purpose of exercising the liberties referred to in Article 1 of the treaty of 1818 entitled to have for those vessels, when duly authorized by the United States in that behalf, the commercial privileges on the treaty coasts accorded by agreement or otherwise to United States trading vessels generally? [1]

These questions are contained in the first article of the Special Agreement, and were the principal questions submitted to the tribunal. The other articles contain some matters which should be considered before the award of the tribunal upon the seven questions be taken up *seriatim.*

The purpose of Mr. Root and of Mr. Bryce was not to enrich the literature of arbitrations by an award on the fisheries question, but to get out of the way those questions which had perplexed the foreign offices of the two countries. It was felt that there might be legislative or executive acts of the two Governments which were claimed to be inconsistent with the true interpretation of the treaty of 1818. Therefore, Article 2 of the Special Agreement provided that acts might be submitted to the tribunal for its examination in order that the arbiters should point out wherein they were inconsistent with the treaty, as interpreted by the tribunal, and each party bound itself in advance to conform to the opinion on this point which might be rendered by the tribunal. The purpose of this was, of course, to have the tribunal determine that legislative or executive acts either were or were not in accord with the treaty, so that, if inconsistent, they would not be issued in the future.

It was foreseen, however, that questions might arise in the argument concerning the reasonableness of regulations which would require an examination of the effect of fishing provisions, or that questions might arise about the fisheries themselves, which could only be passed upon by fishing experts. Therefore, Article 3 of the Special Agreement provided that in such cases a commission, composed of three experts, should be appointed, one by each of the contracting parties and the third, who should not be a national of either country, to be selected by the tribunal itself.

These two articles dealt with past acts, which the contracting parties had already decided to submit to the tribunal, and questions which might

[1] U. S. Statutes at Large, vol. XXXVI, part 2, p. 2141; Malloy, *Treaties, Conventions, International Acts, Protocols and Agreements between the United States of America and other Powers, 1776–1909,* vol. I, pp. 836–837.

arise during the trial of the case. The fourth article of the Special Agreement looks to the future and provides a method for the peaceful settlement of any dispute concerning the fisheries which might arise at any time between the two countries. In such cases, the tribunal was to recommend rules and a method of procedure, by virtue whereof any future dispute might be determined " in accordance with the principles laid down in the award." If the contracting parties adopted the rules, a method would then exist for settling future disputes. If, on the other hand, they did not, after the award, " agree upon such rules and methods " there was no way of settling such disputes as might arise, except through diplomacy, and, upon its failure, through arbitration; but the only agreement to arbitrate was the convention of April 4, 1908, which was limited to a period of five years and which might not be renewed. Mr. Root was unwilling to have the obligation to submit to arbitration depend upon a treaty with a time limit. Therefore, the obligation to submit future fisheries disputes was included, without a time limit, in Article 4, and upon the ratification of the treaty the obligation became binding and could only be abrogated by mutual consent. The questions to be submitted under this clause were any differences relating to the interpretation of the convention of 1818 or to the effects and application of the award of the tribunal, and such differences were to be decided by a special tribunal of three members, in accordance with the summary procedure of the convention for the peaceful settlement of international disputes adopted by the second Hague Peace Conference. This is a treaty in a treaty and provides a method for the settlement of all fisheries disputes when the two countries have failed to agree upon another method, and prevents in the future the procedure in the past, which allowed each country to determine for itself the meaning of the treaty.

Arbitration has become, largely through the exertions of the two countries then in dispute, a favorite method of settling international controversies. They confessed their faith in this method in the Jay Treaty of 1794, which provided that boundary disputes and the claims of British and American merchants should be submitted to mixed commissions in order to be settled by this peaceful and highly satisfactory method of adjustment. The success of the commission organized under the seventh article of the Jay Treaty showed that disputes between nations might be judicially settled by international commissions or tribunals, and the success of the Geneva tribunal of 1872, which decided and got out of the way the so-called Alabama Claims, proved that not merely trifling pecuniary claims, but also the most serious and difficult claims peculiarly liable to produce war, can be settled peacefully by the method of arbitration, if the nations desire peaceable settlement.

As Mr. Root has admirably said in his address on laying the corner stone of the Pan American building on May 11, 1908:

> There are no international controversies so serious that they cannot be settled peaceably if both parties really desire peaceable settlement, while there are few causes of dispute so trifling that they cannot be made the occasion of war if either party really desires war. The matters in dispute between nations are nothing; the spirit which deals with them is everything.[1]

With the century of experience before it, the first Hague Peace Conference was able to say in Article 16 of the peaceful settlement convention that "arbitration is recognized by the signatory Powers as the most effective, and at the same time the most equitable, means of settling disputes which diplomacy has failed to settle." Twenty-six nations signed the convention containing this article in 1899, and, at the second Hague Peace Conference in 1907, forty-four nations confirmed it. It can therefore be said that modern arbitration, the gift of the English-speaking peoples, has been internationalized because of its usefulness, and raised by the two Hague Peace Conferences to the dignity of an international institution.

It was natural, therefore, that Great Britain and the United States should adopt in the Fisheries Arbitration the provisions of the Hague peaceful settlement convention, in so far as its provisions were applicable. This was thus stated in Article 5 of the Special Agreement:

> The Tribunal of Arbitration provided for herein shall be chosen from the general list of members of the Permanent Court at The Hague, in accordance with the provisions of Article XLV of the Convention for the Settlement of International Disputes, concluded at the Second Peace Conference at The Hague on the 18th of October, 1907. The provisions of said Convention, so far as applicable and not inconsistent herewith, and excepting Articles LIII and LIV, shall govern the proceedings under the submission herein provided for.
>
> The time allowed for the direct agreement of the President of the United States and His Britannic Majesty on the composition of such Tribunal shall be three months.[2]

It will be observed that the arbiters were to be selected in accordance with Article 45, and an examination of Articles 53 and 54 of the convention, investing the tribunal with power to draft the Special Agreement or *compromis*, as it is called in the French text, shows that they are not applicable,

[1] See Elihu Root's *Latin America and the United States*, published in this series (1917), pp. 230–231.

[2] U. S. Statutes at Large, vol. XXXVI, part 2, p. 2141; Malloy, *Treaties, Conventions, International Acts, Protocols and Agreements between the United States of America and other Powers, 1776–1909*, vol. I, p. 838.

because the treaty submitting the fisheries dispute to arbitration was itself the Special Agreement or *compromis* of the parties. Article 45 is the method recommended by the second Hague Peace Conference of appointing the members of a temporary tribunal. According to this article, the arbiters are to be selected from the list of members of the so-called Permanent Court designated by the parties to the convention. Article 44 of the convention provides that " each contracting power selects four persons at the most, of known competency in questions of international law, of the highest moral reputation, and disposed to accept the duties of arbitrator." These persons are appointed for a term of six years and the names are arranged in a list and communicated to the powers by the International Bureau which serves as a clerk to the court.

The convention foresaw that the powers in controversy might be able to agree upon the selection of the arbiters to form the temporary tribunal; it also foresaw that they might not agree. Therefore, Article 45 provides the method to be followed when the powers have been unable to agree upon the members of the tribunal, supposing, of course, that the Hague procedure is to be followed. In the event of disagreement, " each party," so Article 45 runs, " appoints two arbitrators, of whom one only can be its national, or chosen from among the persons selected by it as members of the Permanent Court. These arbitrators together choose an umpire."

A method is provided by the convention in Article 45 to select the umpire in case the powers themselves and the arbitrators did not agree upon one. As Great Britain and the United States, however, were able directly to appoint the arbiters, including the umpire, it does not seem necessary to enter into these details. They wisely adopted the provision of the convention permitting each of them to select two members, of whom only one should be their citizen or subject. Great Britain chose as its subject, Sir Charles Fitzpatrick, chief justice of Canada. The United States chose George Gray, judge of the United States Circuit Court of Appeals. Great Britain and the United States chose as the foreign members, A. F. de Savornin Lohman, minister of state of Holland; and Luís María Drago, former minister of foreign affairs of the Argentine Republic. The two countries also agreed upon Dr. Heinrich Lammasch, professor of international law in the University of Vienna and member of the Upper House of the Austrian Parliament. It will be noted that as believers in judicial settlement, each took the national member from the bench. It should also be said that Dr. Lohman had acted as arbiter in the Pious Fund case between Mexico and the United States, in the Muscat-Dhows case between France and Great Britain, and, since the Fisheries Arbitration, he has served in the Canevero case between Italy and Peru.

Although Dr. Drago had not heretofore acted as an arbitrator, he was and is a distinguished lawyer of large practice. His appointment was designed to show the willingness of the United States to have Latin American publicists sit in judgment upon its disputes and its confidence in their ability and integrity. It was expected that Mr. Root, as Secretary of State, would confess his faith in Pan American publicists when opportunity permitted and it was also to be expected that Mr. Bryce and his country would share this faith. But Dr. Drago's appointment was the joint act of both countries, not of one of them.

Professor Lammasch had, like Dr. Lohman, already served as arbiter in the Venezuelan preferential case, as umpire in the Muscat-Dhows case, as well as in the Fisheries Tribunal, and, upon its adjournment, he acted as umpire in the Orinoco Steamship Company case between the United States and Venezuela.

Proceedings before an international tribunal differ from the procedure of ordinary courts of justice. The parties to a suit before a national court may be the state on the one hand and a private citizen on the other (except that in the United States, state may sue state in the Supreme Court) and individual versus individual. The state or person beginning the suit is called the plaintiff and the person answering the suit, the defendant. Under municipal law the plaintiff can begin suit with or without the consent of the defendant and, if it be one of which the court has jurisdiction, may prosecute the case to judgment in the absence of the defendant, if the defendant, properly summoned, has not appeared. The judgment, if it be a case against an individual, will be executed by force if necessary.

Between nations litigation is not as yet a matter of course. In the first place, there is no court, as the so-called Permanent Court of Arbitration of The Hague is only a panel or list of persons from which or from whom the requisite number of arbiters can be selected to form a temporary tribunal. Nation cannot sue nation in an international court, because, as has been said, such a court does not exist, and for the further reason that nations cannot be sued, even by nations, without consent. It is therefore necessary that the nations agree to litigate their dispute, that they create the tribunal in which it is to be tried and appoint the arbiters or judges who are to pass upon it.

Nations can, of course, agree, as the states of the American judicial union have agreed, to allow themselves to be sued, and it is to be hoped that the nations as a whole or the most civilized of them will one day create a court for that purpose. But, if they do, it is believed that the procedure will be different from that of a private case and will approach very closely, if it does not follow in all respects, the procedure of the Supreme Court of the United States in suits between states of the American union. In the absence of judges, a nation cannot be haled into court by a plaintiff state, and it is believed that when an international court is created nations will not for many a day to come allow themselves to be compelled by force to appear before the court, although they may and indeed will permit themselves to be invited. But an invitation under the pressure of public opinion will be much the same thing as a command, as the experience of the United States has shown, for although a subpœna issues out of the Supreme Court of the United States in a suit against a state, the defendant is not compelled by force to appear.

A nation, if it does not consent to litigate, and if it does not appear, is not a party to the proceedings, for, as previously stated, there is neither a court nor a judge without the coöperation of the nations in litigation, and a judgment cannot as in the case of national courts be prosecuted to judgment in the absence of the defendant, although in the Supreme Court of the United States the plaintiff state may obtain judgment in the absence of the defendant state duly summoned to appear. There is no agreement or guarantee for the execution of the judgment of an international court other than the good faith of the nations involved, and here again it is likely that the nations will follow the experience of the Supreme Court of the United States in not requiring a judgment against a defendant state to be executed by force. The individual is subject to the power of his state, which, invested by him and his fellows with the power of a superior, establishes the court and determines the procedure thereof. There is no superior in the society of nations. Each is sovereign, independent and equal, and, while sovereign, independent, and equal states may be invited, they cannot, consistently with existing theory and practice, be compelled to submit a case, to litigate a case, and to execute a judgment had in a case. The difference in procedure in suits between nations and suits between individuals is that the nations are sovereign whereas the individuals are subordinated to the sovereign will of the state which they have created and endowed with sovereign power. Within the nations this sovereign power imposes its will upon native and alien within its jurisdiction, determines the law to be observed, the courts within which disputes are to be tried, and the procedure to be followed. The consent of the defendant to a suit is not necessary, as the law prescribes the right of the plaintiff and the duty of the defendant in the premises. In the society of nations, the absence of a superior renders this procedure inapplicable. The national statute creates or imposes a duty. Between nations, the right or duty is created by treaty between the two nations in dispute, consent taking the place of command. The nations may agree generally to submit their disputes to arbitration and to create a permanent court in which they may be decided. They tried to agree upon a treaty of arbitration which would bind the nations at the first Hague Peace Conference and they tried to do it again at the second Hague Peace Conference, but each attempt failed, owing to the opposition of Germany. At the second Hague Peace Conference an agreement was reached with the coöperation of Germany upon the establishment of a permanent court of arbitral justice, but unfortunately the nations did not agree upon a method of appointing the judges, which they relegated to diplomatic channels after the adjournment of the Conference, and — diplomacy is proverbially slow.

There fortunately exists a treaty of arbitration between Great Britain and the United States, of April 4, 1908, obliging the two countries to submit their differences of a legal nature or relating to the interpretation of their existing treaties to arbitration at The Hague. This provision, however, is not self-acting. It requires the negotiation of a special agreement, called in French "*compromis*," "defining," to use the language of Article 2 of the treaty, "clearly the matter in dispute, the scope of the powers of the arbitrators, and the periods to be fixed for the formation of the Arbitral Tribunal and the several stages of the procedure." This Special Agreement is regarded by the Senate of the United States as in the nature of a treaty and by Article 2 of the arbitration convention the Special Agreement requires the advice and consent of the Senate.

In the absence, therefore, of a general treaty of arbitration, and even in the case of a treaty of arbitration to which the United States is a party, there must be a Special Agreement submitting the case or cases to arbitration. In other words, the parties in conflict must agree upon each and every case to be submitted to arbitration and they must create for each and every case the temporary tribunal by mutual consent.

It was hoped that the method of constituting the temporary tribunal from the Hague list or panel and the procedure to be followed in the trial of a case would commend itself to and be followed by the nations. This expectation has been justified by the event. As far as the Fisheries case is concerned, the Special Agreement expressly adopted the method and procedure laid down in the pacific settlement convention except as otherwise determined in the Special Agreement.

The final clause of Article 5 of the Special Agreement, providing that the tribunal shall be constituted within three months from the ratification thereof, needs no comment other than to say that a provision of this kind appears to be a necessary spur to diplomacy.

But, supposing that the nations have agreed to submit the dispute to arbitration, that they have negotiated the Special Agreement and that they have created the temporary tribunal, the nations must in the present unorganized condition of the society of nations determine the procedure to be followed in the preparation of the case and in its presentation before the Tribunal.

In the case of a suit in a municipal court there are two stages: The first is the preparation of the case before it is tried in court, and the second is the trial itself.

In international procedure, there are likewise two stages: First, the written pleadings prepared by the parties before the case is tried in court, and the oral discussions, meaning the procedure before the judges in the trial of the case.

Article 63 of the revised pacific settlement convention thus states the procedure recommended to the nations:

> As a general rule, arbitration procedure comprises two distinct phases: pleadings and oral discussions.
>
> The pleadings consist in the communication, by the respective agents to the members of the Tribunal and the opposite party, of cases, counter-cases, and, if necessary, of replies; the parties annex thereto all papers and documents called for in the case. This communication shall be made either directly or through the intermediary of the International Bureau, in the order and within the time fixed by the "*compromis*."
>
> The time fixed by the "*compromis*" may be extended by mutual agreement by the parties, or by the Tribunal when the latter considers it necessary for the purpose of reaching a just decision.
>
> The discussions consist in the oral development before the Tribunal of the arguments of the parties.[1]

It will be observed that this article supposes a *compromis*, called in English the Special Agreement, in which the details necessary to give effect to the article are to be settled. Accordingly, Article 2 of the Special Agreement dealt with these matters.

Each nation prepares its case, that is to say, each nation makes a statement of the facts involved in the controversy, accompanying these facts with the principles of law applicable or restricting itself to the statement of facts as each may think best. This requires time, the time is stated in the Special Agreement, and in practice the delivery of the case is arranged in such a way that neither party has the advantage of seeing the case of the other, for the cases are to be delivered within a fixed time to the proper authorities of the litigating nations and also to the arbiters. There is an old English proverb to the effect that one story is good until another is told, and this applies between nations as between individuals. Each nation prepares an answer to the case of the other, which answer is not inappropriately called in the Special Agreement the "counter-case." This again may be a restatement of the facts which each country believes to be involved, but it is in practice a restatement of the case in the light of the case made by the adverse party. Here, again, the Special Agreement

[1] U. S. Statutes at Large, vol. XXXVI, part 2, p. 2228; Malloy, *Treaties, Conventions, International Acts, Protocols and Agreements between the United States of America and other Powers, 1776–1909*, vol. II, p. 2239.

fixes the date when the counter-case is to be delivered to the appropriate authorities of the nations in dispute and also to the arbiters.

The next step in due process of law between nations is the preparation and presentation of the argument, called in the pacific settlement convention " replies," but " argument " in the Special Agreement. In like manner, each of the nations in controversy prepares an argument, using for such purpose the cases and counter-cases, designed to show the principles of law which each nation believes are applicable to the facts of the case and which will decide the controversy in its favor. In the same way, the time is fixed for the delivery of the argument to the proper authorities of the litigating nations and to the arbiters of the temporary tribunal. These are called the written pleadings, because they are prepared, printed and delivered in advance of the meeting of the tribunal. The arbiter has thus received them and should have read them and mastered them before the second stage, consisting of the trial of the case, which is called in the peaceful settlement convention the oral discussions.

It may be well to make some observations of a general nature in regard to these matters. The procedure contemplated by the Hague Peace Conferences recognizes that the nations shall be represented in the conduct and trial of the case by certain persons known as agent and counsel and the duties of each are specified in Article 62 of the revised convention as follows:

> The parties are entitled to appoint special agents to attend the Tribunal to act as intermediaries between themselves and the Tribunal.
>
> They are further authorized to retain for the defence of their rights and interests before the Tribunal counsel or advocates appointed by themselves for this purpose.
>
> The members of the Permanent Court may not act as agents, counsel, or advocates except on behalf of the Power which appointed them members of the Court.

The agent is therefore a political officer and the counsel or advocates are legal functionaries, or lawyers, as we say in the United States. The agent for the United States was the Honorable Chandler P. Anderson; for Great Britain, the Honorable Sir Allen B. Aylesworth, then minister of justice of Canada. The agent is intrusted by his government with the preparation of the case, for which purpose he is assisted by counsel, appointed by each of the nations in controversy. The agent, however, is, as the article says, the representative of his country in matters concerning the case. He confers with the agent of the other country, who has a like representative capacity, and between them, with the concurrence of their governments, they arrange the details for the trial of the case, and pass upon the many questions which are bound to arise from time to time. The agent is, on the other hand, the representative of his country before the tribunal, and, as a political agent or diplomatic person, his word binds his country, which the word of the advocate or counsel does not. The agent may or may not argue the case. In the Fisheries dispute neither did.

In regard to counsel, it is only necessary to mention that Mr. Root, at that time United States senator, was chief counsel on behalf of the United States, and his chief assistants were former Senator George Turner of Washington who argued questions 1 to 4; Samuel J. Elder of Boston who argued questions 6 and 7, and Charles B. Warren of Detroit who argued question 5. The chief counsel on behalf of Great Britain was Sir William Robson, then attorney-general; his chief assistant was Sir Robert Finlay, a former attorney-general, and said to be the leader of the English bar, both of whom argued the entire case and their chief assistants were Sir James Winter of Newfoundland who argued questions 1 and 5, and John S. Ewart who dealt with questions 1, 2, 5 and 7.

It is a very remarkable, if not a unique, circumstance, that Mr. Root, who had conducted the negotiations resulting in the submission of the fisheries dispute to arbitration, should as counsel on behalf of the United States have argued the case which he had made as Secretary of State.

The preparation of the case would be difficult, if indeed adequate preparation would be possible, if each country had to rely upon the evidence in its possession. In an ordinary lawsuit in a national court, evidence in the possession of the opponent can be produced by an order of the court, because the court is an agent of the sovereign will in the trial of the case and orders the litigants before it to conduct themselves according to law and directs them to produce the evidence which the law requires. The relation is that of sovereign and subject. In the society of nations there is, as has been stated, no sovereign and no subject, as the nations are sovereign, independent, and equal states. Therefore, it is necessary for the nations in controversy to consent to produce the evidence which they may have bearing upon the case. It is not to be supposed, however, that the defendant in an ordinary case offers of his own free will the evidence which the plaintiff may need, but upon the demand of the plaintiff in appropriate cases the evidence requested should be forthcoming. Likewise, it is not to be expected that a nation would by its own motion open its archives to the country with which it was in controversy. But the submission of the case to arbitration pledges the good faith of the nation implicitly as well as expressly, and it is the custom of nations upon the request of the country with which they are in litigation to produce evidence necessary to the trial and disposition of the case.

Great Britain and the United States followed this practice and regulated it by Article 7 of the Special Agreement. The submission of the case means the submission of evidence necessary to its decision, and it is thus specifically stated in Article 75 of the pacific settlement convention:

> The parties undertake to supply the Tribunal, as fully as they consider possible, with all the information required for deciding the case.

Therefore the convention provides in Article 63 that the parties annex to the various written pleadings " all papers and documents called for in the case." Article 68 empowers the tribunal " to take into consideration new papers or documents to which its attention may be drawn by the agents or counsel of the parties." And Article 69 authorizes the tribunal itself to call for such evidence as it may deem relevant and necessary to the decision of the case. This article, a very important one, is thus worded:

> The Tribunal can, besides, require from the agents of the parties the production of all papers, and can demand all necessary explanations. In case of refusal the Tribunal takes note of it.

Good faith, of course, requires that a document referred to by either nation must be forthcoming upon request of the other, because it should not have the benefit of evidence which it does not disclose. The important point in the Fisheries arbitration was to learn the meaning which the negotiators of the convention of 1818 put upon the fisheries article. The United States presented the official reports of Messrs. Gallatin and Rush dated October 20, 1818, the day of signing, and also the supplementary report of Mr. Gallatin written in Paris upon return to his post, dated November 6, 1818, in which he spoke of the fishing liberty as a *servitude*. And it is interesting to observe that in the original report to his Government in his own handwriting, Mr. Gallatin italicizes servitude. The United States produced these reports and could not very well have refused to do so, because they had been published and were therefore public property. Great Britain would have produced them if the United States had not done so, and, as a matter of fact, Great Britain did produce them as well as the United States. Great Britain, on the contrary, disclosed certain preliminary reports of its negotiators, and agent and counsel were careful in their written pleadings to abstain from a reference to a final report of the negotiators, much less to quote any passage to be found therein, as this would have required them to produce the report or to lose the benefit of the reference to or passage from it. Great Britain has hitherto abstained from publishing the final report of its negotiators, although such an one is known to exist. The United States might have made a demand for the production of this report. It did not do so. It might have asked the tribunal under Article 69 to require His Britannic Majesty's agent to produce the report. It did not, although the fact was referred to in the trial that Great Britain had failed to produce the report. Why did Great Britain not do so ? Why did the United States not insist that it be produced ?

As far as American counsel were concerned Mr. Root at the close of his argument was about to take up the question of withholding this evidence when the President of the tribunal interrupted him by abruptly beginning his closing address. Mr. Root and the American agent conferred hurriedly as to the advisability of interrupting the President for the purpose of dealing with this question, but they decided, in view of the unexpected turn affairs had taken that it would be inadvisable to do so, as they could insist upon the production of the Report if the decision of the tribunal should be against the American contention or if further differences should arise calling for the interpretation of the treaty in subsequent arbitrations to be held under Article 4 of the special agreement.

It was reasonably certain that the Report of the British negotiators was still in existence because British counsel would have assigned its loss as a reason for not producing it, and American counsel knew enough about its character and description to be able to demand its production in any future proceedings. It seemed to American counsel, therefore, that this knowledge and the power to compel the production of the report would be a great advantage in dealing with any future questions of difference about the fisheries, because they felt that Great Britain would, in view of the circumstances, prefer to make very extensive concessions rather than be put in the position of having to produce a document which would or might tend to show that British counsel had been guilty of the discreditable act of winning the case — which, however, they did not win — by the suppression of material evidence which would or might have supported American contentions.

The Special Agreement provides for the revision of the award, to which many partisans of arbitration are opposed, on the theory that the award is to be final, and that any provision for its reopening is destructive of this finality. The answer to this is, of course, that of President Lincoln, that nothing is settled until it is settled right, and national courts universally recognize the fallibility of inferior judges. After much debate, the first Hague Peace Conference refused to allow a revision as a matter of right, but by way of compromise, permitted, what could not be withheld from sovereign states, the right to reserve in the *compromis* the revision of the award. Opponents of revision tried to reopen this question at the second Conference and to withdraw even this slight concession to international justice, but the Conference wisely confirmed the original compromise.

The Special Agreement in Article 10 allows two grounds for the revision of the award, the first being that of Article 55 of the original and Article 83 of the revised pacific settlement convention, namely, " the discovery of some new fact calculated to exercise a decisive influence upon the Award and which was unknown to the tribunal and to the party which demanded the revision at the time the discussion was closed." The term " discussion " in this connection means, of course, the oral proceedings.

The second ground is that the award " does not fully and sufficiently, within the meaning of this Agreement determine any question or questions submitted." There were no new facts found after the discussion had closed and the award of the tribunal fully and sufficiently determined all questions submitted to it, including one not submittd, namely, the nature of the French fishing liberty, and, when it felt that the determination of a question was beyond its jurisdiction, but within its power to recommend, fully and sufficiently made recommendations covering the matter in question.

The tribunal opened its sessions with the trial of the case on June 1, 1910, and closed its sessions on August 12, 1910, after the case had been exhaustively, not to say exhaustingly, argued. It met again on the 7th day of September and, as is required by Article 80 of the pacific settlement convention, announced its award in the presence of agents and counsel duly notified to be present. Great Britain opened the case. The United States closed it, and the published volumes of the oral arguments on trial are mute witnesses to the fact that unstinted use was made of Article 70 of the revised pacific settlement convention, that " the agents and the counsel of the parties are authorized to present orally to the Tribunal all the arguments they may consider expedient in defense of their case."

Mr. Root argued the entire case for the United States in the sense that he argued each of the questions, contenting himself with a contemptuous reference to the sixth question instead of dwelling upon it, and his argument was not only the closing argument for his country, but it was the final argument in the trial of the case.

It is not, as already stated, the purpose of this introduction to argue the case, as Mr. Root has done this and his argument is at the disposal of the reader. Nor is it the purpose of the introduction to consider the evidence and to examine the questions submitted in the light of the facts presented to the tribunal and the principles of law invoked as applicable to and decisive of the case. This the judges of the tribunal did and their award is contained in the present volume. It is at the disposal of the reader who may care to consult this volume. It is, however, thought advisable to state the questions and the holding of the tribunal in a general way, in order that the reader may be in a better position to read, to enjoy, and to profit by Mr. Root's argument.

There are three episodes in the oral argument before the tribunal which should be mentioned, indeed called to the reader's attention, because they produced an agreement as to the binding nature and effect of the fourth article of the Special Agreement and laid the basis for the settlement not merely of the first question but of all questions between the two countries concerning the exercise of the fishing liberty under the convention of 1818, a settlement consistent with the sovereignty of Great Britain in its territorial waters and the protection of American fishermen plying their calling within British jurisdiction.

The first and third of these episodes deal with the nature and unlimited duration of Article 4 of the Special Agreement; the second, with the right of the United States to be consulted as to the reasonableness of imperial or colonial regulations affecting American fishermen in the exercise of the fishing liberty. To show the process by which the agreement on these important points was reached, some quotations are made from the official record of the proceedings before the tribunal. The first extract is from the official record of June 14, 1910.

Sir Robert Finlay: Most fortunately, we have the most complete provision contained in this treaty, first, for dealing with any Acts which already have been passed, and which are complained of and, secondly, for legislating in future in accordance with the principles to be laid down by this Tribunal. The award of the Tribunal on this occasion will be a very worthy one, for it will not only solve the differences which have already occurred, but will provide the principles and a method of procedure for disposing of any question which may arise in the future with regard to the application of those principles to any particular enactment.

The President: I understand there is some difference between article 2 and article 4; that the award of the Tribunal under article 1 and article 2, and under article 4, is decidedly different.

Sir Robert Finlay: Yes.

The President: What the Tribunal shall pronounce under article 4 is only a recommendation to the Governments ?

Sir Robert Finlay: Yes.

The President: But if the Governments should decide not to follow this recommendation, they have submitted themselves beforehand to the summary procedure under the Act of 1907 ?

Sir Robert Finlay: Precisely.

The President: And there is this difference between article 1 and article 2, on the one hand, and article 4, on the other hand ?

Sir Robert Finlay: Yes; and, of course, that difference was inherent in the nature of the subject. Where it relates to something that has already occurred the Tribunal can be asked to decide. Where it relates to possible differences emerging in the future, then all that can be done is to provide for the recommendation of a method of procedure, and if that should not be followed with success the matter is to be summarily adjusted in accordance with the regulations of this Tribunal, chapter 4. . . .

So that I think the Court will be of opinion that, though I put it very shortly, I did not put it too high when I said that the means was provided for adjusting any difference of that kind, — whether it relates to what is already done or what may be done in the future —

for adjusting any difference as to the reasonableness of regulations by the machinery of this Tribunal. The Tribunal decides in this reference on what has already taken place. It provides the means of deciding any similar difference which may arise in the future; and while, of course, as a general rule, differences between nations can be referred to arbitration only by consent, yet we have got that consent, first, under the general treaty, and, secondly, under the very special provisions of the agreement which was entered into for reference of these differences to this Tribunal upon the present occasion.[1]

It will be observed that in this colloquy British counsel appealed to Article 4 of the Special Agreement as the way out of the difficulty. The views of British counsel did not fall on deaf ears, although no notice was taken of them at the time. Later, during the course of the trial, to be specific, on August 5, 1910, American counsel, represented by Mr. Root, returned to the subject, as appears from the following extract from the official record of that day:

Senator Root: There might well be a question, and I think we are bound to consider the possibility of there being a question raised, as to whether the provisions of article 4 of this Special Agreement under this treaty would survive the end of that treaty. Do I make that clear ?

Sir Charles Fitzpatrick: Do you think there can be much doubt about that ?

Senator Root: My own opinion is that they do.

The President: Your opinion is that they do survive ?

Senator Root: My own opinion is that the provisions of article 4 constitute, in effect, a new treaty.

The President: In article 4 they speak of any differences which may arise in the future, without any limitation of time. That seems to settle one of the points.

Senator Root: I think, both because, as the President has said, they expressly relate to any differences which arise in the future, and because they go outside of the function of a *compromis* that

[1] North Atlantic Coast Fisheries Arbitration at The Hague, Oral Argument before the Tribunal constituted under an Agreement signed at Washington on the 27th day of January, 1909, between His Britannic Majesty and the United States of America, part I, pp. 200, 201 (London, 1910); North Atlantic Coast Fisheries, Proceedings in the North Atlantic Coast Fisheries Arbitration before the Permanent Court of Arbitration at The Hague under the provisions of the General Treaty of Arbitration of April 4, 1908, and the Special Agreement of January 27, 1909, between the United States of America and Great Britain, vol. IX, part I, pp. 339–341 (Washington, 1912).

they constitute in effect a new treaty, and that they would survive the death of the treaty under which the Special Agreement was made. I refer to the question now chiefly in order that I may show that that is the view taken by the United States; and I understand the counsel for Great Britain to express, in behalf of Great Britain, the same view.

SIR CHARLES FITZPATRICK: That was clearly the intention of the parties.

SENATOR ROOT: I think it was. I understand the counsel for Great Britain to take that position; and, in behalf of the United States, I accept for the United States that position taken by the counsel for Great Britain, and express the agreement of the United States with that view.

THE PRESIDENT: May I ask counsel for Great Britain whether we understood the former enunciation by counsel for Great Britain in that sense? Perhaps it would be convenient to the Attorney-General to make another declaration. . . .

THE ATTORNEY-GENERAL: In reference to the question that the President was good enough to put to me, . . . I understand it to be as to whether the limit of five years, which appears in the general treaty of 1908, would put any term to the provisions of the Special Agreement of 1909.

THE PRESIDENT: Yes.

THE ATTORNEY-GENERAL: It seems to me that, so far as article 4 is concerned, certainly not. Article 4 is not limited by any term, but is expressly agreed between the parties as relating to the future, generally; so that it would not be a terminable article at all, so far as affects the subject-matter of that article.[1]

In an earlier part of this introduction it has been mentioned that the agents not counsel bound their respective governments. It was therefore not enough that counsel should agree upon this important point. Mr. Root wanted the understanding of court and counsel to be made a part of the record, saying:

[1] North Atlantic Coast Fisheries Arbitration at The Hague, Oral Argument before the Tribunal constituted under an Agreement signed at Washington, on the 27th day of January, 1909, between His Britannic Majesty and the United States of America, part II, pp. 1209, 1210 (London, 1910); North Atlantic Coast Fisheries, Proceedings in the North Atlantic Coast Fisheries Arbitration before the Permanent Court of Arbitration at The Hague under the provisions of General Treaty of Arbitration of April 4, 1908, and the Special Agreement of January 27, 1909, between the United States of America and Great Britain, vol. XI, pp. 1997–2000 (Washington, 1912).

> My object in referring to the question here was to clear away possible doubt which might cause controversy in the future, and to do it now before the award of the Arbitrators, because I should think that it might be very well in the award to fix the rights of the parties with some reference to this provision, so that it would not be left an open question.[1]

It is betraying no confidence to state that Article 4 of the Special Agreement was drafted by Mr. Root in the hope and with the confident expectation that it would appeal to the British Government as the way out of the difficulties that beset its advocates in the trial and disposition of the case, and that it would be proposed by Great Britain during the argument as the solution of future fishing disputes.

The next episode really decided the case, because, accepting Article 4 of the Special Agreement as a binding and continuing treaty between Great Britain and the United States — "the treaty" as Mr. Root was accustomed to call it — an understanding was reached by virtue of which the reasonableness of fishing regulations to which the United States objected was to be tested by the procedure contained in Article 4 of the Special Agreement. The understanding and the way in which it was reached are set forth in the proceedings of the official record, under date of August 4, 1910, from which the material portion is quoted:

> Senator Root: If any question arises regarding the exercise of the liberties referred to in the treaty of 1818 . . . it may be determined in accordance with the principles laid down in the award. The Tribunal is to "recommend, for the consideration of the contracting parties, rules and a method of procedure under which all questions which may arise in the future regarding the exercise of the liberties by them referred to may be determined in accordance with the principles laid down in the award."
>
> If the rules are not adopted —
>
> "then any differences which may arise in the future between the High Contracting Parties relating to the interpretation of the Treaty of 1818 or to the effect and application of the award of the Tribunal

[1] North Atlantic Coast Fisheries Arbitration at The Hague, Oral Argument before the Tribunal constituted under an Agreement signed at Washington, on the 27th day of January, 1909, between His Britannic Majesty and the United States of America, part II, p. 1210 (London, 1910); North Atlantic Coast Fisheries. Proceedings in the North Atlantic Coast Fisheries Arbitration before the Permanent Court of Arbitration at The Hague under the provisions of General Treaty of Arbitration of April 4, 1908, and the Special Agreement of January 27, 1909, between the United States of America and Great Britain, vol. XI, p. 1999 (Washington, 1912).

shall be referred informally to the Permanent Court at The Hague for decision." . . .

THE PRESIDENT: According to the fourth article, the solution would be that either this Court would propose some method of procedure to which both governments would accede, by their free-will — they are not obliged, at all, to accede to them; it is a pure recommendation — or if they do not accede, then both parties have bound themselves by article 4 to submit future contestations to the decision of The Hague Tribunal in the summary procedure.

Would it not seem that both parties would gain by this method ?

SENATOR ROOT: Precisely; both parties would gain by this method. . . .

SIR CHARLES FITZPATRICK: Do I understand you to say, then, that if you object, and the principle is adopted that in case of your objection the regulation would not have effect until such time as it would be submitted to The Hague Tribunal, that you would be satisfied with that ?

SENATOR ROOT: Precisely. Certainly. That is what we are contending for. And I think that this treaty grant draws clearly the line within which that principle applies; that Great Britain has full and unrestrained scope of sovereignty until she comes to that clear and definite line, that is, of the exercise of the right of fishing, as granted in the terms of the grant; but when she comes to that narrow field, wishing to change the situation by making a new limitation, that was not in the treaty, a limitation upon the times or manner, then that ought to be in practical good sense the subject of consultation between both owners of the common right; and if they cannot agree, let it be determined before it is made effective and our fishermen's vessels are seized under it. My objection to the British theory is that they propose to make these things effective by virtue of their sovereignty, *ex proprio vigore*, before anybody has decided. Sir Robert Finlay says they have not the right to decide; that they do not claim the right to decide; that they ought not to decide — but they propose to make effective these limitations by deciding.

THE PRESIDENT: Your rights, as you consider them, would be safeguarded by conceding to you a suspensive veto ? . . .

SENATOR ROOT: Precisely. Before this treaty was made, what we claimed was that instead of going ahead and putting your regulations, extending your sovereignty, over the modification of this right without saying anything to us, you should consult us first, just as you did with Mr. Marcy, when these laws were brought down to him and he approved them. And in order to obviate the claim that that might lead to a deadlock, and might put Great Britain in a most disagreeable situation, because she has got this colony behind her, pressing always for extreme views and extreme action, we make this agreement, under which, if we cannot agree upon what ought to be put into force, we will go to The Hague Tribunal, and we will have an arrangement, perhaps a more convenient and practical arrangement, proposed by the Tribunal, for determining whether they ought to be put into effect or not.

SIR CHARLES FITZPATRICK: Or the parties can arrange it themselves?

SENATOR ROOT: Certainly; and they will arrange it. There is no trouble about making the arrangement. The great trouble is, and the best thing that can be done for Great Britain — I know my friends on the other side will smile at me when I say it, but I say it not proposing to arrogate to myself the position of a guardian for Great Britain — the best thing that can be done for Great Britain is to give a line of right here so that she will not be in the position of having either to assent to unjust and extreme positions taken by her colony, in the spirit that has been exhibited here, against her own feeling of what is really due to us on the one hand, or to overrule them and have her colony feel that she has been unkind towards the colony, and has been deciding against it of her own will. . . .[1]

It is thus seen as a result of the exchange of views between Mr. Root and Sir Charles Fitzpatrick that the basis of settlement was struck off in the heat of argument between counsel and judge, as is so often the case in the courts of the English speaking peoples.

The award of the tribunal determines the right of the United States under the convention of 1818 and enables the Government to inform American fishermen of their rights and duties, thus settling old controversies and preventing new ones, and in determining the rights of Great Britain under the same convention enables the British Government to hold the colonies to the strict observance of their duties as defined by the award without the suggestion of undue imperial interference or dictation. The award is therefore mutually beneficial to the two countries so recently contending at The Hague, even although it may not have given to either

[1] North Atlantic Coast Fisheries Arbitration at The Hague, Oral Argument before the Tribunal constituted under an Agreement signed at Washington on the 27th day of January, 1909, between His Britannic Majesty and the United States of America, part II, pp. 1206–1208 (London, 1910); North Atlantic Coast Fisheries, Proceedings in the North Atlantic Coast Fisheries Arbitration before the Permanent Court of Arbitration at The Hague under the provisions of General Treaty of Arbitration of April 4, 1908, and the Special Agreement of January 27, 1909, between the United States of America and Great Britain, vol. XI, pp. 1992–1996 (Washington, 1912).

the full extent of its claims. The example to the world is greater than the benefit to either litigant and the advantage to each transcends the terms of the award.

In the final position assumed in submitting the case to arbitration, the Government of Great Britain contended for the right directly or indirectly through Canada or Newfoundland, to make regulations applicable to American fishermen in treaty waters without the consent of the United States, in respect of (1) the hours, days, or seasons when fish may be taken on the treaty coast; (2) the method, means, and implements to be used in the taking of fish or in the carrying on of fishing operations on such coasts, provided such regulations were " reasonable, as being for instance, appropriate or necessary for the protection and preservation of such fisheries; desirable on grounds of public order and morals; equitable and fair as between local fishermen and the inhabitants of the United States."

The United States, on the other hand, denied the right of Great Britain to make such regulations "unless their appropriateness, necessity, reasonableness, and fairness be determined by the United States and Great Britain by common accord and the United States concurs in their enforcement."

The fishing regulations were thus by the submission of both parties to be reasonable; but who was to pass upon the question of reasonableness? The tribunal affirmed the right of Great Britain " to make regulations without the consent of the United States " but lays down that " such regulations must be made *bona fide* and must not be in violation of the said treaty "; and that " regulations which are appropriate or necessary for the preservation of such fisheries, or desirable or necessary on grounds of public order and morals without unnecessarily interfering with the fishery itself, and in both cases equitable and fair as between local and American fishermen, and not so framed as to give an advantage to the former over the latter class, are not inconsistent with the obligation to execute the treaty in good faith, and are therefore not in violation of the treaty."

So far the award is squarely in favor of Great Britain, but the award goes further and holds that, if the reasonableness of a regulation is contested, Great Britain is not to be the judge of what is or what is not reasonable. The language of the award on this crucial point is as follows:

> By reason, however, of the form in which Question I is put, and by further reason of the admission of Great Britain by her counsel before this Tribunal that it is not now for either of the parties to the treaty to determine the reasonableness of any regulation made by Great Britain, Canada, or Newfoundland, the reasonableness of any such regulation, if contested, must be decided not by either of the parties, but by an impartial authority in accordance with the principles herein-

above laid down, and in the manner proposed in the recommendations made by the Tribunal in virtue of Article IV of the agreement.[1]

But as the present purpose is not to examine the recommendations drawn up by the tribunal and inserted in the award, it is sufficient to state that Great Britain is no longer to be the judge of the reasonableness of a contested regulation and that the reasonableness or unreasonableness of future regulations is henceforth to be determined by impartial authority instead of by partial authority as in the past. This provision of the award thus seems to grant substantially the result for which the United States contended.

The necessity of submission to " impartial authority " in case of a contested regulation may well result in practice in the amicable discussion by the interested parties of proposed regulations so as to prevent the delay and expense likely to result from a reference to the " impartial authority " provided for by the award.

The award on the first question is thus in substance a victory for the United States.

Question II involving the right of the United States to employ as members of the fishing crews non-inhabitants of the United States is decided in favor of the right of the United States. The reservation in the second paragraph of the award negatives any treaty rights in aliens, who derive their rights solely from their employer.

In the exercise of the fishing-rights under the convention of 1818, the United States claimed that its inhabitants were not, without its consent, to be subjected " to the requirements of entry or report at custom-houses or the payment of light or harbor dues, or to any other similar requirement or condition or exaction."

The decision of the tribunal on this point raised by Question III is very reasonable and satisfactory to both parties. The duty to report is not unreasonable, if the report may be made conveniently either in person or by telegraph. If no reasonably convenient opportunity be provided, then the American vessel need not report.

The second and final clause of the award on this point is admirably clear and concise: " But the exercise of the fishing liberty by the inhabitants of the United States should not be subjected to the purely commercial formalities of report, entry and clearance at a custom-house, nor to light, harbor or other dues not imposed upon Newfoundland fishermen."

The United States always admitted and stated in the presentation of its case that American fishing vessels exercising their treaty rights might properly be called upon to make known their presence and exhibit their credentials by a report to custom-houses, but on the other hand, the United

[1] Official Report published by the Bureau of the Permanent Court of Arbitration in the North Atlantic Coast Fisheries case, arbitrated at The Hague, 1910, p. 126.

States always denied that such vessels could be subjected to the customs regulations imposed upon other vessels, or required to pay light, harbor or other dues not imposed upon local fishing vessels. The award, therefore, sustains the American contention to its fullest extent.

The convention of 1818 permitted American fishermen to enter the bays or harbors of the non-treaty coast covered by the renunciatory clause " for the purpose of shelter and of repairing damages therein, of purchasing wood, and of obtaining water, and for no other purpose whatever." The treaty specifically subjected American fishermen to such restrictions as might be necessary to prevent them from abusing the privilege thus reserved.

Great Britain contended as to this question (Question IV), that vessels seeking these non-treaty ports were to be treated as ordinary vessels, subject to local ordinances and regulations, whereas the United States maintained that the ports were to be treated as ports of refuge and that the subjection of fishing vessels to the prerequisite of entering and reporting at custom-houses, or of paying light, harbor or other dues would unjustly impair and limit the privileges which the clause meant to concede. The tribunal adopted the American contention as in accord with the " duties of hospitality and humanity which all civilized nations impose upon themselves."

To prevent the abuse of the privileges, the tribunal holds that if the American vessel remains in such ports for more than forty-eight hours, Great Britain may require such vessel to report either in person or by telegraph, at a custom-house or to a customs official, if reasonably convenient opportunity therefor is afforded. Question IV is thus decided in favor of the American contention.

By the convention of 1818 the United States renounced the right " to take, dry, or cure fish on, or within three marine miles of any of the coasts, bays, creeks, or harbours of His Britannic Majesty's dominions in America " not included within the limits specified by the treaty. Great Britain contended that the United States renounced by this clause the right to fish within all bays and within three miles thereof, whereas the United States maintained that it renounced merely the right to fish within such bays as formed part of His Majesty's dominions; that only such bays whose entrance was less than double the marine league were renounced, and that in such cases the three marine miles were to be measured from a line drawn across the bays where they were six miles or less in width. In other words, Great Britain argued that " bays " were used in both a geographical and territorial sense, thereby excluding American fishermen from all bodies of water on the non-treaty coast known as bays on the maps of the period, whereas the United States insisted that " bays " were used in the territorial sense, and therefore limited to small bays.

Question V asked " from where must be measured the ' three marine miles of any of the coasts, bays, creeks or harbors ' referred to in the said Article ? " The tribunal adopted the British contention only to the extent of holding that the word " bays " must be interpreted as applying to geographical bays. " In case of bays the three marine miles are to be measured from a straight line drawn across the body of water at the place where it ceases to have the configuration and characteristics of a bay. At all other places the three marine miles are to be measured following the sinuosities of the coast."

A body of water, geographically called a bay, may cease to have " the configuration and characteristics of a bay " and at this point the line is to be drawn. This would leave each bay to be considered by itself, and the tribunal recognized that the terms of its award would be too general. Therefore to avoid this difficulty it conceded in part the contention of the United States and recommended the ten-mile provision found in recent fishery treaties and drew the lines in the most important bays of the non-treaty coast in general accordance with the unratified treaty of 1888 between Great Britain and the United States, with, however, very considerable modifications in favor of the United States.

Without indulging in criticism of the award, attention is called to the very able dissenting opinion of Dr. Drago from the Award of the tribunal on this question.

The attempt of Great Britain under Question VI to exclude American fishermen from " the bays, harbours and creeks " of the treaty coast, which would have worked irreparable injury to American fishing interests, signally failed, and the final question (Question VII) was likewise resolved in favor of the United States, for it is held that its inhabitants are entitled to have for their vessels " the commercial privileges on the treaty coasts accorded by agreement or otherwise to United States trading vessels generally," provided that " the commercial privileges are not exercised concurrently " with the exercise of treaty rights.

With the exception of Question V, the award of the tribunal was unanimous.

An examination of the special agreement will show that the tribunal was authorized by Article 4 to recommend for the consideration of the high contracting parties rules and a method of procedure under which all questions which might arise in the future regarding the exercise of the liberties above referred to may be determined in accordance with the principles laid down in the award. The tribunal complied with this authorization and made a series of recommendations covering the matter.

It was foreseen, however, that the contracting parties might not adopt the rules and method of procedure as they were recommended, or that they might adopt them with sundry modifications, or that they might wholly reject them, in which event, as has already been pointed out, " any differences . . . relating to the interpretation of the treaty of 1818 or to the effect and application of the award of the tribunal " were to be referred informally to the summary procedure of the revised peaceful settlement convention of 1907.

Again, the tribunal felt that its award on the fifth question, concerning the point from which " the three marine miles of any of the coasts, bays, creeks, or harbors " should be measured, was unsatisfactory, as it contented itself with saying that " in case of bays the three marine miles are to be measured from a straight line drawn across the body of water at the place where it ceases to have the configuration and characteristics of a bay. At all other places the three miles are to be measured following the sinuosities of the coast."

The commission held itself justified by Article 4 of the special agreement to make a recommendation where it did not feel itself authorized to make an award. It therefore recommended that only bays of ten miles width should be considered as those wherein fishing is reserved to nationals, and it recommended that lines should be drawn from specified points in certain enumerated bays of the Dominion of Canada and of the Colony of Newfoundland. The tribunal might indeed impose its award, because the parties had agreed to abide by it unless a revision were demanded in accordance with the terms of the Special Agreement. But no revision was requested, and each agent on behalf of his government accepted the award.

The two governments, therefore, took up the question of the recommendations and adopted the spirit, although they modified the letter. On July 20, 1912, the Honorable Chandler P. Anderson, agent of the United States in the fisheries case and then counselor for the Department of State, and Alfred Mitchell Inness, Esquire, Chargé d'affaires of His Majesty's Embassy at Washington, reached an agreement in behalf of their Governments, adopting, with certain modifications, the recommendation of the tribunal, and apparently providing permanent and adequate machinery for the settlement of such fishing disputes as are likely to arise between the two countries.

This agreement, which is contained in this volume and follows the award of the tribunal, provides that imperial or colonial laws, ordinances, or regulations of the fisheries affecting the time, the method, the implements or means of fishing, or other regulations of a similar character " shall be promulgated and come into operation within the first fifteen days of November in each year; provided, however, in so far as any such law, ordinance, or rule shall apply to a fishery conducted between the first day of November and the first day of February, the same shall be promulgated at least six months before the first day of November in each year." The purpose of this article is to inform the United States of British laws or ordinances before they go into effect, in order that the United States might object to them if they were held to be inconsistent with the convention of 1818, and in order that the information should become public property they were to be published in the London Gazette, in the Canadian Gazette and in the Newfoundland Gazette. The United States was authorized by Section 2, Article 1 of this very important agreement " to notify the Government of Great Britain within forty-five days after the publication above referred to, and may require that the same be submitted to and their reasonableness, within the meaning of the award, be determined by the permanent mixed fishery commission " which the two countries agreed to constitute.

The purpose of this provision is to give the United States forty-five days within which to determine whether a regulation is, in its opinion, reasonable and consistent with the treaty of 1818 as interpreted by the award of the tribunal, inasmuch as, if the United States did not object, the law or regulation would go into effect. If, on the contrary, the United States objected, then the question whether the law or regulation was reasonable or consistent with the treaty of 1818 and the award of the tribunal, was to be passed upon by a permanent fishery commission for Canada and Newfoundland, as contemplated by the special agreement of January 27, 1909.

The commission is to consist of three members, appointed for a period of five years. Each of the countries appoints a member and, in case of a failure to agree upon the third member, who is to act as umpire, he is to be nominated by Her Majesty, the Queen of the Netherlands. At the request of the United States, Great Britain obligates itself to summon the two national members of the appropriate permanent commission within thirty days from the request of the United States, and upon failure of the national members to agree, the full commission, under the presidency of the umpire, is to be convened within thirty days thereafter "to decide all questions upon which the two national members disagreed." It is further provided that the commission is to deliver its decision, in the absence of a contrary agreement, " within forty-five days after it is convened," and in order that there may be no time lost in agreeing upon procedure, Article 1 of the agreement further provides that the summary procedure of the pacific settlement convention of 1907 is to be followed, except in so far as the present agreement provides otherwise. There is no doubt that a majority decision is binding, but, in order that there may be no uncertainty, the seventh clause of the first article provides that " the unanimous decision of the two national commissioners, or the majority decision of the umpire and one commissioner, shall be final and binding."

The meaning of this agreement is too clear to be misunderstood. It is a formal recognition by the two Governments that neither is competent to determine, in such a way as to bind the other, the question whether any law or regulation issued by Great Britain or its self-governing dominion or colony is reasonable or consistent with the treaty of 1818, as interpreted by the award of The Hague Tribunal. It recognizes the right of Great Britain to issue laws and regulations, a right inherent in sovereignty; but it recognizes, on the other hand, that the exercise of this right is inconsistent or may be inconsistent with the convention of 1818. Great Britain maintains its sovereignty, but the exercise of it in the matter of fisheries is put in commission.

Passing now to the recommendations dealing with Question 5, the two Governments expressly adopted in Article 2 the recommendations of the tribunal regarding the Canadian bays. The Newfoundland bays are not included within the terms of the agreement and it is to be presumed that, in view of the permanent fisheries commission, there is little likelihood of troubles arising between the two countries because of the Newfoundland bays.

It is difficult to see how disputes concerning the fisheries can arise between two countries without being promptly ended by this pacific method. The negotiation of the Special Agreement was a great triumph to Mr. Root as Secretary of State, and the acceptance of the Agreement of July 20, 1912, is a great tribute to the reasonableness and conciliatory desires of the British Government.

Both the United States and Great Britain are to be congratulated upon the award and the final agreement giving effect to the recommendations of the tribunal. The real importance of the outcome of the fisheries dispute, greater than the issues involved to the fishermen of the two countries, lies in its international bearings; for it furnishes an example of the peaceful and harmonious settlement of international disputes which will not, it is to be hoped, be without influence upon the world at large when it feels and responds, as in the course of time it must, to the pressure of an irresistible and enlightened public opinion in favor of the judicial settlement of justiciable disputes.

APPENDIX TO THE FOREWORD

TREATY OF PARIS, SEPTEMBER 3, 1783, BETWEEN GREAT BRITAIN AND UNITED STATES [1]

Definitive Treaty of Peace and Friendship between His Britannic Majesty and the United States of America Signed at Paris, the 3rd of September, 1783

Art. III. It is agreed that the people of the United States shall continue to enjoy unmolested the right to take fish of every kind on the Grand Bank, and on all the other banks of Newfoundland; also in the gulph of St. Lawrence, and at all other places in the sea, where the inhabitants of both countries used at any time heretofore to fish; and also that the inhabitants of the United States shall have liberty to take fish of every kind on such part of the coast of Newfoundland as British fishermen shall use (but not to dry or cure the same on that island); and also on the coasts, bays and creeks of all other of his Britannic Majesty's dominions in America; and that the American fishermen shall have liberty to dry and cure fish in any of the unsettled bays, harbors and creeks of Nova Scotia, Magdalen Islands, and Labrador, so long as the same shall remain unsettled; but so soon as the same or either of them shall be settled, it shall not be lawful for the said fishermen to dry or cure fish at such settlement, without a previous agreement for that purpose with the inhabitants, proprietors or possessors of the ground.

CONVENTION OF OCTOBER 20, 1818, BETWEEN GREAT BRITAIN AND THE UNITED STATES [2]

Art. 1. Whereas differences have arisen respecting the liberty claimed by the United States, for the inhabitants thereof, to take, dry, and cure fish, on certain coasts, bays, harbors, and creeks, of his Britannic Majesty's dominions in America, it is agreed between the high contracting parties, that the inhabitants of the said United States shall have, forever, in common with the subjects of his Britannic Majesty, the liberty to take fish of every kind on that part of the southern coast of Newfoundland, which extends from Cape Ray to the Rameau Islands, on the western and northern coast of Newfoundland, from the said Cape Ray to the Quirpon

[1] U. S. Statutes at Large, vol. VIII, p. 80.

[2] U. S. Statutes at Large, vol. VIII, p. 248.

Islands, on the shores of the Magdalen Islands, and also on the coasts, bays, harbors, and creeks, from Mount Joly, on the southern coast of Labrador, to and through the Straights of Belleisle, and thence northwardly indefinitely along the coast, without prejudice, however, to any of the exclusive rights of the Hudson Bay Company: And that the American fishermen shall also have liberty, forever, to dry and cure fish in any of the unsettled bays, harbors, and creeks, of the southern part of the coast of Newfoundland, hereabove described, and of the coast of Labrador; but so soon as the same, or any portion thereof, shall be settled, it shall not be lawful for the said fishermen to dry or cure fish at such portion so settled, without previous agreement for such purpose, with the inhabitants, proprietors, or possessors, of the ground. And the United States hereby renounce, forever, any liberty heretofore enjoyed or claimed by the inhabitants thereof, to take, dry, or cure fish, on or within three marine miles of any of the coasts, bays, creeks, or harbors, of his Britannic Majesty's dominions in America, not included within the abovementioned limits: Provided, however, that the American fishermen shall be admitted to enter such bays or harbors, for the purpose of shelter and of repairing damages therein, of purchasing wood, and of obtaining water, and for no other purpose whatever. But they shall be under such restrictions as may be necessary to prevent their taking, drying, or curing, fish therein, or in any other manner whatever abusing the privileges hereby reserved to them. . . .

ARBITRATION CONVENTION BETWEEN THE UNITED STATES AND GREAT BRITAIN [1]

The President of the United States of America and His Majesty the King of the United Kingdom of Great Britain and Ireland and of the British Dominions beyond the Seas, Emperor of India, desiring in pursuance of the principles set forth in Articles 15–19 of the Convention for the pacific settlement of international disputes, signed at The Hague July 29, 1899, to enter into negotiations for the conclusion of an Arbitration Convention, have named as their Plenipotentiaries, to wit:

The President of the United States of America, Elihu Root, Secretary of State of the United States, and

His Majesty the King of the United Kingdom of Great Britain and Ireland and of the British Dominions beyond the Seas, Emperor of India, The Right Honorable James Bryce, O. M., who, after having communicated to one another their full powers, found in good and due form, have agreed upon the following articles:

Art. I. Differences which may arise of a legal nature or relating to the interpretation of treaties existing between the two Contracting Parties and

[1] U. S. Statutes at Large, vol. XXXV, pt. 2, p. 1960.

which it may not have been possible to settle by diplomacy, shall be referred to the Permanent Court of Arbitration established at The Hague by the Convention of the 29th of July, 1899, provided, nevertheless, that they do not affect the vital interests, the independence, or the honor of the two Contracting States, and do not concern the interests of third Parties.

ART. II. In each individual case the High Contracting Parties, before appealing to the Permanent Court of Arbitration, shall conclude a special Agreement defining clearly the matter in dispute, the scope of the powers of the Arbitrators, and the periods to be fixed for the formation of the Arbitral Tribunal and the several stages of the procedure. It is understood that such special agreements on the part of the United States will be made by the President of the United States, by and with the advice and consent of the Senate thereof; His Majesty's Government reserving the right before concluding a special agreement in any matter affecting the interests of a self governing Dominion of the British Empire to obtain the concurrence therein of the Government of that Dominion.

Such Agreements shall be binding only when confirmed by the two Governments by an Exchange of Notes.

ART. III. The present Convention shall be ratified by the President of the United States of America by and with the advice and consent of the Senate thereof, and by His Britannic Majesty. The ratifications shall be exchanged at Washington as soon as possible, and the Convention shall take effect on the date of the exchange of its ratifications.

ART. IV. The present Convention is concluded for a period of five years, dating from the day of the exchange of its ratifications.

Done in duplicate at the City of Washington, this fourth day of April, in the year 1908.

ELIHU ROOT [SEAL]
JAMES BRYCE [SEAL]

SPECIAL AGREEMENT FOR THE SUBMISSION OF QUESTIONS RELATING TO FISHERIES ON THE NORTH ATLANTIC COAST UNDER THE GENERAL TREATY OF ARBITRATION CONCLUDED BETWEEN THE UNITED STATES AND GREAT BRITAIN ON THE 4th DAY OF APRIL, 1908 [1]

ART. I. Whereas, by Article I of the Convention signed at London on the 20th day of October, 1818, between the United States and Great Britain, it was agreed as follows:

> Whereas differences have arisen respecting the Liberty claimed by the United States for the Inhabitants thereof, to take, dry and cure Fish on Certain Coasts, Bays, Harbours, and Creeks of His Britannic

[1] U. S. Statutes at Large, vol. XXXVI, pt. 2, p. 2141.

Majesty's Dominions in America, it is agreed between the High Contracting Parties, that the Inhabitants of the said United States shall have forever, in common with the Subjects of His Britannic Majesty, the Liberty to take Fish of every kind on that part of the Southern Coast of Newfoundland which extends from Cape Ray to the Rameau Islands, on the Western and Northern Coast of Newfoundland, from the said Cape Ray to the Quirpon Islands on the shores of the Magdalen Islands, and also on the Coasts, Bays, Harbours, and Creeks from Mount Joly on the Southern Coast of Labrador, to and through the Straits of Belleisle and thence Northwardly indefinitely along the Coast, without prejudice however, to any of the exclusive Rights of the Hudson Bay Company; and that the American Fishermen shall also have liberty forever, to dry and cure Fish in any of the unsettled Bays, Harbours, and Creeks of the Southern part of the Coast of Newfoundland hereabove described, and of the Coast of Labrador; but so soon as the same, or any Portion thereof, shall be settled, it shall not be lawful for the said Fishermen to dry or cure Fish at such Portion so settled, without previous agreement for such purpose with the Inhabitants, Proprietors, or Possessors of the ground. — And the United States hereby renounce forever, any Liberty heretofore enjoyed or claimed by the Inhabitants thereof, to take, dry, or cure Fish on, or within three marine Miles of any of the Coasts, Bays, Creeks, or Harbours of His Britannic Majesty's Dominions in America not included within the above mentioned limits; provided, however, that the American Fishermen shall be admitted to enter such Bays or Harbours for the purpose of Shelter and of repairing Damages therein, of purchasing Wood, and of obtaining Water, and for no other purpose whatever. But they shall be under such Restrictions as may be necessary to prevent their taking, drying or curing Fish therein, or in any other manner whatever abusing the Privileges hereby reserved to them.

And, whereas, differences have arisen as to the scope and meaning of the said Article, and of the liberties therein referred to, and otherwise in respect of the rights and liberties which the inhabitants of the United States have or claim to have in the waters or on the shores therein referred to:

It is agreed that the following questions shall be submitted for decision to a tribunal of arbitration constituted as hereinafter provided:

Question 1. To what extent are the following contentions or either of them justified?

It is contended on the part of Great Britain that the exercise of the liberty to take fish referred to in the said Article, which the inhabitants of the United States have forever in common with the subjects of His Britannic Majesty, is subject, without the consent of the United States, to reasonable regulation by Great Britain, Canada, or Newfoundland in the form of municipal laws, ordinances, or rules, as, for example, to regulations in respect of (1) the hours, days, or seasons when fish may be taken on the treaty coasts; (2) the method, means, and implements to be used in the taking of fish or in the carrying on of fishing operations on such coasts; (3) any other matters of a similar character relating to fishing; such regulations being reasonable, as being, for instance —

(*a*) Appropriate or necessary for the protection and preservation of such fisheries and the exercise of the rights of British subjects therein and of the liberty which by the said Article I the inhabitants of the United States have therein in common with British subjects;

(*b*) Desirable on grounds of public order and morals;

(*c*) Equitable and fair as between local fishermen and the inhabitants of the United States exercising the said treaty liberty and not so framed as to give unfairly an advantage to the former over the latter class.

It is contended on the part of the United States that the exercise of such liberty is not subject to limitations or restraints by Great Britain, Canada, or Newfoundland in the form of municipal laws, ordinances, or regulations in respect of (1) the hours, days, or seasons when the inhabitants of the United States may take fish on the treaty coasts, or (2) the method, means, and implements used by them in taking fish or in carrying on fishing operations on such coasts, or (3) any other limitations or restraints of similar character —

(*a*) Unless they are appropriate and necessary for the protection and preservation of the common rights in such fisheries and the exercise thereof; and

(*b*) Unless they are reasonable in themselves and fair as between local fishermen and fishermen coming from the United States, and not so framed as to give an advantage to the former over the latter class; and

(*c*) Unless their appropriateness, necessity, reasonableness, and fairness be determined by the United States and Great Britain by common accord and the United States concurs in their enforcement.

Question 2. Have the inhabitants of the United States, while exercising the liberties referred to in said Article, a right to employ as members of the fishing crews of their vessels persons not inhabitants of the United States?

Question 3. Can the exercise by the inhabitants of the United States of the liberties referred to in the said Article be subjected, without the consent of the United States, to the requirements of entry or report at custom-houses or the payment of light or harbor or other dues, or to any other similar requirement or condition or exaction?

Question 4. Under the provision of the said Article that the American fishermen shall be admitted to enter certain bays or harbors for shelter, repairs, wood, or water, and for no other purpose whatever, but that they shall be under such restrictions as may be necessary to prevent their taking, drying, or curing fish therein or in any other manner whatever abusing the privileges thereby reserved to them, is it permissible to impose restrictions making the exercise of such privileges conditional upon the payment of light or harbor or other dues, or entering or reporting at custom-houses or any similar conditions ?

Question 5. From where must be measured the "three marine miles of any of the coasts, bays, creeks, or harbors" referred to in the said Article ?

Question 6. Have the inhabitants of the United States the liberty under the said Article or otherwise, to take fish in the bays, harbors, and creeks on that part of the southern coast of Newfoundland which extends from Cape Ray to Rameau Islands, or on the western and northern coasts of Newfoundland from Cape Ray to Quirpon Islands, or on the Magdalen Islands ?

Question 7. Are the inhabitants of the United States whose vessels resort to the treaty coasts for the purpose of exercising the liberties referred to in Article I of the treaty of 1818 entitled to have for those vessels, when duly authorized by the United States in that behalf, the commercial privileges on the treaty coasts accorded by agreement or otherwise to United States trading vessels generally ?

Art. II. Either Party may call the attention of the Tribunal to any legislative or executive act of the other Party, specified within three months of the exchange of notes enforcing this agreement, and which is claimed to be inconsistent with the true interpretation of the treaty of 1818; and may call upon the Tribunal to express in its award its opinion upon such acts, and to point out in what respects, if any, they are inconsistent with the principles laid down in the award in reply to the preceding questions; and each Party agrees to conform to such opinion.

Art. III. If any question arises in the arbitration regarding the reasonableness of any regulation or otherwise which requires an examination of the practical effect of any provisions in relation to the conditions surrounding the exercise of the liberty of fishery enjoyed by the inhabitants of the United States, or which requires expert information about the fisheries themselves, the Tribunal may, in that case, refer such question to a commission of three expert specialists in such matters; one to be designated by each of the Parties hereto, and the third, who shall not be a national of either Party, to be designated by the Tribunal. This Commission shall examine into and report their conclusions on any question or questions so referred to it by the Tribunal and such report shall be considered by the Tribunal and shall, if incorporated by them in the award, be accepted as a part thereof.

Pending the report of the Commission upon the question or questions so referred and without awaiting such report, the Tribunal may make a separate award upon all or any other questions before it, and such separate award, if made, shall become immediately effective, provided that the report aforesaid shall not be incorporated in the award until it has been considered by the Tribunal. The expenses of such Commission shall be borne in equal moieties by the Parties hereto.

Art. IV. The Tribunal shall recommend for the consideration of the High Contracting Parties rules and a method of procedure under which all questions which may arise in the future regarding the exercise of the liberties above referred to may be determined in accordance with the principles laid down in the award. If the High Contracting Parties shall not adopt the rules and method of procedure so recommended, or if they shall not, subsequently to the delivery of the award, agree upon such rules and methods, then any differences which may arise in the future between the High Contracting Parties relating to the interpretation of the treaty of 1818 or to the effect and application of the award of the Tribunal shall be referred informally to the Permanent Court at The Hague for decision by the summary procedure provided in Chapter IV of The Hague Convention of the 18th of October, 1907.

Art. V. The Tribunal of Arbitration provided for herein shall be chosen from the general list of members of the Permanent Court at The Hague, in accordance with the provisions of Article XLV of the Convention for the Settlement of International Disputes, concluded at the Second Peace Conference at The Hague on the 18th of October, 1907. The provisions of said Convention, so far as applicable and not inconsistent herewith, and excepting Articles LIII and LIV, shall govern the proceedings under the submission herein provided for.

The time allowed for the direct agreement of the President of the United States and His Britannic Majesty on the composition of such Tribunal shall be three months.

Art. VI. The pleadings shall be communicated in the order and within the time following:

As soon as may be and within a period not exceeding seven months from the date of the exchange of notes making this agreement binding the printed case of each of the Parties hereto, accompanied by printed copies of the documents, the official correspondence, and all other evidence on which each Party relies, shall be delivered in duplicate (with such additional copies as may be agreed upon) to the agent of the other Party. It shall be sufficient for this purpose if such case is delivered at the British Embassy at Washington or at the American Embassy at London, as the case may be, for transmission to the agent for its Government.

Within fifteen days thereafter such printed case and accompanying evidence of each of the Parties shall be delivered in duplicate to each member of the Tribunal, and such delivery may be made by depositing within the stated period the necessary number of copies with the International Bureau at The Hague for transmission to the Arbitrators.

After the delivery on both sides of such printed case, either Party may, in like manner, and within four months after the expiration of the period above fixed for the delivery to the agents of the case, deliver to the agent of the other Party (with such additional copies as may be agreed upon), a printed counter-case accompanied by printed copies of additional documents, correspondence, and other evidence in reply to the case, documents, correspondence, and other evidence so presented by the other Party, and within fifteen days thereafter such Party shall, in like manner as above provided, deliver in duplicate such counter-case and accompanying evidence to each of the Arbitrators.

The foregoing provisions shall not prevent the Tribunal from permitting either Party to rely at the hearing upon documentary or other evidence which is shown to have become open to its investigation or examination or available for use too late to be submitted within the period hereinabove fixed for the delivery of copies of evidence, but in case any such evidence is to be presented, printed copies of it, as soon as possible after it is secured, must be delivered, in like manner as provided for the delivery of copies of other evidence, to each of the Arbitrators and to the agent of the other Party. The admission of any such additional evidence, however, shall be subject to such conditions as the Tribunal may impose, and the other Party shall have a reasonable opportunity to offer additional evidence in rebuttal.

The Tribunal shall take into consideration all evidence which is offered by either Party.

ART. VII. If in the case or counter-case (exclusive of the accompanying evidence) either Party shall have specified or referred to any documents, correspondence, or other evidence in its own exclusive possession without annexing a copy, such Party shall be bound, if the other Party shall demand it within thirty days after the delivery of the case or counter-case respectively, to furnish to the Party applying for it a copy thereof; and either Party may, within the like time, demand that the other shall furnish certified copies or produce for inspection the originals of any documentary evidence adduced by the Party upon whom the demand is made. It shall be the duty of the Party upon whom any such demand is made to comply with it as soon as may be, and within a period not exceeding fifteen days after the demand has been received. The production for inspection or the furnishing to the other Party of official governmental publications, publishing, as authentic, copies of the documentary evidence referred to, shall be a sufficient compliance with such demand, if such governmental publications shall have been published prior to the 1st day of January, 1908. If the demand is not complied with, the reasons for the failure to comply must be stated to the Tribunal.

Art. VIII. The Tribunal shall meet within six months after the expiration of the period above fixed for the delivery to the agents of the case, and upon the assembling of the Tribunal at its first session each Party, through its agent or counsel, shall deliver in duplicate to each of the Arbitrators and to the agent and counsel of the other Party (with such additional copies as may be agreed upon) a printed argument showing the points and referring to the evidence upon which it relies.

The time fixed by this Agreement for the delivery of the case, counter-case, or argument, and for the meeting of the Tribunal, may be extended by mutual consent of the Parties.

Art. IX. The decision of the Tribunal shall, if possible, be made within two months from the close of the arguments on both sides, unless on the request of the Tribunal the Parties shall agree to extend the period.

It shall be made in writing, and dated and signed by each member of the Tribunal, and shall be accompanied by a statement of reasons.

A member who may dissent from the decision may record his dissent when signing.

The language to be used throughout the proceedings shall be English.

Art. X. Each Party reserves to itself the right to demand a revision of the award. Such demand shall contain a statement of the grounds on which it is made and shall be made within five days of the promulgation of the award, and shall be heard by the Tribunal within ten days thereafter. The Party making the demands shall serve a copy of the same on the opposite Party, and both Parties shall be heard in argument by the Tribunal on said demand. The demand can only be made on the discovery of some new fact or circumstance calculated to exercise a decisive influence upon the award and which was unknown to the Tribunal and to the Party demanding the revision at the time the discussion was closed, or upon the ground that the said award does not fully and sufficiently, within the meaning of this Agreement, determine any question or questions submitted. If the Tribunal shall allow the demand for a revision, it shall afford such opportunity for further hearings and arguments as it shall deem necessary.

Art. XI. The present Agreement shall be deemed to be binding only when confirmed by the two Governments by an exchange of notes.

In witness whereof this Agreement has been signed and sealed by the Secretary of State of the United States, Elihu Root, on behalf of the United States, and by His Britannic Majesty's Ambassador at Washington, The Right Honorable James Bryce, O. M., on behalf of Great Britain.

Done at Washington on the 27th day of January, one thousand nine hundred and nine.

Elihu Root [seal]
James Bryce [seal]

AWARD OF THE TRIBUNAL[1]

PERMANENT COURT OF ARBITRATION AT THE HAGUE. THE NORTH ATLANTIC COAST FISHERIES

PREAMBLE. Whereas a Special Agreement between the United States of America and Great Britain, signed at Washington the 27th January, 1909, and confirmed by interchange of Notes dated the 4th March, 1909, was concluded in conformity with the provisions of the General Arbitration Treaty between the United States of America and Great Britain, signed the 4th April, 1908, and ratified the 4th June, 1908;

And whereas the said Special Agreement for the submission of questions relating to fisheries on the North Atlantic Coast under the general treaty of Arbitration concluded between the United States and Great Britain on the 4th day of April, 1908, is as follows:

ART. I. Whereas by Article I of the Convention signed at London on the 20th day of October, 1818, between Great Britain and the United States, it was agreed as follows: —

> Whereas differences have arisen respecting the liberty claimed by the United States for the Inhabitants thereof, to take, dry and cure Fish on Certain Coasts, Bays, Harbours and Creeks of His Britannic Majesty's Dominions in America, it is agreed between the High Contracting Parties, that the Inhabitants of the said United States shall have forever, in common with the Subjects of His Britannic Majesty, the Liberty to take Fish of every kind on that part of the Southern Coast of Newfoundland which extends from Cape Ray to the Rameau Islands, on the Western and Northern Coast of Newfoundland, from the said Cape Ray to the Quirpon Islands, on the shores of the Magdalen Islands, and also on the Coasts, Bays, Harbours, and Creeks from Mount Joly on the Southern Coast of Labrador, to and through the Straits of Belleisle and thence Northwardly indefinitely along the coast, without prejudice, however, to any of the exclusive Rights of the Hudson Bay Company; and that the American Fishermen shall also have liberty forever, to dry and cure Fish in any of the unsettled Bays, Harbours, and Creeks of the Southern part of the Coast of Newfoundland hereabove described, and of the Coast of Labrador; but so soon as the same, or any Portion thereof, shall be settled, it shall not be lawful for the said Fishermen to dry or cure Fish at such Portion so settled, without previous agreement for such purpose with the Inhabitants, Proprietors, or Possessors of the ground. — And the United States hereby renounce forever, any Liberty heretofore enjoyed or

[1] Official Report published by the Bureau of the Permanent Court of Arbitration in the North Atlantic Coast Fisheries Case, arbitrated at The Hague, 1910, p. 104.

claimed by the Inhabitants thereof, to take, dry, or cure Fish on, or within three marine Miles of any of the Coasts, Bays, Creeks, or Harbours of His Britannic Majesty's Dominions in America not included within the above-mentioned limits; provided, however, that the American Fishermen shall be admitted to enter such Bays or Harbours for the purpose of Shelter and of repairing Damages therein, of purchasing Wood, and of obtaining Water, and for no other purpose whatever. But they shall be under such Restrictions as may be necessary to prevent their taking, drying or curing Fish therein, or in any other manner whatever abusing the Privileges hereby reserved to them.

And, whereas, differences have arisen as to the scope and meaning of the said Article, and of the liberties therein referred to, and otherwise in respect of the rights and liberties which the inhabitants of the United States have or claim to have in the waters or on the shores therein referred to:

It is agreed that the following questions shall be submitted for decision to a tribunal of arbitration constituted as hereinafter provided: —

Question 1. To what extent are the following contentions or either of them justified?

It is contended on the part of Great Britain that the exercise of the liberty to take fish referred to in the said Article, which the inhabitants of the United States have forever in common with the subjects of His Britannic Majesty, is subject, without the consent of the United States, to reasonable regulation by Great Britain, Canada, or Newfoundland in the form of municipal laws, ordinances, or rules, as, for example, to regulations in respect of (1) the hours, days, or seasons when fish may be taken on the treaty coasts; (2) the method, means, and implements to be used in the taking of fish or in the carrying on of fishing operations on such coasts; (3) any other matters of a similar character relating to fishing; such regulations being reasonable, as being, for instance —

(*a*) Appropriate or necessary for the protection and preservation of such fisheries and the exercise of the rights of British subjects therein and of the liberty which by the said Article I the inhabitants of the United States have therein in common with British subjects;

(*b*) Desirable on grounds of public order and morals;

(*c*) Equitable and fair as between local fishermen and the inhabitants of the United States exercising the said treaty liberty and not so framed as to give unfairly an advantage to the former over the latter class.

It is contended on the part of the United States that the exercise of such liberty is not subject to limitations or restraints by Great Britain, Canada, or Newfoundland in the form of municipal laws, ordinances, or regulations in respect of (1) the hours, days, or seasons when the inhabitants of the United States may take fish on the treaty coasts, or (2) the method, means, and implements used by them in taking fish or in carrying on fishing operations on such coasts, or (3) any other limitations or restraints of similar character —

(*a*) Unless they are appropriate and necessary for the protection and preservation of the common rights in such fisheries and the exercise thereof; and

(*b*) Unless they are reasonable in themselves and fair as between local fishermen and fishermen coming from the United States, and not so framed as to give an advantage to the former over the latter class; and

(*c*) Unless their appropriateness, necessity, reasonableness, and fairness be determined by the United States and Great Britain by common accord and the United States concurs in their enforcement.

Question 2. Have the inhabitants of the United States, while exercising the liberties referred to in said Article, a right to employ as members of the fishing crews of their vessels persons not inhabitants of the United States ?

Question 3. Can the exercise by the inhabitants of the United States of the liberties referred to in the said Article be subjected, without the consent of the United States, to the requirements of entry or report at custom-houses or the payment of light or harbour or other dues, or to any other similar requirement or condition or exaction ?

Question 4. Under the provision of the said Article that the American fishermen shall be admitted to enter certain bays or harbours for shelter, repairs, wood, or water, and for no other purpose whatever, but that they shall be under such restrictions as may be necessary to prevent their taking, drying, or curing fish therein or in any other manner whatever abusing the privileges thereby reserved to them, is it permissible to impose restrictions making the exercise of such privileges conditional upon the payment of light or harbour or other dues, or entering or reporting at custom-houses or any similar conditions ?

Question 5. From where must be measured the " three marine miles of any of the coasts, bays, creeks, or harbours " referred to in the said Article ?

Question 6. Have the inhabitants of the United States the liberty under the said Article or otherwise to take fish in the bays, harbours, and creeks on that part of the southern coast of Newfoundland which extends from Cape Ray to Rameau Islands, or on the western and northern coasts of Newfoundland from Cape Ray to Quirpon Islands, or on the Magdalen Islands ?

Question 7. Are the inhabitants of the United States whose vessels resort to the treaty coasts for the purpose of exercising the liberties referred to in Article I of the treaty of 1818 entitled to have for those vessels, when duly authorized by the United States in that behalf, the commercial privileges on the treaty coasts accorded by agreement or otherwise to United States trading-vessels generally ?

ART. II. Either Party may call the attention of the Tribunal to any legislative or executive act of the other Party, specified within three months of the exchange of notes enforcing this agreement, and which is claimed to be inconsistent with the true interpretation of the Treaty of 1818; and may call upon the Tribunal to express in its award its opinion upon such acts, and to point out in what respects, if any, they are inconsistent with the principles laid down in the award in reply to the preceding questions; and each Party agrees to conform to such opinion.

ART. III. If any question arises in the arbitration regarding the reasonableness of any regulation or otherwise which requires an examination of the practical effect of any provisions in relation to the conditions surrounding the exercise of the liberty of fishery enjoyed by the inhabitants of the United States, or which requires expert information about the fisheries themselves, the Tribunal may, in that case, refer such question to a Commission of three expert specialists in such matters; one to be designated by each of the Parties hereto, and the third, who shall not be a national of either Party, to be designated by the Tribunal. This Commission shall examine into and report their conclusions on any question or questions so referred to it by the Tribunal and such report shall be considered by the Tribunal and shall, if incorporated by them in the award, be accepted as a part thereof.

Pending the report of the Commission upon the question or questions so referred and without awaiting such report, the Tribunal may make a separate award upon all or any other questions before it, and such separate award, if made, shall become immediately effective, provided that the report aforesaid shall not be incorporated in the award until it has been considered by the Tribunal. The expenses of such Commission shall be borne in equal moieties by the Parties hereto.

ART. IV. The Tribunal shall recommend for the consideration of the High Contracting Parties rules and a method of procedure under which all questions which may arise in the future regarding the exercise of the liberties above referred to may be determined in accordance with the principles laid down in the award. If the High Contracting Parties shall not adopt the rules and method of procedure so recommended, or if they shall not, subsequently to the delivery of the award, agree upon such rules and methods, then any differences which may arise in the future between the High Contracting Parties relating to the interpretation of the Treaty of 1818 or to the effect and application of the award of the Tribunal shall be referred informally to the Permanent Court at The Hague for decision by the summary procedure provided in Chapter IV of The Hague Convention of the 18th October, 1907.

ART. V. The Tribunal of Arbitration provided for herein shall be chosen from the general list of members of the Permanent Court at The Hague, in accordance with the provisions of Article XLV of the Convention for the Settlement of International Disputes, concluded at the Second

Peace Conference at The Hague on the 18th of October, 1907. The provisions of said Convention, so far as applicable and not inconsistent herewith, and excepting Articles LIII and LIV, shall govern the proceedings under the submission herein provided for.

The time allowed for the direct agreement of His Britannic Majesty and the President of the United States on the composition of such Tribunal shall be three months.

ART. VI. The pleadings shall be communicated in the order and within the time following:

As soon as may be and within a period not exceeding seven months from the date of the exchange of notes making this agreement binding the printed case of each of the Parties hereto, accompanied by printed copies of the documents, the official correspondence, and all other evidence on which each Party relies, shall be delivered in duplicate (with such additional copies as may be agreed upon) to the agent of the other Party. It shall be sufficient for this purpose if such case is delivered at the British Embassy at Washington or at the American Embassy at London, as the case may be, for transmission to the agent for its Government.

Within fifteen days thereafter such printed case and accompanying evidence of each of the Parties shall be delivered in duplicate to each member of the Tribunal, and such delivery may be made by depositing within the stated period the necessary number of copies with the International Bureau at The Hague for transmission to the Arbitrators.

After the delivery on both sides of such printed case, either Party may, in like manner, and within four months after the expiration of the period above fixed for the delivery to the agents of the case, deliver to the agent of the other Party (with such additional copies as may be agreed upon), a printed counter-case accompanied by printed copies of additional documents, correspondence, and other evidence in reply to the case, documents, correspondence, and other evidence so presented by the other Party, and within fifteen days thereafter such Party shall, in like manner as above provided, deliver in duplicate such counter-case and accompanying evidence to each of the Arbitrators.

The foregoing provisions shall not prevent the Tribunal from permitting either Party to rely at the hearing upon documentary or other evidence which is shown to have become open to its investigation or examination or available for use too late to be submitted within the period hereinabove fixed for the delivery of copies of evidence, but in case any such evidence is to be presented, printed copies of it, as soon as possible after it is secured, must be delivered, in like manner as provided for the delivery of copies of other evidence, to each of the Arbitrators and to the agent of the other Party. The admission of any such additional evidence, however, shall be subject to such conditions as the Tribunal may impose, and the other

Party shall have a reasonable opportunity to offer additional evidence in rebuttal.

The Tribunal shall take into consideration all evidence which is offered by either Party.

Art. VII. If in the case or counter-case (exclusive of the accompanying evidence) either Party shall have specified or referred to any documents, correspondence, or other evidence in its own exclusive possession without annexing a copy, such Party shall be bound, if the other Party shall demand it within thirty days after the delivery of the case or counter-case respectively, to furnish to the Party applying for it a copy thereof; and either Party may, within the like time, demand that the other shall furnish certified copies or produce for inspection the originals of any documentary evidence adduced by the Party upon whom the demand is made. It shall be the duty of the Party upon whom any such demand is made to comply with it as soon as may be, and within a period not exceeding fifteen days after the demand has been received. The production for inspection or the furnishing to the other Party of official governmental publications, publishing, as authentic, copies of the documentary evidence referred to, shall be a sufficient compliance with such demand, if such governmental publications shall have been published prior to the 1st day of January, 1908. If the demand is not complied with, the reasons for the failure to comply must be stated to the Tribunal.

Art. VIII. The Tribunal shall meet within six months after the expiration of the period above fixed for the delivery to the agents of the case, and upon the assembling of the Tribunal at its first session each Party, through its agent or counsel, shall deliver in duplicate to each of the Arbitrators and to the agent and counsel of the other Party (with such additional copies as may be agreed upon) a printed argument showing the points and referring to the evidence upon which it relies.

The time fixed by this Agreement for the delivery of the case, counter-case, or argument, and for the meeting of the Tribunal, may be extended by mutual consent of the Parties.

Art. IX. The decision of the Tribunal shall, if possible, be made within two months from the close of the arguments on both sides, unless on the request of the Tribunal the Parties shall agree to extend the period.

It shall be made in writing, and dated and signed by each member of the Tribunal, and shall be accompanied by a statement of reasons.

A member who may dissent from the decision may record his dissent when signing.

The language to be used throughout the proceedings shall be English.

Art. X. Each Party reserves to itself the right to demand a revision of the award. Such demand shall contain a statement of the grounds on which it is made and shall be made within five days of the promulgation of the award, and shall be heard by the Tribunal within ten days thereafter. The Party making the demand shall serve a copy of the same on the opposite Party, and both Parties shall be heard in argument by the Tribunal on said demand. The demand can only be made on the discovery of some new fact or circumstance calculated to exercise a decisive influence upon the award and which was unknown to the Tribunal and to the Party demanding the revision at the time the discussion was closed, or upon the ground that the said award does not fully and sufficiently, within the meaning of this Agreement, determine any question or questions submitted. If the Tribunal shall allow the demand for a revision, it shall afford such opportunity for further hearings and arguments as it shall deem necessary.

Art. XI. The present Agreement shall be deemed to be binding only when confirmed by the two Governments by an exchange of notes.

In witness whereof this Agreement has been signed and sealed by His Britannic Majesty's Ambassador at Washington, the Right Honourable James Bryce, O. M., on behalf of Great Britain, and by the Secretary of State of the United States, Elihu Root, on behalf of the United States.

Done at Washington on the 27th day of January, one thousand nine hundred and nine.

James Bryce [seal]
Elihu Root [seal]

And whereas, the parties to the said Agreement have by common accord, in accordance with Article V, constituted as a Tribunal of Arbitration the following Members of the Permanent Court at The Hague: Mr. H. Lammasch, Doctor of Law, Professor of the University of Vienna, Aulic Councillor, Member of the Upper House of the Austrian Parliament; His Excellency Jonkheer A. F. De Savornin Lohman, Doctor of Law, Minister of State, Former Minister of the Interior, Member of the Second Chamber of the Netherlands; the Honourable George Gray, Doctor of Laws, Judge of the United States Circuit Court of Appeals, former United States Senator; the Right Honourable Sir Charles Fitzpatrick, Member of the Privy Council, Doctor of Laws, Chief Justice of Canada; the Honourable Luis Maria Drago, Doctor of Law, former Minister of Foreign Affairs of the Argentine Republic, Member of the Law Academy of Buenos-Aires;

And whereas, the Agents of the Parties to the said Agreement have duly and in accordance with the terms of the Agreement communicated to this Tribunal their cases, counter-cases, printed arguments and other documents;

And whereas, counsel for the Parties have fully presented to this Tribunal their oral arguments in the sittings held between the first assembling of the Tribunal on 1st June, 1910, to the close of the hearings on 12th August, 1910;

Now, therefore, this Tribunal having carefully considered the said Agreement, cases, counter-cases, printed and oral arguments, and the documents presented by either side, after due deliberation makes the following decisions and awards:

QUESTION I. To what extent are the following contentions or either of them justified?

It is contended on the part of Great Britain that the exercise of the liberty to take fish referred to in the said Article, which the inhabitants of the United States have forever in common with the subjects of His Britannic Majesty, is subject, without the consent of the United States, to reasonable regulation by Great Britain, Canada, or Newfoundland in the form of municipal laws, ordinances, or rules, as, for example, to regulations in respect of (1) the hours, days, or seasons when fish may be taken on the treaty coasts; (2) the method, means, and implements to be used in the taking of fish or in the carrying on of fishing operations on such coasts; (3) any other matters of a similar character relating to fishing; such regulations being reasonable, as being, for instance —

(*a*) Appropriate or necessary for the protection and preservation of such fisheries and the exercise of the rights of British subjects therein and of the liberty which by the said Article I the inhabitants of the United States have therein in common with British subjects;

(*b*) Desirable on grounds of public order and morals;

(*c*) Equitable and fair as between local fishermen and the inhabitants of the United States exercising the said treaty liberty, and not so framed as to give unfairly an advantage to the former over the latter class.

It is contended on the part of the United States that the exercise of such liberty is not subject to limitations or restraints by Great Britain, Canada, or Newfoundland in the form of municipal laws, ordinances, or regulations in respect of (1) the hours, days, or seasons when the inhabitants of the United States may take fish on the treaty coasts, or (2) the method, means, and implements used by them in taking fish or in carrying on fishing operations on such coasts, or (3) any other limitations or restraints of similar character —

(*a*) Unless they are appropriate and necessary for the protection and preservation of the common rights in such fisheries and the exercise thereof; and

(*b*) Unless they are reasonable in themselves and fair as between local fishermen and fishermen coming from the United States, and not so framed as to give an advantage to the former over the latter class; and

(*c*) Unless their appropriateness, necessity, reasonableness, and fairness be determined by the United States and Great Britain by common accord and the United States concurs in their enforcement.

Question I, thus submitted to the Tribunal, resolves itself into two main contentions:

1st. Whether the right of regulating reasonably the liberties conferred by the Treaty of 1818 resides in Great Britain;

2d. And, if such right does so exist, whether such reasonable exercise of the right is permitted to Great Britain without the accord and concurrence of the United States.

The Treaty of 1818 contains no explicit disposition in regard to the right of regulation, reasonable or otherwise; it neither reserves that right in express terms, nor refers to it in any way. It is therefore incumbent on this Tribunal to answer the two questions above indicated by interpreting the general terms of Article I of the Treaty, and more especially the words " the inhabitants of the United States shall have, forever, in common with the subjects of His Britannic Majesty, the liberty to take fish of every kind." This interpretation must be conformable to the general import of the instrument, the general intention of the parties to it, the subject matter of the contract, the expressions actually used and the evidence submitted.

Now in regard to the preliminary question as to whether the right of reasonable regulation resides in Great Britain:

Considering that the right to regulate the liberties conferred by the Treaty of 1818 is an attribute of sovereignty, and as such must be held to reside in the territorial sovereign, unless the contrary be provided; and considering that one of the essential elements of sovereignty is that it is to be exercised within territorial limits, and that, failing proof to the contrary, the territory is coterminous with the Sovereignty, it follows that the burden of the assertion involved in the contention of the United States (viz. that the right to regulate does not reside independently in Great Britain, the territorial Sovereign) must fall on the United States. And for the purpose of sustaining this burden, the United States have put forward the following series of propositions, each one of which must be singly considered.

It is contended by the United States:

(1) That the French right of fishery under the treaty of 1713 designated also as a liberty, was never subjected to regulation by Great Britain, and therefore the inference is warranted that the American liberties of fishery are similarly exempted.

The Tribunal is unable to agree with this contention:

(*a*) Because although the French right designated in 1713 merely " an allowance," (a term of even less force than that used in regard to the American fishery) was nevertheless converted, in practice, into an exclusive right, this concession on the part of Great Britain was presumably made because France, before 1713, claimed to be the sovereign of Newfoundland, and, in ceding the Island, had, as the American argument says, " reserved for the benefit of its subjects the right to fish and to use the strand " ;

(*b*) Because the distinction between the French and American right is indicated by the different wording of the Statutes for the observance of Treaty obligations towards France and the United States, and by the British Declaration of 1783;

(*c*) And, also, because this distinction is maintained in the Treaty with France of 1904, concluded at a date when the American claim was approaching its present stage, and by which certain common rights of regulation are recognized to France.

For the further purpose of such proof it is contended by the United States:

(2) That the liberties of fishery, being accorded to the inhabitants of the United States " forever," acquire, by being in perpetuity and unilateral, a character exempting them from local legislation.

The Tribunal is unable to agree with this contention:

(*a*) Because there is no necessary connection between the duration of a grant and its essential status in its relation to local regulation; a right granted in perpetuity may yet be subject to regulation, or, granted temporarily, may yet be exempted therefrom; or being reciprocal may yet be unregulated, or being unilateral may yet be regulated: as is evidenced by the claim of the United States that the liberties of fishery accorded by the Reciprocity Treaty of 1854 and the Treaty of 1871 were exempt from regulation, though they were neither permanent nor unilateral;

(*b*) Because no peculiar character need be claimed for these liberties in order to secure their enjoyment in perpetuity, as is evidenced by the American negotiators in 1818 asking for the insertion of the words " forever." International law in its modern development recognizes that a great number of Treaty obligations are not annulled by war, but at most suspended by it;

(*c*) Because the liberty to dry and cure is, pursuant to the terms of the Treaty, provisional and not permanent, and is nevertheless, in respect of the liability to regulation, identical in its nature with, and never distinguished from, the liberty to fish.

For the further purpose of such proof, the United States allege:

(3) That the liberties of fishery granted to the United States constitute an International servitude in their favour over the territory of Great Britain, thereby involving a derogation from the sovereignty of Great Britain, the servient State, and that therefore Great Britain is deprived, by reason of the grant, of its independent right to regulate the fishery.

The Tribunal is unable to agree with this contention:

(*a*) Because there is no evidence that the doctrine of International servitudes was one with which either American or British Statesmen were conversant in 1818, no English publicists employing the term before 1818, and the mention of it in Mr. GALLATIN's report being insufficient;

(*b*) Because a servitude in the French law, referred to by Mr. GALLATIN, can, since the Code, be only real and cannot be personal (Code Civil, art. 686);

(*c*) Because a servitude in International law predicates an express grant of a sovereign right and involves an analogy to the relation of a *praedium dominans* and a *praedium serviens;* whereas by the Treaty of 1818 one State grants a liberty to fish, which is not a sovereign right, but a purely economic right, to the inhabitants of another State;

(*d*) Because the doctrine of International servitude in the sense which is now sought to be attributed to it originated in the peculiar and now obsolete conditions prevailing in the Holy Roman Empire of which the *domini terrae* were not fully sovereigns; they holding territory under the Roman Empire, subject at least theoretically, and in some respects also practically, to the Courts of that Empire; their right being, moreover, rather of a civil than of a public nature, partaking more of the character of *dominium* than of *imperium*, and therefore certainly not a complete sovereignty. And because in contradistinction to this quasi-sovereignty with its incoherent attributes acquired at various times, by various means, and not impaired in its character by being incomplete in any one respect or by being limited in favor of another territory and its possessor, the modern State, and particularly Great Britain, has never admitted partition of sovereignty, owing to the constitution of a modern State requiring essential sovereignty and independence;

(*e*) Because this doctrine being but little suited to the principle of sovereignty which prevails in States under a system of constitutional government such as Great Britain and the United States, and to the present International relations of Sovereign States, has found little, if any, support from modern publicists. It could therefore in the general interest of the Community of Nations, and of the Parties to this Treaty, be affirmed by this Tribunal only on the express evidence of an International contract;

(*f*) Because even if these liberties of fishery constituted an International servitude, the servitude would derogate from the sovereignty of the servient State only in so far as the exercise of the rights of sovereignty by the servient State would be contrary to the exercise of the servitude right by the dominant State. Whereas it is evident that, though every regulation of the fishery is to some extent a limitation, as it puts limits to the exercise of the fishery at will, yet such regulations as are reasonable and made for the purpose of securing and preserving the fishery and its exercise for the common benefit, are clearly to be distinguished from those restrictions and "molestations," the annulment of which was the purpose of the American demands formulated by Mr. ADAMS in 1782, and such regulations consequently cannot be held to be inconsistent with a servitude;

(*g*) Because the fishery to which the inhabitants of the United States were admitted in 1783, and again in 1818, was a regulated fishery, as is evidenced by the following regulations:

Act 15 Charles II, Cap. 16, s. 7 (1663) forbidding " to lay any seine or other net in or near any harbour in Newfoundland, whereby to take the spawn or young fry of the Poor-John, or for any other use or uses, except for the taking of bait only," which had not been superseded either by the order in council of March 10th, 1670, or by the statute 10 and XI Wm. III, Cap. 25, 1699. The order in council provides expressly for the obligation " to submit unto and to observe all rules and orders as are now, or hereafter shall be established," an obligation which cannot be read as referring only to the rules established by this very act, and having no reference to anteceding rules " as are now established." In a similar way, the statute of 1699 preserves in force prior legislation, conferring the freedom of fishery only " as fully and freely as at any time heretofore." The order in council, 1670, provides that the Admirals, who always were fishermen, arriving from an English or Welsh port, " see that His Majesty's rules and orders concerning the regulation of the fisheries are duly put in execution " (sec. 13). Likewise the Act 10 and XI, Wm. III, Cap. 25 (1699) provides that the Admirals do settle differences between the fishermen arising in respect of the places to be assigned to the different vessels. As to Nova Scotia, the proclamation of 1665 ordains that no one shall fish without license; that the licensed fishermen are obliged " to observe all laws and orders which now are made and published, or shall hereafter be made and published in this jurisdiction," and that they shall not fish on the Lord's Day and shall not take fish at the time they come to spawn. The judgment of the Chief Justice of Newfoundland, October 26th 1820, is not held by the Tribunal sufficient to set aside the proclamations referred to. After 1783, the statute 26 Geo. III, Cap. 26, 1786, forbids " the use, on the shores of Newfoundland, of seines or nets for catching cod by hauling on shore or taking into boat, with meshes less than 4 inches "; a prohibition which cannot be considered as limited to the bank fishery. The act for regulating the fisheries of New Brunswick, 1793, which forbids " the placing of nets or seines across any cove or creek in the Province so as to obstruct the natural course of fish," and which makes specific provision for fishing in the Harbour of St. John, as to the manner and time of fishing, cannot be read as being limited to fishing from the shore. The act for regulating the fishing on the coast of Northumberland (1799) contains very elaborate dispositions concerning the fisheries in the bay of Miramichi which were continued in 1823, 1829 and 1834. The statutes of Lower Canada, 1788 and 1807, forbid the throwing overboard of offal. The fact that these acts extend the prohibition over a greater distance than the first marine league from the shore may make them nonoperative against foreigners without the territorial limits of Great Britain, but is certainly no reason to deny their obligatory character for foreigners within these limits;

(*h*) Because the fact that Great Britain rarely exercised the right of regulation in the period immediately succeeding 1818 is to be explained by various circumstances and is not evidence of the non-existence of the right;

(*i*) Because the words " in common with British subjects " tend to confirm the opinion that the inhabitants of the United States were admitted to a regulated fishery;

(*j*) Because the statute of Great Britain, 1819, which gives legislative sanction to the Treaty of 1818, provides for the making of " regulations with relation to the taking, drying and curing of fish by inhabitants of the United States in ' common.' "

For the purpose of such proof, it is further contended by the United States, in this latter connection:

(4) That the words " in common with British subjects " used in the Treaty should not be held as importing a common subjection to regulation, but as intending to negative a possible pretention on the part of the inhabitants of the United States to liberties of fishery exclusive of the right of British subjects to fish.

The Tribunal is unable to agree with this contention:

(*a*) Because such an interpretation is inconsistent with the historical basis of the American fishing liberty. The ground on which Mr. ADAMS founded the American right in 1782 was that the people then constituting the United States had always, when still under British rule, a part in these fisheries and that they must continue to enjoy their past right in the future. He proposed " that the subjects of His Britannic Majesty and the people of the United States shall continue to enjoy unmolested the right to take fish . . . where the inhabitants of both countries used, at any time heretofore, to fish." The theory of the partition of the fisheries, which by the American negotiators had been advanced with so much force, negatives the assumption that the United States could ever pretend to an exclusive right to fish on the British shores; and to insert a special disposition to that end would have been wholly superfluous;

(*b*) Because the words " in common " occur in the same connection in the Treaty of 1818 as in the Treaties of 1854 and 1871. It will certainly not be suggested that in these Treaties of 1854 and 1871 the American negotiators meant by inserting the words " in common " to imply that without these words American citizens would be precluded from the right to fish on their own coasts and that, on American shores, British subjects should have an exclusive privilege. It would have been the very opposite of the concept of territorial waters to suppose that, without a special treaty-provision, British subjects could be excluded from fishing in British waters.

Therefore that cannot have been the scope and the sense of the words " in common ";

(*c*) Because the words " in common " exclude the supposition that American inhabitants were at liberty to act at will for the purpose of taking fish, without any regard to the co-existing rights of other persons entitled to do the same thing; and because these words admit them only as members of a social community, subject to the ordinary duties binding upon the citizens of that community, as to the regulations made for the common benefit; thus avoiding the " bellum omnium contra omnes " which would otherwise arise in the exercise of this industry;

(*d*) Because these words are such as would naturally suggest themselves to the negotiators of 1818 if their intention had been to express a common subjection to regulations as well as a common right.

In the course of the Argument it has also been alleged by the United States:

(5) That the Treaty of 1818 should be held to have entailed a transfer or partition of sovereignty, in that it must in respect to the liberties of fishery be interpreted in its relation to the Treaty of 1783; and that this latter Treaty was an act of partition of sovereignty and of separation, and as such was not annulled by the war of 1812.

Although the Tribunal is not called upon to decide the issue whether the treaty of 1783 was a treaty of partition or not, the questions involved therein having been set at rest by the subsequent Treaty of 1818, nevertheless the Tribunal could not forbear to consider the contention on account of the important bearing the controversy has upon the true interpretation of the Treaty of 1818. In that respect the Tribunal is of opinion:

(*a*) That the right to take fish was accorded as a condition of peace to a foreign people; wherefore the British negotiators refused to place the right of British subjects on the same footing with those of American inhabitants; and further, refused to insert the words also proposed by Mr. ADAMS — " continue to enjoy " — in the second branch of Art. III of the Treaty of 1783;

(*b*) That the Treaty of 1818 was in different terms, and very different in extent, from that of 1783, and was made for different considerations. It was, in other words, a new grant.

For the purpose of such proof it is further contended by the United States:

(6) That as contemporary Commercial Treaties contain express provisions for submitting foreigners to local legislation, and the Treaty of 1818 contains no such provision, it should be held, *a contrario*, that inhabitants of the United States exercising these liberties are exempt from regulation.

The Tribunal is unable to agree with this contention:

(*a*) Because the Commercial Treaties contemplated did not admit foreigners to all and equal rights, seeing that local legislation excluded them from many rights of importance, e. g. that of holding land; and the purport of the provisions in question consequently was to preserve these discriminations. But no such discriminations existing in the common enjoyment of the fishery by American and British fishermen, no such provision was required;

(*b*) Because no proof is furnished of similar exemptions of foreigners from local legislation in default of Treaty stipulations subjecting them thereto;

(*c*) Because no such express provision for subjection of the nationals of either Party to local law was made either in this Treaty, in respect to their reciprocal admission to certain territories as agreed in Art. III, or in Art. III of the Treaty of 1794; although such subjection was clearly contemplated by the Parties.

For the purpose of such proof it is further contended by the United States:

(7) That, as the liberty to dry and cure on the Treaty coasts and to enter bays and harbours on the non-treaty coasts are both subjected to conditions, and the latter to specific restrictions, it should therefore be held that the liberty to fish should be subjected to no restrictions, as none are provided for in the Treaty.

The Tribunal is unable to apply the principle of "*expressio unius exclusio alterius*" to this case:

(*a*) Because the conditions and restrictions as to the liberty to dry and cure on the shore and to enter the harbours are limitations of the rights themselves, and not restrictions of their exercise. Thus the right to dry and cure is limited in duration, and the right to enter bays and harbours is limited to particular purposes;

(*b*) Because these restrictions of the right to enter bays and harbours applying solely to American fishermen must have been expressed in the Treaty, whereas regulations of the fishery, applying equally to American and British, are made by right of territorial sovereignty.

For the purpose of such proof it has been contended by the United States:

(8) That Lord Bathurst in 1815 mentioned the American right under the Treaty of 1783 as a right to be exercised "at the discretion of the United States"; and that this should be held as to be derogatory to the claim of exclusive regulation by Great Britain.

But the Tribunal is unable to agree with this contention:

(*a*) Because these words implied only the necessity of an express stipulation for any liberty to use foreign territory at the pleasure of the grantee, without touching any question as to regulation;

(*b*) Because in this same letter Lord Bathurst characterized this right as a policy "temporary and experimental, depending on the use that might be made of it, on the condition of the islands and places where it was to be exercised, and the more general conveniences or inconveniences from a military, naval and commercial point of view"; so that it cannot have been his intention to acknowledge the exclusion of British interference with this right;

(c) Because Lord BATHURST in his note to Governor Sir C. HAMILTON in 1819 orders the Governor to take care that the American fishery on the coast of Labrador be carried on *in the same manner* as previous to the late war; showing that he did not interpret the Treaty just signed as a grant conveying absolute immunity from interference with the American fishery right.

For the purpose of such proof it is further contended by the United States:

(9) That on various other occasions following the conclusion of the Treaty, as evidenced by official correspondence, Great Britain made use of expressions inconsistent with the claim to a right of regulation.

The Tribunal, unwilling to invest such expressions with an importance entitling them to affect the general question, considers that such conflicting or inconsistent expressions as have been exposed on either side are sufficiently explained by their relations to ephemeral phases of a controversy of almost secular duration, and should be held to be without direct effect on the principal and present issues.

Now with regard to the second contention involved in Question I, as to whether the right of regulation can be reasonably exercised by Great Britain without the consent of the United States:

Considering that the recognition of a concurrent right of consent in the United States would affect the independence of Great Britain, which would become dependent on the Government of the United States for the exercise of its sovereign right of regulation, and considering that such a co-dominium would be contrary to the constitution of both sovereign States; the burden of proof is imposed on the United States to show that the independence of Great Britain was thus impaired by international contract in 1818 and that a co-dominium was created.

For the purpose of such proof it is contended by the United States:

(10) That a concurrent right to coöperate in the making and enforcement of regulations is the only possible and proper security to their inhabitants for the enjoyment of their liberties of fishery, and that such a right must be held to be implied in the grant of those liberties by the Treaty under interpretation.

The Tribunal is unable to accede to this claim on the ground of a right so implied:

(a) Because every State has to execute the obligations incurred by Treaty *bona fide*, and is urged thereto by the ordinary sanctions of International Law in regard to observance of Treaty obligations. Such sanctions are, for instance, appeal to public opinion, publication of correspondence, censure by Parliamentary vote, demand for arbitration with the odium attendant on a refusal to arbitrate, rupture of relations, reprisal, etc. But no reason has been shown why this Treaty, in this respect, should be considered as different from every other Treaty under which the right of a State to regulate the action of foreigners admitted by it on its territory is recognized;

(*b*) Because the exercise of such a right of consent by the United States would predicate an abandonment of its independence in this respect by Great Britain, and the recognition by the latter of a concurrent right of regulation in the United States. But the Treaty conveys only a liberty to take fish in common, and neither directly nor indirectly conveys a joint right of regulation;

(*c*) Because the Treaty does not convey a common right of fishery, but a liberty to fish in common. This is evidenced by the attitude of the United States Government in 1823, with respect to the relations of Great Britain and France in regard to the fishery;

(*d*) Because if the consent of the United States were requisite for the fishery a general veto would be accorded them, the full exercise of which would be socially subversive and would lead to the consequence of an unregulatable fishery;

(*e*) Because the United States cannot by assent give legal force and validity to British legislation;

(*f*) Because the liberties to take fish in British territorial waters and to dry and cure fish on land in British territory are in principle on the same footing; but in practice a right of coöperation in the elaboration and enforcement of regulations in regard to the latter liberty (drying and curing fish on land) is unrealizable.

In any event, Great Britain, as the local sovereign, has the duty of preserving and protecting the fisheries. In so far as it is necessary for that purpose, Great Britain is not only entitled, but obliged, to provide for the protection and preservation of the fisheries; always remembering that the exercise of this right of legislation is limited by the obligation to execute the Treaty in good faith. This has been admitted by counsel and recognized by Great Britain in limiting the right of regulation to that of reasonable regulation. The inherent defect of this limitation of reasonableness, without any sanction except in diplomatic remonstrance, has been supplied by the submission to arbitral award as to existing regulations in accordance with Arts. II and III of the Special Agreement, and as to further regulation by the obligation to submit their reasonableness to an arbitral test in accordance with Art. IV of the Agreement.

It is finally contended by the United States:

That the United States did not expressly agree that the liberty granted to them could be subjected to any restriction that the grantor might choose to impose on the ground that in her judgment such restriction was reasonable. And that while admitting that all laws of a general character, controlling the conduct of men within the territory of Great Britain, are effective, binding and beyond objection by the United States, and competent to be made upon the sole determination of Great Britain or her colony, without accountability to anyone whomsoever; yet there is somewhere a line, beyond which it is not competent for Great Britain to go, or beyond which she cannot rightfully go, because to go beyond it would be an invasion of the right granted to the United States in 1818. That the legal effect of the grant of 1818 was not to leave the determination as to where that line is to be drawn to the uncontrolled judgment of the grantor, either upon the grantor's consideration as to what would be a reasonable exercise of its sovereignty over the British Empire, or upon the grantor's consideration of what would be a reasonable exercise thereof towards the grantee.

But this contention is founded on assumptions, which this Tribunal cannot accept for the following reasons in addition to those already set forth:

(*a*) Because the line by which the respective rights of both Parties accruing out of the Treaty are to be circumscribed, can refer only to the right granted by the Treaty; that is to say to the liberty of taking, drying and curing fish by American inhabitants in certain British waters in common with British subjects, and not to the exercise of rights of legislation by Great Britain not referred to in the Treaty;

(*b*) Because a line which would limit the exercise of sovereignty of a State within the limits of its own territory can be drawn only on the ground of express stipulation, and not by implication from stipulations concerning a different subject-matter;

(*c*) Because the line in question is drawn according to the principle of international law that treaty obligations are to be executed in perfect good faith, therefore excluding the right to legislate *at will* concerning the subject-matter of the Treaty, and limiting the exercise of sovereignty of the States bound by a treaty with respect to that subject-matter to such acts as are consistent with the treaty;

(*d*) Because on a true construction of the Treaty the question does not arise whether the United States agreed that Great Britain should retain the right to legislate with regard to the fisheries in her own territory; but whether the Treaty contains an abdication by Great Britain of the right which Great Britain, as the sovereign power, undoubtedly possessed when the Treaty was made, to regulate those fisheries;

(*e*) Because the right to make reasonable regulations, not inconsistent with the obligations of the Treaty, which is all that is claimed by Great

Britain, for a fishery which both parties admit requires regulation for its preservation, is not a restriction of or an invasion of the liberty granted to the inhabitants of the United States. This grant does not contain words to justify the assumption that the sovereignty of Great Britain upon its own territory was in any way affected; nor can words be found in the treaty transferring any part of that sovereignty to the United States. Great Britain assumed only duties with regard to the exercise of its sovereignty. The sovereignty of Great Britain over the coastal waters and territory of Newfoundland remains after the Treaty as unimpaired as it was before. But from the Treaty results an obligatory relation whereby the right of Great Britain to exercise its right of sovereignty by making regulations is limited to such regulations as are made in good faith, and are not in violation of the Treaty;

(*f*) Finally to hold that the United States, the grantee of the fishing right, has a voice in the preparation of fishery legislation involves the recognition of a right in that country to participate in the internal legislation of Great Britain and her Colonies, and to that extent would reduce these countries to a state of dependence.

While therefore unable to concede the claim of the United States as based on the Treaty, this Tribunal considers that such claim has been and is to some extent, conceded in the relations now existing between the two Parties. Whatever may have been the situation under the Treaty of 1818 standing alone, the exercise of the right of regulation inherent in Great Britain has been, and is, limited by the repeated recognition of the obligations already referred to, by the limitations and liabilities accepted in the Special Agreement, by the unequivocal position assumed by Great Britain in the presentation of its case before this Tribunal, and by the consequent view of this Tribunal that it would be consistent with all the circumstances, as revealed by this record, as to the duty of Great Britain, that she should submit the reasonableness of any future regulation to such an impartial arbitral test, affording full opportunity therefor, as is hereafter recommended under the authority of Article IV of the Special Agreement, whenever the reasonableness of any regulation is objected to or challenged by the United States in the manner, and within the time hereinafter specified in the said recommendation.

Now therefore this Tribunal decides and awards as follows:

The right of Great Britain to make regulations without the consent of the United States, as to the exercise of the liberty to take fish referred to in Article I of the Treaty of October 20th, 1818, in the form of municipal laws, ordinances or rules of Great Britain, Canada or Newfoundland is inherent to the sovereignty of Great Britain.

The exercise of that right by Great Britain is, however, limited by the said Treaty in respect of the said liberties therein granted to the inhabitants of the United States in that such regulations must be made bona fide and must not be in violation of the said Treaty.

Regulations which are (1) appropriate or necessary for the protection and preservation of such fisheries, or (2) desirable or necessary on grounds of public order and morals without unnecessarily interfering with the fishery itself, and in both cases equitable and fair as between local and American fishermen, and not so framed as to give unfairly an advantage to the former over the latter class, are not inconsistent with the obligation to execute the Treaty in good faith, and are therefore reasonable and not in violation of the Treaty.

For the decision of the question whether a regulation is or is not reasonable, as being or not in accordance with the dispositions of the Treaty and not in violation thereof, the Treaty of 1818 contains no special provision. The settlement of differences in this respect that might arise thereafter was left to the ordinary means of diplomatic intercourse. By reason, however, of the form in which Question I is put, and by further reason of the admission of Great Britain by her counsel before this Tribunal that it is not now for either of the Parties to the Treaty to determine the reasonableness of any regulation made by Great Britain, Canada or Newfoundland, the reasonableness of any such regulation, if contested, must be decided not by either of the Parties, but by an impartial authority in accordance with the principles hereinabove laid down, and in the manner proposed in the recommendations made by the Tribunal in virtue of Article IV of the Agreement.

The Tribunal further decides that Article IV of the Agreement is, as stated by counsel of the respective Parties at the argument, permanent in its effect, and not terminable by the expiration of the General Arbitration Treaty of 1908, between Great Britain and the United States.

In execution, therefore, of the responsibilities imposed upon this Tribunal in regard to Articles II, III and IV of the Special Agreement, we hereby pronounce in their regard as follows:

As to Article II

Pursuant to the provisions of this Article, hereinbefore cited, either Party has called the attention of this Tribunal to acts of the other claimed to be inconsistent with the true interpretation of the Treaty of 1818.

But in response to a request from the Tribunal, recorded in Protocol No. XXVI of 19th July, for an exposition of the grounds of such objections, the Parties replied as reported in Protocol No. XXX of 28th July to the following effect:

His Majesty's Government considered that it would be unnecessary to call upon the Tribunal for an opinion under the second clause of Article II, in regard to the executive act of the United States of America in sending warships to the territorial waters in question, in view of the recognized motives of the United States of America in taking this action and of the relations maintained by their representatives with the local authorities. And this being the sole act to which the attention of this Tribunal has been called by His Majesty's Government, no further action in their behalf is required from this Tribunal under Article II.

The United States of America presented a statement in which their claim that specific provisions of certain legislative and executive acts of the Governments of Canada and Newfoundland were inconsistent with the true interpretation of the Treaty of 1818 was based on the contention that these provisions were not "reasonable" within the meaning of Question I.

After calling upon this Tribunal to express an opinion on these acts, pursuant to the second clause of Article II, the United States of America pointed out in that statement that under Article III any question regarding the reasonableness of any regulation might be referred by the Tribunal to a Commission of expert specialists, and expressed an intention of asking for such reference under certain circumstances.

The Tribunal having carefully considered the counter-statement presented on behalf of Great Britain at the session of August 2nd, is of opinion that the decision on the reasonableness of these regulations requires expert information about the fisheries themselves and an examination of the practical effect of a great number of these provisions in relation to the conditions surrounding the exercise of the liberty of fishery enjoyed by the inhabitants of the United States, as contemplated by Article III. No further action on behalf of the United States is therefore required from this Tribunal under Article II.

As to Article III

As provided in Article III, hereinbefore cited and above referred to, "any question regarding the reasonableness of any regulation, or otherwise, which requires an examination of the practical effect of any provisions surrounding the exercise of the liberty of fishery enjoyed by the inhabitants of the United States, or which requires expert information about the fisheries themselves, may be referred by this Tribunal to a Commission of expert specialists; one to be designated by each of the Parties hereto and the third, who shall not be a national of either Party, to be designated by the Tribunal."

The Tribunal now therefore calls upon the Parties to designate within one month their national Commissioners for the expert examination of the questions submitted.

As the third non-national Commissioner this Tribunal designates Doctor P. P. C. Hoek, Scientific Adviser for the fisheries of the Netherlands and if any necessity arises therefore a substitute may be appointed by the President of this Tribunal.

After a reasonable time, to be agreed on by the Parties, for the expert Commission to arrive at a conclusion, by conference, or, if necessary, by local inspection, the Tribunal shall, if convoked by the President at the request of either Party, thereupon at the earliest convenient date, reconvene to consider the report of the Commission, and if it be on the whole unanimous shall incorporate it in the award. If not on the whole unanimous, i. e., on all points which in the opinion of the Tribunal are of essential importance, the Tribunal shall make its award as to the regulations concerned after consideration of the conclusions of the expert Commissioners and after hearing argument by counsel.

But while recognizing its responsibilities to meet the obligations imposed on it under Article III of the Special Agreement, the Tribunal hereby recommends as an alternative to having recourse to a reconvention of this Tribunal, that the Parties should accept the unanimous opinion of the Commission or the opinion of the non-national Commissioner on any points in dispute as an arbitral award rendered under the provisions of Chapter IV of the Hague Convention of 1907.

As to Article IV

Pursuant to the provisions of this Article, hereinbefore cited, this Tribunal recommends for the consideration of the Parties the following rules and method of procedure under which all questions which may arise in the future regarding the exercise of the liberties above referred to may be determined in accordance with the principles laid down in this award.

1. All future municipal laws, ordinances or rules for the regulation of the fishery by Great Britain in respect of (1) the hours, days or seasons when fish may be taken on the Treaty coasts; (2) the method, means and implements used in the taking of fish or in carrying on fishing operations; (3) any other regulation of a similar character shall be published in the London Gazette two months before going into operation.

Similar regulations by Canada or Newfoundland shall be similarly published in the Canada Gazette and the Newfoundland Gazette respectively.

2. If the Government of the United States considers any such laws or regulations inconsistent with the Treaty of 1818, it is entitled to so notify the Government of Great Britain within the two months referred to in Rule No. 1.
3. Any law or regulation so notified shall not come into effect with respect to inhabitants of the United States until the Permanent Mixed Fishery Commission has decided that the regulation is reasonable within the meaning of this award.
4. Permanent Mixed Fishery Commissions for Canada and Newfoundland respectively shall be established for the decision of such questions as to the reasonableness of future regulations, as contemplated by Article IV of the Special Agreement; these Commissions shall consist of an expert national appointed by either Party for five years. The third member shall not be a national of either Party; he shall be nominated for five years by agreement of the Parties, or failing such agreement within two months, he shall be nominated by Her Majesty the Queen of the Netherlands. The two national members shall be convoked by the Government of Great Britain within one month from the date of notification by the Government of the United States
5. The two national members having failed to agree within one month, within another month the full Commission, under the presidency of the umpire, is to be convoked by Great Britain. It must deliver its decision, if the two Governments do not agree otherwise, at the latest in three months. The Umpire shall conduct the procedure in accordance with that provided in Chapter IV of the Convention for the Pacific Settlement of International Disputes, except in so far as herein otherwise provided.
6. The form of convocation of the Commission including the terms of reference of the question at issue shall be as follows: "The provision hereinafter fully set forth of an Act dated ———, published in the ——— has been notified to the Government of Great Britain by the Government of the United States, under date of ———, as provided by the award of the Hague Tribunal of September 7th, 1910.

"Pursuant to the provisions of that award the Government of Great Britain hereby convokes the Permanent Mixed Fishery Commission for $\frac{\text{(Canada)}}{\text{(Newfoundland)}}$, composed of ——— Commissioner for the United States of America, and of ——— Commissioner for $\frac{\text{(Canada)}}{\text{(Newfoundland)}}$, which shall meet at ——— and render a decision within one month as to whether the provision so notified is reasonable and consistent with the Treaty of 1818, as interpreted by the award of the Hague Tribunal of September 7th, 1910, and if not, in what respect it is unreasonable and inconsistent therewith.

" Failing an agreement on this question within one month the Commission shall so notify the Government of Great Britain in order that the further action required by that award may be taken for the decision of the above question.

" The provision is as follows: ———

7. The unanimous decision of the two national Commissioners, or the majority decision of the Umpire and one Commissioner, shall be final and binding.

Question II

Have the inhabitants of the United States, while exercising the liberties referred to in said Article, a right to employ as members of the fishing crews of their vessels persons not inhabitants of the United States ?

In regard to this question the United States claim in substance:

1. That the liberty assured to their inhabitants by the Treaty plainly includes the right to use all the means customary or appropriate for fishing upon the sea, not only ships and nets and boats, but crews to handle the ships and the nets and the boats;

2. That no right to control or limit the means which these inhabitants shall use in fishing can be admitted unless it is provided in the terms of the Treaty and no right to question the nationality or inhabitancy of the crews employed is contained in the terms of the Treaty.

And Great Britain claims:

1. That the Treaty confers the liberty to inhabitants of the United States exclusively;

2. That the Governments of Great Britain, Canada or Newfoundland may, without infraction of the Treaty, prohibit persons from engaging as fishermen in American vessels.

Now considering (1) that the liberty to take fish is an economic right attributed by the Treaty; (2) that it is attributed to inhabitants of the United States, without any mention of their nationality; (3) that the exercise of an economic right includes the right to employ servants; (4) that the right of employing servants has not been limited by the Treaty to the employment of persons of a distinct nationality or inhabitancy; (5) that the liberty to take fish as an economic liberty refers not only to the individuals doing the manual act of fishing, but also to those for whose profit the fish are taken.

But considering, that the Treaty does not intend to grant to individual persons or to a class of persons the liberty to take fish in certain waters " in common," that is to say in company, with individual British subjects, in the sense that no law could forbid British subjects to take service on American fishing ships; (2) that the Treaty intends to secure to the United States a share of the fisheries designated therein, not only in the interest of a certain class of individuals, but also in the interest of both the United States and Great Britain, as appears from the evidence and notably from the correspondence between Mr. ADAMS and Lord BATHURST in 1815; (3) that the inhabitants of the United States do not derive the liberty to take fish directly from the Treaty, but from the United States Government as party to the Treaty with Great Britain and moreover exercising the right to regulate the conditions under which its inhabitants may enjoy the granted liberty; (4) that it is in the interest of the inhabitants of the United States that the fishing liberty granted to them be restricted to exercise by them and removed from the enjoyment of other aliens not entitled by this Treaty to participate in the fisheries; (5) that such restrictions have been throughout enacted in the British Statute of June 15, 1819, and that of June 3, 1824, to this effect, that no alien or stranger whatsoever shall fish in the waters designated therein, except in so far as by treaty thereto entitled, and that this exception will, in virtue of the Treaty of 1818, as hereinabove interpreted by this award, exempt from these statutes American fishermen fishing by the agency of non-inhabitant aliens employed in their service; (6) that the Treaty does not affect the sovereign right of Great Britain as to aliens, non-inhabitants of the United States, nor the right of Great Britain to regulate the engagement of British subjects, while these aliens or British subjects are on British territory.

Now therefore, in view of the preceding considerations this Tribunal is of opinion that the inhabitants of the United States while exercising the liberties referred to in the said article have a right to employ, as members of the fishing crews of their vessels, persons not inhabitants of the United States.

But in view of the preceding considerations the Tribunal, to prevent any misunderstanding as to the effect of its award, expresses the opinion that non-inhabitants employed as members of the fishing crews of United States vessels derive no benefit or immunity from the Treaty and it is so decided and awarded.

QUESTION III

Can the exercise by the inhabitants of the United States of the liberties referred to in the said Article be subjected, without the consent of the United States, to the requirements of entry or report at custom-houses or the payment of light or harbour or other dues, or to any other similar requirement or condition or exaction ?

The Tribunal is of opinion as follows:

It is obvious that the liberties referred to in this question are those that relate to taking fish and to drying and curing fish on certain coasts as prescribed in the Treaty of October 20, 1818. The exercise of these liberties by the inhabitants of the United States in the prescribed waters to which they relate, has no reference to any commercial privileges which may or may not attach to such vessels by reason of any supposed authority outside the Treaty, which itself confers no commercial privileges whatever upon the inhabitants of the United States or the vessels in which they may exercise the fishing liberty. It follows, therefore, that when the inhabitants of the United States are not seeking to exercise the commercial privileges accorded to trading vessels for the vessels in which they are exercising the granted liberty of fishing, they ought not to be subjected to requirements as to report and entry at custom-houses that are only appropriate to the exercise of commercial privileges. The exercise of the fishing liberty is distinct from the exercise of commercial or trading privileges and it is not competent for Great Britain or her colonies to impose upon the former exactions only appropriate to the latter. The reasons for the requirements enumerated in the case of commercial vessels, have no relation to the case of fishing vessels.

We think, however, that the requirement that American fishing vessels should report, if proper conveniences and an opportunity for doing so are provided, is not unreasonable or inappropriate. Such a report, while serving the purpose of a notification of the presence of a fishing vessel in the treaty waters for the purpose of exercising the treaty liberty, while it gives an opportunity for a proper surveillance of such vessel by revenue officers, may also serve to afford to such fishing vessel protection from interference in the exercise of the fishing liberty. There should be no such requirement, however, unless reasonably convenient opportunity therefor be afforded in person or by telegraph, at a custom-house or to a customs official.

The Tribunal is also of opinion that light and harbour dues, if not imposed on Newfoundland fishermen, should not be imposed on American fishermen while exercising the liberty granted by the Treaty. To impose such dues on American fishermen only would constitute an unfair discrimination between them and Newfoundland fishermen and one inconsistent with the liberty granted to American fishermen to take fish, etc., "in common with the subjects of His Britannic Majesty."

Further, the Tribunal considers that the fulfillment of the requirement as to report by fishing vessels on arrival at the fishery would be greatly facilitated in the interests of both parties by the adoption of a system of registration, and distinctive marking of the fishing boats of both parties, analogous to that established by Articles V to XIII, inclusive, of the International Convention signed at The Hague, 8 May, 1882, for the regulation of the North Sea Fisheries.

The Tribunal therefore decides and awards as follows:

The requirement that an American fishing vessel should report, if proper conveniences for doing so are at hand, is not unreasonable, for the reasons stated in the foregoing opinion. There should be no such requirement, however, unless there be reasonably convenient opportunity afforded to report in person or by telegraph, either at a custom-house or to a customs official.

But the exercise of the fishing liberty by the inhabitants of the United States should not be subjected to the purely commercial formalities of report, entry and clearance at a custom-house, nor to light, harbor or other dues not imposed upon Newfoundland fishermen.

Question IV

Under the provision of the said Article that the American fishermen shall be admitted to enter certain bays or harbours for shelter, repairs, wood, or water, and for no other purpose whatever, but that they shall be under such restrictions as may be necessary to prevent their taking, drying, or curing fish therein or in any other manner whatever abusing the privileges thereby reserved to them, is it permissible to impose restrictions making the exercise of such privileges conditional upon the payment of light or harbour or other dues, or entering or reporting at custom-houses or any similar conditions ?

The Tribunal is of opinion that the provision in the first Article of the Treaty of October 20th, 1818, admitting American fishermen to enter certain bays or harbours for shelter, repairs, wood and water, and for no other purpose whatever, is an exercise in large measure of those duties of hospitality and humanity which all civilized nations impose upon themselves and expect the performance of from others. The enumerated purposes for which entry is permitted all relate to the exigencies in which those who pursue their perilous calling on the sea may be involved. The proviso which appears in the first article of the said Treaty immediately after the so-called renunciation clause, was doubtless due to a recognition by Great Britain of what was expected from the humanity and civilization of the then leading commercial nation of the world. To impose restrictions making the exercise of such privileges conditional upon the payment of light, harbor or other dues, or entering and reporting at custom-houses, or any similar conditions would be inconsistent with the grounds upon which such privileges rest and therefore is not permissible.

And it is decided and awarded that such restrictions are not permissible.

It seems reasonable, however, in order that these privileges accorded by Great Britain on these grounds of hospitality and humanity should not be abused, that the American fishermen entering such bays for any of the four purposes aforesaid and remaining more than 48 hours therein, should be required, if thought necessary by Great Britain or the Colonial Government, to report, either in person or by telegraph, at a custom-house or to a customs official, if reasonably convenient opportunity therefor is afforded. And it is so decided and awarded.

Question V

From where must be measured the "three marine miles of any of the coasts, bays, creeks, or harbours" referred to in the said Article?

In regard to this question, Great Britain claims that the renunciation applies to all bays generally and

The United States contend that it applies to bays of a certain class or condition.

Now, considering that the Treaty used the general term "bays" without qualification, the Tribunal is of opinion that these words of the Treaty must be interpreted in a general sense as applying to every bay on the coast in question that might be reasonably supposed to have been considered as a bay by the negotiators of the Treaty under the general conditions then prevailing, unless the United States can adduce satisfactory proof that any restrictions or qualifications of the general use of the term were or should have been present to their minds.

And for the purpose of such proof the United States contend:

1°. That while a State may renounce the treaty right to fish in foreign territorial waters, it cannot renounce the natural right to fish on the High Seas.

But the Tribunal is unable to agree with this contention. Because though a State cannot grant rights on the High Seas it certainly can abandon the exercise of its right to fish on the High Seas within certain definite limits. Such an abandonment was made with respect to their fishing rights in the waters in question by France and Spain in 1763. By a convention between the United Kingdom and the United States in 1846, the two countries assumed ownership over waters in Fuca Straits at distances from the shore as great as 17 miles.

The United States contend moreover:

2°. That by the use of the term "liberty to fish" the United States manifested the intention to renounce the liberty in the waters referred to only in so far as that liberty was dependent upon or derived from a concession on the part of Great Britain, and not to renounce the right to fish in those waters where it was enjoyed by virtue of their natural right as an independent State.

But the Tribunal is unable to agree with this contention:

(*a*) Because of the term "liberty to fish" was used in the renunciatory clause of the Treaty of 1818 because the same term had been previously used in the Treaty of 1783 which gave the liberty; and it was proper to use in the renunciation clause the same term that was used in the grant with respect to the object of the grant; and, in view of the terms of the grant, it would have been improper to use the term " right " in the renunciation. Therefore the conclusion drawn from the use of the term " liberty " instead of the term " right " is not justified;

(*b*) Because the term " liberty " was a term properly applicable to the renunciation which referred not only to fishing in the territorial waters but also to drying and curing on the shore. This latter right was undoubtedly held under the provisions of the Treaty and was not a right accruing to the United States by virtue of any principle of International law.

3°. The United States also contend that the term " bays of His Britannic Majesty's Dominions " in the renunciatory clause must be read as including only those bays which were under the territorial sovereignty of Great Britain.

But the Tribunal is unable to accept this contention:

(*a*) Because the description of the coast on which the fishery is to be exercised by the inhabitants of the United States is expressed throughout the Treaty of 1818 in geographical terms and not by reference to political control; the Treaty describes the coast as contained between capes;

(*b*) Because to express the political concept of dominion as equivalent to sovereignty, the word " dominion " in the singular would have been an adequate term and not " dominions " in the plural; this latter term having a recognized and well settled meaning as descriptive of those portions of the Earth which owe political allegiance to His Majesty; e. g., " His Britannic Majesty's Dominions beyond the Seas."

4°. It has been further contended by the United States that the renunciation applies only to bays six miles or less in width " inter fauces terrae," those bays only being territorial bays, because the three mile rule is, as shown by this Treaty, a principle of international law applicable to coasts and should be strictly and systematically applied to bays.

But the Tribunal is unable to agree with this contention:

(*a*) Because admittedly the geographical character of a bay contains conditions which concern the interests of the territorial sovereign to a more intimate and important extent than do those connected with the open coast. Thus conditions of national and territorial integrity, of defense, of commerce and of industry are all vitally concerned with the control of the bays penetrating the national coast line. This interest varies, speaking generally in proportion to the penetration inland of the bay; but as no principle of international law recognizes any specified relation between the concavity of the bay and the requirements for control by the territorial sovereignty, this Tribunal is unable to qualify by the application of any new principle its interpretation of the Treaty of 1818 as excluding bays in general from the strict and systematic application of the three mile rule; nor can this Tribunal take cognizance in this connection of other principles concerning the territorial sovereignty over bays such as ten mile or twelve mile limits of exclusion based on international acts subsequent to the treaty of 1818 and relating to coasts of a different configuration and conditions of a different character;

(*b*) Because the opinion of jurists and publicists quoted in the proceedings conduce to the opinion that speaking generally the three mile rule should not be strictly and systematically applied to bays;

(*c*) Because the treaties referring to these coasts, antedating the treaty of 1818, made special provisions as to bays, such as the Treaties of 1686 and 1713 between Great Britain and France, and especially the Treaty of 1778 between the United States and France. Likewise JAY's Treaty of 1794 Art. 25, distinguished bays from the space " within cannon-shot of the coast " in regard to the right of seizure in times of war. If the proposed treaty of 1806 and the treaty of 1818 contained no disposition to that effect, the explanation may be found in the fact that the first extended the marginal belt to five miles, and also in the circumstance that the American proposition of 1818 in that respect was not limited to "bays," but extended to " chambers formed by headlands " and to " five marine miles from a right line from one headland to another," a proposition which in the times of the Napoleonic wars would have affected to a very large extent the operations of the British navy;

(*d*) Because it has not been shown by the documents and correspondence in evidence here that the application of the three mile rule to bays was present to the minds of the negotiators in 1818 and they could not reasonably have been expected either to presume it or to provide against its presumption;

(*e*) Because it is difficult to explain the words in art. III of the Treaty under interpretation " country . . . together with its bays, harbours and creeks " otherwise than that all bays without distinction as to their width were, in the opinion of the negotiators, part of the territory;

(*f*) Because from the information before this Tribunal it is evident that the three mile rule is not applied to bays strictly or systematically either by the United States or by any other Power;

(*g*) It has been recognized by the United States that bays stand apart, and that in respect of them territorial jurisdiction may be exercised farther than the marginal belt in the case of Delaware bay by the report of the United States Attorney General of May 19th 1793; and the letter of Mr. JEFFERSON to Mr. GENET of Nov. 8th 1793 declares the bays of the United States generally to be, "as being landlocked, within the body of the United States."

5°. In this latter regard it is further contended by the United States, that such exceptions only should be made from the application of the three mile rule to bays as are sanctioned by conventions and established usage;

that all exceptions for which the United States of America were responsible are so sanctioned; and that His Majesty's Government are unable to provide evidence to show that the bays concerned by the Treaty of 1818 could be claimed as exceptions on these grounds either generally, or except possibly in one or two cases, specifically.

But the Tribunal while recognizing that conventions and established usage might be considered as the basis for claiming as territorial those bays which on this ground might be called historic bays, and that such claim should be held valid in the absence of any principle of international law on the subject; nevertheless is unable to apply this, *a contrario*, so as to subject the bays in question to the three mile rule, as desired by the United States:

(*a*) Because Great Britain has during this controversy asserted a claim to these bays generally, and has enforced such claim specifically in statutes or otherwise, in regard to the more important bays such as Chaleurs, Conception and Miramichi;

(*b*) Because neither should such relaxations of this claim, as are in evidence, be construed as renunciations of it; nor should omissions to enforce the claim in regard to bays as to which no controversy arose, be so construed. Such a construction by this Tribunal would not only be intrinsically inequitable but internationally injurious; in that it would discourage conciliatory diplomatic transactions and encourage the assertion of extreme claims in their fullest extent;

(*c*) Because any such relaxations in the extreme claim of Great Britain in its international relations are compensated by recognitions of it in the same sphere by the United States; notably in relations with France for instance in 1823 when they applied to Great Britain for the protection of their fishery in the bays on the western coast of Newfoundland, whence they had been driven by French war vessels on the ground of the pretended exclusive right of the French. Though they never asserted that their fishermen had been disturbed within the three mile zone, only alleging that the disturbance had taken place in the bays, they claimed to be protected by Great Britain for having been molested in waters which were, as Mr. Rush stated "clearly within the jurisdiction and sovereignty of Great Britain."

6°. It has been contended by the United States that the words "coasts, bays, creeks or harbours" are here used only to express different parts of the coast and are intended to express and be equivalent to the word "coast," whereby the three marine miles would be measured from the sinuosities of the coast and the renunciation would apply only to the waters of bays within three miles.

But the Tribunal is unable to agree with this contention:

(*a*) Because it is a principle of interpretation that words in a document ought not to be considered as being without any meaning if there is not specific evidence to that purpose and the interpretation referred to would lead to the consequence, practically, of reading the words "bays, creeks and harbours" out of the Treaty; so that it would read "within three miles of any of the coasts" including therein the coasts of the bays and harbours;

(*b*) Because the word "therein" in the proviso — "restrictions necessary to prevent their taking, drying or curing fish therein" can refer only to "bays," and not to the belt of three miles along the coast; and can be explained only on the supposition that the words "bays, creeks and harbours" are to be understood in their usual ordinary sense and not in an artificially restricted sense of bays within the three mile belt;

(*c*) Because the practical distinction for the purpose of this fishery between coasts and bays and the exceptional conditions pertaining to the latter has been shown from the correspondence and the documents in evidence, especially the Treaty of 1783, to have been in all probability present to the minds of the negotiators of the Treaty of 1818;

(*d*) Because the existence of this distinction is confirmed in the same article of the Treaty by the proviso permitting the United States fishermen to enter bays for certain purposes;

(*e*) Because the word "coasts" is used in the plural form whereas the contention would require its use in the singular;

(*f*) Because the Tribunal is unable to understand the term "bays" in the renunciatory clause in other than its geographical sense, by which a bay is to be considered as an indentation of the coast, bearing a configuration of a particular character easy to determine specifically, but difficult to describe generally.

The negotiators of the Treaty of 1818 did probably not trouble themselves with subtle theories concerning the notion of "bays"; they most probably thought that everybody would know what was a bay. In this popular sense the term must be interpreted in the Treaty. The interpretation must take into account all the individual circumstances which for any one of the different bays are to be appreciated, the relation of its width to the length of penetration inland, the possibility and the necessity of its being defended by the State in whose territory it is indented; the special value which it has for the industry of the inhabitants of its shores; the distance which it is secluded from the highways of nations on the open sea and other circumstances not possible to enumerate in general.

For these reasons the Tribunal decides and awards:

In case of bays the three marine miles are to be measured from a straight line drawn across the body of water at the place where it ceases to have the configuration and characteristics of a bay. At all other places the three marine miles are to be measured following the sinuosities of the coast.

But considering the Tribunal cannot overlook that this answer to Question V, although correct in principle and the only one possible in view of the want of a sufficient basis for a more concrete answer, is not entirely satisfactory as to its practical applicability, and that it leaves room for doubts and differences in practice. Therefore the Tribunal considers it its duty to render the decision more practicable and to remove the danger of future differences by adjoining to it a recommendation in virtue of the responsibilities imposed by Art. IV of the Special Agreement.

Considering, moreover, that in treaties with France, with the North German Confederation and the German Empire and likewise in the North Sea Convention, Great Britain has adopted for similar cases the rule that only bays of ten miles width should be considered as those wherein the fishing is reserved to nationals. And that in the course of the negotiations between Great Britain and the United States a similar rule has been on various occasions proposed and adopted by Great Britain in instructions to the naval officers stationed on these coasts. And that though these circumstances are not sufficient to constitute this a principle of international law, it seems reasonable to propose this rule with certain exceptions, all the more that this rule with such exceptions has already formed the basis of an agreement between the two Powers.

Now therefore this Tribunal in pursuance of the provisions of art. IV hereby recommends for the consideration and acceptance of the High Contracting Parties the following rules and method of procedure for determining the limits of the bays hereinbefore enumerated.

1. In every bay not hereinafter specifically provided for the limits of exclusion shall be drawn three miles seaward from a straight line across the bay in the part nearest the entrance at the first point where the width does not exceed ten miles.
2. In the following bays where the configuration of the coast and the local climatic conditions are such that foreign fishermen when within the geographic headlands might reasonably and bona fide believe themselves on the high seas, the limits of exclusion shall be drawn in each case between the headlands hereinafter specified as being those at and within which such fishermen might be reasonably expected to recognize the bay under average conditions.

For the Baie des Chaleurs the line from the Light at Birch Point on Miscou Island to Macquereau Point Light: for the Bay of Miramichi, the line from the Light at Point Escuminac to the Light on the Eastern Point of Tabisintac Gully; for Egmont Bay, in Prince Edward Island, the line from the Light at Cape Egmont to the Light at West Point; and off St. Ann's Bay, in the Province of Nova Scotia, the line from the

Light at Point Anconi to the nearest point on the opposite shore of the mainland.

For Fortune Bay, in Newfoundland, the line from Connaigre Head to the Light on the Southeasterly end of Brunet Island, thence to Fortune Head.

For or near the following bays the limits of exclusion shall be three marine miles seawards from the following lines, namely:

For or near Barrington Bay, in Nova Scotia, the line from the Light on Stoddart Island to the Light on the south point of Cape Sable, thence to the Light at Baccaro Point; at Chedabucto and St. Peter's Bays, the line from Cranberry Island Light to Green Island Light, thence to Point Rouge; for Mira Bay, the line from the Light on the East Point of Scatari Island to the Northeasterly Point of Cape Morien; and at Placentia Bay, in Newfoundland, the line from Latine Point on the Eastern mainland shore, to the most Southerly Point of Red Island, thence by the most Southerly Point of Merasheen Island to the mainland.

Long Island and Bryer Island, on St. Mary's Bay, in Nova Scotia, shall, for the purpose of delimitation, be taken as the coasts of such bays.

It is understood that nothing in these rules refers either to the Bay of Fundy considered as a whole apart from its bays and creeks or as to the innocent passage through the Gut of Canso, which were excluded by the agreement made by exchange of notes between Mr. Bacon and Mr. Bryce dated February 21st 1909 and March 4th 1909; or to Conception Bay, which was provided for by the decision of the Privy Council in the case of the Direct United States Cable Company *v.* The Anglo American Telegraph Company, in which decision the United States have acquiesced.

Question VI

Have the inhabitants of the United States the liberty under the said Article or otherwise, to take fish in the bays, harbours, and creeks on that part of the southern coast of Newfoundland which extends from Cape Ray to Rameau Islands, or on the western and northern coasts of Newfoundland from Cape Ray to Quirpon Islands, or on the Magdalen Islands ?

In regard to this question, it is contended by the United States that the inhabitants of the United States have the liberty under Art. I of the Treaty of taking fish in the bays, harbours and creeks on that part of the Southern Coast of Newfoundland which extends from Cape Ray to Rameau Islands or on the western and northern coasts of Newfoundland from Cape Ray to Quirpon Islands and on the Magdalen Islands. It is contended by Great Britain that they have no such liberty.

Now considering that the evidence seems to show that the intention of the Parties to the Treaty of 1818, as indicated by the records of the negotiations and by the subsequent attitude of the Governments was to admit the United States to such fishery, this Tribunal is of opinion that it is incumbent on Great Britain to produce satisfactory proof that the United States are not so entitled under the Treaty.

For this purpose Great Britain points to the fact that whereas the Treaty grants to American fishermen liberty to take fish " on the coasts, bays, harbours, and creeks from Mount Joly on the Southern coast of Labrador " the liberty is granted to the " coast " only of Newfoundland and to the " shore " only of the Magdalen Islands; and argues that evidence can be found in the correspondence submitted indicating an intention to exclude Americans from Newfoundland bays on the Treaty Coast, and that no value would have been attached at that time by the United States Government to the liberty of fishing in such bays because there was no cod fishery there as there was in the bays of Labrador.

But the Tribunal is unable to agree with this contention:

(*a*) Because the words " part of the southern coast . . . from . . . to " and the words " Western and Northern Coast . . . from . . . to," clearly indicate one uninterrupted coast-line; and there is no reason to read into the words " coasts " a contradistinction to bays, in order to exclude bays. On the contrary, as already held in the answer to Question V, the words " liberty, forever, to dry and cure fish in any of the unsettled bays, harbours and creeks of the Southern part of the Coast of Newfoundland hereabove described," indicate that in the meaning of the Treaty, as in all the preceding treaties relating to the same territories, the words coast, coasts, harbours, bays, etc., are used, without attaching to the word " coast " the specific meaning of excluding bays. Thus in the provision of the Treaty of 1783 giving liberty " to take fish on such part of the coast of Newfoundland as British fishermen shall use"; the word "coast "necessarily includes bays, because if the intention had been to prohibit the entering of the bays for fishing the following words " but not to dry or cure the same on that island," would have no meaning. The contention that in the Treaty of 1783 the word "bays" is inserted lest otherwise Great Britain would have had the right to exclude the Americans to the three mile line, is inadmissible, because in that Treaty that line is not mentioned;

(*b*) Because the correspondence between Mr. ADAMS and Lord BATHURST also shows that during the negotiations for the Treaty the United States demanded the former rights enjoyed under the Treaty of 1783, and that Lord BATHURST in the letter of 30th October 1815 made no objection to granting those " former rights " " placed under some modifications," which latter did not relate to the right of fishing in bays, but only to the " preoccupation of British harbours and creeks by the fishing vessels of the United States and the forcible exclusion of British subjects where the fishery might be most advantageously conducted," and " to the clandestine introduction of prohibited goods into the British colonies." It may be therefore assumed that the word " coast " is used in both Treaties in the same sense, including bays;

(*c*) Because the Treaty expressly allows the liberty to dry and cure in the unsettled bays, etc. of the southern part of the coast of Newfoundland, and this shows that, a fortiori, the taking of fish in those bays is also allowed; because the fishing liberty was a lesser burden than the grant to cure and dry, and the restrictive clauses never referred to fishing in contradistinction to drying, but always to drying in contradistinction to fishing. Fishing is granted without drying, never drying without fishing;

(*d*) Because there is not sufficient evidence to show that the enumeration of the component parts of the coast of Labrador was made in order to discriminate between the coast of Labrador and the coast of Newfoundland;

(*e*) Because the statement that there is no codfish in the bays of Newfoundland and that the Americans only took interest in the codfishery is not proved; and evidence to the contrary is to be found in Mr. JOHN ADAMS' Journal of Peace Negotiations of November 25, 1782;

(*f*) Because the Treaty grants the right to take fish of every kind, and not only codfish;

(*g*) Because the evidence shows that, in 1823, the Americans were fishing in Newfoundland bays and that Great Britain when summoned to protect them against expulsion therefrom by the French did not deny their right to enter such bays.

Therefore this Tribunal is of opinion that American inhabitants are entitled to fish in the bays, creeks and harbours of the Treaty coasts of Newfoundland and the Magdalen Islands and it is so decided and awarded.

QUESTION VII

Are the inhabitants of the United States whose vessels resort to the Treaty coasts for the purpose of exercising the liberties referred to in Article I of the Treaty of 1818 entitled to have for those vessels, when duly authorized by the United States in that behalf, the commercial privileges on the Treaty coasts accorded by agreement or otherwise to United States trading vessels generally ?

Now assuming that commercial privileges on the Treaty coasts are accorded by agreement or otherwise to United States trading vessels generally, without any exception, the inhabitants of the United States, whose vessels resort to the same coasts for the purpose of exercising the liberties referred to in Article I of the Treaty of 1818, are entitled to have for those vessels when duly authorized by the United States in that behalf, the above mentioned commercial privileges, the Treaty containing nothing to the contrary. But they cannot at the same time and during the same voyage exercise their Treaty rights and enjoy their commercial privileges, because Treaty rights and commercial privileges are submitted to different rules, regulations and restraints.

For these reasons this Tribunal is of opinion that the inhabitants of the United States are so entitled in so far as concerns this Treaty, there being nothing in its provisions to disentitle them provided the Treaty liberty of fishing and the commercial privileges are not exercised concurrently and it is so decided and awarded.

Done at the Hague, in the Permanent Court of Arbitration, in triplicate original, September 7th, 1910.

H. Lammasch
A. F. De Savornin Lohman
George Gray
C. Fitzpatrick
Luis M. Drago

Signing the Award, I state pursuant to Article IX clause 2 of the Special Agreement my dissent from the majority of the Tribunal in respect to the considerations and enacting part of the Award as to Question V.

Grounds for this dissent have been filed at the International Bureau of the Permanent Court of Arbitration.

Luis M. Drago

DISSENTING OPINION OF DR. LUIS M. DRAGO [1]

The North Atlantic Coast Fisheries Arbitration. Grounds for the Dissent to the Award on Question V by Dr. Luis M. Drago

Counsel for Great Britain have very clearly stated that according to their contention the territoriality of the bays referred to in the Treaty of 1818 is immaterial because whether they are or are not territorial, the United States should be excluded from fishing in them by the terms of the renunciatory clause, which simply refers to " bays, creeks or harbours of His Britannic Majesty's Dominions " without any other qualification or description. If that were so, the necessity might arise of discussing whether or not a nation has the right to exclude another by contract or otherwise from any portion or portions of the high seas. But in my opinion the Tribu-

[1] Official Report published by the Bureau of the Permanent Court of Arbitration in the North Atlantic Coast Fisheries Case, arbitrated at The Hague, 1910, p. 147.

nal need not concern itself with such general question, the wording of the treaty being clear enough to decide the point at issue.

Article I begins with the statement that differences have arisen respecting the liberty claimed by the United States for the inhabitants thereof to take, dry and cure fish on " certain coasts, bays, harbours and creeks of His Britannic Majesty's Dominions in America," and then proceeds to locate the specific portions of the coast with its corresponding indentations, in which the liberty of taking, drying and curing fish should be exercised. The renunciatory clause, which the Tribunal is called upon to construe, runs thus: " And the United States hereby renounce, forever, any liberty heretofore enjoyed or claimed by the inhabitants thereof, to take, dry or cure fish on, or within three marine miles of any of the Coasts, Bays, Creeks or Harbours of His Britannic Majesty's Dominions in America not included within the above mentioned limits." This language does not lend itself to different constructions. If the bays in which the liberty has been renounced are those " of His Britannic Majesty's Dominions in America," they must necessarily be territorial bays, because in so far as they are not so considered they should belong to the high seas and consequently form no part of His Britannic Majesty's Dominions, which, by definition, do not extend to the high seas. It cannot be said, as has been suggested, that the use of the word " dominions," in the plural, implies a different meaning than would be conveyed by the same term as used in the singular, so that in the present case, " the British dominions in America " ought to be considered as a mere geographical expression, without reference to any right of sovereignty or "*dominion*." It seems to me, on the contrary, that "dominions," or "possessions," or "estates," or such other equivalent terms, simply designate the places over which the " dominion " or property rights are exercised. Where there is no possibility of appropriation or dominion, as on the high seas, we cannot speak of dominions. The " dominions " extend exactly to the point which the " dominion " reaches; they are simply the actual or physical thing over which the abstract power or authority, the *right*, as given to the proprietor or the ruler, applies. The interpretation as to the territoriality of the bays as mentioned in the renunciatory clause of the treaty appears stronger when considering that the United States specifically renounced the " liberty," not the " right " to fish or to cure and dry fish. " The United States renounce, forever, any *liberty* heretofore enjoyed or claimed, to take, cure or dry fish on, or within three marine miles of any of the coasts, bays, creeks or harbours of His Britannic Majesty's Dominions in America." It is well known that the negotiators of the Treaty of 1783 gave a very different meaning to the terms *liberty* and *right*, as distinguished from each other. In this connection Mr. ADAMS' Journal may be recited. To this Journal the British Counter Case refers in the following terms: " From an entry in Mr.

ADAMS' Journal it appears that he drafted an article by which he distinguished the *right* to take fish (both on the high seas and on the shores) and the *liberty* to take and cure fish on the land. But on the following day he presented to the British negotiators a draft in which he distinguishes between the '*right*' to take fish on the high seas, and the '*liberty*' to take fish on the '*coasts*,' and to dry and cure fish on the land. . . . The British Commissioner called attention to the distinction thus suggested by Mr. ADAMS and proposed that the word *liberty* should be applied to the privileges both on the water and on the land. Mr. ADAMS thereupon rose up and made a vehement protest, as is recorded in his Diary, against the suggestion that the United States enjoyed the fishing on the banks of Newfoundland by any other title than that of *right*." . . . "The application of the word *liberty* to the coast fishery was left as Mr. ADAMS proposed." "The incident," proceeds the British Case, "is of importance, since it shows that the difference between the two phrases was intentional." (British Counter Case, page 17.) And the British Argument emphasizes again the difference. "More cogent still is the distinction between the words *right* and *liberty*. The word *right* is applied to the sea fisheries, and the word *liberty* to the shore fisheries. The history of the negotiations shows that this distinction was advisedly adopted." If then a *liberty* is a grant and not the recognition of a *right*; if, as the British Case, Counter Case and Argument recognize, the United States had the right to fish in the open sea in contradistinction with the *liberty* to fish near the shores or portions of the shores, and if what has been renounced in the words of the treaty is the "*liberty*" to fish on, or within three miles of the bays, creeks and harbours of His Britannic Majesty's Dominions, it clearly follows that such *liberty* and the corresponding renunciation refers only to such portions of the bays which were under the sovereignty of Great Britain and not to such other portions, if any, as form part of the high seas.

And thus it appears that far from being immaterial the territoriality of bays is of the utmost importance. The treaty not containing any rule or indication upon the subject, the Tribunal cannot help a decision as to this point, which involves the second branch of the British contention that all so-called bays are not only geographical but wholly territorial as well, and subject to the jurisdiction of Great Britain. The situation was very accurately described on almost the same lines as above stated by the British Memorandum sent in 1870 by the Earl of Kimberley to Governor Sir JOHN YOUNG: "The right of Great Britain to exclude American fishermen from waters within three miles of the coasts is unambiguous, and, it is believed, uncontested. But there appears to be some doubt what are the waters described as within three miles of bays, creeks or harbours. When a bay is less than six miles broad its waters are within the three mile limit, and therefore clearly within the meaning of the treaty; *but when it is more than that breadth, the question arises whether it is a bay of Her Britannic Majesty's Dominions.* This is a question which has to be considered in each particular case with regard to international law and usage. When such a bay is not a bay of Her Majesty's dominions, the American fishermen shall be entitled to fish in it, except within three marine miles of the 'coast'; when it is a bay of Her Majesty's dominions they will not be entitled to fish within three miles of it, that is to say (it is presumed) within three miles of a line drawn from headland to headland." (American Case Appendix, page 629.)

Now, it must be stated in the first place that there does not seem to exist any general rule of international law which may be considered final, even in what refers to the marginal belt of territorial waters. The old rule of the cannon-shot, crystallized into the present three marine miles measured from low water mark, may be modified at a later period inasmuch as certain nations claim a wider jurisdiction and an extension has already been recommended by the Institute of International Law. There is an obvious reason for that. The marginal strip of territorial waters based originally on the cannon-shot, was founded on the necessity of the riparian State to protect itself from outward attack, by providing something in the nature of an insulating zone, which very reasonably should be extended with the accrued possibility of offense due to the wider range of modern ordnance. In what refers to bays, it has been proposed as a general rule (subject to certain important exceptions) that the marginal belt of territorial waters should follow the sinuosities of the coast more or less in the manner held by the United States in the present contention, so that the marginal belt being of three miles, as in the Treaty under consideration, only such bays should be held as territorial as have an entrance not wider than six miles. (See Sir Thomas Barclay's Report to Institute of International Law, 1894, page 129, in which he also strongly recommends these limits.) This is the doctrine which Westlake, the eminent English writer on International Law, has summed up in very few words: "As to bays," he says, "if the entrance to one of them is not more than twice the width of the littoral sea enjoyed by the country in question, — that is, not more than six sea miles in the ordinary case, eight in that of Norway, and so forth — there is no access from the open sea to the bay except through the territorial water of that country, and the inner part of the bay will belong to that country no matter how widely it may expand. The line drawn from shore to shore at the part where, in approaching from the open sea, the width first contracts to that mentioned, will take the place of the line of low water, and the littoral sea belonging to the State will be measured outwards from that line to the distance of three miles or more, proper to the State" (Westlake, Vol. 1, page 187). But the learned author takes care to add: "But although this is the general rule it often meets with an exception in the case of bays which penetrate deep into the land and are called gulfs. Many of these are recognized by immemorial usage as territorial sea of the States into which they penetrate, notwithstanding that their entrance is wider than the general rule for bays would give as a limit for such appropriation." And he proceeds to quote as examples of this kind the Bay of Conception in Newfoundland, which he considers as wholly British, Chesapeake and Delaware Bays, which belong to the United States, and others. (Ibid., page 188.) The Institute of International Law, in its Annual Meeting of 1894, recommended a marginal belt of six miles for the general line of the coast and as a consequence established that for bays the line should be drawn up across at the nearest portion of the entrance toward the sea where the distance between the two sides does not exceed twelve miles. But the learned association very wisely added a proviso to the effect, "that bays should be so considered and measured *unless a continuous and established usage* has sanctioned a greater breadth." Many great authorities are agreed as to that. Counsel for the United States proclaimed the right to the exclusive jurisdiction of certain bays, no matter what the width of their entrance should be, when the littoral nation has asserted its right to take it into their jurisdiction upon reasons which go always back to the doctrine of protection. Lord BLACKBURN, one of the most eminent of English Judges, in delivering the opinion of the Privy Council about Conception Bay in Newfoundland, adhered to the same doctrine when he asserted the territoriality of that branch of the sea, giving as a reason for such finding "that the British Government for a long period had exercised dominion over this bay and its claim had been acquiesced in by other nations, so as to show that the bay had been for a long time occupied exclusively by Great Britain, a circumstance which, in the tribunals of any country, would be very important." "And moreover," he added, "the British Legislature has by Acts of Parliament, declared it to be part of the British territory, and part of the country made subject to the legislation of Newfoundland." (Direct U. S. Cable Co. *v.* The Anglo-American Telegraph Co., Law Reports, 2 Appeal Cases, 374.)

So it may be safely asserted that a certain class of bays, which might be properly called the historical bays such as Chesapeake Bay and Delaware Bay in North America and the great estuary of the River Plate in South America, form a class distinct and apart and undoubtedly belong to the littoral country, whatever be their depth of penetration and the width of their mouths, when such country has asserted its sovereignty over them, and particular circumstances such as geographical configuration, immemorial usage and above all, the requirements of self-defense, justify such a pretension. The rights of Great Britain over the bays of Conception, Chaleur and Miramichi are of this description. In what refers to the other bays, as might be termed the common, ordinary bays, indenting the coasts, over which no special claim or assertion of sovereignty has been made, there does not seem to be any other general principle to be applied than the one resulting from the custom and usage of each individual nation as shown by their Treaties and their general and time honored practice.

The well known words of BYNKERSHOEK might be very appropriately recalled in this connection when so many and divergent opinions and authorities have been recited: "The common law of nations," he says, "can only be learnt from reason and custom. I do not deny that authority may add weight to reason, but I prefer to seek it in a constant custom of concluding treaties in one sense or another and in examples that have occurred in one country or another." (Questiones Jure Publici, Vol. 1, Cap. 3.)

It is to be borne in mind in this respect that the Tribunal has been called upon to decide as the subject matter of this controversy, the construction to be given to the fishery Treaty of 1818 between Great Britain and the United States. And so it is that from the usage and the practice of Great Britain in this and other like fisheries and from Treaties entered into by them with other nations as to fisheries, may be evolved the right interpretation to be given to the particular convention which has been submitted. In this connection the following Treaties may be recited:

Treaty between Great Britain and France. 2nd August, 1839. It reads as follows:

> ARTICLE IX. The subjects of Her Britannic Majesty shall enjoy the exclusive right of fishery within the distance of 3 miles from low water mark along the whole extent of the coasts of the British Islands.
>
> It is agreed that the distance of three miles fixed as the general limit for the exclusive right of fishery upon the coasts of the two countries, shall,with respect to bays, the mouths of which do not exceed ten miles in width, be measured from a straight line drawn from headland to headland.
>
> ARTICLE X. It is agreed and understood, that the miles mentioned in the present Convention are geographical miles, whereof 60 make a degree of latitude.
>
> (HERTSLETT's Treaties and Conventions, Vol. V, p. 89.)

Regulations between Great Britain and France. 24th May, 1843.

> ART. II. The limits, within which the general right of fishery is exclusively reserved to the subjects of the two kingdoms respectively, are fixed (with the exception of those in Granville Bay) at 3 miles distance from low water mark.
>
> With respect to bays, the mouths of which do not exceed ten miles in width, the 3 mile distance is measured from a straight line drawn from headland to headland.

ART. III. The miles mentioned in the present regulations are geographical miles, of which 60 make a degree of latitude.

(HERTSLETT, Vol. VI, p. 416.)

Treaty between Great Britain and France. November 11, 1867.

ART. I. British fishermen shall enjoy the exclusive right of fishery within the distance of 3 miles from low water mark, along the whole extent of the coasts of the British Islands.

The distance of 3 miles fixed as the general limit for the exclusive right of fishery upon the coasts of the two countries shall, with respect to bays, the mouths of which do not exceed ten miles in width be measured from a straight line drawn from headland to headland.

The miles mentioned in the present convention are geographical miles whereof 60 make a degree of latitude.

(HERTSLETT'S Treaties, Vol. XII, p. 1126, British Case App., p. 38.)

Great Britain and North German Confederation. British notice to fishermen by the Board of Trade. Board of Trade, November, 1868.

Her Majesty's Government and the North German Confederation having come to an agreement respecting the regulations to be observed by British fishermen fishing off the coasts of the North German Confederation, the following notice is issued for the guidance and warning of British fishermen:

1. The exclusive fishery limits of the German Empire are designated by the Imperial Government as follows: that tract of the sea which extends to a distance of 3 sea miles from the extremest limits which the ebb leaves dry of the German North Sea Coast of the German Islands or flats lying before it, as well as those bays and incurvations of the coast which are ten sea miles or less in breadth reckoned from the extremest points of the land and the flats, must be considered as under the territorial sovereignty of North Germany.

(HERTSLETT'S Treaties, Vol. XIV, p. 1055.)

Great Britain and German Empire. British Board of Trade, December, 1874.

(Same recital referring to an arrangement entered into between Her Britannic Majesty and the German Government.)

Then the same articles follow with the alteration of the words "German Empire" for "North Germany."

(HERTSLETT'S, Vol. XIV, p. 1058.)

Treaty between Great Britain, Belgium, Denmark, France, Germany and the *Netherlands* for regulating the police of the North Sea Fisheries, May 6, 1882.

II. Les pêcheurs nationaux jouiront du droit exclusif de pêche dans le rayon de 3 milles, à partir de la laisse de basse mer, le long de toute l'étendue des côtes de leurs pays respectifs, ainsi que des îles et des bancs qui en dépendent.

Pour les baies le rayon de 3 milles sera mesuré à partir d'une ligne droite, tirée, en travers de la baie, dans la partie la plus rapprochée de l'entrée, au premier point où l'ouverture n'excédera pas 10 milles.

(HERTSLETT, Vol. XV, p. 794.)

British Order in Council, October 23rd, 1877.

Prescribes the obligation of not concealing or effacing numbers or marks on boats, employed in fishing or dredging for purposes of sale on the coasts of England, Wales, Scotland and the Islands of Guernsey, Jersey, Alderney, Sark and Man, and not going outside;

(*a*) The distance of 3 miles from low water mark along the whole extent of the said coasts;

(*b*) In cases of bays less than 10 miles wide the line joining the headlands of said bays.

(HERTSLETT'S, Vol. XIV, p. 1032.)

To this list may be added the unratified Treaty of 1888 between Great Britain and the United States which is so familiar to the Tribunal. Such unratified Treaty contains an authoritative interpretation of the Convention of October 20th, 1818, *sub-judice:* "The three marine miles mentioned in Article I of the Convention of October 20th, 1818, shall be measured seaward from low-water mark; but at every bay, creek or harbour, not otherwise specifically provided for in this Treaty, such three marine miles shall be measured seaward from a straight line drawn across the bay, creek or harbor, in the part nearest the entrance at the first point where the width does not exceed ten marine miles," which is recognizing the exceptional bays as aforesaid and laying the rule for the general and common bays.

It has been suggested that the Treaty of 1818 ought not to be studied as hereabove in the light of any Treaties of a later date, but rather be referred to such British international Conventions as preceded it and clearly illustrate, according to this view, what were, at the time, the principles maintained by Great Britain as to their sovereignty over the sea and over the coast and the adjacent territorial waters. In this connection the Treaties of 1686 and 1713 with France and of 1763 with France and Spain have been recited and offered as examples also of exclusion of nations by agreement from fishery rights on the high seas. I cannot partake of such a view. The treaties of 1686, 1713, and 1763 can hardly be understood with respect to this, otherwise than as examples of the wild, obsolete claims over the common ocean which all nations have of old abandoned with the progress of an enlightened civilization. And if certain nations accepted long ago to be excluded by convention from fishing on what is to-day considered a common sea, it is precisely because it was then understood that such tracts of water, now free and open to all, were the exclusive property of a particular power, who, being the owners, admitted or excluded others from their use. The Treaty of 1818 is in the meantime one of the few which mark an era in the diplomacy of the world. As a matter of fact it is the very first which commuted the rule of the cannon-shot into the three marine miles of coastal jurisdiction. And it really would appear unjustified to explain such historic document, by referring it to international Agreements of a hundred and two hundred years before when the doctrine of SELDEN'S *Mare Clausum* was at its height and when the coastal waters were fixed at such distances as sixty miles, or a hundred miles, or two days' journey from the shore and the like. It seems very appropriate, on the contrary, to explain the meaning of the Treaty of 1818 by comparing it with those which immediately followed and established the same limit of coastal jurisdiction. As a general rule a Treaty of a former date may be very safely construed by referring it to the provisions of like Treaties made by the same nation on the same matter at a later time. Much more so when, as occurs in the present case, the later Conventions, with no exception, starting from the same premise of the three miles coastal jurisdiction arrive always to an uniform policy and line of action in what refers to bays. As a matter of fact all authorities approach and connect the modern fishery Treaties of Great Britain and refer them to the Treaty of 1818. The second edition of KLUBER, for instance, quotes in the same sentence the Treaties of October 20th, 1818, and August 2, 1839, as fixing a distance of three miles from low water mark for coastal jurisdiction. And FIORI, the well-known Italian jurist, referring to the same marine miles of coastal jurisdiction, says: "This rule recognized as early as the Treaty of 1818 between the United States and Great Britain, and that between Great Britain and France in 1839, has again been admitted in the treaty of 1867." (Nouveau Droit International Public, Paris, 1885, Section 803.)

This is only a recognition of the permanency and the continuity of States. The Treaty of 1818 is not a separate fact unconnected with the later policy of Great Britain. Its negotiators were not parties to such international Convention and their powers disappeared as soon as they signed the document on behalf of their countries. The parties to the Treaty of 1818 were the United States and Great Britain, and what Great Britain meant in 1818 about bays and fisheries, when they for the first time fixed a marginal jurisdiction of three miles, can be very well explained by what Great Britain, the same permanent political entity, understood in 1839, 1843, 1867, 1874, 1878, and 1882, when fixing the very same zone of territorial waters. That a bay in Europe should be considered as different from a bay in America and subject to other principles of international law cannot be admitted in the face of it. What the practice of Great Britain has been outside the Treaties is very well known to the Tribunal, and the examples might be multiplied of the cases in which that nation has ordered its subordinates to apply to the bays on these fisheries the ten mile entrance rule or the six miles according to the occasion. It has been repeatedly said that such have been only relaxations of the strict right, assented to by Great Britain in order to avoid friction on certain special occasions. That may be. But it may also be asserted that such relaxations have been very many and that the constant, uniform, never contradicted, practice of concluding fishery Treaties from 1839 down to the present day, in all of which the ten miles entrance bays are recognized, is the clear sign of a policy. This policy has but very lately found a most public, solemn and unequivocal expression. On a question asked in Parliament on the 21st of February 1907, says PITT COBBETT, a distinguished English writer, with respect to the Moray Firth Case, it was stated that, according to the view of the Foreign Office, the Admiralty, the Colonial Office, the Board of Trade and the Board of Agriculture and Fisheries, the term " territorial waters " was deemed to include waters extending from the coast line of any part of the territory of a State to three miles from the low-water mark of such coast line and the waters of all bays, the entrance to which is not more than *six miles*, and of which the entire land boundary forms part of the territory of the same state. (PITT COBBETT, Cases and Opinions on International Law, Vol. 1, p. 143.)

Is there a contradiction between these six miles and the ten miles of the treaties just referred to ? Not at all. The six miles are the consequence of the three miles marginal belt of territorial waters in their coincidence from both sides at the inlets of the coast and the ten miles far from being an arbitrary measure are simply an extension, a margin given for convenience to the strict six miles with fishery purposes. Where the miles represent sixty to a degree in latitude the ten miles are besides the sixth part of the same degree. The American Government in reply to the observations made to Secretary BAYARD's Memorandum of 1888, said very precisely: " The width of ten miles was proposed not only because it had been followed in Conventions between many other powers, but also because it was deemed reasonable and just in the present case; this Government recognizing the fact that while it might have claimed a width of six miles as a basis of settlement, fishing within bays and harbours only slightly wider would be confined to areas so narrow as to render it practically valueless and almost necessarily expose the fishermen to constant danger of carrying their operations into forbidden waters." (British Case Appendix, page 416.) And Professor JOHN BASSETT MOORE, a recognized authority on International law, in a communication addressed to the Institute of International law, said very forcibly: " Since you observe that there does not appear to be any convincing reason to prefer the ten mile line in such a case to that of double three miles, I may say that there have been supposed to exist reasons both of convenience and of safety. The ten mile line has been adopted in the cases referred to as a practical rule. The transgression of an encroachment upon territorial waters by fishing vessels is generally a grave offense, involving in many instances the forfeiture of the offending vessel, and it is obvious that the narrower the space in which it is permissible to fish the more likely the offense is to be committed. In order, therefore, that fishing may be practicable and safe and not constantly attended with the risk of violating territorial waters, it has been thought to be expedient not to allow it where the extent of free waters between the three miles drawn on each side of the bay is less than four miles. This is the reason of the ten mile line. Its intention is not to hamper or restrict the right to fish, but to render its exercise practicable and safe. When fishermen fall in with a shoal of fish, the impulse to follow it is so strong as to make the possibilities of transgression very serious within narrow limits of free waters. Hence it has been deemed wiser to exclude them from space less than four miles each way from the forbidden lines. In spaces less than this operations are not only hazardous, but so circumscribed as to render them of little practical value." (Annuaire de l'Institut de Droit International, 1894, p. 146.)

So the use of the ten mile bays so constantly put into practice by Great Britain in its fishery Treaties has its root and connection with the marginal belt of three miles for the territorial waters. So much so that the Tribunal having decided not to adjudicate in this case the ten miles entrance to the bays of the treaty of 1818, this will be the only one exception in which the ten miles of the bays do not follow as a consequence the strip of three miles of territorial waters, the historical bays and estuaries always excepted.

And it is for that reason that an usage so firmly and for so long a time established ought, in my opinion, be applied to the construction of the Treaty under consideration, much more so, when custom, one of the recognized sources of law, international as well as municipal, is supported in this case by reason and by the acquiescence and the practice of many nations.

The Tribunal has decided that: "In case of bays the 3 miles (of the Treaty) are to be measured from a straight line drawn across the body of water at the place where it ceases to have the configuration characteristic of a bay. At all other places the three miles are to be measured following the sinuosities of the coast." But no rule is laid out or general principle evolved for the parties to know what the nature of such configuration is or by what methods the points should be ascertained from which the bay should lose the characteristics of such. There lies the whole contention and the whole difficulty, not satisfactorily solved, to my mind, by simply recommending, without the scope of the award and as a system of procedure for resolving future contestations under Article IV of the Treaty of Arbitration, a series of lines, which practical as they may be supposed to be, cannot be adopted by the Parties without concluding a new Treaty.

These are the reasons for my dissent, which I much regret, on Question Five.

Done at The Hague, September 7th, 1910.

LUIS M. DRAGO.

AGREEMENT BETWEEN THE UNITED STATES AND GREAT BRITAIN ADOPTING WITH CERTAIN MODIFICATIONS THE RULES AND METHOD OF PROCEDURE RECOMMENDED IN THE AWARD OF SEPTEMBER 7, 1910, OF THE NORTH ATLANTIC COAST FISHERIES ARBITRATION. — SIGNED AT WASHINGTON, JULY 20, 1912.[1]

The United States of America and His Majesty the King of the United Kingdom of Great Britain and Ireland and of the British Dominions beyond the Seas, Emperor of India, being desirous of concluding an agreement regarding the exercise of the liberties referred to in Article 1 of the treaty of October 20, 1818, have for this purpose named as their plenipotentiaries:

The President of the United States of America:

Chandler P. Anderson, Counselor for the Department of State of the United States;

His Britannic Majesty:

Alfred Mitchell Innes, *Chargé d'Affaires* of His Majesty's Embassy at Washington;

Who, having communicated to each other their respective full powers, which were found to be in due and proper form, have agreed to and concluded the following articles:

ARTICLE I

Whereas the award of the Hague tribunal of September 7, 1910, recommended for the consideration of the Parties certain rules and a method of procedure under which all questions which may arise in the future regarding the exercise of the liberties referred to in Article I of the Treaty of October 20, 1818, may be determined in accordance with the principles laid down in the award, and the Parties having agreed to make certain modifications therein, the rules and method of procedure so modified are hereby accepted by the Parties in the following form:

1. All future municipal laws, ordinances, or rules for the regulation of the fisheries by Great Britain, Canada, or Newfoundland in respect of

[1] U. S. Statutes at Large, vol. XXXVII, pt. 2, p. 1634.

(1) the hours, days, or seasons when fish may be taken on the treaty coasts; (2) the method, means, and implements used in the taking of fish or in carrying on fishing operations; (3) any other regulations of a similar character; and all alterations or amendments of such laws, ordinances, or rules shall be promulgated and come into operation within the first fifteen days of November in each year; provided, however, in so far as any such law, ordinance, or rule shall apply to a fishery conducted between the 1st day of November and the 1st day of February, the same shall be promulgated at least six months before the 1st day of November in each year.

Such laws, ordinances, or rules by Great Britain shall be promulgated by publication in the London Gazette by Canada in the Canada Gazette, and by Newfoundland in the Newfoundland Gazette.

After the expiration of ten years from the date of this Agreement, and so on at intervals of ten years thereafter, either Party may propose to the other that the dates fixed for promulgation be revised in consequence of the varying conditions due to changes in the habits of the fish or other natural causes; and if there shall be a difference of opinion as to whether the conditions have so varied as to render a revision desirable, such difference shall be referred for decision to a commission possessing expert knowledge, such as the Permanent Mixed Fishery Commission hereinafter mentioned.

2. If the Government of the United States considers any such laws or regulations inconsistent with the Treaty of 1818, it is entitled so to notify the Government of Great Britain within forty-five days after the publication above referred to, and may require that the same be submitted to and their reasonableness, within the meaning of the award, be determined by the Permanent Mixed Fishery Commission constituted as hereinafter provided.

3. Any law or regulation not so notified within the said period of forty-five days, or which, having been so notified, has been declared reasonable and consistent with the Treaty of 1818 (as interpreted by the said award) by the Permanent Mixed Fishery Commission, shall be held to be reasonable within the meaning of the award; but if declared by the said Commission to be unreasonable and inconsistent with the Treaty of 1818, it shall not be applicable to the inhabitants of the United States exercising their fishing liberties under the Treaty of 1818.

4. Permanent Mixed Fishery Commissions for Canada and Newfoundland, respectively, shall be established for the decision of such questions as to the reasonableness of future regulations, as contemplated by Article IV of the Special Agreement of January 27, 1909. These Commissions shall consist of an expert national, appointed by each Party for five years; the third member shall not be a national of either Party. He shall be nominated for five years by agreement of the Parties, or, failing such agreement, within two months from the date, when either of the Parties to this Agree-

ment shall call upon the other to agree upon such third member, he shall be nominated by Her Majesty the Queen of the Netherlands.

5. The two national members shall be summoned by the Government of Great Britain, and shall convene within thirty days from the date of notification by the Government of the United States. These two members having failed to agree on any or all of the questions submitted within thirty days after they have convened, or having before the expiration of that period notified the Government of Great Britain that they are unable to agree, the full Commission, under the presidency of the Umpire, is to be summoned by the Government of Great Britain, and shall convene within thirty days thereafter to decide all questions upon which the two national members had disagreed. The Commission must deliver its decision, if the two Governments do not agree otherwise, within forty-five days after it has convened. The Umpire shall conduct the procedure in accordance with that provided in Chapter IV of the Convention for the Pacific Settlement of International Disputes, of October 18, 1907, except in so far as herein otherwise provided.

6. The form of convocation of the Commission, including the terms of reference of the question at issue, shall be as follows:

> The provision hereinafter fully set forth of an act dated...... published in the......Gazette, has been notified to the Government of Great Britain by the Government of the United States under date of......, as provided by the agreement entered into on July 20, 1912, pursuant to the award of the Hague Tribunal of September 7, 1910.
>
> Pursuant to the provisions of that Agreement the Government of Great Britain hereby summons the Permanent Mixed Fishery Commission for
>
> {Canada / Newfoundland} composed of..............Commissioner for the United States of America, and of..............Commissioner for {Canada / Newfoundland} who shall meet at Halifax, Nova Scotia, with power to hold subsequent meetings at such other place or places as they may determine, and render a decision within thirty days as to whether the provision so notified is reasonable and consistent with the Treaty of 1818, as interpreted by the award of the Hague Tribunal of September 7, 1910, and if not, in what respect it is unreasonable and inconsistent therewith.
>
> Failing an agreement on this question within thirty days, the Commission shall so notify the Government of Great Britain in order that the further action required by that award shall be taken for the decision of the above question.
>
> The provision is as follows ....

7. The unanimous decision of the two national Commissioners, or the majority decision of the Umpire and one Commissioner, shall be final and binding.

8. Any difference in regard to the regulations specified in Protocol XXX of the arbitration proceedings, which shall not have been disposed of by diplomatic methods, shall be referred not to the Commission of expert specialists mentioned in the award but to the Permanent Mixed Fishery Commissions, to be constituted as hereinbefore provided, in the same manner as a difference in regard to future regulations would be so referred.

Article II

And whereas the Tribunal of Arbitration in its award decided that —

In case of bays the 3 marine miles are to be measured from a straight line drawn across the body of water at the place where it ceases to have the configuration and characteristics of a bay. At all other places the 3 marine miles are to be measured following the sinuosities of the coast.

And whereas the Tribunal made certain recommendations for the determination of the limits of the bays enumerated in the award;

Now, therefore, it is agreed that the recommendations, in so far as the same relate to bays contiguous to the territory of the Dominion of Canada, to which Question V of the Special Agreement is applicable, are hereby adopted, to wit:

> In every bay not hereinafter specifically provided for, the limits of exclusion shall be drawn three miles seaward from a straight line across the bay in the part nearest the entrance at the first point where the width does not exceed ten miles.
>
> For the Baie des Chaleurs the limits of exclusion shall be drawn from the line from the Light at Birch Point on Miscou Island to Macquereau Point Light; for the Bay of Miramichi, the line from the Light at Point Escuminac to the Light on the eastern point of Tabisintac Gully; for Egmont Bay, in Prince Edward Island, the line from the Light at Cape Egmont to the Light of West Point; and off St. Ann's Bay, in the Province of Nova Scotia, the line from the Light at Point Anconi to the nearest point on the opposite shore of the mainland.
>
> For or near the following bays the limits of exclusion shall be three marine miles seawards from the following lines, namely:
>
> For or near Barrington Bay, in Nova Scotia, the line from the Light on Stoddard Island to the Light on the south point of Cape Sable, thence to the Light at Baccaro Point; at Chedabucto and St. Peter's Bays, the line from Cranberry Island Light to Green Island Light, thence to Point Rouge; for Mira Bay, the line from the Light on the east point of Scatary Island to the northeasterly point of Cape Morien,

Long Island and Bryer Island, on St. Mary's Bay, in Nova Scotia, shall, for the purpose of delimitation, be taken as the coasts of such bays.

It is understood that the award does not cover Hudson Bay.

Article III

It is further agreed that the delimitation of all or any of the bays on the coast of Newfoundland, whether mentioned in the recommendations or not, does not require consideration at present.

Article IV

The present Agreement shall be ratified by the President of the United States, by and with the advice and consent of the Senate thereof, and by His Britannic Majesty, and the ratifications shall be exchanged in Washington as soon as practicable.

In faith whereof the respective Plenipotentiaries have signed this Agreement in duplicate and have hereunto affixed their seals.

Done at Washington on the 20th day of July, one thousand nine hundred and twelve.

Chandler P. Anderson [seal]
Alfred Mitchell Innes [seal]

MR. ROOT'S ARGUMENT

ARGUMENT OF ELIHU ROOT ON BEHALF OF THE UNITED STATES OF AMERICA [1]

MR. PRESIDENT and gentlemen of the Tribunal: I beg you to accept my congratulation upon the approach of the end of this long task which has been imposed upon you, to listen attentively and laboriously to the arguments of counsel. It has been, necessarily, a severe tax, not only upon the time, but upon the powers of the members of the Tribunal, for so long a period to listen and not to act. Yet I cannot doubt that you will feel that the dignity and importance of the controversy which is submitted to you justifies the demands that have been made upon you. It is not alone a controversy that, through lapse of time, has acquired historic interest, that, through the participation of many of the ablest and most honored statesmen of two great nations through nearly a century, has acquired that sanctity which the sentiment of a nation gives to the assertion of its rights, but it is a controversy which involves substantial, and, in some respects, vital interests to portions of the people of each nation.

The fishermen on the coast of Massachusetts and of Maine are poor and simple folk. They live upon the fruit that, with hard toil and danger, they win from the waves. They are not as important a part of the United States today as they

[1] *North Atlantic Coast Fisheries Arbitration at The Hague,* Argument before the Tribunal constituted under an agreement signed at Washington, on the 27th day of January, 1909, between His Britannic Majesty and the United States of America, pt. II, pp. 1167–1349 (London, 1910); *North Atlantic Coast Fisheries,* Proceedings in the North Atlantic Coast Fisheries Arbitration before the Permanent Court of Arbitration at The Hague under the provisions of the General Treaty of Arbitration of April 4, 1908, and the Special Agreement of January 27, 1909, between the United States of America and Great Britain, vol. XI, pp. 1927–2231. (Washington, 1912.)

were in 1783 or in 1818; but, while their comparative weight and importance have declined, their positive importance is as great now as it was then, and greater still. Every consideration that moves a sovereign nation to regard and maintain the interests of its own people urges the United States to press upon you this view of its controversy.

The Attorney-General has pointed out that behind these fishing communities upon the New England coast stand the eighty-five millions of people of the United States. Ah! yes. But behind the fishing communities and traders of Newfoundland stand the hundreds of millions of people of the British Empire — that great empire whose pride and honor it is ever to have safeguarded and maintained the interests of every citizen. And when two great nations, bound to protect the interests of their citizens, however humble, find themselves differing in their views of rights which are substantial, find themselves differing so radically that each conceives itself to have a right which it cannot abandon without humiliation, and cannot maintain without force, a situation arises of the gravest importance and the first dignity. No function can be assumed by any tribunal upon this earth of higher consequence than that which you have now assumed, to substitute your judgment for the war which alone, without such a judgment, could settle the questions of right between these two great countries. I cannot doubt that you will feel, as I feel, that the long, and laborious, and patient, and inconspicuous work of such a proceeding as this is of greater value in the cause of peace among men than a multitude of speeches in congresses and conventions, lauding peace and arbitration to the ears of men who are already satisfied to have peace and arbitration.

The patient attention, the manifest interest of the Tribunal, and the acute and instructive observations which have fallen from the lips of the members of the Tribunal during this argument cannot fail to inspire counsel with a strong desire to contribute something that may be useful to the attainment of a just judgment, as the result of so many and such arduous labors. I shall hope to contribute something. If I fail, it will be my misfortune and not the fault of my intention.

The statement of the first question presents, in authentic form, the real attitude of the two nations in respect of its subject-matter. The form is unusual, peculiar. I have not seen it employed in the presentation of questions to arbitral tribunals.

I will read the article of the treaty to which the question relates, and the question itself.

The article is:

ARTICLE I

Whereas differences have arisen respecting the Liberty claimed by the United States for the Inhabitants thereof, to take, dry and cure Fish on Certain Coasts, Bays, Harbors and Creeks of His Britannic Majesty's Dominions in America, it is agreed between the High Contracting Parties, that the Inhabitants of the said United States shall have forever, in common with the Subjects of His Britannic Majesty, the Liberty to take Fish of every kind on that part of the Southern Coast of Newfoundland which extends from Cape Ray to the Rameau Islands, on the Western and Northern Coast of Newfoundland, from the said Cape Ray to the Quirpon Islands, on the shores of the Magdalen Islands, and also on the Coasts, Bays, Harbors, and Creeks from Mount Joly on the Southern Coast of Labrador, to and through the Straits of Belleisle and thence Northwardly indefinitely along the Coast, without prejudice, however, to any of the exclusive Rights of the Hudson Bay Company; and that the American Fishermen shall also have the liberty forever, to dry and cure Fish in any of the unsettled Bays, Harbors, and Creeks of the Southern part of the Coast of Newfoundland hereabove described, and of the Coast of Labrador; but so soon as the same, or any Portion thereof, shall be settled, it shall not be lawful for the said Fishermen to dry or cure Fish at such Portion so settled without previous agreement for such purpose with the Inhabitants, Proprietors, or Possessors of the ground. And the United States hereby renounce forever, any Liberty heretofore enjoyed or claimed by the Inhabitants thereof, to take, dry, or cure Fish on, or within three marine Miles of any of the Coasts, Bays, Creeks, or Harbors of His Britannic Majesty's Dominions in America not included within the above mentioned limits; provided, however, that the American Fishermen shall be admitted to enter such Bays or Harbors for the purpose of Shelter and of repairing Damages therein, of purchasing Wood, and of obtaining Water, and for no other purpose whatever. But they shall be under such Restrictions as may be necessary to prevent their taking, drying or curing Fish therein, or in any other manner whatever abusing the Privileges hereby reserved to them.

The question is:

Question 1

To what extent are the following contentions or either of them justified ?

It is contended on the part of Great Britain that the exercise of the liberty to take fish referred to in the said article, which the inhabitants of the United States have forever in common with the subjects of His Britannic Majesty, is subject, without the consent of the United States, to reasonable regulation by Great Britain, Canada, or Newfoundland in the form of municipal laws, ordinances, or rules, as, for example, to regulations in respect of (1) the hours, days, or seasons when fish may be taken on the treaty coasts; (2) the method, means and implements to be used in the taking of fish or in the carrying on of fishing operations on such coasts; (3) any other matters of a similar character relating to fishing; such regulations being reasonable, as being, for instance —

(*a*) Appropriate or necessary for the protection and preservation of such fisheries and the exercise of the rights of British subjects therein and the liberty which by the said Article 1 the inhabitants of the United States have therein in common with British subjects;

(*b*) Desirable on grounds of public order and morals;

(*c*) Equitable and fair as between local fishermen and the inhabitants of the United States exercising the said treaty liberty, and not so framed as to give unfairly an advantage to the former over the latter class.

It is contended on the part of the United States that the exercise of such liberty is not subject to limitations or restraints by Great Britain, Canada, or Newfoundland in the form of municipal laws, ordinances, or regulations in respect of (1) the hours, days, or seasons when the inhabitants of the United States may take fish on the treaty coasts, or (2) the method, means, and implements used by them in taking fish or in carrying on fishing operations on such coasts, or (3) any other limitations or restraints of similar character —

(*a*) Unless they are appropriate and necessary for the protection and preservation of the common rights in such fisheries and the exercise thereof; and (*b*) Unless they are reasonable in themselves and fair as between local fishermen and fishermen coming from the United States, and not so framed as to give an advantage to the former over the latter class; and

(*c*) Unless their appropriateness, necessity, reasonableness, and fairness be determined by the United States and Great Britain by common accord and the United States concurs in their enforcement.

The Tribunal will already have observed, of course, that instead of framing the question, the makers of the special agreement, the *compromis*, have stated separately the contention of each party, and have asked the Tribunal to say to what extent these contentions are justified. It may fairly be inferred that neither party to the agreement was willing to state the question in terms of the other's choosing; and that, therefore, there are two separate statements. An examination of the statement of the contentions indicates the reason. The two parties approached the subject of the first question from different points of view. Great Britain approached it from the standpoint of her sovereignty. The United States approached it from the standpoint of her granted right. Great Britain states the question as a question relating to the exercise of her sovereign rights. The United States states the question as relating to the inviolability of her granted right. And the two approaching the subject thus from different points, there comes a line between the two, and it rests with the Tribunal to draw that line.

At the outset of the consideration as to where that line is to be drawn, and how it is to be drawn, there is plainly to be seen one fact, unquestionable, agreed to on all hands: that the contention of the United States does not in any degree whatever thrust the assertion of its right into the field of British sovereignty in general. It does not question the full and unimpeded exercise of the sovereign rights of Great Britain over her territory, and the people within her territory, in all the general affairs of life. It does not question her control, without accountability, over the conduct of all persons who are within the spatial sphere of her sovereignty.

It is a familiar method of dealing with the arguments of an adversary to overstate them, for the purpose of destroying them; and when the claims of the United States are stated as being claims to an abdication of British sovereignty, I cannot help feeling that the statement trenches a little upon that method of argument. It constructs a man of straw, easily overthrown. It creates a certain degree of prejudice against the claim which, stated in such a form, is to remain during the period of a long argument characterized by such a description. We make no such claim. We admit unrestricted and unquestioned sovereignty by Great Britain over persons and their conduct; but our claim questions whether that sovereignty, since the grant to us, extends to a modification of our right. The American inhabitant who goes to the treaty coast for the exercise of his right is absolutely and in the fullest extent subject to the sovereignty of Great Britain; but what is his right? Can Great Britain change his right? His conduct in exercising the right, yes; he must obey the laws. But can it change his right? It is conceded — for certain purposes of argument asserted — asserted in the printed documents, asserted by the counsel for Great Britain here, and repeated over and over again, with emphasis, that there is a line beyond which Great Britain cannot go. Where is the line?

Let me call attention to three expressions as to the existence of the line beyond which Great Britain cannot go, which appear in the record, and which are progressively definitive. I will begin with the circular of Mr. Marcy, with which the Tribunal is very familiar, and which appears in the British Case Appendix at p. 207. The Tribunal will remember that Mr. Marcy, the American secretary of state, upon the revival of the attempt to put into force the temporary and reciprocal treaty of 1854, issued a circular letter to the collectors of customs of the United States in which he said that there were certain acts of the colonial legislatures "intended to prevent the wanton destruction of the fish which frequent the coasts of the colonies and injuries to the fishing." And he said:

> There is nothing in the Reciprocity Treaty between the United States and Great Britain which stipulates for the observance of these regulations by our fishermen; yet, as it is presumed they have been framed with a view to prevent injuries to the fisheries, in which our fishermen now have an equal interest with those of Great Britain, it is deemed reasonable and desirable that both should pay a like respect to those regulations, which were designed to preserve and increase the productiveness and prosperity of the fisheries themselves. It is, consequently, earnestly recommended to our citizens to direct their proceedings accordingly.

That was issued upon the submission to him of the statutes to which he refers, with a statement that they contained no provision inconsistent with the full enjoyment of the American citizens' rights of fishing secured by the treaty. That statement appears in a series of preceding letters, notably the letter of Mr. Crampton to Mr. Manners Sutton, which is to be found on pp. 205 and 206 of the British Case Appendix. It appears from this circular that Mr. Marcy, after examining these statutes, found nothing which he considered to be inconsistent with the full enjoyment of the American citizens' rights of fishing, and he approved the statutes and recommended their observance. Thereupon the British Minister represented to Mr. Marcy that a statement in his circular that there was nothing in the treaty which stipulated for the observance of these regulations would be apt to make trouble with the fishermen; that the American fishermen would not be likely to observe the recommendation which had been made to them, in the face of the statement that there was no stipulation requiring them to obey. That representation appears in the letter of Mr. Crampton of the 25th

April, 1856, which is to be found on p. 210 of the British Case Appendix. And the British Minister asked Mr. Marcy to amend his circular by putting in other words in place of the observation that there was no stipulation requiring obedience. These are the words that the British Minister wished included — I am reading from p. 211 of the British Case Appendix, the italicized words near the foot of the page:

> American citizens would indeed, within British jurisdiction, be liable equally with British subjects to the penalties prescribed by law for a willful infraction of such regulations, but nevertheless should these be so framed or executed as to make any discrimination in favor of the British fishermen or to impair the rights secured to American fishermen by the Reciprocity Treaty, those injuriously affected by them will appeal to this Government for redress.

Mr. Marcy apparently declined to substitute those words for his own. At all events, he did not substitute them, but instead of that he put in a statement, which is the first example of the drawing of the line between what Great Britain could do and what Great Britain could not do, to which I ask your attention. What he put into his circular, in place of the denial of his own first circular, and in the place of the declaration of binding obligation which the British Minister wanted to put in, was: first, a statement of this very general jurisdiction, general sovereign right of Great Britain to which I have already referred; and, secondly, a statement of the limitation in regard to the treaty. What he said was — and I now read from the final circular, on p. 209 of the British Appendix:

> By granting the mutual use of the inshore fisheries neither party has yielded its right to civil jurisdiction over a marine league along its coast. Its laws are as obligatory upon the citizens or subjects of the other as upon its own.

To that proposition we fully subscribe, with the addition which he makes of the particular situation in which the treaty places laws relating to the subject-matter of the treaty. That addition was in these words:

> The laws of the British Provinces not in conflict with the provisions of the Reciprocity Treaty would be as binding upon citizens of the United States within that jurisdiction as upon British subjects.

There is the first statement. It is first in point of being general, and it is first historically. General jurisdiction untouched; laws of the jurisdiction binding upon American citizens as fully as upon British subjects; laws not inconsistent with the treaty, binding; laws that are inconsistent with the treaty, not binding.

But Mr. Marcy does not undertake to point out, indeed the situation did not call upon him to point out, what laws would be consistent and what laws would be inconsistent with the treaty.

I now beg to pass to a second instance which proceeded somewhat further in drawing the line, and that is the letter of Lord Salisbury, to which attention has so often been drawn in his correspondence with Mr. Evarts regarding Fortune Bay.

The President: May I ask you, Senator Root, whether you consider that the following sentences in this circular have no bearing upon the preceding sentences, the sentences:

> Should they be so framed or executed as to make any discrimination in favor of the British fishermen, or to impair the rights secured to American fishermen by the Reciprocity Treaty, those injuriously affected by them will appeal to this Government for redress. In presenting complaints of this kind, should there be cause for doing so, they are requested to furnish the Department of State with a copy of the law or regulation which is alleged injuriously to affect their rights or to make an unfair discrimination.

Senator Root: I do not consider, Mr. President, that they have any bearing at all upon the precise proposition which I am now presenting; that is to say, upon the existence of the line between what Great Britain can do and what she cannot do. But they do have a bearing upon another closely allied question, to which I shall turn my attention in a moment, and that is the procedure which should follow, and the method of determining, practically, the line, as matters stood before this submission, before the making of the treaty of arbitration, or this special agreement. They have a very important bearing upon that.

Lord Salisbury, the Tribunal will remember, became involved in a correspondence with Mr. Evarts regarding the claim of the United States for compensation for certain acts of violence which had been done to American fishermen in Fortune Bay by the British fishermen there. The claim having been made, the British Government answered it in the manner which is ordinarily used in dealing with mere claims, an answer not indicating special consideration, but such as would naturally come from the claims department of a Foreign Office, that this claim could not be allowed because the American fishermen who suffered the injury were guilty of three distinct violations of the laws of Newfoundland; that they were on shore when they had no right to be on shore; that they were in-barring herring when the law prohibited it; and that they were taking herring with a seine during the period between October and May, when the statute prohibited it. In response to that, Mr. Evarts called attention to the fact that these laws were, in his view, not binding upon American fishermen, and he said, in a letter of the 28th September, 1878, which appears in the United States Case Appendix at p. 652, from which I read on p. 655:

> In transmitting to you a copy of Captain Sullivan's report, Lord Salisbury says: "You will perceive that the report in question appears to demonstrate conclusively that the United States fishermen on this occasion had committed three distinct breaches of the law."
>
> In this observation of Lord Salisbury, this Government cannot fail to see a necessary implication that Her Majesty's Government conceives that in the prosecution of the right of fishing accorded to the United States by

Article XVIII of the treaty our fishermen are subject to the local regulations which govern the coast population of Newfoundland in their prosecution of their fishing industry, whatever those regulations may be, and whether enacted before or since the Treaty of Washington.

And he said, in the third paragraph below the one which I have read:

It would not, under any circumstances, be admissible for one government to subject the persons, the property, and the interests of its fishermen to the unregulated regulation of another government upon the suggestion that such authority will not be oppressively or capriciously exercised, nor would any government accept as an adequate guaranty of the proper exercise of such authority over its citizens by a foreign government, that, presumptively, regulations would be uniform in their operation upon the subjects of both governments in similar case. If there are to be regulations of a common enjoyment, they must be authenticated by a common or joint authority.

And he concluded his letter by some paragraphs which I will read from p. 657:

So grave a question, in its bearing upon the obligations of this Government under the treaty makes it necessary that the President should ask from Her Majesty's Government a frank avowal or disavowal of the paramount authority of Provincial legislation to regulate the enjoyment by our people of the inshore fishery, which seems to be intimated, if not asserted, in Lord Salisbury's note.

Before the receipt of a reply from Her Majesty's Government, it would be premature to consider what should be the course of this Government should this limitation upon the treaty privileges of the United States be insisted upon by the British Government as their construction of the treaty.

In response to that plain challenge, Lord Salisbury proceeded to draw the line which, as I conceive, it is to be your function to draw. In his reply of the 7th November, 1878, United States Case Appendix, p. 657, he said, in a paragraph which I shall read from p. 658:

I hardly believe, however, that Mr. Evarts would in discussion adhere to the broad doctrine which some portion of his language would appear to convey, that no British authority has a right to pass any kind of laws binding Americans who are fishing in British waters; for if that contention be just, the same disability applies *a fortiori* to any other power, and the waters must be delivered over to anarchy.

There he stated what I have stated, and what Mr. Marcy had stated, as to the general jurisdictional power of Great Britain over her colony.

And subsequently, Mr. Evarts, rather sharply, and with language which indicated that no such idea ought to be imputed to him or suggested as conceived by him, repudiated any such view.

Lord Salisbury went on to state the other side of the question. Having stated in this form what, clearly, Great Britain can do, and having been challenged in due form to make a frank avowal or disavowal of the paramount authority of provincial legislation to regulate the enjoyment by our people of the inshore fisheries, he proceeded to state what Great Britain cannot do.

"On the other hand," he said, "Her Majesty's Government will readily admit — what is, indeed, self-evident — that British sovereignty, as regards those waters, is limited in its scope by the engagements of the Treaty of Washington, which cannot be modified or affected by any municipal legislation."

And, in his further correspondence, after arguing that acts passed before the treaty was made did not come within this limitation, he supplemented his former statement in his letter of the 3d April, 1880 (United States Case Appendix, p. 683), by a further statement which I read from that letter on p. 687:

Mr. Evarts will not require to be assured that Her Majesty's Government, while unable to admit the contention of the United States Government on the present occasion, are fully sensible of the evils arising from any difference of opinion between the two governments in regard to the fishery rights of their respective subjects. They have always admitted the incompetence of the colonial or the imperial legislature to limit by subsequent legislation the advantages secured by treaty to the subjects of another power.

It still remains, however, after the drawing of this line by Lord Salisbury declaring on the one hand what Great Britain clearly could do, and on the other hand what Great Britain clearly could not do, to further define the position of the line beyond the generality of the terms used by Lord Salisbury. And that further definition was made in the correspondence relating to the Newfoundland treaty legislation of 1873 and 1874.

You will remember that the Treaty of Washington of 1871 provided that it should apply to Newfoundland, in case the Legislature of Newfoundland passed a law making it applicable, and they did pass a law in 1873. It appears in the British Case Appendix at p. 705, " An Act relating to the Treaty of Washington, 1871." In the first article of that statute they include a proviso (p. 706):

> Provided that such Laws, rules and regulations, relating to the time and manner of prosecuting the Fisheries on the Coasts of this Island, shall not be in any way affected by such suspension.

A very definite claim, a distinct assertion:

> Provided that such Laws, rules and regulations, relating to the time and manner of prosecuting the Fisheries on the Coasts of this Island, shall not be in any way affected by such suspension.

When that was called to the attention of the American Government, Mr. Fish, the American secretary of state, wrote a letter, dated the 25th June, 1873, which appears on p. 252 of the British Case Appendix, in which, concerning the Treaty of Washington, he said, as we say of this treaty of 1818:

> The Treaty places no limitation of time, within the period during which the Articles relating to the fisheries are to remain in force, either upon the right of taking fish on the one hand, or of the exemption from duty of fish and fish oil (as mentioned therein).
>
> I regret, therefore, that the Act of the Legislature of Newfoundland which reserves a right to restrict the American right of fishing within certain periods of the year, does not appear to be such consent on the part

of the Colony of Newfoundland to the application of the stipulations and provisions of Articles 18 to 25 of the Treaty, as is contemplated by the Act of Congress to which you refer, and in accordance with which the Proclamation of the President is to issue.

There Mr. Fish stated the proposition which we press upon you here. " The treaty places no limitation of time within the period during which the articles relating to the fisheries are to remain in force ", and " the Act which reserves a right to restrict the American right of fishing within certain periods of the year is not such a consent as is contemplated by the Act of Congress ", and so on.

That is supplemented by the conversation with Mr. Fish, reported by Sir Edward Thornton, the British minister in Washington, in which he said on p. 253 of the British Case Appendix:

Mr. Fish replied that he could state confidentially his understanding that the jurisdiction gave the right of laying down reasonable police regulations, and that as a matter of course such regulations would be observed by all who fished in the waters in question;

that is the general jurisdiction as I have stated it; as Mr. Marcy stated it; and as Lord Salisbury stated it;

but

he proceeded to say —

the permission to fish granted by the treaty was accompanied by no restriction except so far as to define the localities in which the fishing was to be carried on.

That is the basis.

And upon that the Legislature of Newfoundland passed a new enactment omitting the attempted reservation of the right to regulate in respect of the time and manner of fishing which had been declared contrary to the treaty, and substituted in place of it their Act of the 28th March, 1874, which appears at p. 706 of the British Appendix, and which says the articles of the Treaty of Washington shall come into full force, operation and effect, in this Colony, so far as the same are applicable, and shall thenceforth so continue in full force, operation and effect, during the period mentioned in Article thirty-three of the said Treaty, recited in the Schedule to this Act, any law of this Colony to the contrary notwithstanding.

Both of these correspondences I shall refer to again for other purposes. I refer to them now with the sole purpose of attempting to give definition to the line which I conceive must be drawn between what it is competent for Great Britain to do in the exercise of her general sovereignty, and what it is incompetent for Great Britain to do in respect of the modification of our right.

Now, to return to the question which the president asked as to the concluding words of Mr. Marcy's circular advising the fishermen to appeal to their own Government in case they found discrimination or interference with their right.

Of course it follows from the fact that Great Britain has the general right of sovereignty, and the general right to pass laws within that jurisdiction, that there may be, as Lord Salisbury justly observes, an inadvertent overstepping of the line. That is always possible, wherever you draw the line, and of course those lines are not to be passed upon by fishermen, the statutes are to be respected, and, as Mr. Marcy instructs the fishermen, appeal must be made to their own Government; as Lord Salisbury says in the letter to which I have referred, the subject is to be taken up by the Governments.

No one on the part of the United States has ever been so lost to all considerations of the way in which government must be conducted as to claim anything to the contrary of that.

Wherever there is doubt as to whether a law is within or not within the competency of the government which has general sovereignty over the territory in which the law is to be applied, that doubt must be resolved in a decent and orderly manner, in accordance with the customs of nations, not by having individuals take the law into their own hands and say, I will obey or I will not obey. That is true, wherever the line is drawn.

But, there still remains the question, when the two governments come to consider whether a law that has been passed does overstep the line of competency, where are they to find the line of competency, what rule are they to apply ?

If you were to find, as I hope you will, that it is competent for Great Britain to make police regulations to control the conduct of persons within this territory, although it is not competent for her to modify our right, or the rights which Americans go there to exercise, nevertheless there must always be a question, what is a police regulation ? We have had a good illustration here, in this subject of net interference. That was referred to in some one of the American printed papers as not being a police regulation. Mr. Turner stated in his opening argument for the United States that he thought it was. Sir Robert Finlay said he thought it was. I agree with both of them that it is a police regulation; but suppose a fisherman in Newfoundland had been of the opinion that that was not a police regulation, it was not his business to determine his conduct according to his view: that is a matter the government must consider: Is it a police regulation ?

And so, wherever the line is drawn, the question as to which side of the line statutes fall must be raised, not by individuals, but by the government whose rights may be or are alleged to be affected.

The President: May I ask, Mr. Senator Root, would there be any difference in the decision of the question whether the laws have been overstepped in regard to this treaty, or in regard to any other treaty ? Is this treaty in a peculiar situation or of a peculiar character in this respect ?

SENATOR ROOT: I think, Mr. President, it belongs to a special class of treaties, and the considerations regarding it must proceed upon somewhat different principles from the treaties of any other class; and assigning to this treaty its proper place in the class to which I think it belongs will be the function of another portion of my argument.

Let me state what I think is the question involved in the drawing of this line.

Granted that all laws of a general character, controlling the conduct of men within the territory of Great Britain, are effective, binding, and, beyond objection by the United States, competent to be made upon the sole determination of Great Britain or her colony, without accountability to any one whomsoever; granting that there is somewhere a line beyond which it is not competent for Great Britain to go, or beyond which she cannot rightfully go, because to go beyond it would be an invasion of the right granted to the United States in 1818; was the legal effect of the grant of 1818 to leave the determination as to where that line is to be drawn to the uncontrolled judgment of the grantor, either upon the grantor's consideration as to what would be a reasonable exercise of its sovereignty over the British Empire, or upon the grantor's consideration of what would be reasonable towards the grantee ?

Or, was the legal effect of the grant to establish a right which by its own terms drew the line beyond which the grantor could not rightfully go with statutes modifying or restricting the right, or the exercise of the right, without consulting the grantee whose rights were to be affected ?

I have said, in stating this question, that it was whether the line was to be drawn upon the uncontrolled judgment of the grantor, either upon what would be a proper exercise of the grantor's sovereignty over the British Empire, or upon what would be reasonable towards the grantee, as coming under both heads, both branches, in both aspects, under the category of uncontrolled judgment. It seems that no argument is necessary to sustain that. I must, however, revert to the statement of the British contention, which appears to impose upon Great Britain in express terms the limitation of reasonableness.

That certainly does impose a limitation. And the limitation is the limitation of what is reasonable. It is, what *is* reasonable, what *is* appropriate or necessary for the protection and preservation of the fishery, what *is* desirable on grounds of public order and morals, what *is* equitable and fair as between local fishermen and the inhabitants of the United States, and so on. And so Sir Robert Finlay, in his most comprehensive and able argument, assumed it to be, at one point in the argument; for he says " it never has for one moment been contended by Great Britain that regulations of the kind indicated there giving a preference to British fishermen as against fishermen of the United States would be defensible. The liberty given by the treaty cannot be taken away by regulation, and Great Britain could not so contend; Great Britain never contended that regulations might be framed which would put the natives of the dominion concerned in a better position than the United States fishermen who have been admitted to share in the benefits of the fishery."

But, when the counsel for Great Britain are confronted by the manifest unfairness of having a right vested in us which cannot be affected or modified by any legislation or regulation on the part of the grantor of the right which is not reasonable, fair, appropriate and necessary, and at the same time arrogating to the grantor the right itself alone to determine what is reasonable, fair, appropriate, and necessary, he seeks refuge from the consequence by the proposition which I will now read from the copy of his argument at p. 176:

It is not claimed for the British Government, or for the Colonial Governments, that they can determine the question whether any regulation is reasonable. All that they claim is the right to make reasonable regulations, and if the point is raised as to whether any regulation is reasonable or not, it is not for the Colonial Government, it is not for the British Government, it is not for the United States Government to determine whether that regulation is or is not reasonable. It is for this Tribunal, to which the parties can, if such a difference arises, come.

Where did the right stand before the year 1908? What are you to adjudge the rights to be under the treaty of 1818? Under any arbitration proceeding, in any determination which you may make under the articles of this treaty following the ones submitting the question, in any determination which may be made under the rules of procedure which you may frame and which may possibly be accepted, or under the short form of procedure at The Hague, provided for by article 4, what must be the foundation but an ascertainment of the rights of the parties under the treaty of 1818, and a procedure based upon the award which determines those rights? And, in determining what those rights are under the treaty of 1818, of course you must proceed without any reference whatever to the fact that, recognizing the inequity of their own position, recognizing that that position would be revolting to the sense of justice of an international tribunal, Great Britain has recourse to the fact that under this recent agreement a tribunal may do what it would have been unjust for Great Britain to do, that is to say, to pass herself alone upon the rights in which another was equally interested, to be the judge in her own case.

Of course I need not argue that the assertion of such an uncontrolled right is in its legal effect wholly destructive of the limitation which is stated in the contention of Great Britain under the first question of the special agreement.

How does Great Britain arrive at the conclusion that, while the grant of 1818 limits the scope of sovereignty, excludes her from legislation which modifies or affects our right, she alone is entitled to be the judge as to what is desirable, appropriate, necessary, and fair for her purposes to lead to a modification and restriction and limitation of our right? She does it by appealing to her sovereignty. It is not because there is any fairness as between two common owners of a right, that one should be the judge of limitations and modifications to be imposed upon the right; she does it by an appeal to her sovereignty. It is because she is sovereign there.

I shall deal hereafter with the question as to whether there is any foundation for that appeal. I refer to it now, however, for the purpose of pointing to the practical effect of the ground on which she claims the right to decide. That is, the ground upon which she claims that she had the right to decide prior to the making of this special agreement, for the ninety years before the treaty of 1908 came into existence.

What is the practical effect of Great Britain establishing her right to determine alone herself as to what limitations may and should be imposed upon our right, upon the ground of her sovereignty? Why, it is that the right granted to us is subject to her right of sovereignty. And what is the scope of the right of sovereignty?

It is to do what she pleases. It is that she may, if she will, go to any length whatever in restricting, limiting, impeding, or practically destroying the right which has been granted, for there is no limitation upon the right of sovereignty, and whatever authority is to be inferred from that is an authority without limit.

Now, I have endeavored to state what I think to be the attitude of the two parties in regard to Question One, and to draw from the record definitions, in so far as seems to be useful for the moment, as to what Great Britain can do and what Great Britain cannot do. It is my purpose, as best I may, first, to dispose of certain rather narrow questions relating to the meaning of terms in the grant of 1818; second, to show the practical bearing of the decision of the first question on the substantial rights of the United States; third, to examine the nature of the right granted and the consequences and legal effect of that nature; fourth, to show the understanding and intent of the negotiators as to the meaning and effect of the article and the terms used in it; fifth, to show the construction that has been put upon the article of the treaty of 1818 in question by the parties — the construction that was put upon it for more than sixty years after it was made — and, sixth, to show the relations to this case, to this right created by this article, of the accepted rules of international law which have grown up in the consideration and treatment of cases embodying the same fundamental characteristics and having a generic relation to the grant of the right under the treaty of 1818, as I hope to make it plain to you.

First, as to the meaning of some of the terms in the article. Fortunately, we have for our assistance in the elucidation of these terms at the outset the fact that this agreement was an agreement in settlement of an old controversy. It was a settlement of questions which arose under the former treaty of 1783, and the terms used, wherever there is any question, may be considered with all the light thrown upon them that comes from the terms of the former treaty, the negotiations and correspondence relating to it, the practice under it, and the evidence of understanding by the parties as to what that treaty meant.

Words are like those insects that take their color from their surroundings. Half the misunderstanding in this world comes from the fact that the words that are spoken or written are conditioned in the mind that gives them forth by one set of thoughts and ideas, and they are conditioned in the mind of the hearer or reader by another set of thoughts and ideas, and even the simplest forms of expression are frequently quite open to mistake, unless the hearer or reader can get some idea of what were the conditions in the brain from which the words come.

We are fortunate in having a clear guide to the solution of many of the questions which may arise regarding the words of this article of the treaty of 1818. The first term used in the article regarding which there has been a question is the word " liberty." I hesitate to refer to the case of Wickham *vs.* Hawker, of which my learned friend Sir Robert Finlay thought so lightly, but I will, partly because during more than forty years' practice at the American bar I have learned to have great respect and reverence for the decisions of those great English courts, and I should not like to see the utterances of Baron Parke allowed to rest in this Tribunal under the ignominy which seems to have been cast upon them; and partly because the case does present a use of the word " liberty " very illuminating for our purpose in getting at the meaning of the first article of the treaty of 1818. In turning to this case we find that there was a term used in the English law regarding a subject about which every English gentleman is perfectly familiar. It was the name of a particular class of rights. The liberty of fowling has been described, in the words of Baron Parke, to be a *profit à prendre.* The liberty of fishing, he says, appears to be of the same nature. It implies that the person who takes the fish takes for his own benefit. It is a common of fishing. This case was decided in 1840. It cites the Duchess of Norfolk's case from the *Year Book,* and it states what the law has been from the earliest or from very early times in England. The liberties, that is a particular class of rights known to the English law, to Englishmen and to Americans in the year 1818, were interests in land, they were those particular kinds of interest classified as *profits à prendre.* They might be appurtenant when they were attached to another estate; they might be *en gros* when they were conferred upon an individual irrespective of his ownership of another estate. Therefore, the word meant a right which could be conveyed by deed, inheritable, giving to a man and to his heirs no license, no mere privilege, no mere accommodation, no consent or acquiescence, but a right which passed out of a grantor to a grantee, and was then his and his heirs' if the grant so expressed.

I say that was known to every English gentleman and every American, for the subject was a subject most interesting, certainly most interesting to all men of the Anglo-Saxon race, something not left to lawyers alone as a matter of interest. Now, there was this distinction carried by the use of the word " liberty " which was not necessarily carried by the general word " right." The liberty came by grant from the general owner of the estate in which the fishing, the hawking, or the hunting was to take place. It implied that the grantee of the liberty had acquired it from the general owner.

When the treaty of 1783 came to be made, John Adams claimed that the United States was equal in title with Great Britain to the fisheries which, you will remember, he speaks of as being one whole fishery on the banks and coasts. Great Britain, willing to concede that the United States had, irrespective of any grant from her, the right to fish on the banks, in the Gulf of St. Lawrence, in other places in the sea, was unwilling to concede that the United States had, without a grant from her, the right to fish upon the coasts. At that time the old vague claims to well-nigh universal control over the seas were beginning to fade away. The new idea of a protective right over a limited territorial zone had not yet become distinct, certain, and fixed; but Great Britain was willing to abandon her claims to exclude any other independent nation from the Banks of Newfoundland and from the Gulf of St. Lawrence, as she had so long sought to exclude, and with great success, France and Spain. She was willing to concede the right, and did concede the right, to the United States as an independent nation to use that fishery. But she insisted upon using in the grant of the right to fish on the coasts a word which connoted the acquisition of the right by the United States from her, and not as incident to the independence of the United States. That was very well explained by Lord Bathurst in his letter of the 30th October, 1815, which is found in the United States Case Appendix at p. 273. I will read a few words from the paragraph at the foot of p. 276. He said:

It is surely obvious that the word *right* is, throughout the treaty, —

that is, the treaty of 1783 —

used as applicable to what the United States were to enjoy, in virtue of a recognized independence; and the word *liberty* to what they were to enjoy, as concessions strictly dependent on the treaty itself.

You will remember that, in some of these letters, there is a statement of one of the negotiators speaking of the word " right " as being unpleasing to the English people in that relation because it would indicate that the United States did not get it from them but held it by original title as against them; not that the word " right " itself was unpleasant. There is no word, perhaps, so pleasing to the English ear as the word " right ", but it was because of the inference that would be drawn from its use. So the word " liberty " was applied to this particular kind of right that must come by grant from another. The same distinction is very well stated by Mr. Webster in that unfinished memorandum of which we have heard. I read from p. 526 of the United States Case Appendix. He says:

It is admitted that by these treaties,—

that is, the preliminary treaty of 1782 and the treaty of 1783 —

> the right of approaching immediately to, and using the shore for drying fish, is called a *liberty*, throughout this discussion it is important to keep up constantly the plain distinction between an acknowledged right and a conceded *liberty*.

The words were taken into the treaty of 1818 from the treaty of 1783, and they were taken into the treaty of 1783 from the French-English treaty of 1763. The treaty of 1763, United States Case Appendix, vol. I, p. 52, says:

> The Subjects of France shall have the liberty of Fishing and Drying, on a part of the coasts of the Island of Newfoundland, such as is specified in Article XIII of the Treaty of Utrecht.

The relations between these French treaties and the American treaty of 1783 were very peculiar. You will remember that the two treaties — the one between Great Britain and France and the one between Great Britain and the United States—were made on the 3d September, 1783. They ended a war in which France and the United States were allies against Great Britain, and they were the product of a connected negotiation. The preamble of the treaty between Great Britain and the United States of the 3d September, 1783, recites, p. 23 of the American Appendix:

> And having for this desirable end —

that is, peace —

> already laid the foundation of peace and reconciliation by the provisional articles, signed at Paris, on the 30th of Nov'r, 1782, by the commissioners empowered on each part, which articles were agreed to be inserted in and to constitute the treaty of peace proposed to be concluded between the Crown of Great Britain and the said United States, but which treaty was not to be concluded until terms of peace should be agreed upon between Great Britain and France, and His Britannic Majesty should be ready to conclude such treaty accordingly; and the treaty between Great Britain and France having since been concluded.

So you have these two treaties interdependent, necessarily because of the subject-matter, making a peace in which the two are allied against the third, in the same terms, made upon the same day and both treating of the subject of the fisheries, the treaty with France expressly continuing, with certain modifications, the rights, the liberty, granted in 1763, which continued, with certain modification, the right granted in 1713, and the same word used in the American treaty to describe the right granted, which was used in the French treaties to describe the right granted. I will not weary the court by arguing that in 1783, or in 1818, it was well known to the negotiators that the words " shall have the liberty to take fish " in the French treaty of 1763 conferred a right on France, that it was no mere acquiescence or temporary concession, or good-natured assent, but that it was the grant of a right and of a right that France had been asserting with a degree of boldness and uncompromising insistence against Great Britain for three generations — for one hundred and five years before this treaty of 1818 was made.

So it is quite clear that the word " liberty " was understood by the negotiators to be descriptive of a right, and whenever the representatives of the two countries come to use the word, in such circumstances that there is no occasion to make this discrimination as to the origin of the right, they use the two words interchangeably. If you look at the treaty of 1854, which is in the United States Case Appendix, p. 25, you will see in the first article that there was provision for the appointment of commissioners to settle the limits within which the liberty conferred by that treaty was to be exercised. The treaty of 1854, you will remember, conferred the liberty to take, cure, and dry fish, using the same words in the granting clause as the treaty of 1818. The first article of the treaty of 1854 provided for the appointment of commissioners to fix the limits within which the liberty was to be exercised, and if you will be kind enough to look at the foot of p. 26 of the United States Case Appendix you will see that the commissioners were directed to

> make and subscribe a solemn declaration that they will impartially and carefully examine and decide, to the best of their judgment, and according to justice and equity, without fear, favor, or affection to their own country, upon all such places as are intended to be reserved and excluded from the common liberty of fishing under this and the next succeeding article.

Now, if you will look at the paragraph just above the middle of p. 27 you will see what these commissioners were directed to do:

> Such commissioners shall proceed to examine the coasts of the North American provinces and of the United States, embraced within the provisions of the first and second articles of this treaty, and shall designate the places reserved by the said articles from the common right of fishing therein.

"Liberty" and "right" were regarded by both countries in making the treaty as interchangeable terms. Otherwise the commissioners were to take oath to do one thing and they were required by the treaty to do another and quite a different thing. You will find the same interchangeable use of the words "right" and "liberty" in the treaty of 1871. I will call your attention to but one more use of the term and that was by the British negotiators of the treaty of 1818 themselves. In the British Case Appendix, p. 86, there is a letter from Messrs. Robinson and Goulburn to Lord Castlereagh, dated September. The letter contains internal evidence that it was written on the 17th September, because it encloses copies of the protocol "of this day's conference." They speak of it as a protocol of this day's conference, and if you look at the protocols you will see that they are protocols of the 17th September; so that, although this date is blank, you could, with absolute certainty, write in the date the 17th. These gentlemen are making a formal report:

We have the honor to report to your Lordship that we had yesterday agreeably to appointment a further conference with the commissioners of the United States

and so forth. It tells of certain things which the United States commissioners said, and then, in the paragraph at the top of p. 87, says:

They concluded their observations on the subject of the fishery by adverting to that part of the proposed article in which the right to fish within the limits prescribed is conveyed permanently to the United States.

I think that is all I want to trouble the Tribunal with upon the subject of the meaning of the word "liberty."

THE PRESIDENT: Have you finished your argument upon this point?

SENATOR ROOT: I am entirely in the hands of the Tribunal. I think perhaps we might as well adjourn.

THE PRESIDENT: We shall be pleased to have you continue your argument upon this question today. I was under the impression that you had finished it.

SENATOR ROOT: I have finished in regard to this particular subject of the meaning of the word "liberty."

THE PRESIDENT: The court will adjourn until Thursday at 10 o'clock.[1]

THE PRESIDENT: Mr. Senator Root, will you kindly continue your address? [2]

SENATOR ROOT (resuming): I wish to add a single observation as to what I said regarding the meaning of the word "liberty" before the adjournment.

In stating the meaning of the word as it was used in ordinary municipal affairs, I did not wish to be understood as contending, of course, that it would necessarily have the

[1] Thereupon, at 4.30 o'clock P.M., the Tribunal adjourned until Thursday, the 4th August, 1910, at 10 o'clock A.M.

[2] Thursday, August 4, 1910. The Tribunal met at 10 A.M.

same effect when used internationally. I should not contend for any such proposition.

When, on the other hand, I stated that the term "shall have liberty", used in the treaty of 1783 and in the treaty of 1818, was taken from the French-British treaty of 1763, I did mean to be understood as indicating that it would have the same meaning, especially in view of the peculiarly close and intimate relations between the treaties.

I now pass to the words "in common." I do not think there is much, if any, difference between the two sides as to the meaning of the term "in common." I think the difference is rather as to the legal effect of the use of the term in the combination of words which we find in this treaty.

The ordinary use of the term "in common" as an English term, is stated in the printed argument of the United States, pp. 39 and 40. Examples are given, and no criticism has been made, that I observe, and no difference appears to exist between counsel upon the two sides.

The particular use of the term "in common" as opposed to "exclusive" in this treaty was a matter which had some antecedents, and some circumstances naturally pointing towards it.

In the United States Case Appendix you will find at p. 286 some observation by Mr. Adams contained in a letter to Lord Bathurst, dated the 22d January, 1816. I read from just above the middle of the page:

> By the British municipal laws, which were the laws of both nations, the property of a fishery is not necessarily in the proprietor of the soil where it is situated. The soil may belong to one individual and the fishery to another. The right to the soil may be exclusive while the fishery may be free or held in common. And thus, while in the partition of the national possessions in North America, stipulated by the treaty of 1783, the jurisdiction over the shores washed by the waters where this fishery was placed was reserved to Great Britain, the fisheries themselves, and the accommodations essential to their prosecution, were, by mutual compact, agreed to be continued in common.

That letter was one of the series of letters passing between the two governments that settled and defined the matter in controversy, which was settled, which was adjusted, by the treaty of 1818. It was one of the series of letters which exhibited in authentic form the positions taken by the two countries, and which were adjusted in that treaty of 1818. It is no casual remark. It is the formal statement of the pleadings of the parties in the controversy which came to settlement in the treaty. And this letter was in the hands of the negotiators on each side in the making of the treaty of 1818.

So that there was a formal statement on the American side of the view as to the relation of the parties under the treaty of 1818 as being the holders of the fishery " in common ", and that was not dissented from, but was the general view.

If we turn to the British Counter-Case Appendix, at p. 71, we find Mr. Oswald, the chief negotiator of the treaty of 1783 and the preliminary treaty of 1782, writing to Mr. Townshend, his chief in the Foreign Office of Great Britain, under date of the 2d October, 1783, adding a postscript:

> Drying fish in Newfoundland, I find, is to be claimed as a privilege in common, we being allowed the same on their shores.

And on p. 78 there is a note in a letter from Mr. Jay to Mr. Livingston. Mr. Jay, you will remember, was one of the negotiators on the American side in the treaty of peace of 1783, and he writes home to Washington, under date of the 24th October, 1782, speaking of a conversation with M. Rayneval, the French negotiator:

> He inquired [that is, M. Rayneval] what we demanded as to the fisheries. We answered that we insisted on enjoying a right in common to them with Great Britain.

That was Mr. Jay's conception of what was demanded and what was received by the Americans in the treaty of 1783, corresponding precisely to Mr. Adams' statement of it in his letter in 1816 to Lord Bathurst.

In the same British Counter-Case Appendix at p. 110 there is a letter dated the 4th December, 1782, from Count de Vergennes to M. de Rayneval. At the beginning of the very last line on p. 110, and running on to the top of p. 111, it says:

> The perusals of the preliminaries of the Americans will make you feel how important it is that their concessions should be free from ambiguity in respect to the exclusive exercise of our rights of fishing —

the French right of fishing. He proceeds:

> The Americans acquiring the right to fish in common with the English fishermen, they should have no occasion or pretext for troubling us.

Near the very beginning of the British Argument, p. 6, Great Britain cites a paper which was interposed by Mr. Rush in the negotiations with Great Britain which followed the French interference with American rights on the coast in 1820, 1821, and 1822, in which Mr. Rush refers to the French right of fishing on the coast as being a right in common, and that view was the view always taken by the British regarding the French rights of fishing on that coast, always denied by the French, always asserted by the British.

JUDGE GRAY: Mr. Root, in order that I may fully understand your position, your contention is that the use of the words " in common " in the citations that you have just made from M. Rayneval and Comte de Vergennes was such as to contra-distinguish it, in those instances, to exclusiveness.

SENATOR ROOT: Precisely, sir.

THE PRESIDENT: Please, Mr. Root, do not some of these quotations — not all — but some of them, apply to the first draft of the treaty of 1782 or 1783, in which it was said:

> That the subjects of His Britannic Majesty and the people of the said United States shall continue to enjoy unmolested the right

and so on, and at the end of that passage:

And His Britannic Majesty and the said United States will extend equal privileges and hospitality to each other's fishermen as to their own ?

In this draft there was considered a reciprocity which, at a later stage, was omitted. Now, perhaps some of these quotations refer to this suggestion of a considered reciprocity?

SENATOR ROOT: That may be, Mr. President. For the purpose of my present contention that would not make any difference. What I am endeavoring to point out is that " in common " which is inserted in this treaty of 1818, was a phrase which had been customarily used in describing the non-exclusive character of the rights which were negotiated about, granted, and exercised under these previous treaties, so that it was a natural use of terms. When they talked about the fishery right that was being negotiated in 1782, they talked about and wrote about it as being a right in common, and whether it was in the same terms as the final draft or not, they were using that expression to indicate that thing. That is precisely the point.

I do not conceive that it is necessary to argue that the right under the final treaty of 1783 was, in fact, a right " in common ", because the undisputed practice of the two countries treated it as a right " in common ", and the references upon both sides to it as being a right in common leave that beyond dispute. I am addressing myself now to the meaning of the words " in common ", and showing that the term had a customary use prior to its being put into the treaty of 1818 as excluding the idea of exclusiveness.

SIR CHARLES FITZPATRICK: That is to say, if that word had not been used, it was conceivable that the treaty might be so construed as to be an exclusive grant to the Americans ?

SENATOR ROOT: Of course it is conceivable, but I do not, by saying that it is conceivable, mean that it could properly have been so considered.

SIR CHARLES FITZPATRICK: That is not your argument ?

SENATOR ROOT: Not at all. I think that Sir Robert made a very just observation when he said that the meaning would have been the same without the words "in common." I think that without those words, that the right was "in common" would have been implied, and that the insertion of the words "in common" merely expressed what would have been implied.

SIR CHARLES FITZPATRICK: And therefore it does not exclude the idea of exclusiveness, to use your own words?

SENATOR ROOT: It does. It expresses the negation of exclusiveness, instead of leaving that negation to implication. While it is the plain and ordinary use of the words, it is not necessary to look far for the reason why it was expressed instead of being left to implication; I think it is easy to find it.

The French right which the British had always contended to be "in common", a right "in common" and not exclusive, had been asserted by the French to be exclusive and not "in common" and I beg you to observe that that assertion by the French did not depend upon any Declaration of 1783, it depended upon the terms of the Treaty of Utrecht and the treaty of 1763, which used the precise words of the treaty of 1783 and the treaty of 1818. The assertion of exclusiveness was prior to the making of the treaty of 1783, in which Americans and French and English were all concerned. It was upon the basis of the grant of the treaty of 1763 which says "the subjects of France shall have the liberty of fishing." The same words. Upon that the French asserted an exclusive and not a common right, and the United States in their treaty of 1778 with France, made five years before the Declaration of 1783, had assented to that exclusive interpretation. So that Great Britain, making this new treaty of 1818, was using words of grant which had been interpreted by France as granting an exclusive right, and which had received the assent of the United States, so far as the French were concerned, as granting an exclusive right.

Now, in view of what we have seen here of the possibilities of new and varied constructions presenting themselves to the human mind in the course of years, when contemplating the treaty, it was but ordinary prudence that it should occur to some British negotiator that they had better put in an expression of the common right, rather than leave it to implication, which in regard to the very same words had been denied by the French with the assent of the Americans.

It may be, I think it is quite probable, there was another motive urging them. Of course it is but conjecture. But, in the treaty of 1783, the British included a phrase which saved them from ever being charged with having undertaken to grant away a second time rights that they had granted to the French.

Their grant in 1783 was in regard to Newfoundland to take fish of every kind " on such parts of the coast of Newfoundland as British fishermen shall use." Now, that saved them from any controversy on the part of the French claiming that the British had undertaken to sell what was not theirs, and on the part of the Americans from any claim that the British had sold something that they did not have, which they had already sold to the French.

It would seem quite natural that in framing the treaty of 1818, when they came to substitute definite limits on the Newfoundland coast for the description of such parts as British fishermen should use, thus dropping out that safeguard against the French, and when instead of saying " such part . . . as British fishermen shall use " they said, " you may go from the Quirpon Islands to Cape Ray ", it should occur to them before they finished that they had dropped out that element of protection against the French; and the words, " in common with British fishermen " may well have been inserted in order to save them from interference with the French right of fishing. So that, if the French fishermen were in fact entitled, or if it should turn out that France could maintain her right to exclusiveness under her treaty, the American right should not go beyond the right that the British in fact had.

There is a certain support for that view, not merely in the natural disposition that men would have to protect themselves, but in the negotiations of 1824.

You will remember after the French had warned the Americans off the coast of Newfoundland, there was a claim made by the United States to which reference has already been made. The claim runs in this way, in words that have already been read to the Tribunal, and I will not ask you to turn to them again, on the part of the United States:

> It is obvious that if Great Britain cannot make good the title which the United States hold under her to take fish on the western coast of Newfoundland it will rest with her to indemnify them for the loss.

And, upon that, in the negotiations which included some other things, in 1824 there was a protocol which appears on p. 126 of the United States Counter-Case Appendix. It is the very last paragraph on that page:

> The citizens of the United States were clearly entitled, under the convention of October, 1818, to a participation with His Majesty's subjects in certain fishing liberties on the coasts of Newfoundland; the Government of the United States might, therefore, require a declaration of the extent of those liberties as enjoyed by British subjects under any limitations prescribed by treaty with other powers, and protection in the exercise of the liberties so limited, in common with British subjects, within the jurisdiction of His Majesty as sovereign of the island of Newfoundland.

I do not know of anything in the treaty which would justify that statement unless it be the words "in common." I think the words "in common" do justify it. It is an important part of the treaty. There is the limitation upon the right granted, the limit upon the right possessed by Great

Britain, and that is of importance in determining what the right is. So I think it is fair to infer that that purpose may have led to the insertion of these words.

So much for the meaning of " in common ", which is all I am addressing myself to now, and not to the legal effect of the words in combination with the other words of this article. The words have an ordinary, natural, undisputed significance as negativing exclusion and carrying into the right granted the limits of the rights possessed by the grantor; the first, certainly, because that is the use that the parties had been making of the phrase in writing and speaking about the subject; and the second, possibly, perhaps probably, because it was natural in view of the situation in which the grantor nation was.

I pass to the meaning of the word " inhabitants." Some point has been made about that. I think it is used as an equivalent for " subjects " or " citizens " in a general way, as indicating the great body of human beings who make up the organized civil society called the United States. There was a rational explanation for the use of the term " inhabitants " instead of " subjects " or " citizens." Of course it was taken into the treaty of 1818 from the treaty of 1783 and the preliminary articles of 1782. In 1782 the relations of the individuals to the organized civil society were quite vague and unsettled. Men were very much accustomed to group the members of the different divisions of an empire or kingdom under the head of subjects. The person of the sovereign was the nexus. In 1782 they were cutting off the head of this organized society in which the king of Great Britain had united the people living in these thirteen colonies, the people living in the British Islands and the people living in the northern colonies in America, and they had not quite settled how the relations between the individuals should be described in lieu of describing them as subjects of this king who was no longer uniting them. In the Articles of Confederation, which appear in the British Counter-Case Appendix, p. 7, you will see that uncertainty:

> Articles of Confederation and Perpetual Union between the States of New Hampshire, Massachusetts Bay,

and so forth. The date is the 9th July, 1778.

> Article I. The style of this confederacy shall be, "the United States of America."
>
> Art. II. Each state retains its sovereignty, freedom, and independence, and every power, jurisdiction, and right, which is not by this confederation expressly delegated to the United States in Congress assembled.
>
> Art. IV. The better to secure and perpetuate mutual friendship and intercourse among the people of the different states in this Union, the free inhabitants of each of these states, paupers, vagabonds, and fugitives from justice excepted, shall be entitled to all the privileges and immunities of free citizens in the several states.

Then the articles go on to put into the United States of America the entire treaty-making power, making the United States sovereign internationally. But you will perceive that there rather the dominant idea was that citizenship was citizenship of the several states, and that the relation to the international organization was that of the inhabitants of the country who were citizens of the several states.

Indeed, they had little to guide them. You go back to the Roman state and citizenship; the privilege of *civis Romanus sum* related but to the little town on the banks of the Tiber rather than to the great world-wide political organization, and vast numbers of people — the great majority of the people who really made up the political organization of the Roman Empire — had no privileges of citizenship. Go farther back, to the Greeks, and there was no such thing as citizenship of the Achæan League or the Delian Confederacy; and people then were very much in the habit of thinking about what they had done in Rome and Greece. They were trying to work out a theory of government, of association, without a sovereign, and about the best models they could get were those drawn from classical precedents.

Now a type has emerged. When, in 1787, the people in the United States came to make a new constitution, they found that this loosely compacted organization, in which municipal sovereignty was deemed everything, was too weak, and that they must make a stronger central sovereign, and from that came the type of national sovereignty, national citizenship. But they had not reached that point then, and so they used a comprehensive word which went just as far as their conception of organization had gone, endeavoring to cover the same idea which would have described the people of Austria and Hungary as subjects of Francis Joseph, and which would have described the people of Scotland, England, and Wales, and Berwick-on-Tweed as subjects of His Majesty King George.

I will call your attention to the fact that when these negotiators of 1824 met to make a formal protocol about the rights of the United States under the treaty of 1818, the protocol I have just referred to, they said, " The citizens of the United States were clearly entitled under the convention of October, 1818," etc. That was signed by Mr. Rush, one of the negotiators of 1818, and Mr. Huskisson and Mr. Stratford Canning, who were most skillful and fully informed negotiators, on the part of Great Britain, and it shows that they regarded the terms as being convertible.

The President: Would it be possible to say, having reference to Article 4 of the Articles of Confederation, that in the sense of the treaty of 1818 only the citizens of the thirteen states were to be considered as inhabitants of the United States? Then the concept of " inhabitants of the United States " would be identical with the concept of citizens of one of the thirteen states; or, notwithstanding this Article 4, and notwithstanding the protocol you have just referred to, would the concept of "inhabitants of the United States" be a larger one than the concept of the citizens of the thirteen states?

SENATOR ROOT: I should think that there was no idea of limitation to the citizens of the thirteen states, for several reasons. In the first place, it was well known that in 1783 the territory which was included within the boundaries then established by that treaty covered a vast area not included within the limits of the original states. The inhabitants of the United States, or the inhabitants who were to have this right, included a great area not strictly within the state limits. It was property held under the rights of the different states and ceded to the United States. Then, when you come to 1818, there had already been an enormous enlargement beyond that. Louisiana had been purchased in 1803, and there was the great Louisiana territory and the northwest territory stretching out to the west with indefinite limits that no one knew, unsurveyed, to a great extent unexplored, being part of the territory of the United States, and the inhabitants of those different states all pushing out into it. Then it is of the nature of a state to change its territories, and the loosely compacted organization of 1778, which existed when the 1783 treaty was made, had disappeared in 1818, and there was this closely compacted empire whose citizens were quite independent of residence in one state or another and had scattered widely over this great area. So I hardly think that we can find any limitation to a specific territory.

THE PRESIDENT: So that, in 1818, the term "inhabitants of the United States" embraced also persons who were not citizens of one of the different states if they had a residence in the territory of the United States?

SENATOR ROOT: Yes.

DR. DRAGO: May I draw your attention to the fact that in the treaty of peace of 1783, article 3, the words "people of the United States" and "inhabitants of the United States" are used as convertible terms?

SENATOR ROOT: That is true.

DR. DRAGO: Article 3 says that

> the People of the United States shall continue to enjoy unmolested the right to take Fish of every kind.

It further says:

> And also that the inhabitants of the United States shall have liberty to take fish of every kind.

> the Inhabitants of both Countries

shall have the liberty to take fish, etc., and then proceeds:

> the Inhabitants of the United States shall have liberty to take fish of every kind, etc.

You can see that all these denominations are used as equivalent terms.

SENATOR ROOT: There is a third — "that the American fishermen shall have liberty to dry and cure fish."

DR. DRAGO: Yes. So that we have here that "the people of the United States" shall have liberty to take fish, then "the inhabitants of the United States" shall have liberty to take fish, and, in the third place, "the American fishermen" shall have liberty to dry and cure fish.

SENATOR ROOT: I think that supports the view that I have taken that these were interchangeable terms.

THE PRESIDENT: Have all these terms the same significance as being expressive of an identical idea, or do they express different purposes?

SENATOR ROOT: I think they have the same subject-matter, but it was viewed from different aspects. I think that when they say "people of the United States" they are thinking rather of the right which came by virtue of independence.

JUDGE GRAY: A sovereign right?

Senator Root: The right which appertained to a sovereign independent state. I think that when they were speaking about the "inhabitants of the United States" they were thinking rather of how the right which they were granting to the United States was to be exercised by individuals, as a business enterprise that individuals must enter upon. And when they spoke of "American fishermen" they had reference to the method by which the right was to be exercised — that is, by vessel.

Sir Charles Fitzpatrick: Only a limited class of Americans would exercise the privilege, and that class would come under the description of American fishermen.

Senator Root: Well, that may be.

Sir Charles Fitzpatrick: They would be the only people who would require to land and dry fish?

Senator Root: Bankers, merchants, and clergymen would not be there. But they did, in fact, know that it would be the American fishermen, and when they were speaking about the practical exercise of the privilege they spoke about the people who would be there.

Sir Charles Fitzpatrick: Each one of these words has a meaning when read in the context. Whoever drafted that clause gave a special meaning to each of these words.

Senator Root: I do not doubt that. Now, a further word about the meaning of "American fishermen." Plainly it is a personification of the vessel which is owned and manned by Americans, just as these British statutes which have been cited here so fully speak of vessels receiving bounties and of vessels carrying on the fishery. Take the Act of 1775, British Case Appendix, p. 545 — I hardly think it is worth while to look it up, for it is a perfectly simple thing, but I will read from Article 7:

> All vessels fitted and cleared out as fishing ships in pursuance of this act —

that is, the Act 10 and 11 Wm. III, having reference to Newfoundland —

shall not be liable to any restraint or regulation with respect to days or hours of working.

There is the ordinary personification of a ship. The vessels shall not be liable to any restraint or regulation. At p. 565 of the same British Case Appendix you will see that the Act of 1819, passed to put this treaty into effect, in the second article provides

that if any such foreign ship, vessel or boat; or any persons on board thereof, shall be found fishing, etc.

THE PRESIDENT: Does the term "inhabitants of the United States" embrace persons who are not citizens of the United States; or does it embrace also British subjects resident in the United States? Can a British subject resident in the United States be, under the terms of the treaty of 1818, an inhabitant of the United States?

SENATOR ROOT: I should think so. Ideas were then quite vague and indefinite about what was the connection between the great body of the people in the territory who made up the political organization. Indeed, there are still states, portions of the United States, in which aliens have the right to vote.

THE PRESIDENT: If a British subject resident in the United States goes, under his treaty right as an inhabitant, into British waters to fish, would he be entitled also to the privileges which the inhabitants of the United States have, and would he be exempt from British fishery legislation?

SENATOR ROOT: Mr. President, that opens a pretty wide field — a field upon which the Foreign Office of the United States and the Foreign Offices in most of the countries of Europe have been engaged in discussion for a good part of a century, as to the extent to which old allegiance may be thrown off and new taken on, and the effect of that change upon the rights and powers of control of the country of origin over the person.

The President: You mean the Bancroft treaties ?

Senator Root: Yes, and there have been a great many situations of this kind which have arisen. The problem still remains to a certain extent in discussing the question of military service. It still remains in the discussion of the effect upon a Russian subject who goes to the United States and becomes naturalized and then goes home to Russia. There it is a criminal offense and he can be punished still under their law, if they apply their law, for having gone away. I do not think that on the spur of the moment I could solve the question you ask, but, of course, these gentlemen, in making these treaties, were not thinking about questions of that kind. That whole subject was in a very vague and indefinite position at that time, whether the original bond of allegiance between the Government of Great Britain and one of its nationals would be so completely destroyed by his going to the United States and becoming an inhabitant that, when he returned, he would not be subject to the entire control of his original government, and whether he could claim as a right under the treaty exemption from that control, are questions perhaps not easy of solution. It is quite clear he could claim no right whatever against the Government of Great Britain personally; no one could make any claim in respect of it except the Government of the United States. If the Government of the United States chose to assert to Great Britain that it had a right under this treaty to have that inhabitant, although a citizen of Great Britain, exercise certain rights, then the question would arise and it might be a difficult one.

One single word about the meaning of " bays, harbors, and creeks." I merely desire to make an observation regarding the ordinary use of the words as English words. It seems to me quite plain that the word " gulf " is used only to indicate very large indentations in the land — the Gulf of Bothnia, the Gulf of Finland, the Gulf of Genoa, the Gulf of St. Lawrence, the Gulf of Mexico. The word " bays " seems to be used either for very large indentations, which might be called gulfs, or very small ones, there being a wide range. For instance, there are the Bay of Biscay and Hudson Bay, which might well be called gulfs; the Bay of New York, the Bay of Fundy, Conception Bay, the Bay of Chaleur, the Bay of Naples, the Bay of Rio, Bahía Blanca (in Argentina), Bahía Honda (in Cuba), Bahia (in Brazil), Bantry Bay, Bay of Islands, and Bonne Bay, all of which are less than six miles wide, and there is not a bay on the western coast of Newfoundland which is more than six miles wide, except St. George's Bay. All the bays out of which the Americans were ordered by the French on this occasion that has been referred to were bays less than six miles wide, except St. George's Bay — so I am instructed; I have not been there to measure them.

Let me now say something about the practical bearing of your decision on the profitable use of the treaty right. I shall make some observations regarding the course of legislation in Newfoundland. I wish to impress upon the Tribunal this disclaimer, that I do not say a single word of fault-finding with Newfoundland or its Government. They are and have been for many years protecting their interests, which is very much the duty of the government, and have been following the natural and commendable instincts of human nature in doing it. I find no fault with them. I am going to challenge a judge; I am going to put to the judgment of the Tribunal the question whether the Government of Newfoundland, constituted as it is, inspired by the motives that it has, can be properly a judge upon our rights, which are its burdens, and left to draw the line which was intended to be established by the grant of this treaty. And I am going to urge upon you that the result which is developed by the application of the British theory to this case up to this time is a powerful argument against the soundness of the theory and against the view that the negotiators, in making the treaty, meant to have it construed as Great Britain now construes it.

I need not devote much time to urging upon the Tribunal the importance of the right. The Tribunal will remember that it was a *sine qua non* of the treaty of peace. John Adams declared he would never put his hand to the treaty unless this fishery right was provided for. He, and with him Franklin and Jay, were willing to stake the issues of peace and war upon having that right. Adams says so; Strachey wrote home to London so; Oswald wrote home to London so; Fitzherbert wrote home to London so. Our friends on the other side minimize it. They think little of it. Of course that is their privilege. Probably it is their duty to take that view of it. But not so these men who established it. One thing about it our friends on the other side have said that is certainly true: the value of it was not for the few miserable herring to be taken upon the shore of Newfoundland, nor was it for the cod-fish, the chief value that could be taken along the headlands or along the south shore; nor was it for the other fish, the hake, the halibut, the sea-cows, the great variety of fish that could be taken along the coast of Newfoundland. The great value of it was the bank fishery. And old John Adams, who knew his subject well, for he himself had been a participator in the fishing, as he tells us here, spoke of it as being one fishery; and it was one fishery. Why? Because the bank fishery cannot be prosecuted without bait. The herring, the capelin, the squid, were the seed corn of the harvest of the sea, which made the livelihood and the prosperity of the New England coast, and which still do make its livelihood and its prosperity.

The value of the bank fishery is quite apparent, I think. I will refer the Tribunal to a single statement in our Counter-Case Appendix, at p. 554, where the British counsel at the Halifax discussion presented the results of what was undoubtedly a careful inquiry into the facts. I will read from just below the middle of p. 554. They said:

> Secondly. There has also been conceded to the United States the enormous privilege of the use of the Newfoundland coast as a basis for the prosecution of those valuable fisheries in the deep sea on the banks of that island capable of unlimited development, and which development must necessarily take place to supply the demand of extended and extending markets. That the United States are alive to the importance of this fact, and appreciate the great value of this privilege, is evidenced by the number of valuable fishing-vessels already engaged in this branch of the fisheries.

That is to say, in 1877, and with the rights of the treaty of 1818 only. They said, further:

> We are warranted in assuming the number at present so engaged as at least 300 sail, and that each vessel will annually take, at a moderate estimate, fish to the value of 10,000 dollars. The gross annual catch made by United States fishermen in this branch of their operations cannot, therefore, be valued at less than 3,000,000 dollars.

That bait is an absolute necessity for the continuance of that important industry is also shown by the statements of these Halifax counsel. They said, at p. 551 of the same Counter-Case Appendix, beginning near the foot of the page:

> It is impossible to offer more convincing testimony as to the value to United States fishermen of securing the right to use the coast of Newfoundland as a basis of operations for the bank fisheries than is contained in the declaration of one who has been for six years so occupied, sailing from the ports of Salem and Gloucester, in Massachusetts, and who declares that it is of the greatest importance to United States fishermen to procure from Newfoundland the bait necessary for those fisheries, and that such benefits can hardly be overestimated; that there will be, during

the season of 1876, upwards of 200 United States vessels in Fortune Bay for bait, and that there will be upwards of 300 vessels from the United States engaged in the Grand Bank fishery; that owing to the great advantage of being able to run into Newfoundland for bait of different kinds, they are enabled to make four trips during the season.

Further down on the page, they said:

It is evident from the above considerations that not only are the United States fishermen almost entirely dependent on the bait supply from Newfoundland, now open to them for the successful prosecution of the Bank fisheries, but also that they are enabled, through the privileges conceded to them by the Treaty of Washington, to largely increase the number of their trips, etc.

But Sir Robert Bond himself has given evidence on that subject. I read from his speech of the 12th April, 1905, beginning near the foot of p. 447 of the United States Counter-Case Appendix:

I hold in my hand papers relating to Canada and Newfoundland, printed by order of the Canadian parliament in the session of 1892, and on page 28 of that report I find a letter addressed by C. Edwin Kaulbach, esq., to the Hon. Charles H. Tupper, minister of marine and fisheries at Ottáwa, under date 17th of April, 1890. This gentleman, who hails from Lunenburg, Nova Scotia, and who is a member of the Canadian parliament, wrote as follows in respect to the restrictions which the government of this colony had placed on Canadian vessels visiting our shores for bait in that year: "Our men are in terrible straits to know what to do under these circumstances, as their bait for the Grand Bank for our summer trip is almost wholly obtained on the south side of Newfoundland. The Grand Bank has been the summer resort of our fishermen for many years, and from various bays on the south coast of Newfoundland their supply of bait has been drawn, these being much less of distance and a greater certainty of bait than Canadian waters. We have hitherto enjoyed the privilege of obtaining bait in Newfoundland to the fullest extent, paying only such internal fees and taxes as were proper. The result of the action of the Newfoundland government will be most disastrous, and one season alone will prove its dire effects on the fishing fleet of Nova Scotia and the shipyards now also so busy and prosperous."

It is after that that Sir Robert Bond made this declaration:

This communication is important evidence as to the value of the position we occupy as mistress of the northern seas so far as the fisheries are concerned. Herein was evidence that it is within the power of the legislature of this colony to make or mar our competitors to the North Atlantic fisheries. Here was evidence that by refusing or restricting the necessary bait supply we can bring our foreign competitors to realize their dependence upon us.

This record is full of reports and correspondence showing that the French had for their bank fishery depended upon the procurement of bait in Newfoundland, and disclosing attempts by the Newfoundlanders to prevent the French from getting it, with the constant prohibition on the part of the Government of Great Britain, which regarded the effect that it would have upon her relations with her neighbor across the Channel to cut off such an important supply.

Of course there is also an element of value in this fishery, in the cod-fishing on the coast of Labrador, which is a very great fishery; and for that bait is necessary for the Americans. The Newfoundlanders carry on trap fishing there. They are on shore, and they run their traps out. But our fishermen use bait; they use a bultow. Then there is, of course, the cod-fishing on the south coast, as Sir James Winter has told the Tribunal. There is also the winter herring fishery, which has a relation to the bank fishery in this: the bank fishery is a summer fishery. The ships leave the Massachusetts and Maine coasts at the very end of winter, the beginning of spring, the last of February or the first of March, and they go up to the banks, take as many fish as they can with the bait that they can carry and keep, and then they go to the nearest point to get bait, and back to the banks. When they have exhausted the supply of bait, which is limited not merely by carrying capacity, but by keeping capacity, they go back again, and to and fro for bait. Even if bait were unlimited down on the Massachusetts coast, the long voyage for a sailing vessel to get it and back again would exhaust the time which they should spend in catching cod-fish. The bank season ends along in the autumn, and the vessels which are employed in it must either lie up, and the men employed in it sit idle, until the next spring, or some other occupation must be found. This winter herring fishery affords occupation for vessels and men during the off-season of the bank fishery, and so enables that fishery to be prosecuted profitably; and it has been of very material effect in making possible the profitable prosecution of the bank fishery.

There have been, in regard to these fishing rights in Newfoundland, two lines of action on the part of the Newfoundland Government, both constituting the expressions of a single policy: a line of legislation relating to the sale of bait, and a line of legislation regarding the taking of fish, both constituting but expressions of a single policy, which is the policy stated by Sir Robert Bond — the control of the bait supply, compelling competitors to recognize Newfoundland as " the mistress of the northern seas " in respect of fishing.

I shall ask the Tribunal to bear with me while I trace those two lines of action, begging the members of the Tribunal to keep in mind what I have said: that no one act is to be treated by itself, that neither line of action is to be taken by itself, but that the whole grand policy of Newfoundland is to be considered and the separate acts are to be relegated to their proper positions under that policy.

The first consideration in tracing this policy is one which has frequently been referred to here in respect of the purchase of bait. Our fishermen would rather buy bait in Newfoundland than take it, and there are several reasons for that. The first natural reason is that they could better use their time catching cod-fish than in catching bait; and it is more convenient and inexpensive, either by purchase or employment, to have the Newfoundlanders provide them with the supply of bait, and to go on to the fishing fields, where they can spend their time taking cod-fish. And, as Sir James Winter tells us, they have always bought bait. There never was any practical limitation upon the buying of bait until the Bait Act of 1887, the first Bait Act, which merely prescribed a license, evincing a purpose to take into the hands of the Government control of the business of selling and buying bait. But the licenses were issued until 1905, when they were cut off. During all that long course of years a population grew up along the western and southern coast — a sterile coast, as you will see before long, selected for the locus of the grant to the United States in 1818 because it was sterile and afforded no invitation to population. A population grew up on the basis of the business of catching and selling bait to French and to Americans. It was their means of livelihood. The quotations from the reports of Captain Anstruther, the British naval officer that Mr. Elder referred to, show what the situation was. The only money that these poor fellows on the coast ever got they got from the Americans. As Captain Anstruther says, what they had been doing before was to work under the trade or barter system, with such local business concerns as would buy from them. They would bring in their fish and get a credit, and buy a pair of boots, or an oiler, or molasses, or pork, and have it charged, and so on. The first money they ever got, and the only money they got, came from the Americans. But all that is in Captain Anstruther's report, and I shall not dwell on it. But a custom, a practice, and a population finding their means of livelihood from this trade had grown up on the treaty coast, until down came the axe in 1905 and cut that means off.

As an incident to the fact that these people, father and son, had come to live upon this industry or trade with the Americans, there came an assertion on their part of a right to take the fish themselves, and to profit by the industry; and that was the basis of the Fortune Bay difficulty. I will read from some of the affidavits about the Fortune Bay affair, in the United States Case Appendix, pp. 694 and 695.

The Tribunal will remember that after the Treaty of Washington was made, under which the United States, pursuant to the Halifax award, paid 5,500,000 dollars to Great Britain for the privilege of fishing, a lot of American fishing-vessels went into Fortune Bay to exercise the privilege, and they undertook to do so and were prevented by the inhabitants. I read from p. 694 of the United States Appendix:

> The examination of James Tharnell, of Anderson's Cove, Long Harbor, taken upon oath, and who saith: " I am a special constable for this neighborhood."

That is, a special officer of Newfoundland at that point in Fortune Bay. I now read from the foot of p. 694, and over on to p. 695, what he says about the Fortune Bay affair:

> The people were not aware that it was illegal to set the seines that time of the year, and were only prompted to their act by the fact that it was Sunday. We all consider it to be the greatest loss to us for the Americans to bring those large seines to catch herring. The seines will hold 2,000 or 3,000 barrels of herring, and, if the soft weather continues, they are obliged to keep them in the seines for sometimes two or three weeks, until the frost comes, and by this means they deprive the poor fishermen of the bay of their chance of catching any with their small nets, and then, when they have secured a sufficient quantity of their own, they refuse to buy of the natives.
>
> If the Americans had been allowed to secure all the herrings in the bay for themselves, which they could have done that day, they would have filled all their vessels, and the neighboring fishermen would have lost all chance the following week-days. The people believe that they (the Americans) were acting illegally in thus robbing them of their fish.

On p. 699 I read from the affidavit of John Cluett, of Fortune Bay:

> The Americans, by hauling herring that day when the Englishmen could not, were robbing them of their lawful and just chance of securing their share in them, and further, had they secured all they had barred they could have, I believe, filled every vessel of theirs in the bay. They would have probably frightened the rest away, and it would have been

useless for the English to stay, for the little left for them to take they could not have sold.

On p. 700 Charles Dagle, American master, says in his affidavit:

If I had been allowed the privilege guaranteed by the Washington Treaty, I could have loaded my vessel and all the American vessels could have loaded. The Newfoundland people are determined that the American fishermen shall not take herring on their shores. The American seines being very large and superior in every respect to the nets of the Newfoundlanders, they cannot compete with them.

And there was another affair which illustrates what I am now trying to make clear to the Tribunal, and that is that the Newfoundland fishermen came to deem that they had rights in this trade which the Americans ought not to interfere with by taking the fish themselves. In 1880 some American vessels undertook to take their own bait up in Conception Bay. That was while the Treaty of Washington was still in force. I will read from the affidavit of John Dago, on p. 715, at the foot of the page. He says he left Gloucester on the 1st April, 1880, then says:

On the 9th August, 1880, we went into a cove in Conception Bay, called Northard Bay, for squid. I put out four dories and attempted to catch my bait with the squid jigs or hooks used for that purpose.

Now, turning over to the top of p. 716 of the United States Case Appendix, I read:

My men went into the immediate vicinity of where the local shore boats were fishing for squid, but in a short time they returned and reported to me that they were not allowed to fish by the men on board the shore boats, and not wishing any trouble they returned on board. I then manned my lines on the vessel and commenced to catch squid; the men in the shore boats seeing us fishing came off to us to the number of sixteen boats, with some thirty men. These men demanded that I should stop fishing or leave, or else buy squid from them. They were very violent in their threats, and to avoid trouble I bought my squid, paying them one hundred and fifty dollars for the squid, which I could easily have taken if I had not been interfered with.

Wherever I have been in Newfoundland I find the same spirit exists, and that it is impossible for any American vessel to avail herself of the privileges conferred by the Treaty of Washington.

There, on the same page, is an affidavit by Joseph Bowie, master of the American schooner "Victor". He went into Musquito, Newfoundland, three times for bait, he says, and bought capelin from the local fishermen. He continues, at the bottom of p. 716:

The next time I went to a place called Devil's Cove on the chart, but it is called Job's Cove by the people; this was on the 4th of August, and the only bait to be obtained was squid. I anchored in the cove about $\frac{1}{4}$ of a mile from the shore, and commenced to catch squid with the common hooks or jigs used for that purpose. I had no nets or seines on my vessel. I had been fishing about fifteen minutes when some sixty boats that had been fishing inshore from us, manned by at least one hundred and fifty men, rowed up alongside of us and forbade our taking any squid.

The President: If you please, Mr. Senator Root, where is this Musquito? Is that on the treaty coast or the non-treaty coast?

Senator Root: I think it is not on the treaty coast. It was under the Treaty of Washington.

The President: Oh, yes; under the Treaty of Washington.

Sir Charles Fitzpatrick: They were all treaty coast at that time.

The President: Yes.

Senator Root: They appeared to have been in the habit of buying their bait, until the Treaty of Washington came along, and there was all this talk about the value of the fishery, and the Halifax award had determined that we were to pay 5,500,000 dollars for the privilege of fishing. Apparently, then, the American vessels tried to fish, and this was the obstacle that they met from the local inhabitants.

This same affidavit goes on to say that the natives prevented their fishing, and finally they bought their bait and went their way.

JUDGE GRAY: Do you know, sir, as a matter of fact, whether, outside of the Treaty of Washington, when it was open, the Americans were in the habit of resorting to what would now be called the non-treaty waters to buy bait?

SENATOR ROOT: I think the indications are that they went to the most convenient port, treaty or non-treaty coast, to buy bait. The fishermen find out where they are most likely to get it, and they run into one place or another place, as the case may be. Sometimes it is very plentiful in one place, and then again the horn of plenty will be poured out in another direction. They go where they think they can get it. But so long as they were buying it, it made no difference whether they were on treaty coast or non-treaty coast. That is not very definite, but that is my inference, from reading all this great mass of documents.

Now, *pari passu* with this practice of purchase which had been continued time out of mind, and under which the local population had come to conceive that they had rights against the substitution of taking for purchasing, there ran a series of shore protection statutes and executive acts. The first of that series to which I ask your attention is the denial to American fishermen of any shore rights whatever, under the treaty of 1818. They were denied back in 1839, by that opinion of the Law Officers of the Crown in which, like the Colossus of Rhodes, they fell off the headlands into the sea. They, being asked whether the American fishermen had any right to use the strand of the Magdalen Islands for the purpose of hauling their nets, answered No, with the admirable logic involved in the proposition that because the treaty granted American fishermen rights to go ashore on the south coast of Newfoundland to dry and cure their fish, therefore there was a necessary implication that they could not draw their nets on the strand of the Magdalen Islands. That opinion the Tribunal will find referred to many times afterwards in the correspondence. The Halifax British counsel stated what was considered to be the situation at p. 538 of the United States Counter-Case Appendix — the situation, I mean, as to American shore rights. I read now from just below the middle of p. 538, where they say:

> The Convention of 1818 entitled United States citizens to fish on the shores of the Magdalen Islands, but denied them the privilege of landing there. Without such permission the practical use of the inshore fisheries was impossible.

I hope the Tribunal will observe the progressive effect of these different things which I am going to refer to, to the ultimate end of crowding us out of any opportunity of any benefit whatever under this treaty of 1818, the exercise of a right under which is the key to the great bank fishery. They said, in the last paragraph on p. 538:

> In the case of the remaining portions of the sea-board of Canada, the terms of the Convention of 1818 debarred United States citizens from landing at any part for the pursuit of operations connected with fishing. This privilege is essential to the successful prosecution of both the inshore and deep-sea fisheries.

Lord Salisbury, in a letter which has been much referred to, of the 3d April, 1880, refers to the same subject. I read from p. 684 of the United States Case Appendix. That is in his correspondence with Mr. Evarts, in which they got down to an understanding, or supposed they got down to an understanding, as to what the rights of the parties were under the treaty, with the exception of certain definite points on which they agreed to disagree. Lord Salisbury says there, just below the middle of the page:

> Thus whilst absolute freedom in the matter of fishing in territorial waters is granted, the right to use the shore for four specified purposes alone is mentioned in the treaty articles, from which United States fishermen derive their privileges, namely, to purchase wood, to obtain water, to dry nets, and cure fish.
>
> The citizens of the United States are thus by clear implication absolutely precluded from the use of the shore in the direct act of catching fish.

This view was maintained in the strongest manner before the Halifax Commission, etc.

And that statement of Lord Salisbury is based upon both the treaty of 1818 and the treaty of 1871. He has just referred to both of them as the basis of that conclusion. Sir Robert Bond, in his speech of the 7th April, 1905, refers to the same subject, and reasserts the position.

It is true that this view that we were excluded from the shore was denied by Mr. Evarts, and that the United States has never assented to it; but it has been the practical treatment of the subject by Great Britain that she has denied to the United States any use of the shore; and, as a practical matter, any attempt to overcome that would be met by this insuperable, or practically insuperable, obstacle of the opposition of the shore population, so that the attention of American fishermen has been directed not to undertaking to get ashore and have a fight with the inhabitants, but to getting their bait in the best way they could. And so long as they could buy it, down to 1905, it was a matter of comparatively little consequence. When I come to discuss the British view of the inferences to be drawn from the fact that the fishing is in common, I am going to say something more about this question of shore rights. But what I have said serves my present purpose, which is to enumerate the successive steps by which the shore of Newfoundland was protected against us. The shore fishermen, in the exercise of their industry protested against the foreigner coming there, and the foreigner was compelled to purchase until, in 1905, the right to purchase was cut off, and he found himself with this barrier against the exercise of the treaty right of taking fish standing before him, both being in pursuance of a general purpose to shut him out from getting bait which would enable him to compete with Newfoundlanders in the bank fishery.

The Tribunal will perceive that by itself this exclusion from the shore made it inevitable that the kind of fishery that the Americans prosecuted should be a different kind of fishery from that which the Newfoundlanders prosecuted. It made the necessary working of the industry such that it was aptly described by Mr. Evarts when he said that it was impossible that the rights of the strand fishermen and the vessel fishermen should be turned over entirely to the determination of either one of them.

There was a series of statutes, I have said, and we have —

THE PRESIDENT: The exclusion from the shores of the Magdalen Islands was reported at the Halifax Commission by the United States agent himself?

SENATOR ROOT: Yes.

THE PRESIDENT: In the course of the argument.

SENATOR ROOT: Of course counsel there were dealing with a practical situation, and it was their tendency to minimize as much as possible what was coming from Great Britain.

THE PRESIDENT: Those tactics were observed on both sides.

SIR CHARLES FITZPATRICK: There was a tendency to exaggerate on one side and minimize on the other.

THE PRESIDENT: Yes.

SENATOR ROOT: As to all this long series of statutes, Sir James Winter has told us how they were made.

I turn to p. 3427 of the typewritten copy of his argument [p. 568, *supra*], where he says:

> Newfoundland has such legislation as it considers desirable, after having considered the matter most carefully, and after having had the experience and the opinion of the best qualified authorities in the country.

That is, in the country of Newfoundland. Then he proceeds, after an interval, to say:

> Among other things, those who are entrusted with these powers and duties —

that is, of legislation —

have come to the conclusion that in certain places bultows are objectionable, that they have a bad effect upon the fishing operations of these localities, and the result is, without going into details, as has already been stated, at certain places which are marked on the maps, which I believe are being put in for the information of the Tribunal, these regulations against the use of bultows are in force.

Let me observe that " bultow " is a corruption of the English word " bulter " — a long line to which shorter lines with hooks and bait are attached. I saw one of them the other day out on the pier at Scheveningen, and there were a number of them there. I saw one of them drawn in from the sea. It had been carried out to a distance, and this long line stretched out into the water, and at intervals of a few inches only there were little short lines depending with hooks on them, that had been baited; and as the man drew it in, for the amusement of the people resorting there, there was a long row of little lost soles hanging on to these short lines. That is the " bulter " — what they call in Newfoundland the " bultow " — a long line, which has short lines depending from it, with hooks and bait, and which is weighted down so as to run nearly to the bottom, and which is connected with a line at the surface which is buoyed up; and the vessel puts out these long lines, of tremendous length, almost as long as the drift nets that are used in the Holland and Scotch herring fisheries; they put these out, baited, and after they have been left there long enough for the fish to have taken their luncheon, the fishermen go round and draw the lines in and take the fish off.

The local fishermen in certain localities objecting to these bultows, Sir James says they prohibited the bultows in those localities. Over on p. 3431 of the record [p. 570, *supra*] Sir James says:

The same general observations that I have made about bultows apply to seining, with this exception, that there is more unanimity of opinion on the matter of seines than there is to bultows. The fact that bultows are prohibited in a number of places on the coast is because, on account of local circumstances, the reasons are different, and it is generally left to those who have the best information on these matters in each of the localities to decide and to help the legislators. It is generally upon their opinions and views that these regulations are made; in other words, they are made to suit the circumstances, views, and opinions of the people. It is a sort of what is called local option, and from this it results that the prohibition of bultows is not general or universal. But, it is different with seining.

There you have stated, upon unimpeachable authority, with great frankness, and an accuracy which is supported by a reading of this record, the way in which Newfoundland makes these regulations which Great Britain wishes you to say constitute and will constitute an adequate protection for the very rights that the local fishermen in these localities are seeking to protect themselves against.

Now, as to the specific statutes: In the first place, the legislation began with the Act of 1862, which the Tribunal will remember prohibited the taking of herring by seines between the 20th October and the following April:

That no person shall haul, catch, or take Herrings in any Seine, on or near any part of the Coast of this Island, or of its Dependencies on the Coast of Labrador, or in any of the Bays, Harbors, or any other places therein, at any time between the Twentieth day of October and the Twelfth day of April in any year.

I think there is satisfactory evidence in the case that that statute was passed with no idea of applying it to Americans. It is not very important, but I think that will be quite clear as I go on in developing certain facts under other heads. And they put into the statute, under Article 10:

Provided always, That nothing in this Act contained shall in any way affect or interfere with the rights and privileges granted by Treaty to the Subjects or Citizens of any State or Power in amity with Her Majesty.

I must say, and I think the Tribunal will agree, that the legislature of Newfoundland in passing that statute considered that that saving clause excluded Americans from the purview of the Act. What it did was to put the prohibition down during the French off-season. I hope the Tribunal will understand what I mean by the "French off-season."

THE PRESIDENT: The season in which the French are not permitted to fish — the winter season?

SENATOR ROOT: Yes; the season closes the 20th October.

THE PRESIDENT: Yes.

SENATOR ROOT: From the 20th October until the French come back again they put down this statute.

THE PRESIDENT: Yes. One section begins with the 20th October, and the second section begins with the 20th December. The first section would coincide with the French off-season, whereas the second section would, perhaps, not totally coincide with it.

SENATOR ROOT: I do not know why they fixed those dates in this second section.

THE PRESIDENT: You do not know why the dates are fixed?

SENATOR ROOT: No, I do not. I merely observed that the first section did coincide with the period during which the French do not fish.

THE PRESIDENT: Yes.

SENATOR ROOT: It is a shore-protection statute, because it is limited to seines; and it is expressly provided that it shall not prevent the taking of herrings by nets, which is the natural and customary implement of the shore fishery — not necessarily exclusive, but the customary and ordinary implement of shore fishery. It would have excluded Canadians and it would exclude from the shore fishermen, Newfoundlanders, coming from other parts of the country. Such is the nature of fishermen that they do not like to have their own local fishing interfered with by anybody. He may be friend and brother, but they want their own fishing for themselves;

and this is a shore-protection statute. As I go on with these I am not going to contend that they had specific interference with the American right in their minds in passing each of these statutes. In some of them later I think they included American rights in what they meant to exclude, to bar out; but they are following, in all this series of statutes, the natural impulse of mankind, of fishermankind, to protect their own fishing at their own doors. It is the same impulse that every boy has about the stream that runs through his father's farm; and it is an impulse that is inevitable, and not at all discreditable.

The next statute that I would like to bring to the attention of the Tribunal is the provision which now exists as section 25 of the regulations of 1908. My reference to it is in the United States Appendix, p. 202.

JUDGE GRAY: The last statute was in 1862, about ?

SENATOR ROOT: Yes; and that was continued along and included in the consolidated statutes of 1872, and along in the second consolidation of 1892, and this provision I am about to refer to comes down from previous acts of legislation; but the most convenient form in which to find it is in this provision in the 1908 regulations.

The 1908 regulations were a reprint in this respect, and in most respects, merely of regulations of previous years. It was rather an edition than a new set of regulations. It is a new 1908 edition of long-standing regulations. The provision is:

> No herring seine or herring trap shall be used for the purpose of taking herring on that part of the coast from Cape La Hune on the West Coast, and running by the west and north through the Straits of Belle Isle to Cape St. John.

Now, here is Cape La Hune in here (indicating on map) just about twenty miles east of the Ramea Islands; and this stretch takes in the whole of the American treaty coast, the south and the west, and runs down to Cape St. John down here somewhere, which is the end of the French treaty coast. So that it includes the whole American treaty coast, and the whole French coast, and about twenty miles in addition. That is a clear shore protection statute. It would not be so singular if it did not omit the great stretch of the free fishing coast of Newfoundland, imposing no limitation to the taking of herring by the seine anywhere in these great herring bays, Fortune and Placentia, or upon any of the great fishing coast of the east side.

THE PRESIDENT: What other means of taking herring would be permitted on that part of the coast?

SENATOR ROOT: Nets.

THE PRESIDENT: Are nets used principally by the inhabitants?

SENATOR ROOT: Principally by the inhabitants; yes; that is the principal implement used by the inhabitants.

THE PRESIDENT: By Newfoundlanders?

SENATOR ROOT: Yes. But this provision does not stand alone. Under the heading "Herring Fishery," on p. 202, first paragraph, is:

> Herring may be caught in nets or hauled in seines, and other contrivances, under the conditions and in the manner prescribed by these rules, and not otherwise.
>
> No herring trap shall be used in the waters of the district of Placentia and St. Mary's or Fortune Bay

and so on. But there still exists, and existed when these regulations were made, the Act of 1884, which provided that Newfoundlanders, for purposes of bank fishing, might take herring at any time and in any manner, "notwithstanding any law to the contrary" (p. 709 of the British Case Appendix):

> Notwithstanding any law to the contrary, it shall be lawful for the owner of any vessel owned and registered in this Colony, which shall be

fully fitted out, supplied and ready to prosecute the Bank fishery, and shall have obtained a Customs Clearance for the said fishery to haul, catch, and take herring at any time and by any means, except by inbarring or enclosing such herring in a cove, inlet, or other place, to an extent not exceeding sixty barrels for any one voyage, to be used as bait in prosecuting the said Bank fishery in the said vessel.

Now, Sir James Winter explained that very frankly as being called for by the necessities of the Newfoundland bank fishermen. They had to have bait, and accordingly here was the statute authorizing them to take bait — no seine limitation, no Sunday limitation — "any law to the contrary notwithstanding." Newfoundland bank fishermen may take their bait as best they can, and when they can.

Yet upon the full length of the treaty coast no one but a Newfoundland fisherman is at liberty to take bait with a seine or herring trap. Everywhere off the treaty coast Newfoundlanders can take herring for any purpose, with herring traps and herring seines, if they see fit. And everywhere — treaty coasts or non-treaty coasts — Newfoundlanders engaged in the bank fishing may take their bait.

Now, there is a shore protection statute—a statute for the protection of Newfoundland fishermen against all the world. I do not know that they had Americans particularly in view in that discrimination which they made, but the fact that they did include the whole American treaty coast in this prohibition would seem to indicate it. They certainly meant to stand for Newfoundland fishermen against all the rest of mankind; and they did it, and they did it effectively if the British theory be true that the grant of the treaty of 1818 to the United States is subject to the British right of legislation.

The Sunday provision, introduced in 1876, is another illustration. It was not religious fervor, because it did not prohibit the taking of cod-fish, and cod-fish is the great industry of Newfoundland. The great mass of this population are taking cod-fish. They can do that on Sunday. But it is the practice and the custom of the herring fishers who go to the places where the herring come in in schools, to want their day in the week to go home to their families; and they do not want anybody competing with them when they do go home to their families. And they put this prohibition upon this particular industry to keep competitors from taking the herring while they wanted to stay at home. They were not resting fish, they were resting Newfoundlanders.

Let me observe here that this provision in the regulations of 1891 which was discovered during the course of Sir James Winter's argument, and suggested to him, which he, with all his intimate knowledge of the situation, did not know of, was there but one year. When the commissioner came to make up regulations in 1891, he changed the old rule about nets on Sunday. The old rule was that they could not set the nets on Sunday and they could not haul them on Sunday, but there was nothing to prevent their being set on Saturday and left there to work, like money at interest, while one slept, to work all day Sunday catching fish, and let them be taken out on Monday. There was nothing in the law to prevent that until 1891, when those new regulations were made. And the commissioner making the regulations put in that the nets should not be left in the water over Sunday. The next year it was taken out, and in these regulations now it does not appear. They have gone back to the old law.

The Sunday provision is a curious one in another way. That also, you will observe, is subject to the exceptions of this controlling Act of 1884, which, notwithstanding any law to the contrary, gives the Newfoundlander the right to take his bait at any time and in any way. So that the Sunday provision applies only to bait, and does not apply to Newfoundlanders taking bait for the bank fishery, but only to the persons who, as Bret Harte says in one of his stories of life in a Western village, are regarded by the inhabitants as having the defective moral quality of being foreigners.

Then there is another interesting circumstance which you will find by looking at paragraph 78 of these same 1898 regulations, on page 209 of the American Case Appendix, at the end of the page. This enlarges the Sunday prohibition, so that it applies not merely to herring but to any bait fish:

> No person shall between the hours of twelve o'clock on Saturday night and twelve o'clock on Sunday night, take or catch in any manner whatsoever any herring, capelin, squid, or any other bait fish, or set or put out any contrivance whatsoever for the purpose of taking or catching herring, capelin, squid or other bait fish. Capelin may be taken for fertilizing purposes by farmers or their employees during the usual season.

That is to say, when capelin come in in such quantities that human nature cannot stand it and the farmers can make good use of them, they can take them on Sunday. But when the herring come in in such quantities that American human nature cannot stand it, and they see the opportunity to make their whole voyage profitable and support for themselves and their families for the whole year to come, by availing themselves of the opportunity on the Sunday, American human nature must conform itself to the Revised Statutes of Newfoundland. The Newfoundlanders are protecting themselves; they are giving latitude to themselves to correspond to their own wants and their own wishes. The stern and severe rule of exclusion is to be applied to the foreigner, whoever he is.

That ends what I have to say about the Sunday provision.[1]

THE PRESIDENT: Senator Root, will you kindly continue your address?[2]

[1] Whereupon, at 12.15 o'clock P.M., the Tribunal took a recess until 2.15 o'clock P.M.

[2] Thursday, August 4, 1910, 2.15 P.M.

SENATOR ROOT (resuming): The next provision to which I refer is section 9 of the Consolidated Statutes of 1892 of Newfoundland. It appears on p. 176 of the United States Appendix. It will be found a little below the middle of that page:

> No person shall, between the tenth day of May and the twentieth day of October in any year, haul, catch or take herrings or other bait for exportation within one mile measured by the shore or across the water of any settlement situate between Cape Chapeau Rouge and Point Enragee, near Cape Ray, under a penalty of two hundred dollars

and so on. You will perceive that this time, between the 10th May and the 20th October, covers the period during which bank fishermen would wish to resort to the coast of Newfoundland to obtain bait, and this provision prohibits the taking of bait by any one in any way within a mile of settlements.

There is a curious similarity in that to a treaty to which I expect to call your attention hereafter upon another point.

JUDGE GRAY: Will you point on the map where that is, Senator ?

SENATOR ROOT: Cape Chapeau Rouge is over here, near the western entrance to Placentia Bay, and Point Enragee is up here quite near Cape Ray, so that this covers the entire southern treaty coast, and it also covers that part of the coast which is in proximity to the French Islands of St. Pierre and Miquelon.

THE PRESIDENT: May I ask you, Mr. Root, how long does the fishing season on the banks last ?

SENATOR ROOT: I think it ends about November — October or November. The 1st November, I am told.

THE PRESIDENT: Thank you.

SENATOR ROOT: You see this covers the practical resort for bait. Our vessels leave the New England coast about the 1st March; they take their first baiting with them, or pick it up somewhere along the route, along Nova Scotia; but when they have used up that first bait, then they want to go to the nearest place where they can get it, and get it as quickly as possible, and get back.

I was about to refer to a curious similarity between this provision and the treaty of 1878 between Austria and Italy, which I was intending to refer to upon another point. In that treaty in which Austria accorded to Italy rights of fishing upon the Dalmatian coast, the east coast of the Adriatic, there is a margin of one mile. Treaty rights are not allowed to come within one mile.

These gentlemen here have made a new treaty. They have put into their statute the same kind of limitation which Austria put into a treaty, protecting these people who dwell upon the coast for a mile from all their settlements, from the incursion of any one to take bait; protecting their industry, protecting the sale of bait.

The next provision is a provision relating to purse seines.

JUDGE GRAY: When you say there is a discrimination, will you be good enough to point out just what it is in that ninth section? The president and myself both would like an explanation.

SENATOR ROOT:

> No person shall, between the tenth day of May and the twentieth day of October in any year, haul, catch or take herrings or other bait for exportation within one mile measured by the shore or across the water of any settlement situate between Cape Chapeau Rouge and Point Enragee.

That bars the Americans from the convenient and approximate treaty coast entirely, but it leaves the great body of Newfoundland open, where the Americans cannot go — open to the taking of bait for the purposes of sale.

SIR CHARLES FITZPATRICK: Is what you say now affected at all by section 28 which is found at the foot of p. 178?

Senator Root: That depends upon the meaning and force which they give to that clause.

As I have already said, it is quite clear from the other evidence in the case, when the original Act of 1862 was passed, I do not think they had any idea of its applying to Americans, but there did come a time when that view changed.

Lord Salisbury in his correspondence with Mr. Evarts regarding the Fortune Bay affair took the view that these statutes did apply to Americans; and while he abandoned the view that statutes passed after the treaty of 1871 applied under that treaty, he still maintained that statutes passed before the treaty did apply to rights under the treaty; and when they went a step farther, and Lord Granville wrote his letter of 1880, he took the position that the statutes of Newfoundland generally applied, and I do not know whether when they passed this law they thought that this saving clause did apply to Americans, or did not apply.

Sir Charles Fitzpatrick: Would that not appear fairly obvious? If that section is to have any effect whatever, it must apply to the treaty rights of the Americans.

Senator Root: It must?

Sir Charles Fitzpatrick: Yes, section 28; does it not say:

> Nothing in this chapter shall affect the rights and privileges granted by treaty to the subjects of any state or power in amity with Her Majesty?

Senator Root: Well, that clause is in all these statutes. That clause is in the statutes which the British are here claiming to apply to Americans. It is in the statute which Lord Granville asserted to apply to Americans. It is in the statutes which were the subject of negotiation to secure agreement or regulation as between Lord Granville and Mr. Blaine, following the year 1880. And it is obvious that the question — whether that applies or how far it applies — depends upon what you say the rights of the Americans are;

and if you say, as Great Britain now says here, that the rights of Americans are subject to the right of municipal legislation by Newfoundland, then application of it to American fishing-vessels is no interference and has no effect upon the rights and privileges granted by treaty to the subjects of any state in amity, and so on.

SIR CHARLES FITZPATRICK: I did not quite understand it that way. I was under the impression that the position taken by those who represented Great Britain was that the Americans were subject to the municipal laws of the province of Newfoundland in so far as these laws did not violate the treaty rights of the American. That is what I have understood their position to be as stated here.

SENATOR ROOT: But when they come to say what the treaty rights of the Americans are, they say, and the whole British argument here is based upon the proposition, that there is an implied reservation of the right of municipal legislation. And if there is such an implied reservation, then the exercise of the power of municipal regulation does not infringe upon American rights. It is all there, as to the construction you give to the treaty grant.

I am arguing the very proposition that your honor has put. I am arguing that this treaty grant was a grant of a definite and certain right, with a line drawn round it by the terms of the treaty grant, so that this clause would except — must be deemed to except — American vessels from the application of such a statute. But, Great Britain says that there is no such line, that the treaty grant is subject to the right of municipal legislation, subject to the exercise of the sovereignty of Great Britain; that there is an implied reservation of the right of municipal legislation, because that is British territory. And, if that is so, then the line for which I am contending is wiped out, and these rights are subject to this legislation, and this clause does not save them.

Now I pass to the provision about purse seines. The use of purse seines is prohibited.

THE PRESIDENT: May I ask one question, sir? A close season has the special purpose of protecting the spawning period?

SENATOR ROOT: That is natural.

THE PRESIDENT: And how long is the spawning season? Can you tell me how long it is?

SENATOR ROOT: I suppose but a few weeks. Certainly it does not last all winter.

THE PRESIDENT: Nor all summer. Probably not as long as from the 10th May to the 20th October?

SENATOR ROOT: Certainly not. Of course, different fish spawn at different times. My understanding is that the herring spawn in May. Mr. Lansing says they spawn in May, and that the spawning period lasts about a month.

Now, I will refer to purse seines. A purse seine is a kind of seine that is adapted to use by vessels, as distinguished from the seine adapted for use by men who can draw the seine on the shore. It is simply a seine with a cord running through rings at the bottom so that when fishermen have to use it who have not any bottom to use it on, who cannot go ashore and draw their seines so that the fish will be kept in by being drawn along the bottom, they can make a bottom for themselves by pulling in the foot of the seine. That is a simple little device to enable vessels that cannot go to shore to utilize seines.

Upon this general subject of " seines " I would like to call your attention to the report of Mr. Joncas, read at the International Fisheries Exhibition in London in 1883. Mr. Joncas, I believe, was a Canadian.

SIR CHARLES FITZPATRICK: A Canadian, I understand.

SENATOR ROOT: At p. 606 of the United States Counter-Case Appendix he tells about the implements used. He says:

The nets used by our fishermen are generally thirty fathoms long by five or six wide.

They are set in the evening, and in the morning early the fishermen visit them, take out the fish, and if necessary take the net ashore to clean it. Generally, in the spring, when the fishing is good, each net will take from five to ten barrels of fish during one night.

But there is a much more expeditious mode of taking herrings than with nets, and that is with seines. Seines for this purpose must be of large dimensions, say from one hundred to one hundred and fifty fathoms long, by from eight to eleven fathoms wide, with braces of two hundred fathoms long. These seines are expensive and require many hands to work them, so that it is not every fisherman that can have one. There are also the purse seines which are used to fish the herrings on the banks, sometimes twenty and thirty miles from the shore.

Now, you will see that all this legislation, while directed at the seine, is protection of those on shore. The fishermen Sir James Winter and other counsel told us about, who live in their little fishermen's huts, who have little capital, who have a hard life—and they must elicit the sympathy of every one (they certainly have mine)—they have not the money to buy expensive seines, either the ordinary kind of seine or purse seines, and they feel a natural antipathy to the people who come from a distance with these more efficacious implements for the taking of fish, and taking their bread and butter out of their mouths. The purse seine, Sir James Winter very frankly told us, is objectionable because it is more efficacious than other kinds of seines. It is also more expensive. It is more peculiarly the implement of the foreigner who comes. No one can complain of the shore fishermen having that feeling. Putting ourselves in their places, how should we feel, dependent for the support of our families upon taking fish as they come into the shallow waters of our bays and inlets, to see great fishing-vessels coming, whether from France, from New England, or from Canada, with the most modern and approved appliances, and taking the fish before they get in to us, instead of coming in to buy the fish from us?

I am not going into the question here as to whether there is any other reason against the use of a purse seine than that it is more efficacious. I am not going into the discussion of the question as to whether purse seines are injurious to fish, or any kind of seines injurious to fish. I am endeavoring to show to your honors that this is another step, together with those I have already mentioned, in which the protection of the shore fishery against the vessel fishery is embodied in the policy of the government of Newfoundland. The question whether a purse seine has any other objection than its efficacy still must be determined by experts, for whom we have asked, and whose appointment I understand our friends upon the other side have objected to.

Another statute which is not referring to herring fishery, or bait, but which breathes the same spirit, is the prohibition against the use of bultows on the south shore. That is to be found in its present form on p. 208, section 62 of the Regulations of 1908, into which it comes from some period in the past:

No bultows shall be used on the fishing grounds from Cape La Hune to Cape Ray, both inclusive, in the district of Burgeo and La Poile.

Cape La Hune was the limit of one of the other provisions, just east of the end of the treaty coast. Now Sir James Winter has told us that the only place on Newfoundland itself where cod-fish are taken in any considerable number is on the south coast. The way cod-fish may be taken is with the hand lines, by the shore fisherman, or with traps, which, as described by Sir James Winter, are those having four sides, set down to the bottom, with a leader that runs up to the shore, so that as fish pass along the shore they run against this leader, that is, a net running up to the shore, they run against that, and follow that along down, and go into the trap, and there they are when the fisherman goes out in the morning. That is purely the shore fisherman's concern. He sets it out from the shore. It is not a vessel fisherman's plan. The way in which the vessel fishermen take cod-fish on this south shore, and also upon the Labrador shore, is by the bultow, these long lines; and here is the provision which prohibits the use of that kind of fishing on the very coast and the only part of the coast to which Americans may resort for cod-fishing purposes. There are other little places where there are local regulations, where there is a similar prohibition, depending, as Sir James said, on local option, people wanting to keep anybody else from coming and interfering with their fisheries. You see they are protecting the shore fishermen against people coming from outside.

When you get up on to the Labrador coast there is another provision contained in the very next section on p. 208. That section provides:

> No person shall place in the waters of the Labrador Coast, any cod-trap, or cod-trap leader or mooring, nor shall it be lawful for any person to put out any contrivance whatsoever for the purpose of securing a trap-berth on that portion of the coast: — From Blanc Sablon to Gull Island, near the north-east point of Square Island, before noon of the first day of June.

Then in regard to another portion of the Labrador coast, before the 5th of June; another the 10th June; another before the 20th June, and so on down to the 10th July. So that the times for setting these cod-traps and cod-trap leaders, which are used by the Newfoundland fishermen on the Labrador coast for the taking of cod-fish, are set at different dates from the 1st June to the 10th July. That is supposed to prevent anybody from coming in and taking an unfair advantage, and getting a location for his cod-traps. You will notice it refers not only to placing the cod-traps, but to placing any contrivance for the purpose of securing a trap-berth.

There are other provisions which make it possible for a man to take and hold a cod-trap berth by putting up poles. That is regulated in section 54 of the same regulation which appears on p. 206:

> Two poles or buoys moored to indicate the position in which it is intended a cod-trap is to be set,

and so on. That is a regulation of Newfoundland fishing with reference to the securing of these locations for the taking of cod-fish and, of course, by the 10th July the great army of Newfoundland cod-fishermen who go to the Labrador coast, have got up there and they have got their cod-traps set and their cod-trap location preëmpted. Then, on p. 209:

> No bultows or trawls shall be used before the fifteenth day of August in any year on the fishing grounds within three miles of the Coast of Labrador or Islands on said Coast between a line to be drawn south-east from Cape Charles and a line drawn from east and west from White Islands in Domino Run.

That is from a line somewhere down here (indicating on map) running up off this map. So that the best location for taking cod-fish is preëmpted for nearly two months by the Newfoundland fisherman with his cod-trap and contrivances, before the American fisherman, who uses the bultow, is at liberty to go up on that coast and set out his bultow. When he gets there he finds the places where he would put his bultows for the purpose of taking cod-fish preëmpted by the cod-traps, again protecting the shore fisherman as against the vessel fisherman.

As I have said before, I am not blaming these people for wanting to protect themselves, but that is what they are doing, and the effect of it all is to substitute a fishery dictated by the wants, the opinions, the local option of these dwellers in these little fishing communities along the coasts, for the great fishing interests you have illustrated upon the shores of Holland and Scotland, to substitute the little humble fishers' daily tale of fish for a great fishery such as that which has built up the power and strength of Holland, and is one of the great sources of the wealth of Scotland, England, and Ireland today.

That is prohibited to us because these laws are the laws of shore fishermen, dictated by their wants and unrestrained by the large considerations which would apply to the whole of this fishery if it were the fishery of a single nation, and a single government were to weigh in the balance the broader and the narrower interests.

Now, we come to still further expressions of purpose, a little different in origin, not originating with the fishermen, but originating with the Government of Newfoundland. This has reference to Sir Robert Bond's Question Six proposition. He has discovered that the Americans are not at liberty to go into any bays, or harbors, or inlets, or creeks on the coast of Newfoundland, and it is his purpose, he says, to keep them out. I read from p. 414 of the United States Counter-Case Appendix. He says:

I venture to go further than the learned counsel for the United States in his admission —

he is referring to an admission made in the Halifax Case —

and to express the opinion, after very careful consideration, that American fishermen not only have no right to land and seine herrings, but they have no right to enter into the harbors, creeks, or coves from Cape Ray to Rameau Islands, and from Cape Ray to Quirpon Islands, for the purpose of buying herrings or fishing for them. . . . If the position that I have taken up in regard to this section of the coast of this colony is correct, the exclusive rights to the winter herring fishery are under the British flag today, and always have been so ever since the dominion of the British flag was first established in North America.

I am not at this moment going to take up the argument of Question Six. I refer to the attitude of the Government of Newfoundland upon it as one of the group of circumstances illustrating the spirit and purpose of the Government of Newfoundland. It is set up here to be the judge of our rights, and it is to be the judge of our rights unless our construction of this treaty, which makes a definite line, be a correct construction.

Sir Robert Bond, says the counsel, has been turned out of office. Aye, but the Government of Newfoundland is here by counsel asserting, maintaining, the attitude of Sir Robert Bond. Says Sir James Winter:

> But the fact that the question is now raised for the first time is because, up to the present time, they have never done cod-fishing, as it was expected and contemplated when the treaty was made, and they now come in to prosecute a business to which the Newfoundland Government, at any rate, very strongly object. namely, the fishing for herring in the bays on the west coast.

I am reading from p. 3582 of the typewritten argument [p. 597, *supra*]. Sir James proceeds:

> When they set up this claim for the first time it becomes necessary to inquire strictly into their legal rights. Then, for the first time, we examine into their title deeds to see what their title is to exercise this new fishery, to carry on a new business which it is the object and purpose of the Newfoundland Government, for the present at any rate, to prohibit altogether.

Nor is it a new purpose, a new policy with Sir Robert Bond. That very excellent gentleman's name has come into prominence in the discussion because it happened to be he who made this great discovery, which discovery was but one of the incidents of the execution of that policy. In his speech of the 12th April, 1905, reading from p. 413 of the United States Counter-Case Appendix, I find Sir Robert Bond saying:

> My memory as a member of this Legislature goes back now for nearly a quarter of a century, and I do not remember that the position was ever before taken in this house that our fishermen could not compete with either the American or French fishermen on an equal footing. The object of every bill that has been introduced into this Legislature in relation to

foreign fishermen has been with the sole view to bring about an alteration in the foreign bounty system or the reduction of prohibitive duties.

I am not finding fault with Sir Robert Bond or with Newfoundland for attempting to bring about a change in the bounty system or in the protective duties of another country. I am urging upon you that this is not the attitude of a judge, that that purpose which has inspired the consistent policy of the Government of Newfoundland for a quarter of a century, as Sir Robert Bond says, is wholly inconsistent with what my honorable friends on the other side call the fair regulation of our rights. I am saying that if there is no line of demarcation set by this treaty grant upon our rights, but they are left to the unrestrained judgment, the discretion, the legislative authority of the Government of Newfoundland, our rights are gone; and all this right, for which John Adams was willing to refuse peace, for which John Quincy Adams threatened war to Bagot in 1816, was an idle fantasy, a delusion, unprotected by the terms of the instrument they were so insistent upon.

Still further, what is the meaning of these laws about the employment of Newfoundland fishermen, about the shipment of Newfoundland fishermen, or of any fishermen within the jurisdiction? What is the meaning of the provisions of the Acts of 1905 and 1906? They do not relate to the purchase of bait. Here the two lines come together. They relate to the taking of fish. Let us, for the present, assume that they are justified — under some construction of the treaty they would be justified — let us assume that Newfoundland had a perfect right to prohibit the shipment of any sailor, of any fisherman in a fishing crew within the territory of Newfoundland, let us assume that they had a right to prohibit any British subject from fishing from an American vessel within the territory of Newfoundland, let us assume that they had a right to prohibit any Newfoundlander to go outside of Newfoundland territory for the purpose of shipping upon an American vessel — why did they do it? They did it for no other purpose, or conceivable purpose, than to limit, restrict, interfere with, and prevent the successful prosecution of the American fishery. It was the spirit of competition, it was the determination to destroy a competitor's enterprise that dictated these laws. Granted, if you please, that they had a perfect legal right to make those provisions, they exhibited the spirit which I am discussing, and it was exhibited in their regulation of our fishery as well as in the particular statute to which I refer.

We are not without much evidence as to this spirit and purpose. It was intense, it was controlling, it made the Government of Newfoundland willing to ignore the interests and wishes of their own fishermen. It was not a fisherman's policy, but it was a trading policy which was outcropping for the benefit of the great fishing and trading firms of St. John's, and it was the same policy which led Great Britain into the statutes which you have read, that endeavored to keep Newfoundland unpopulated, and inflicted penalties upon people endeavoring to live in Newfoundland and fish — a roast when they wanted raw and a raw when they wanted roast policy. Here is the way in which the fishermen looked at it: United States Counter-Case Appendix, p. 380. The fishermen of the Ferryland district — observe, not on the treaty coast — send a petition to the Legislature in which they say:

That your petitioners are engaged in the cod-fishery on the southern shore, and until two years ago added to their earnings from that avocation by the sale of bait to American vessels.

That this bait business was one which enabled your petitioners to earn considerable money, and that the visits of these American vessels resulted in the circulation of considerably larger amounts to the sale of ice, stores, fishing outfits, shipping men, and proving a means of circulating at least $40,000 per year to the people of this district.

They strenuously object to this new policy of the Government of Newfoundland in so far as that branch of it goes which is concerned with preventing the sale of bait. They say:

That this traffic has become so profitable to the people of these Nova Scotia ports that they are advocating the abolishing of the license fees altogether, and allowing free entry to the American fishermen, without any restrictions, for the sake of the trade they bring. . . .

And that your petitioners, therefore, humbly pray that this Legislature in its wisdom will terminate the present policy of hostility towards the American fishermen, and return to that under which the people of this district and other districts of the Colony were able to earn food for their families by carrying on legitimate traffic with the Americans, instead of being, as they are now, obliged to emigrate to foreign lands to obtain a livelihood denied them at home.

The Bay of Islands fishermen held a monster mass meeting, in which they passed a resolution protesting against the new policy. They say, at p. 386 of the United States Counter-Case Appendix:

We beg to state most emphatically that the people of this coast are unanimous in condemning this policy as one which is injurious to the best interests of the Colony as a whole, and ruinous to the livelihood of the people of this Western Coast.

Governor MacGregor, forwarding that in a letter of the 4th of April, 1907, to the Colonial Office, says that the newspaper which reports it represents that this resolution was adopted at a meeting which was well attended and that "the resolution was adopted with practical unanimity, and expresses the deliberate opinion of the community." There was a protest from Bonne Bay, which appears at p. 389. The fishermen, in what they say, point to the real origin of this policy:

If ever the Americans are effectually excluded, it may be that the West Coast merchants who engage in the Bank fishery will come to the front; but before killing the goose that laid the golden egg the substitute or successor should have been found.

Governor MacGregor writes, p. 390:

> At the same time it is impossible to conceal from oneself the fact that the people of Bonne Bay and of Bay of Islands are those that are most directly interested in, and dependent on, this particular herring fishery, in which practically no others, except the people of St. George's Bay, participate.

There were a number of others that I will not detain you with. Mr. Elder has read to you what Sir James Winter said in a formal public interview regarding this policy as being a policy directed against the interests and against the protests of the fishermen themselves. Now, here is the explanation of it — United States Counter-Case Appendix, p. 446. Sir Robert Bond reads, in his speech to the Newfoundland Legislature, a communication which he has received, dated the 23d March, 1905, signed by a list of merchants of St. John's, and containing this resolution:

> *Resolved*, That, in the opinion of the meeting, —

it seems they had had a meeting —

> it is expedient and highly important that immediate steps should be taken to prohibit American fishermen from obtaining supplies of bait fishes in the harbors or upon the coast of Newfoundland, and that a copy of these resolutions, bearing signatures, be forwarded forthwith to the Right Honorable Sir Robert Bond.

On the preceding page, 445, he quotes the Hon. Edgar Bowring, of the firm of Bowring Brothers, Limited, as follows:

> The Hon. Edgar Bowring, of the firm of Messrs. Bowring Brothers, Limited, than whom there is no firm in the colony more largely interested in the fisheries, addressed me a letter in reply, in which the following occurs:
>
> "I have to say that I think it is of paramount importance that the government should take immediate steps to prevent the Americans from obtaining bait supplies."

There are many other places in the record which show that this is a trade policy pursued as against the fishermen's interests, and I beg you to bear in mind that that policy is a policy that cannot be carried out except by preventing both the purchase and the taking of bait fish. Of course the great trading firms of Newfoundland do not want our competition with their source of supply. Until the American fishing-vessels came to buy from those poor fellows on the shore, the trading firms of Newfoundland had the fishermen in their hands; they could dictate the price, they could give as many gallons of molasses or as many rubber boots or oilers to the fisherman for every quintal of fish he brought in as they pleased; but now, with the American competition, the fisherman gets his opportunity of making his price. If he can get a better price from the Americans he sells to them instead of selling to the Newfoundland firms; and we find in Captain Anstruther's report a communication stating that some sell to the Newfoundland traders and some to the Americans, not to accommodate the Americans, but because they get a better price. It is for the interest of the trader to prevent competition, it is for the interest of the fishermen to have competition; but the Government of Newfoundland, answering to the impulse of the trader, shows its purpose not of fairly regulating the fisheries, but of preventing the Americans from having bait for the bank fishery in order to compel a commercial concession, and also shows that for that purpose it is willing to ride down and over the interests of the fisherfolk for whom our sympathies are invoked here.

Not only that, but they are willing to flout the power of England. In a score of communications which have been read to you here and in which Sir William MacGregor addressed the Colonial Office he advisedly used the expression: "My responsible advisers" think so and so; that wise and capable man excluding himself from participation. In the score of communications that appear in this record the colony of Newfoundland treats the Government of Great Britain with scant courtesy, with persistent condemnation, and in a contumacious spirit. They are willing to violate the traditional policy of the British Empire, so designated here, which never permitted the withdrawal from France of the ordinary trading privileges as to the purchase of bait. They are willing to do that for this sole purpose, that involves necessarily the prevention of our fishing rights under the treaty of 1818 as well as the prevention of our purchase under the ordinary comity of nations.

And Sir James Winter does not hesitate to say, after his review of the whole situation, that the American treaty right is worthless. After discussing this Question No. 6, the president says that it was worthless as regards herring, and Sir James Winter says: Yes, it is to a certain extent worthless as regards herring, and practically also worthless as regards cod-fish on that part of the coast.

Sir Robert Bond, of course, boldly avows the same position in 1905, in the extract relating to Newfoundland being the mistress of the northern seas. She is mistress, his proposition is; and if the British theory of this grant is right, so she is. If we are prevented from buying and we are prevented from taking, we hold this great industry upon the banks at their will and in their power, and I suppose we must abandon it or we must pay over again for the opportunity of getting bait to prosecute the industry.

I am not going to discuss protective tariffs. We have a tariff policy under our system of government. The national government is practically assigned to indirect revenues, the field of direct revenues is practically occupied by the separate states for local purposes, and in the raising of revenues by indirect means we have built up a tariff and we have applied to it a principle which largely obtains now throughout the world, that we shall raise our revenue by putting our duties upon such things as involve competition with our industries at home.

I do not think we are open to the charge of being very selfish, because we have opened our shores and all the wealth of our country to the millions of all the nations of Europe. We have given to them freely, without thought of their competition, of all the benefits that the richness of our land and the security of our government could afford; but we have said that in raising our necessary revenue we will impose the tax so that it shall contribute to the food, the prosperity of those who come to us. And I submit that there ought not to be a construction put upon this treaty which will deprive us of the benefit of it unless we are willing to buy the benefit over again by changing the general fiscal policy of our government for the benefit of the government of Newfoundland.

I pass to another proposition, passing off the narrow field of the particular situation in which we are involved in Newfoundland through the execution of this purpose that could be executed only by destroying our treaty right, to a more general consideration. It is that this situation is the situation that must always be anticipated in the case of grants of this character — I mean of this generic character; grants which constitute a perpetual burden granted to one country upon the territory of another.

A question has been raised as to why such grants need exemption from the power of municipal regulation and limitation by municipal legislation, while trading rights do not. It is because of the ingrained, innate distinction between the two. Trading rights are temporary. The vast number of trading treaties, all, so far as I know, are temporary. When circumstances change they expire. They are made for periods when no change is to be anticipated. One can make an agreement for ten years, five years, or perhaps for fifteen or twenty years, forecasting what the course of development may be, and with reasonable certainty that no change of conditions will make a stipulation that is advantageous to one's country today disadvantageous before the period ends. Such agreements are reciprocal and mutually beneficial. An undue restriction upon one side immediately meets with some restriction upon the other side; and the advantage that is obtained by one country cannot be restricted, limited, modified, changed, taken away, in whole or part, without a similar treatment derogating from or taking away the advantage to the other country. All the conditions of the trading right urge the people of each country towards its preservation and continuance in its full force, because upon the preservation of the other country's benefits depends the preservation of their own benefits. But a right like this, perpetual as against all the changing conditions of the changing years, always a burden, is sure to become vexatious, the cause of irritation and of resentment, with no interest on the part of the people of the country on which the burden rests for its preservation, for nothing more comes to them. The trading right in its nature urges to preservation. The perpetual burden in its nature urges to destruction. And the course of conduct on the part of the Government of Newfoundland which I have been detailing, without criticism or condemnation, is but the subjection of our right to the inevitable working of human nature which must apply to every such right as this, and which must demand for the efficacy of the grant of the right an exemption from the opportunity for municipal legislation to control, limit, restrict, or modify the right.

THE PRESIDENT: If I understand you well, Mr. Senator Root, you base the claim that this right is quite of an exceptional character, that it is different from the regular treaty rights, on its perpetuity ?

SENATOR ROOT: It is different from the regular treaty rights of trading, for instance, the kind of rights that I am speaking about, in two respects: one that it is perpetual and therefore must meet the changing conditions of the country to which it applies, and the other that it is a one-sided burden.

JUDGE GRAY: That it is unilateral.

SENATOR ROOT: That it is unilateral, and has to sustain it no continuing benefit whatever coming to the country upon which it is a burden.

THE PRESIDENT: How would it have been with the rights of the American fishermen in British territorial waters according to the treaties of 1854 and 1871? Were these rights the same or were they different?

SENATOR ROOT: They were different in respect of the necessity in regard to which I am speaking now. In the making of temporary and reciprocal fishing arrangements there is not the imperative necessity for exemption from regulation that there is regarding a right of this kind, and that is one of the reasons why many competent writers of authority do not apply the doctrine of servitudes to temporary treaties.

THE PRESIDENT: So your conclusion would be that the American fishermen, under the treaties of 1854 and 1871, were not exempted?

SENATOR ROOT: No; I beg pardon. I do not think that. I think they stood upon the same ground. I think they were exempted from the power of legislation, but the urgent necessity for exemption which applies here did not apply to those treaties. I shall take up the nature of the right hereafter, and of course the right might have existed, although it might not have been necessary for it to exist. If one were arguing the question whether the exemption existed under those treaties, one would not have the ground of argument which I have just been urging regarding the treaty of 1818, that is all.

THE PRESIDENT: There would be another basis?

SENATOR ROOT: There would be another basis which applies both to the treaty of 1818 and to those, but this basis of argument would be wanting.

THE PRESIDENT: Yes.

SENATOR ROOT: It might well be that one could find the exemption here and not find it there, although I think that it exists in both cases.

THE PRESIDENT: In the American Argument it is in some place expressed that the treaty of 1871, in its grant of fishing rights, is in effect the same as the treaty of 1818.

SENATOR ROOT: Yes. I suppose that is designed to refer to the terms of the grant.

THE PRESIDENT: Yes. It refers to the terms of the grant. But, therefore, one might conclude that, also under the treaty of 1854 and 1871, American fishermen were exempted from the British regulations.

SENATOR ROOT: I think they were; but not on this ground.

THE PRESIDENT: Not on this ground, because these treaties were not perpetual?

SENATOR ROOT: Precisely.

THE PRESIDENT: And were not unilateral?

SENATOR ROOT: Precisely.

I have said something about sympathy with the Newfoundland fishermen. Of course one cannot help it. This is a burden. But there is a right way and there is a wrong way to get rid of a burden. The right way is to do as Great Britain did with France — make a new agreement with her, and to the extent that the burden is relieved by cutting down the right that was burdensome, to make compensation for it, as she did in 1904. The wrong way is to do what is being done here, to whittle away, wear away, fritter away the right so that it is worthless, and it will no longer be profitable to maintain it as a burden.

Let me call attention to the fact that when fishermen are let alone, they settle the difficulty. They have settled it whenever they were left to themselves. It is no necessary burden upon Newfoundland, because when the fishermen were left alone they settled it by — what ? By substituting for the treaty burden a profitable trade for themselves. And everything went merrily as a marriage bell until the Government of Newfoundland undertook to close down, with its purpose to use the trading right in order to affect our fiscal policy. And when we came to the *modus vivendi* of 1906, Great Britain and the United States agreed upon it, and on the suggestion coming from fishermen we put into the *modus*, or letter, or instrument containing it, a clause that other arrangements might be made on the coast — I do not remember the exact words; but there was that permission, that the local people might adjust matters; and they did; they substituted a *modus* of their own for ours, and it went on. If they can only be let alone they will adjust the matter. Great Britain did the same thing to France; in addition to giving her territory in other parts of the world, she gave the right to purchase bait, the ordinary trading right, adapted to the uses of fishermen.

So there is no very serious burden and no real cause for special sympathy, except that the fishermen have a government that cares more about the interest of the St. John's traders than it does about the interests of the fishermen.

Where does all this leave us ? The British theory of their right is, as I have said over and over again, that the treaty grant is subject to the implied reservation of the British right to legislate. That is stated without any reserve. The obligation of reasonableness is not an obligation of sovereignty. If their theory is correct, if the treaty grant is subject to the right of legislation, it is subject to a right that is under no obligation of reasonableness towards us. That is of the essence of sovereignty — itself to determine what is the policy to be enacted into law. The policy of the empire is to find its expression in the legislation of the empire and all its legislative bodies. I need not trouble the Tribunal with citations from the argument. Sir Robert Finlay stated it at the outset:

Subjection to British legislative control was inherent in and formed an essential part of the very subject-matter of the treaty.

He said [p. 213]:

The right to make such regulations springs out of the sovereignty which the British government retained over the coast and the territorial waters.

It is not because of anything that is found in the treaty that that statement is made. It is because Great Britain is sovereign, and the right to which our treaty grant is subject is the right of sovereignty. Nothing that counsel can say here can impose a limit upon that right of sovereignty. We know well what it is.

I am laying aside now, for the moment, what is said in the statement of the question about reasonableness. I am merely pursuing the British argument, the theory upon which the argument is based, for the purpose of testing the soundness of the proposition that the grant is subject to British sovereignty. If there is an implied reservation of the powers of sovereignty and our grant is subject to it, Americans must be subject to the same restrictions by law as British subjects are; and that is what Great Britain says. The power of Great Britain over our treaty must be commensurate with her power of legislative control. If the treaty grant is subject to the sovereign power, the sovereign power cannot be subject to the treaty grant. One or the other must be controlling. The proposition of Great Britain is that her sovereignty is controlling and, therefore, not the treaty grant.

Every government, of course, considers itself under a certain obligation to be reasonable, to be fair, to be just;

but it is an imperfect obligation. It is to be reasonable, to be fair, to be just according to its own conception of what is reasonable and fair and just. It is a law unto itself. That is sovereignty. And the subjection of the government to the law or reasonableness is a subjection to its own will, controlled by its own idea; and if the grievous situation of the traders of Newfoundland makes it reasonable that limitations should be imposed or impairment visited upon any fishing privilege or right upon the coast, that is competent to government. The standard to be applied to us is the standard to be applied to British subjects, we are told; we are subject to regulation because they are subject to regulation, because our right is subject to the sovereign right which regulates them; and if our right is subject to the sovereign right of legislation, then there is nothing unreasonable in imposing such limitations upon our right as, in the exercise of their sovereign judgment, they see fit to impose. It is not unreasonable for them so to limit and restrict our right as to subserve the whole interests of the colony of Newfoundland or the British Empire. If our right is subject to their sovereignty, it is no impairment of our right for them to say: "No herring shall be taken upon the west coast for six months, for six years, for sixty years" or "no cod-fish shall be taken upon the south coast." They can do what they did do in the treaty of 1857 with France, which did not take effect, because the Newfoundland legislature never passed the necessary legislation to make it applicable; a treaty concluded and ratified, and effective as between Great Britain and France, but never becoming applicable for lack of legislation. There they did give France, in express terms, the exclusive right to fish upon the north coast, from Quirpon Island to Cape Norman, and at five separate points down on the west coast, all on the treaty coast — Port au Port and a variety of other places that I do not recall at this moment. If the American treaty grant was subject to the legislative power of Great Britain, there would be nothing unreasonable in their exercising their right to impose that same limitation upon us which they imposed then in favor of France. There is nothing unreasonable in a country's asserting its rights. There is but one way in which the grant of 1818 can be protected against the sovereign power of Great Britain, with all the scope of that sovereign power, and that is by drawing the line of the grant as against the sovereign power; and the moment that you assert that the grant is subject to the sovereign power, it is completely under the control of the sovereign power. No obligation of reasonableness, which is to be in the judgment of the sovereign, is any protection to any extent whatever.

THE PRESIDENT: Do I understand you, Mr. Senator Root, that you now base the claim of the American right being not subject to British regulations, not as you did before on the unilateral or the perpetual character of this treaty, but that you base this claim now upon a more general ground, upon general ideas of international law and general ideas concerning the binding effect of treaties?

SENATOR ROOT: No; if you will permit me to explain —

THE PRESIDENT: That is the object of my question. I want to understand you exactly.

SENATOR ROOT: I am now addressing my remarks to the character of the right as claimed by Great Britain. I am not now arguing on the character of our right. I shall address myself to that presently. I am endeavoring to describe and exhibit the true character of the British claim, and the effect which that claim will have upon the treaty right, if you accord it the approval of your award.

THE PRESIDENT: That was a description of the consequences the British contestation would have?

SENATOR ROOT: Precisely, yes; and I shall presently take up the other view and present what seems to be our right — the nature of the right granted and the legal effects of that nature.

My present proposition is that the British right, as stated and argued by them, involving and based upon the assertion in the fullest possible form that the treaty grant is subject to British sovereignty, is necessarily in its effect destructive; that is to say, it is at their will to make it destructive.

Take a practical situation: What is the United States to do? A law is passed which American fishermen think seriously interferes with the profitable prosecution of their industry. The law, in the ordinary course of events, will become effective before the fishermen ever hear of it. They know of it only when some local officer tells them they cannot do thus and so. What are we to do? Appeal to the Government of Newfoundland? Well, the Government of Newfoundland is possessed of this spirit and purpose which I have been describing to the Tribunal. We get nothing. Appeal to the Government of Great Britain? No one can have a higher respect or a warmer regard for any body politic than I have for the Government of Great Britain; and no one, certainly, could ever have experienced more courtesy or kinder treatment than I have always experienced from the representatives of that great Power. Nevertheless, one cannot blind oneself to the fact that a change has taken place in the relations between the Government of Great Britain and her colonies in recent years. The change began with this American revolution, which was ended by the treaty of peace in 1783. The Attorney-General, I think it was, referred to it as the civil war, and I rather like that way of describing it; for it was a civil war among the people of Great Britain. It was that which first taught Great Britain how to treat colonies. She has profited by the lesson, and our friends in Canada and Newfoundland and Australia and all over the world have been benefiting by it. And from that time to this the colonies of Great Britain have gradually grown more and more self-governing, and nearer and nearer to an independent attitude. The ties between them and Great Britain have come to be largely voluntary — ties of voluntary adherence, of sentiment, of loyalty. And it has become more and more evident that they would not survive deep and long-continued resentment.

Sir Robert Finlay rather protested against reference to the colonies as being different from Great Britain, and said they are one. They are one, in a juristic sense. They are one as they appear in this proceeding and before this Tribunal. Nevertheless, for the purpose of dealing with a practical situation it must be realized that they are far from one; that Great Britain has handed over general legislative power to this other body, this self-governing colony of Newfoundland, which proceeds in accordance with its will, and if officers of the Government of Great Britain undertake to interfere, talks about violation of the constitution of Newfoundland, and talks pretty sharply and stiffly, too.

Great Britain has vested in the government of this self-governing country the power to exercise the discretion of sovereignty; that is to say, the power to exercise this very discretion subject to which the British argument places our treaty grant. It is not quite, but almost, equivalent to a change of sovereignty. And when we appeal to Great Britain against a decision by Newfoundland in a certain law establishing a close season, prohibiting us from fishing thus and so, or now and then, what do we find ? We are appealing to Great Britain against the exercise by this self-governing colony of the very power that Great Britain has vested her with. What is Great Britain to do ? Take away her constitutional power, or declare that the exercise of it has been a violation of the treaty ? Ah! But on the British theory it is not a violation of the treaty, because the treaty is subject to the exercise of that very power.

Suppose Great Britain were of the opinion that comity, kindly feeling, good relations with the United States called upon her to review the action of the self-governing colony of Newfoundland as to whether this power with which the colony had been invested had not been abused. Ah! There we have it. We have to prove, and to secure any action from Great Britain we must prove, that there has been an abuse of the power, and that is very difficult. It must be a case gross, extreme, outrageous, to lead the mother-country to face the inevitable resentment of her colony which would follow a condemnation for an abuse of its constitutional powers. Hardly a practical relief.

THE PRESIDENT: But was it not practised in 1906 — withholding the royal sanction to the Act of 1906 ?

SENATOR ROOT: Yes, it was; for the purposes of this arbitration, and when Newfoundland imposed conditions upon her consent to entry into the arbitration; that is, the conditions of including in the arbitration Sir Robert Bond's Question Six and also the trading question. But you will remember with what indignation that was received by Newfoundland.

THE PRESIDENT: Yes.

SENATOR ROOT: And it was justified by Great Britain in this correspondence, not as a reversal, not as a final judgment, but as a necessary *modus*, to make it possible to secure an adjustment by arbitration between the two countries.

Now, as to arbitration; the practical bearing of that. Of course I am talking now only about the practical situation that we would be in, and therefore I refrain from any reference at this time to the fact that you are first to pass upon rights as they existed under the treaty of 1818, which would be the basis of further arbitration. But there is one preliminary thing to be considered, and that is: What is the scope and continuance of Article 4 of the agreement ? First, as to its scope, if any question arises regarding the exercise of the liberties referred to in the treaty of 1818 (this is on p. 6 of the United States Case Appendix) it may be determined in accordance with the principles laid down in the award. The Tribunal is to " recommend, for the consideration of the contracting parties, rules and a method of procedure under which all questions which may arise in the future regarding the exercise of the liberties by them referred to may be determined in accordance with the principles laid down in the award." If the rules are not adopted

then any differences which may arise in the future between the High Contracting Parties relating to the interpretation of the Treaty of 1818 or to the effect and application of the award of the Tribunal shall be referred informally to the Permanent Court at The Hague for decision

and so on. Now, I say, as to the scope. The Permanent Court at The Hague, if we get there ever, and I hope it will never be necessary to go under this Article, will have to make their decision upon the interpretation of the treaty of 1818 and the effect and application of the award of this Tribunal. Suppose this Tribunal makes an award which affirms the contention of Great Britain here, that is to say, that the treaty grant is subject to the sovereign power of municipal legislation. What is the new Tribunal going to say when that power has been exercised ? That is the award. That is the law for the parties. It has been the exercise of a sovereign power that we are subject to. Suppose you add that it must be reasonable, and that is for the Tribunal to determine. Then we have got to prove that there has been an abuse of the discretion. We have got to make a proof of the negative. Instead of the United States going upon the treaty coast to exercise a liberty granted in 1818 as it had been exercised time out of mind, as it was exercised without interference for half a century after the treaty of 1818, and meeting an assertion that now the exercise of that liberty ought to be restricted, an assertion that there is good reason for restricting it in time or in manner, and the establishment of that to somebody's satisfaction, the United States must go to this Tribunal and prove that there was not any reason for restricting — a very difficult thing to do; in a majority of cases quite impossible to prove that there is no occasion. It is a complete reversal of the rights. Our rights are to be our rights as granted; and if there were anywhere a right to change them, the burden of justifying, giving grounds, reasons for the change, should be upon the person who proposes to change them. If the British theory is maintained by your award, there is a complete reversal, and we have got to make the negative proof. Our right as it was originally granted and originally exercised is to be assumed to be all wrong, and a different situation and a different method is to be assumed to be right, and we are to disprove it. I do not know whether anybody can prove that a limitation against the use of purse seines ought to be imposed or not, and I do not know whether anybody can prove that the limitation against the use of purse seines is unreasonable or not; but I do know that there is an immense difference between having somebody else prove it to be necessary and having yourself to prove that it is unnecessary; and in the majority of cases that difference of the burden of proof would probably be controlling.

The President: I beg pardon for so often interrupting you, Senator Root, but I really think it is necessary. These are now the last days that we have the benefit of the assistance of counsel, and therefore we must make use of the opportunity — perhaps it might seem that we are abusing it; I hope not.

The contention of the United States is that they have a *liberum veto* of objecting to particular regulations. The contention of the United States is that if you consider one of the British regulations as contrary to the treaty, you may object to it, and then the matter is at an end; Great Britain has no longer the power of enacting those regulations. And the British contention now, as it stands, is that Great Britain has a right to make the regulations. You have the right to make diplomatic remonstrances, but if Great Britain will not listen to these remonstrances the matter is again at an end. Great Britain says: " We do not want your objections. We do not consider your objections."

According to the fourth article, the solution would be that either this court would propose some method of procedure to which both governments would accede, by their free-will — they are not obliged, at all, to accede to them; it is a pure recommendation — or if they do not accede, then both parties have bound themselves by Article 4 to submit future contestations to the decision of The Hague Tribunal in the summary procedure. Would it not seem that both parties would gain by this method ?

Senator Root: Precisely; both parties would gain by this method. But I beg the Tribunal to observe that it works both ways. If the United States refuses its assent to proposed limitations, that can go to the Tribunal just as much as if Great Britain on the other theory imposed regulations to which the United States objected.

The President: I should think there would be no victorious party and no vanquished party, in that case.

Senator Root: If the line is drawn according to the American contention, there is an assertion on one side that there ought to be this regulation for the common benefit; there is a refusal to assent to that on the other, and they go and get a determination. But, under the British theory, that our grant is subject to their right of municipal legislation, the exercise of their right in the first instance establishes the regulation.

SIR CHARLES FITZPATRICK: Do I understand you to say that if a regulation is made, and if you object to it, then it would be the right of the British Government to hale you before The Hague Tribunal, under Section 4 ?

SENATOR ROOT: Undoubtedly.

SIR CHARLES FITZPATRICK: Then it is the exercise of sovereignty that made it ?

SENATOR ROOT: I do not quite get your question.

SIR CHARLES FITZPATRICK: Then do you not necessarily admit the right of the British Government to make the regulation ?

SENATOR ROOT: No.

SIR CHARLES FITZPATRICK: Subject to your objection ?

SENATOR ROOT: No. Because my proposition is, the regulation shall not take effect until it has been determined that it ought to take effect.

SIR CHARLES FITZPATRICK: That is right.

SENATOR ROOT: My proposition is, that the application of the British theory here is that by force of British sovereignty they can make a regulation which is imposed, which does take effect, upon which they have decided — they, and they alone, have decided — in the exercise of their sovereign power, and have made it effective, and that it shall stand there until we have appealed to an arbitral tribunal for the purpose of reversing their decision.

SIR CHARLES FITZPATRICK: Do I understand you to say, then, that if you object, and the principle is adopted that in case of your objection the regulation would not have effect until such time as it would be submitted to The Hague Tribunal, that you would be satisfied with that ?

SENATOR ROOT: Precisely. Certainly. That is what we are contending for. And I think that this treaty grant draws clearly the line within which that principle applies; that Great Britain has full and unrestrained scope of sovereignty until she comes to that clear and definite line, that is, of the exercise of the right of fishing, as granted in the terms of the grant; but when she comes to that narrow field, wishing to change the situation by making a new limitation, that was not in the treaty, a limitation upon the times or manner, then that ought to be in practical good sense the subject of consultation between both owners of the common right; and if they cannot agree, let it be determined before it is made effective and our fishermen's vessels are seized under it. My objection to the British theory is that they propose to make these things effective by virtue of their sovereignty, *ex proprio vigore*, before anybody has decided. Sir Robert Finlay says they have not the right to decide; that they do not claim the right to decide; that they ought not to decide — but they propose to make effective these limitations by deciding.

THE PRESIDENT: Your rights, as you consider them, would be safeguarded by conceding to you a suspensive veto ?

SENATOR ROOT: Precisely.

THE PRESIDENT: A suspensive veto, until the decision of an impartial tribunal ?

SENATOR ROOT: Precisely. Before this treaty was made, what we claimed was that instead of going ahead and putting your regulations, extending your sovereignty, over the modification of this right without saying anything to us, you should consult us first, just as you did with Mr. Marcy when these laws were brought down to him and he approved them.

And in order to obviate the claim that that might lead to a deadlock and might put Great Britain in a most disagreeable situation, because she has got this colony behind her, pressing always for extreme views and extreme action, we make this agreement, under which, if we cannot agree upon what ought to be put into force, we will go to The Hague Tribunal, and we will have an arrangement, perhaps a more convenient and practical arrangement, proposed by the Tribunal, for determining whether they ought to be put into effect or not.

SIR CHARLES FITZPATRICK: Or the parties can arrange it themselves?

SENATOR ROOT: Certainly; and they will arrange it. There is no trouble about making the arrangement. The great trouble is, and the best thing that can be done for Great Britain — I know my friends on the other side will smile at me when I say it, but I say it not proposing to arrogate to myself the position of a guardian for Great Britain — the best thing that can be done for Great Britain is to give a line of right here so that she will not be in the position of having either to assent to unjust and extreme positions taken by her colony, in the spirit that has been exhibited here, against her own feeling of what is really due to us on the one hand, or to over-rule them and have her colony feel that she has been unkind towards the colony, and has been deciding against it of her own will.

The only way in which to bring about a practical solution of these difficulties is to fix this line of right and give to Great Britain the protection of an obligation imposed by the award to have a just judgment upon the proposed regulations before they are put into effect.[1]

[1] Thereupon, at 4.15 o'clock P.M., the Tribunal adjourned until the next day, Friday, the 5th August, 1910, at 10 o'clock A.M.

THE PRESIDENT: Will you please continue your argument, Mr. Senator Root?[1]

SENATOR ROOT: Before the adjournment I had referred to the question of the continuance of the arbitration provision in Article 4. I refer to it rather for the purpose of precluding the question than of arguing the question. The Tribunal has already observed, of course, that this Special Agreement under which we are now proceeding is in terms a

Special Agreement for the submission of questions relating to fisheries on the North Atlantic Coast under the general treaty of Arbitration concluded between the United States and Great Britain on the 4th day of April, 1908.

That general treaty of arbitration appears at p. 11 of the United States Case Appendix, and that is a treaty which, the Tribunal will perceive by Article 4, is concluded for a period of five years. I have no reason to doubt that it will be renewed at the expiration of the five years; but, nevertheless, it is a treaty which terminates by its own terms in three years from this time; and there might be a question whether the provisions of Article 4 of this Special Agreement, which is an agreement made under the treaty, would survive the treaty under which it is made.

In Article 2 of the treaty itself, on p. 11, there is a provision for the Special Agreement. The treaty says:

In each individual case the High Contracting Parties, before appealing to the Permanent Court of Arbitration, shall conclude a special Agreement defining clearly the matter in dispute, the scope of the powers of the Arbitrators, and the periods to be fixed for the formation of the Arbitral Tribunal and the several stages of the procedure.

Then it goes on to say:

It is understood that such special agreements on the part of the United States will be made by the President of the United States, by and with the advice and consent of the Senate thereof; His Majesty's Government reserving the right before concluding a special agreement in any matter

[1] Friday, August 5, 1910. The Tribunal met at 10 o'clock A.M.

affecting the interests of a self-governing Dominion of the British Empire to obtain the concurrence therein of the Government of that Dominion.

Now, as I say, there might well be a question, and I think we are bound to consider the possibility of there being a question raised, as to whether the provisions of Article 4 of this Special Agreement under this treaty would survive the end of that treaty. Do I make that clear?

SIR CHARLES FITZPATRICK: Do you think there can be much doubt about that?

SENATOR ROOT: My own opinion is that they do.

THE PRESIDENT: Your opinion is that they do survive?

SENATOR ROOT: My own opinion is that the provisions of Article 4 constitute, in effect, a new treaty.

THE PRESIDENT: In Article 4 they speak of any differences which may arise in the future, without any limitation of time. That seems to settle one of the points.

SENATOR ROOT: I think, both because, as the president has said, they expressly relate to any differences which arise in the future and because they go outside of the function of a *compromis*, that they constitute in effect a new treaty, and that they would survive the death of the treaty under which the Special Agreement was made. I refer to the question now chiefly in order that I may show that that is the view taken by the United States; and I understand the counsel for Great Britain to express, in behalf of Great Britain, the same view.

SIR CHARLES FITZPATRICK: That was clearly the intention of the parties.

SENATOR ROOT: I think it was. I understand the counsel for Great Britain to take that position; and, in behalf of the United States, I accept for the United States that position taken by the counsel for Great Britain, and express the agreement of the United States with that view.

THE PRESIDENT: May I ask counsel for Great Britain whether we understood the former enunciation by counsel for

Great Britain in that sense? Perhaps it would be convenient to the Attorney-General to make another declaration.

THE ATTORNEY-GENERAL: I am sorry to say that I was engaged in another duty; I was writing a letter, and I did not catch Mr. Root's remarks, but I will make myself acquainted with their purport, and then I will make some further observation to the Tribunal.

THE PRESIDENT: If you please.

JUDGE GRAY: You will observe, Senator, that Article 2 of the treaty of 1908 provides that

> the high contracting parties, before appealing to the Permanent Court of Arbitration, shall conclude a special agreement defining clearly the matter in dispute, the scope of the powers of the arbitrators, etc.

That has some significance, has it not?

SENATOR ROOT: That, I suppose, would apply —

JUDGE GRAY: To the dispute?

SENATOR ROOT: I suppose it would apply primarily to the powers of this Tribunal.

SIR CHARLES FITZPATRICK: Yes, that is it.

SENATOR ROOT: That was the idea.

THE PRESIDENT: Has not that which in the regular cases is the object of the Special Agreement to be made under Article 2 of the general treaty been done already by Article 4 for this purpose?

> the matter in dispute, the scope of the powers of the arbitrators

are defined by Article 4,

> the periods to be fixed for the formation of the Arbitral Tribunal and the several stages of the procedure

are also fixed by Article 4. In referring to Article 87 of The Hague Act, on p. 121, Article 4 says that these contestations are to be referred to The Hague Court for decision by the summary procedure provided in Chapter 4 of The Hague

Convention. And if we look at this Chapter 4, "Arbitration by Summary Procedure", on p. 21 of the United States Case Appendix, there is, in Article 88, this provision:

In the absence of any previous agreement, the Tribunal, as soon as it is formed, settles the time within which the two parties must submit their respective cases to it.

So that although this matter, which, according to Article 2 of the general treaty, has to be defined by the special agreement, is regulated by Article 88 of the summary procedure, as under special provisions for the time being fixed, the Tribunal itself fixes precisely this time. There is nothing left open. There is no question left open, I should think, to be fixed by the Special Agreement, and therefore it would not be necessary in that case.

SENATOR ROOT: The questions have got to be stated.

THE PRESIDENT: Yes; but is not that provided by Article 4 already? Every difference which arises under these circumstances is to be submitted.

SENATOR ROOT: But you have got to define what the difference is, which is frequently a rather difficult thing to do. However that may be, that can be settled when it is reached. My object in referring to the question here was to clear away possible doubt which might cause controversy in the future, and to do it now before the award of the arbitrators, because I should think that it might be very well in the award to fix the rights of the parties with some reference to this provision, so that it would not be left an open question.

DR. DRAGO: Perhaps this Article 4 could be considered as disposing of the matter. It has been made under the provisions of the general treaty of arbitration. The general treaty of arbitration will expire after five years, and may or may not be renewed. But this Article, created in virtue of the treaty which is to disappear, shall continue to exist. The treaty could in that sense and in what refers to this particular matter be called *dispositive*, as the jurists say; it disposes of the matter; it is *transitory*, as they also call it, with a somewhat misleading name, inasmuch as there is no necessity of any other provision afterwards. The treaty of arbitration may pass, but the right or juristic relation created by it under Article 4 shall continue to exist as a separate fact.

SENATOR ROOT: Precisely.

DR. DRAGO (continuing): And the position of the parties as to future contentions which might occur relating to these fisheries will be regulated by it. I do not know whether I have made myself quite clear.

SENATOR ROOT: You have made yourself quite clear, sir, and I fully agree with that; and I hope the Attorney-General does.

THE ATTORNEY-GENERAL: In reference to the question that the president was good enough to put to me, which I am sorry I missed at the time, owing to my attention being directed elsewhere, I understand it to be as to whether the limit of five years, which appears in the general treaty of 1908, would put any term to the provisions of the Special Agreement of 1909.

THE PRESIDENT: Yes.

THE ATTORNEY-GENERAL: It seems to me that, so far as Article 4 is concerned, certainly not. Article 4 is not limited by any term, but is expressly agreed between the parties as relating to the future, generally; so that it would not be a terminable article at all, so far as affects the subject-matter of that article.

SENATOR ROOT: Now, may it please the Tribunal, I have, in a very informal way, examined the effect of the British theory presented here in argument upon the practical situation as it exists in Newfoundland, and for that purpose have considered the nature of the British right as contended for by Great Britain.

I now ask the attention of the Tribunal to some consideration of the other side of the picture — the nature of the American right, as contended for by the United States, and the legal effect, as bearing upon the practical rights of the parties, in the prosecution of the industry to which the treaty relates, of the nature of the right of the United States as we deem it to be.

The first consideration which it seems to me lies at the bottom of any just view of the right of the United States is that it is a national right, and not a right of individuals. The treaty is a treaty made between sovereign and independent nations. The grant which the treaty contains is a grant to the United States. There is no privity of contract or estate between Great Britain and the inhabitants of the United States, or between the United States and the subjects of Great Britain.

We speak in a colloquial way about the grant of a fishing right, about the treaty granting the right to fish, and about the inhabitants of the United States receiving from the treaty the right to fish, but it is a colloquial use of terms. Using terms with the precision that is appropriate to a consideration of the legal consequences that flow from their use in a formal solemn instrument like a treaty, we must reject that very general and colloquial expression or series of expressions and consider what this treaty actually does. The contracting party with Great Britain is the United States of America, the nation, the sovereign and independent nation. What does it get under the contract made with it by Great Britain ? It gets something, of course. It is plain upon the face of the contract what it gets. It gets the right that its inhabitants shall have forever, in common with the subjects of His Britannic Majesty, the liberty to take fish of every kind upon the treaty coast. The United States gets by the treaty granted to it the right that its inhabitants shall forever have this liberty, a right of the highest national importance. The individual opportunity for profit is but incidental, subordinate. The thing granted, the great subject-matter of the treaty, what passed from one contracting party to the other contracting party, is the right of the United States to have this door of opportunity forever open to its inhabitants; the great national right, subserving the great national interest, which led Great Britain, in this series of statutes before you, for a long period of years, before 1818, before 1783, to pay bounties, to induce its people to engage in this industry of fishing; so strictly national that Great Britain, and France, and the United States all tax the whole body of their inhabitants to raise the funds to induce citizens to pursue the industry. It is the national interest of forever having open to the people of the nation the opportunity for profitable industry and trade; the national interest for which sovereigns in all the period of modern history have fitted out expeditions and made wars and treaties of reciprocity, and have subsidized steamship lines; and for which all over the world nations have been seeking to open doors to the inhabitants of their countries, holding open the door of the Orient, under common agreement with all other countries, in order that the inhabitants of our countries may have the opportunity to enter into the profitable trade of the East. That is the national interest that was subserved, and that is the national right that was granted. It was also the right to a perpetual source of food supply for the people of the United States, the right to a nursery for seamen to defend the coasts of the United States, very great national interests that today are leading Great Britain to spend hundreds of millions in the creation of the greatest navy of the world to protect her food supply and to protect her coasts. That is what was granted by the treaty to the nation with which the treaty was made.

This was to a sovereign. And it follows necessarily, from the nature of sovereignty, that the right was held by the sovereign with the powers of a sovereign. It was its right. It was the right of the United States. There is a perhaps apparent analogy to a trust in form, but it is the trust of sovereignty. It is that great trust under which all the powers of sovereignty are held, a trust which differs from all municipal trusts in that there is no power to supervise or control it.

My friend the Attorney-General criticized a gentleman who was introduced here by Sir Robert Finlay as a very learned author, Mr. Clauss. Sir Robert was specially solicitous to know that the Tribunal had the book written by Mr. Clauss, and he quoted to the Tribunal not mere statements of fact by Mr. Clauss, but an expression of opinion regarding the construction of instruments which were supposed to create servitudes, as being well worthy the attention of the Tribunal. And he describes Mr. Clauss as a learned author. Now when it appears that in this book, which the Tribunal has, there were statements of fact, of a great range of facts, and expressions of opinion which do not suit the British Case, my learned friend the Attorney-General flouts Mr. Clauss, and he rather criticizes him for shrinking from giving a definition of sovereignty. The Attorney-General goes on to make a definition of sovereignty, and I am bound to say that when I read his definition I am inclined to think Mr. Clauss was wise, for the Attorney-General's definition is either defective or no definition at all. The definition by the Attorney-General [p. 1033] is:

Sovereignty is the supreme governing power vested in some defined person or persons over all persons and things within the limit or under the control of a state. That is the modern view of sovereignty.

If that means by the expression " within the limit of a state " within the spatial territorial sphere of the state, it excludes the very important range of sovereignty which is maintained generally on the Continent, that is, the control over the person, the subject, the citizen, wherever he goes, and which we certainly do exercise, all of us, all countries in the Western civilized world, within the range of extra-territoriality, in the Oriental countries. If the words "within the limit of a state" do not refer to spatial extent, then we have no definition, because this amounts merely to saying that sovereignty is the power to govern all persons and things within the power of government; and the addition of the words "or under the control of a state" adds nothing to the definition, because it is merely expressing the same idea in different words.

Now, let me join Sir William in rushing in where Mr. Clauss feared to tread. I do it with more confidence, because there is no counsel to come after me, and I am sure that the court will be judicial in its treatment of the subject. I am going to state what seems to me to be the modern idea of sovereignty, the universal idea, and base it upon the definition of a very great English thinker — I should say, although, of course, it is open to difference of opinion and dispute, the most accurate English thinker of modern times — and that is John Austin. Basing the definition upon what he says, I should say: Sovereignty is the power to control, without accountability, all persons constituting an organized political community and the territory occupied by them, and all persons and things within that territory.

The essential quality of the definition, which is Austin's, is the freedom from accountability to any one, and that is the same idea, I suppose, which is carried into the Attorney-General's definition by the word "supreme." That is the characteristic essential quality of the artificial person to which this grant is made, the nation, the United States. And the United States holds this great national right concerning a subject-matter of special interest to all sovereigns under the powers of sovereignty, which involve no accountability to any power on earth. It follows, necessarily, that this right of the United States, that its inhabitants shall have the liberty to take fish, is a right which the United States can, so far as it and its inhabitants are concerned, deal with at its will. It can impose upon its inhabitants conditions to the exercise of the liberty that they may have; it may say to them, You shall exercise that liberty only upon complying with such and such conditions. It may exclude part of them from it. It may include part of them in it. It may say, You shall exercise it only at such times, and not at other times. It may say to them, You shall exercise it only in such ways, and not in other ways. That is necessarily the result of this national right being granted to this sovereign, to be held under the trust of sovereignty, without accountability, for the benefit of its inhabitants.

SIR CHARLES FITZPATRICK: Is there not another necessary result — to protect them in the exercise of the right ?

SENATOR ROOT: Only as every sovereign has a right to protect all its citizens in the exercise of their rights. But that is not a right of the treaty. It is not a right under the treaty. Wherever a citizen of Great Britain, or of France, or of the United States may go he is entitled to have the protection of his government for his rights. Whatever national right may exist, the nation has internationally the right to protect it, but not a right derived from a treaty — a right inherent in the independence of nations. When a British ship sails the ocean and is arrested, is attacked, the power of Great Britain can be used to protect it. It needs no treaty to give that power; the protection of it may be war — not the exercise of a treaty right. When France gave notice to Great Britain, in the correspondence that is here, and that Mr. Turner referred to, that she proposed to enforce her rights on the treaty coast — rather a peremptory correspondence, the Tribunal will remember — and Great Britain answered back that she proposed to enforce hers, that did not mean the exercise of treaty rights. It meant war. When Mr. Evarts had this correspondence here with Lord Granville about the question as to whether we would be compelled to send ships of war to the treaty coast, that did not mean the exercise of a treaty right. It meant war. The treaty right, and the full extent of the sovereign right that comes to the United States under the treaty, is to deal with its own inhabitants.

SIR CHARLES FITZPATRICK: The power to regulate its own inhabitants?

SENATOR ROOT: Its own inhabitants, yes. We do not claim any right over British subjects that we deny to Great Britain over ours. I mean, we do not in respect of this very treaty right. Of course, we do not claim any such right in that vast field of jurisdiction which exists because that is British territory, and which is not affected at all by this question.

JUDGE GRAY: The sovereign to whom this right is granted may also, following out your own line of argument, relinquish or destroy it by renouncing the treaty?

SENATOR ROOT: Precisely; it may relinquish or destroy it, and in this treaty it does renounce and destroy the right which it claimed to have, and had had under the treaty of 1783, in regard to the great extent of British treaty coasts other than this special reservation.

SIR CHARLES FITZPATRICK: Going back to the legal proposition, the power to regulate a treaty right to be exercised in foreign territory seems to me necessarily to involve the power to protect that treaty right, to protect the inhabitant in the exercise of that treaty right. Sovereignty must include that, surely, as a legal proposition?

SENATOR ROOT: It involves, not by grant of the treaty, but as the existence of every right involves, the right to make war in its defense; not a right granted by the treaty, but the superior and all-embracing right of independence to defend one's rights. We claim under this treaty no right whatever to the exercise of force in British waters. We say that as to this treaty right, with its narrow powers of sovereignty over the exercise of a liberty by our own citizens, and with regard to every right that the United States possesses, there may come a time when we shall be compelled to defend our rights; but we appeal to no treaty as the basis of that defense; it is because we are an independent nation, and it is essential to independence that at times a nation shall be ready to maintain its independence by maintaining its rights.

THE PRESIDENT: If you please, Mr. Senator Root: Is your proposition that American fishermen, in exercising their industry in British waters, only depend upon American sovereignty, and not upon the territorial sovereignty of Great Britain ?

SENATOR ROOT: My contention is that American fishermen, exercising the liberty in British waters so far as regards the entire range of personal conduct, are under British sovereignty.

THE PRESIDENT: Yes, I forgot to qualify the question.

SENATOR ROOT: But so far as the method and time and manner of exercising that liberty, and the conditions upon which they shall exercise it are concerned, they are dependent upon their own government. They take no right from Great Britain. They take the right from their own government, which received from Great Britain the power to give them that right.

THE PRESIDENT: In this respect, the exercise of this industry would be different from the exercise of any other industry in British territory? If American subjects exercise any other industry in British territory, they are dependent upon the British laws concerning this industry; and with respect to the fishing industry, they are not dependent upon the British regulations concerning this specific industry ?

SENATOR ROOT: I will show, I think with great distinctness, the reason of the difference, in a very short time. There is a clear and distinct line to be drawn. I indicated yesterday one element of difference.

THE PRESIDENT: The perpetual and unilateral character of the grant was one difference ?

SENATOR ROOT: That was the difference upon which I based my submission that for the preservation of this kind of right it is necessary to have freedom from control, while for the preservation of the other kind of right it is not. That is one difference, and I shall presently come to the further differences.

It follows necessarily from what I have said regarding what the right was that passed to the United States under the contract, that there was in it no element of a transaction between juristic persons. Upon that both parties here are fully agreed, and the statements by counsel are quite unequivocal. I turn to one by the Attorney-General, who says [p. 1020]:

> No, we did not part with the right to fish; . . . We consented not to exercise our sovereign right of exclusion against them for that purpose.

That is the Attorney-General's description of what was done. The very full and frank statements by the counsel for Great Britain as to the limitation upon their sovereignty, which have characterized the entire argument of the case, standing upon Lord Salisbury's position as to limitation upon sovereignty, are quite inconsistent with the idea that this is a transaction merely between two juristic persons; because, of course, the mere passing of a private title is no limitation of sovereignty at all; absolutely none. But the subject is important, and it was raised by suggestions and questions from the bench, and I think that perhaps I ought to assign a rational basis for the agreement of counsel on both sides regarding it.

Under the Roman law we all know the sea was free to every one, clear to the edge of the shore, and no one could acquire ownership or special rights in it. When the dreadful and brutal, selfish period of the Middle Ages came in Europe, and the advanced juristic learning of Rome was in a great measure forgotten, the different sovereigns reached out for general control over as great a part of the sea as they could accomplish — narrow seas, and closed seas, and broad seas, and great stretches running out into the ocean, and this in some cases even went so far as to extend, practically, to a claim over the entire ocean.

But when the great duel between *mare liberum* and *mare clausum* was ended, when Grotius and his followers, representing the newly awakening spirit of commercial freedom that ushered in the civilization of our day, had overcome the conservatism and principle of exclusion represented by Selden, with all his learning and ability, when the principle of modern freedom had conquered, and the old claims to control and possession and ownership over the sea disappeared, they disappeared entirely: it is not that there was a residuum left; it is that they were gone. A very great English judge has stated what happened, in the case of the Queen *vs.* Keyn, already referred to here, in the 2d Exchequer Division. Lord Chief Justice Cockburn says:

> All these vain and extravagant pretensions have long since given way to the influence of reason and common sense. If, indeed, the sovereignty thus asserted had a real existence, and could now be maintained, it would, of course, independently of any question as to the three-mile zone, be conclusive of the present case. But the claim to such sovereignty, at all times unfounded, has long since been abandoned. No one would now dream of asserting that the sovereign of these realms has any greater right over the surrounding seas than the sovereigns on the opposite shores; or that it is the especial duty and privilege of the Queen of Great Britain to keep the peace in these seas. . . . It is in vain, therefore, that the an-

cient assertion of sovereignty over the narrow seas is invoked to give countenance to the rule now sought to be established, of jurisdiction over the three-mile zone. . . . To invoke as its foundation, or in its support, an assertion of sovereignty which, for all practical purposes, is, and always has been, idle and unfounded, and the invalidity of which renders it necessary to have recourse to the new doctrine, involves an inconsistency, on which it would be superfluous to dwell.

That is to say, these vague and unfounded claims disappeared entirely, and there was nothing of them left as the basis for any claim of ownership or sovereignty or jurisdiction over any portion of the sea beyond the line that adjoins the land. The sea became, in general, as free internationally as it was under the Roman law. But the new principle of freedom, when it approached the shore, met with another principle — the principle of protection; not a residuum of the old claim, but a new independent basis and reason for modification, near the shore, of the principle of freedom. The sovereign of the land washed by the sea asserted a new right to protect his subjects and citizens against attack, against invasion, against interference and injury; to protect them against attack threatening their peace, to protect their revenues, to protect their health, to protect their industries. That is the basis and the sole basis on which is established the territorial zone that is recognized in the international law of today. War-ships may not pass without consent into this zone, because they threaten. Merchant-ships may pass and repass, because they do not threaten. But merchant-ships may not enter into the coast trade from port to port without consent, because they interfere with the industry of the people, the natural right of the people to carry on the intercourse between their own ports. Fishing ships may not come to engage in fishing, because they interfere with the natural industry of the people on the coast, the natural, immemorial right of the dwellers by the sea. Back in the remotest times, in all times, whatever be the rule of freedom of the sea, however free it may be, it is deeply embedded in human nature that the men who dwell on the shore of the sea consider that they have a natural right to win their support from the waters at their doors; and they look with natural resentment at one coming from a distance to interfere with that right; and that immemorial, natural right of the coastal population to secure support from the sea is an object of the right of protection by the sovereign.

That is essentially a relation of sovereignty. Efforts have been made at times by monarchs in former days, when the old theory of ownership prevailed, to separate some portions of the opportunity and grant them to individuals or corporations — special rights to fish, seldom, I think, out in the marginal seas or territorial seas, but in interior waters. However, those instances have been exceptional. The attempt unduly to restrict this great natural right of his subjects, and to create monopolies in particular places, was one of the great things that cost Charles I his head. Universally, now, the relation of the state to the fishing of its coastal population is the sovereign right of protection; and we are certified in this treaty that that is the relation of Great Britain, for in it she declares that this liberty which the inhabitants of the United States are to have forever is to be in common with the subjects of Great Britain.

Now, I say we are agreed upon this, and perhaps I should not discuss it further. It is the subject-matter of countless treaties regulating these rights; sovereign acts, the North Sea Convention, treaties with France of 1839, treaties of various and many powers with each other, all in the exercise of this sovereign right of protection.

The Act of 1878 of Great Britain puts the matter on a sound basis, the Territorial Waters Act. It is in the British Appendix, p. 574. The second section of that Act says that an offense committed by a person on the open sea within the territorial waters of Her Majesty's dominions shall be punished, and so on, and then at the foot of that page there is a definition:

> The territorial waters of Her Majesty's dominions, in reference to the sea, means such part of the sea adjacent to the coast of the United Kingdom, or the coast of some other part of Her Majesty's dominions, as is deemed by international law to be within the territorial sovereignty of Her Majesty.

That is Section 7 of this Act of 1878, the Territorial Waters Act, British Appendix, p. 574.

Despagnet has stated the rule very accurately in the work which is already in the hands of the court. He says in Section 411 of his work:

> But the reasons which justify the sovereignty of the state beyond the limits of its terrestrial territory are always the same.
>
> Perels summarizes them in three principles:
>
> First. The security of the adjacent state requires that it shall have exclusive possession of its shores and that it may protect the approaches.
>
> Second. The surveillance of vessels which enter, leave, or sojourn in its territorial waters is imposed by the guaranty of efficient police and the advancement of its political, commercial, and fiscal interests.
>
> Third. Finally, the exclusive enjoyment of the territorial waters, *e.g.*, for fishing and coastal trade, may be necessary to secure the existence of coastal populations.

The conclusions of the Institute of International Law at the meeting of 1894 contain what is supposed to be a correct statement of the relation of the state to this kind of right. The resolution adopted there is as follows:

> The state has a right of sovereignty over a zone of sea which washes the shore, subject to the right of innocent passage reserved in Article 5. This zone bears the name " territorial sea."

The president of the Tribunal will perhaps remember that in the debate which took place at that meeting of the Institute of International Law the original report of this resolution was a little broader, and it took the form " a state has the right of sovereignty", and that was modified in the final resolution by substituting "a" for "the", so that it read "has a right of sovereignty."

DR. DRAGO: I think a marginal breadth of six miles was recommended.

SENATOR ROOT: The Institute fixed upon a margin of six miles, I think.

JUDGE GRAY: Recommended.

SENATOR ROOT: Yes, recommended a margin of six miles. Of course, I am referring to it with reference to the character of the relation of the state to the zone, whatever it is.

DR. DRAGO: Was there not a difference mentioned in the discussion between the right of property on the marginal water and the imperium over it or right of sovereignty, so that the state could have the imperium but not the ownership?

SENATOR ROOT: That I understand to be the effect of the conclusion reached by the Institute of International Law.

Before leaving this subject let me put a third proposition. I have stated that this was a grant of a national right from one sovereign to another, that the relation which was involved was in no sense a relation of two juristic persons with each other, but the relation of two sovereigns dealing with the subject-matter of the sovereignty.

The third proposition is that this grant of this treaty must be construed and interpreted with reference to the fact that it was the settlement of a claim to a national right of the highest importance. That is the relevancy and materiality of the discussion regarding partition of empire, and that is all. The bearing of that discussion is upon the construction which is to be placed upon this treaty, upon what we must consider to have been in the minds of the makers of the treaty, and as presenting the great salient fact with reference to the presence of which in the minds of the makers of the treaty we must construe and interpret their words.

This was the settlement of a controversy in which the United States had claimed that she was entitled for her people to equal rights upon these coasts with Great Britain for her people, and in this treaty a part of the rights regarding which that claim was made and that controversy waged were surrendered and a part were continued, regranted.

The renunciation refers expressly to the matter in controversy. Observe the recital:

Whereas differences have arisen respecting the liberty claimed by the United States for the inhabitants thereof.

Now the renunciation:

And the United States hereby renounce forever any liberty heretofore enjoyed or claimed by the inhabitants thereof . . .

a direct reference to the statement of the subject-matter of the controversy —

by the inhabitants thereof to take, dry or cure fish, on or within three marine miles of any of the coasts, bays, creeks or harbors of His Britannic Majesty's dominions in America, not included within the above-mentioned limits.

And the new grant of the treaty covered a portion of the liberty claimed, and the renunciation of the treaty covered all the remainder of the liberty claimed. So I say it is not to be supposed that the makers of this treaty considered that they were going very far in making a grant of a right affecting this small portion of the coasts involved in the controversy as a right of the highest order of dignity.

The true nature of this right could not be better stated than it was stated by Lord Bathurst in his letter to Mr. Adams of the 30th October, 1815, which appears in the United States Case Appendix, and from which I will read, p. 274.

First let me say a word about the significance of the letter. As we all know, Great Britain claimed, after the end of the War of 1812, that the right of the United States within her maritime jurisdiction had been destroyed by the war. We all know that Mr. Adams controverted this very vehemently, and this letter is the statement of the British ground upon which it maintained that position and refused to permit the United States to exercise the liberty which it had held under the treaty of 1783.

This is the formal authentic statement of the position of Great Britain under which she justified herself — was ready to justify herself to the world — for the denial of the rights which she had solemnly granted by the treaty of 1783 to the United States. It was the formal statement of the position of Great Britain in that controversy.

Mr. Adams, you will remember, had claimed that, because of this original right of the United States under the partition of empire theory, the grant of the liberty or the right of 1783 was not ended by the war, but that it was an original right which continued, war or no war. That was Mr. Adams's position.

Lord Bathurst is here controverting that position and stating the contrary position on which Great Britain stood, and he says in the first paragraph on p. 274:

> The minister of the United States appears, by his letter, to be well aware that Great Britain has always considered the liberty formerly enjoyed by the United States of fishing within British limits, and using British territory, as derived from the third article of the treaty of 1783, and from that alone; and that the claim of an independent state to occupy and use at its discretion any portion of the territory of another, without compensation or corresponding indulgence, cannot rest on any other foundation than conventional stipulation.

That is the basis of Great Britain's position in ending the "liberties" granted in 1783.

He proceeds:

> It is unnecessary to inquire into the motives which might have originally influenced Great Britain in conceding such liberties to the United States, or whether other articles of the treaty wherein these liberties are

specified did, or did not, in fact afford an equivalent for them, because all the stipulations profess to be founded on reciprocal advantages and mutual convenience. If the United States derived from that treaty privileges from which other independent nations, not admitted by treaty were excluded, the duration of the privileges must depend on the duration of the instrument by which they were granted; and if the war abrogated the treaty, it determined the privileges.

You will perceive how material and necessary to the argument was this definition of the nature of the right that Great Britain had granted to the United States. Other nations might exercise privileges at the discretion of Great Britain by acquiescence, subject always to be withdrawn or modified. Other nations might exercise privileges in the territory of Great Britain accorded by statute, always in the discretion of Great Britain to alter, amend, or repeal, but that an independent state shall occupy and use, *at its discretion*, any portion of the territory of Great Britain without compensation or corresponding indulgence cannot rest on any other foundation than conventional stipulation.

THE PRESIDENT: But then, must it not be expressed in the conventional stipulation that this right is to be exercised at the discretion of the party entitled ?

SENATOR ROOT: The conventional stipulation which he is describing contained no such stipulation. He is ascribing that quality to the grant of 1783, which contained no such express stipulation.

On the following page (276) Lord Bathurst argues that this grant was temporary and experimental, and depending on the use that might be made of it, and so on, and on the condition of the island and the place where it was to be exercised, and on the general convenience and inconvenience, from a naval, military, or commercial point of view, resulting from *the access of an independent nation* to such island and places — further characterization of the same description of the grant of 1783. And, as my learned friend the Attorney-

General has argued so cogently here, the grant of 1818 was a continuance or renewal of a portion of the same grant as that of 1783.

Now I will come to another consideration, which is of primary importance in the construction of this grant, and that is the quality imported into it by the use of the word "forever" — the quality of permanency. If you will remember, the United States insisted that this quality existed in the grant of 1783, and Lord Bathurst, in the letters which I have read, insisted that it did not exist in the grant, but the right was liable to be terminated by war.

You will remember the vehement assertion of John Adams in 1782 regarding the rights of the United States and his unwillingness to enter into any treaty except one which secured these fishery rights.

The New England States in 1783 and in 1818 were poor, their soil was sterile, the great grain fields of the West had not been opened, the manufacturing which has grown to such great extent was in its infancy, and the fisheries were a matter of primary vital importance to the people of the United States, and especially to the people of New England.

Now, when the War of 1812 was ended, a war waged over the question of impressments and not affecting the fisheries or involving as a matter of controversy the fisheries in any degree — when that war ended without settling the question of impressments, without any particular credit to either side, the people of New England awoke to the startling and shocking realization of the fact that their fisheries, their great industry, were gone, provided Great Britain could maintain that position, unanticipated, unexpected, and a cause for chagrin.

That is the explanation of the vehemence of John Quincy Adams in conducting the controversy and the meaning of his deep feeling and indignation. The proposition of Great Britain that the grant of this right was not permanent was a blow at the vital interest of the New England seaboard, and an absolute prerequisite and *sine qua non* of the settlement of that controversy on the part of the United States was that, while she was forced to give up, while, under this argument of Lord Bathurst, she was out-faced, borne down, and compelled to give up the greater part of the rights she had held under the treaty of 1783, the little remnant that she saved was to be made permanent beyond any possibility of doubt. That is a dominant feature in the article of the treaty of 1818, and it is one to which no court can fail to give effect. It must receive effect, and it must receive the effect that all the conditions and circumstances show it was intended to have. The American instructions to the negotiators, which appear on p. 304 of the United States Appendix, are:

> The President authorizes you to agree to an article whereby the United States will desist from the liberty of fishing and curing and drying fish, within the British jurisdiction *generally*, upon condition that it shall be secured as *a permanent right;* not liable to be impaired by any future war.

THE PRESIDENT: What is the connection between the perpetuity, the permanent character, of the right, and its exemption from regulation by the state in whose territory it is to be exercised?

SENATOR ROOT: The connection is this. I assume I may now pass from demonstrating the importance and pressing nature of the demand for permanency and for the inclusion of the word "forever", which, in numerous documents appearing here, is shown to have been a consideration in the negotiation. For example, in the letter from Mr. Robinson to Lord Castlereagh of the 10th October, 1818, the British negotiator reported, British Case Appendix, p. 92, that permanency was an indispensable condition on the American part; in the letter of Messrs. Gallatin and Rush to Mr. Adams of the 20th October, 1818, United States Case

Appendix, p. 307, Mr. Gallatin says the insertion of the word "forever" was strenuously resisted; in Mr. Gallatin's letter of the 6th November, 1818, British Case Appendix, p. 97, he says that they could have secured more territory at the expense of giving up the word "forever", and the report of Messrs. Robinson and Goulburn of the 17th September, 1818, British Case Appendix, p. 86, refers to the right permanently conveyed. Now, the connection of that with the right of regulation is that there is only one way to give effect to this absolutely essential feature of the grant, and that is to regard it, not as an obligation, but as a conveyance of the right from Great Britain to the United States; so that it becomes the right of the United States, and not a mere obligation of Great Britain, for all obligations are ended by war and all obligations are ended by transfer of sovereignty.

THE PRESIDENT: Could there not be a perpetual obligation without a transfer of sovereignty?

SENATOR ROOT: There could not be a perpetual obligation not ended by war. The obligation ends with war, and the same obligation ends with a transfer of sovereignty. It must be remembered that sovereignty had been transferred as to thirteen British colonies, and it always must have been in contemplation that it might be transferred as to another. Lord Salisbury, in his speech in the House of Lords in 1891, declared, of the French right, that Newfoundland was mistaken in considering that the burden of the right was due to her continued allegiance to Great Britain, that wherever Newfoundland went that right would still persist, and I say there is no other way to give effect to this essential quality of the grant than to regard it as being not a mere obligation, but to regard it as being a transfer of the right from Great Britain to the United States, so that it became the right of the United States and not the right of Great Britain. To that feature of the article we are all bound to give effect, and we cannot put any construction on the article which leaves the right open to be destroyed either by war, or by a transfer of sovereignty, or by any other agency, unless it be the voluntary act of the grantee.

THE PRESIDENT: Then the consequence of the fact that this right has been acknowledged as a permanent right would be that the character of the right would be enlarged beyond the words of the grant itself? The grant itself speaks of the right of the United States to take fish, and in consequence of the fact that the right has been granted forever, it extends to participation by the United States in the legislation and administration of Great Britain concerning the exercise of the right?

SENATOR ROOT: No, the right was not a grant to the inhabitants of the United States.

THE PRESIDENT: No, it was a grant to the United States for the benefit of the inhabitants of the United States.

SENATOR ROOT: It is a grant to the United States, and a right granted to the United States, of course, belongs to the United States. It is its right.

THE PRESIDENT: Is it not the essence of every international right that it belongs to the state? When you say that a treaty is made for the benefit of the inhabitants of the state, you mean that it confers the right on the state and not on the inhabitants? It is a contract, not between the inhabitants, but between the two states?

SENATOR ROOT: Precisely. This is a right of the United States, and it is a right which must persist forever. The grant of a right forever, independent of the promise of the grantor, made so by impressing upon it the quality of perpetuity, is a conveyance and is not a mere obligation. That is my proposition.

THE PRESIDENT: So that every right conferred on a state in perpetuity would be a conveyance and not a mere obligation; would convey a part of the sovereignty to the grantee state?

SENATOR ROOT: Every right conveyed to the state in perpetuity, so that it is not open to destruction, or impairment by the grantor, and relating to the use of the territory of the grantor, made in perpetuity, is a conveyance.

JUDGE GRAY: It no longer rests in promise, but it is an executed grant.

SENATOR ROOT: It no longer rests in promise, but is an executed grant. There is no other way to give effect to that quality that was imported, or expressed, by the word "forever." Of course, Great Britain stands upon the proposition that the territorial zone and the bays, creeks, inlets, and harbors to which this right relates is a portion of her territory, over which she exercises sovereignty. That is the basis of her position, and I need not stop to argue it. So that the right which was conveyed to the United States is the right of one independent nation to make use forever, for its own benefit in a prescribed area, of the territory of another independent nation. That is just as Lord Bathurst described it. It is in the nature of an international, real right; it is a *jus in re aliena*. We have here another reason why this should not be regarded as a mere municipal right, or a transaction between two juristic persons, because that has none of the elements of indestructibility. One of the essential qualities of this grant, and one which cannot be denied to it without violence to the terms of the grant, is that it is removed from the exercise of the powers of sovereignty of Great Britain, put beyond the exercise of that power, and is vested alone in the sovereign to which the grant was made. The sovereignty to which the grant was made, exercising its sovereign right, its sovereign control over its own right, not going beyond it, not arrogating to itself the right to interfere with British jurisdiction, or with the British exercise of a common right, but arrogating to itself the right to control its own inhabitants, to condition the right to them, is exercising that which is the right of the sovereign to which it is granted, and not the right of the sovereign making the grant. That is the proposition I make.

Now, a further proposition upon which we are all agreed is that this grant did limit British sovereignty. That is agreed by counsel on both sides, and I suppose I need not spend any time over it. Originally, Great Britain had the right to reserve to her own subjects, for fishing purposes, the exclusive use of that portion of the earth's surface which we call the treaty coast. She had the right to exclude all other persons from it. She had the right to dispose freely as sovereign, of the opportunity for its use among her own subjects, to condition its exercise, and to say that they shall do so and so; that these may go there and that those may not. She had the right to admit to the beneficial use such aliens as she saw fit. She had the right to say to the people of Massachusetts, You may come here and fish, and to the people of Maine and New Hampshire, You may not; or the people of New York may go and fish and the people of Massachusetts may not. But when she made the grant she parted to a material extent with the power to do those acts of sovereignty. She could no longer exclude this great class of men who are described as "inhabitants of the United States." It rested with the United States to exclude them or to prohibit them from entering that territory and fishing. She could no longer say to one, You may go, and to another, You may not. She could no longer dispose of the entire opportunity for fishing, as she had been able to do before.

Now, these are limitations upon the sovereign powers of Great Britain, and, while not extensive or alarming or a matter of practical disturbance of British sovereignty, the

United States, in conditioning her own inhabitants, saying, You may be admitted, and you not, those who comply with the conditions may be admitted, and others not, was entitled to exercise the same right of sovereignty which Great Britain had theretofore been able to exercise, and had exercised. So, sovereignty was limited.

Now, there cannot be an implied reservation in the grant of the very thing that the grant excludes; that is to say, when the grant limited British sovereignty it excluded British sovereignty from the field of operation commensurate with the right granted according to its terms. It is not an exact use of words to call it an implied reservation. There cannot be any reservation implied of a right which the essential quality of the grant is to exclude. There is a limit to the grant, and beyond that limit sovereignty remains intact, unimpaired, and you must go to the grant to find what the limit is. If you find a limit in the grant there can be no implied reservation within it of any sovereign right, for to the extent of its limits the grant must limit the sovereignty, or the sovereignty must limit the grant. They cannot both limit each other. One must be superior and the other inferior. The grant, to the extent of the terms of the grant, is superior because it limits the sovereignty, and when you have gone to the grant and found how far the terms of the grant go and the extent to which sovereignty is excluded, to that extent there can be no implied reservation of sovereignty whatever.

The President: If it can be said on one side that there can be no implied reservation of sovereignty, can it not be said on the other side that there can be no implied abdication of sovereignty? The consequence would be that one must stick to the words of the treaty, and consider that it confers only that right which is expressed by *ipsissimis verbis* of the treaty.

SENATOR ROOT: That is undoubtedly true. The words of the treaty must be construed according to what is found to be their true meaning, and giving effect to all the words which are of consequence or of importance in the treaty. Of course, you have to find there an exclusion of sovereignty in the grant reasonably construed. The terms of the grant are general and without any limit except the limit of territory, and the limit carried by the fact that the rights are in common. The grant carries the right, to be held in common with British subjects, to take fish of every kind within this territory, and there is in it no power on the part of any one to say that the right shall not be exercised except where I choose that it shall be exercised, when I choose that it shall be exercised, or in the way that I choose it shall be exercised. That is the grant, and to that extent it excludes, pushes back the power of British sovereignty. Within that extent there can be no implied reservation. It rests with whoever claims to find in the terms of the grant authority on the part of the grantor to say to the grantee, You shall not do this except when I say, or as I say, or where I say, to show reason for it, to show ground for it.

Now, I will ask you to consider some of the grounds of such a claim which are presented. One of them, and one which has been pressed somewhat, is that there is an implication from the fact that the liberty is a liberty in common with British subjects. It is claimed by Great Britain that from that fact results a right of Great Britain to say that the citizens of the United States are to be subject to the same legislative control as the citizens of Great Britain. We must discriminate a little now. The personal conduct, of course, of the Americans who go upon the treaty coast is subject to the same control, but that is the result, not of the fact that the right which they go there to exercise is a right in common, but of the fact that they are in British territory; and the great field of control by Great Britain results not from the common quality of the right which they go there to exercise, but from the fact that they are there within British jurisdiction. In the next place, it should be observed, that it is the *right* that the inhabitants of the United States are to have in common; it is not that it is to be *exercised* in common with British subjects. As Chief Justice Fitzpatrick observed yesterday in regard to the terms of the treaty of 1783, words were not used here loosely or carelessly. The men who drafted and settled this knew what they meant by the words that they used, and, of course, this right of the United States had been the subject of very careful and critical analysis. The United States was being compelled to surrender a large part of its right, and they, of course, used words with the greatest care for the purpose of securing a definite, and perpetual, and effective right. It was not by mere accident that they used the words " the inhabitants of the said United States shall have,forever, in common with the subjects of His Britannic Majesty, the liberty to take fish of every kind."

The natural inference from the fact that two nations have rights in common is not that one of them shall have entire control of both rights and shall determine when it is desirable for the common interest that the rights shall be limited or modified. That is not the natural inference. The natural inference from the legal effect of the fact that two nations have common rights is that they shall have a common voice in modifying or changing the rights, and the real ground upon which the claim is made for an exclusive right in Great Britain to say what modifications shall be made in both of these common rights is not that the rights are common, but it is that it is her soil, her territory. The inference is not aided or added to in the slightest degree by the fact that the rights are in common: the inference from the fact that the rights are in common is all the other way.

I think I have already disposed of the idea that there is to be any inference, any implication, from the fact that it is within British territory, that British sovereignty controls the exercise of the right. I think I have disposed of that, and that is the sole ground for the contention that Great Britain can control the common right. The fact that the right is common adds nothing whatever to it.

But, let us examine a little further this idea, that the common quality of the rights of the two nations justifies one of them in controlling both. They are equal, and they are held by two equal independent sovereign states. The rights of one are of as great sanctity and dignity as the rights of the other. Great Britain is the sole judge of the time when, the places where, and the manner in which her rights shall be exercised. There is no equality whatever in having the subjects of Great Britain exercise their common right, or, to put it in the other form, in having Great Britain exercise her common right when she chooses, where she chooses, and as she chooses, and having the United States exercise her equal common right, not where, and when and as she chooses, but where and when and as Great Britain chooses. That is repugnant to the idea of equal common rights held by equal, independent states.

It is to be remembered that there are no limitations imposed upon the subjects of Great Britain by any superior power. The right of Great Britain is as ample and full to-day, after all these statutes, and notwithstanding these statutes, as it was the day after this treaty was made, when there were no regulations, no statutes whatever, affecting the fishing upon this treaty coast. The people of Great Britain, called subjects, who may exercise Great Britain's right, are not different from the law-making power of Great Britain. The laws are made by the Commons of England, the Parliament. They are stated, in theoretical form, as though made by the king, the traditional form coming down from great antiquity when kings were supposed to hold by divine right the power to impose laws upon the people. But that is no longer the fact, and it was not when this treaty was made. If there be a statute passed by Parliament, or by any agency authorized by Parliament, such as a colonial legislature or a fish commission, to the effect that herring shall not be taken between October and April in a particular place, that does not affect the right of the people of Great Britain in any degree whatever. It is merely that they, of their own will, impose upon each individual member of that organized society this limitation upon the exercise of the right. They may repeal it tomorrow. There is still the right. The people of Great Britain may determine to exercise their right or not to exercise it — to exercise it in one way or another. It does not affect their right, and it does not affect our right. We may determine that we will not exercise our right; the United States may forbid its citizens to take fish on the coast of Newfoundland in October or May, or to take fish on Sunday or on Monday; that is voluntary; it has no effect and can have no effect upon the national right. The right persists, and the voluntary abstention, the self-denying ordinance, has no effect whatever upon the right of Great Britain and its subjects to take fish whereever they choose, how they choose, and however they choose upon the treaty coasts. It is no concern of ours, and it has no effect on our right, and affords no measure of our right whether they choose to take or not to take.

SIR CHARLES FITZPATRICK: Do you read the grant as conveying to the United States a right in the fish before they are taken ?

SENATOR ROOT: I should hardly think so.

SIR CHARLES FITZPATRICK: It is a right to reduce the fish into possession?

SENATOR ROOT: Yes, I think so.

SIR CHARLES FITZPATRICK: Until such fish are taken from the water they are the property of the territorial sovereign?

SENATOR ROOT: I would think that they were nobody's property.

SIR CHARLES FITZPATRICK: They are under the jurisdiction of the territorial sovereign.

SENATOR ROOT: They are within the special —

SIR CHARLES FITZPATRICK: They are within the territorial jurisdiction of the British sovereign?

SENATOR ROOT: Yes. We did try very hard to establish the idea of property in regard to fur seals, but Great Britain succeeded in defeating us in it.

SIR CHARLES FITZPATRICK: The right acquired was a right to take fish from the water and reduce them into possession.

SENATOR ROOT: The right we acquired was the right to have our inhabitants take fish from the water. Of course, when the fish is taken it becomes the property of the man who takes it.

SIR CHARLES FITZPATRICK: When it is reduced into possession it becomes the property of the inhabitant of the United States who takes it?

SENATOR ROOT: Yes.

THE PRESIDENT: Do you consider the right to be a right in common to the fishing territory between the United States and Great Britain, or is it rather that the inhabitants of the United States may take fish from British waters in common with the subjects of Great Britain?

SENATOR ROOT: It is a right in common of both states, because it is a right held in common for the inhabitants or citizens of both. They use the general expression that they shall have the liberty in common.

SIR CHARLES FITZPATRICK: I thought you said that the property in the fish, in so far as there can be property in it, and in so far as it is in the territorial jurisdiction of England, would be vested in British subjects, subject to your right.

SENATOR ROOT: After the fish had been taken.

SIR CHARLES FITZPATRICK: But until such time as the fish are taken, who has jurisdiction over the fish ?

SENATOR ROOT: Great Britain has jurisdiction over the water and over the vessels and over the land. I do not know that she has any jurisdiction over the fish.

SIR CHARLES FITZPATRICK: And over the taking of the fish ?

SENATOR ROOT: Yes, she has over the person who takes the fish.

THE PRESIDENT: Is there anything in the treaty which says that the right of the United States and the right of Great Britain is a right common to both states, so that the right of one state is equal to the right of the other state according to the subject-matter ?

SENATOR ROOT: I think it follows necessarily from the fact that the right which they have is expressed to be a common right. Great Britain, under that clause of the treaty, has the right to have her subjects exercise the liberty, and the United States acquires the right to have her subjects exercise the liberty, and that liberty is a liberty that they are to have forever in common.

THE PRESIDENT: The court will adjourn until a quarter-past two.[1]

[1] Thereupon, at 12.15 o'clock, the Tribunal took a recess until 2.15 P.M.

THE PRESIDENT: Will you kindly continue, Mr. Senator Root? [1]

SENATOR ROOT: It follows from the nature of the right that was granted to the United States, quite independently of the question whether the grant to the United States must be treated as a conveyance by reason of the peremptory requirement of perpetual existence imported in the word "forever", and from the fact that this grant was to the United States, that when the inhabitants of the United States go upon the treaty coast for the purpose of exercising the liberty that they have, they go there by virtue of the authority which they derive from their own government, not by virtue of an authority derived by them from the British government, availing themselves of a right which their country has internationally as against the general sovereign of the territory, by virtue of the grant which that general sovereign has made to their sovereign. The right which they exercise is a right that is therefore beyond the competency of the general sovereign of the territory — that is to say, Great Britain — to destroy or to impair or to change. It is a right which it is competent only for their own government to destroy or to impair or to change. That is equivalent to saying, in another form, that the right which they exercise is a right that they hold under their sovereign, and which that sovereign has acquired from Great Britain.

Under the way in which the exercise of this right has been treated by Britain, and in which it is the claim of Great Britain to be entitled to treat it, the American fishermen constitute a separate class by themselves, who, although Great Britain claims them to be subject to all her rights of municipal legislation, because the right that they have is a right in common, nevertheless are excluded from the real common exercise of the right. I hope I make it plain. It

[1] Friday, August 5, 1910, 2.15 P.M.

is that when the inhabitants of the United States go upon the treaty coast and exercise the liberty that is the subject of this grant to their country, under the view which Great Britain takes of the force of the words "in common", of the fact that the liberty is in common, they are treated as being a special class by themselves, not mingling with the population as in case of ordinary trade and travel rights, not really exercising rights in common, but exercising a special kind of right as a separate class, denied real rights of exercise in common; they are not permitted to use the shore as British subjects can use it; they are not permitted to exercise the liberty of fishing in common with British subjects in so far as the exercise of the right of fishing involves the use of the shore for the drawing of nets or the setting out of traps, the drawing of seines; they are not permitted to use the shores for the purpose which was mentioned by one of the counsel for Great Britain here the other day as being important and serious, the disposal of the offal resulting from the dressing of the fish; they are not permitted to use the shore for the drying of their nets as British fishermen may — for the purpose that we can see illustrated any day here as we go towards the coast, by the great stretches covered with nets laid out to dry. They must confine themselves to their ships and their boats, and their seines or nets may rot through not being dried, or they must find some way to dry them as best they can on shipboard. They are excluded from the opportunity to employ labor as British fishermen may. They are excluded from the opportunity of obtaining supplies as British fishermen may, excluded from the opportunity to procure bait as British fishermen may. And in this great variety of ways they are prohibited from the real common exercise of the right of fishing. The inference from the fact that the right is in common is, in the view of Great Britain, an inference that it is to be common for purposes of restriction, and not common for the purposes of opportunity.

If the Tribunal should be of the opinion that the British view is correct, that the fact that this liberty is a liberty held in common with subjects of Great Britain means or requires the inference that its exercise is to be in common with the exercise of the liberty by British fishermen, so that the laws or regulations or rules imposed upon British fishermen may also be imposed upon American fishermen in respect of their right, then I submit that the Tribunal must find also that that common quality extends to the opportunities of British fishermen as well as to the limitations upon British fishermen.

There is a very good illustration, which I will ask permission to hand to the court, and copies will be given to the counsel for Great Britain, of the way to make a real common exercise of the right of fishing, in the Russo-Japanese Convention concerning fisheries, of the 15th July, 1907. I submit it to the Tribunal as an illustration of the view which I am now presenting. In that treaty it is provided:

Article I. The Imperial Government of Russia grants to Japanese subjects, in accordance with the provisions of the present convention, the right to fish, catch, and prepare all kinds of fish and aquatic products, except fur seals and sea otters, along the Russian coasts of the seas of Japan, Okhotsk, and Behring, with the exception of the rivers and inlets. . . .

Article II. Japanese subjects are authorized to engage in fishing and in the preparation of fish and aquatic products in the fishing tracts specially designated for this purpose, situated both at sea and on the coasts, and which shall be leased at public auction without any discrimination between Japanese and Russian subjects, either for a long term or for a short term. Japanese subjects shall enjoy in this respect the same rights as Russian subjects who have acquired fishing tracts in the regions specified in Article I of the present convention.

The dates and places appointed for these auctions, as well as the necessary details relative to the leases of the various fishing tracts shall be officially notified to the Japanese consul at Vladivostok at least two months before the auctions. . . .

Article III. Japanese subjects who shall have acquired fishing tracts by lease in accordance with the provisions of Article II of the present convention shall have, within the limits of these tracts, the right to make free use of the coasts which have been granted to them for the purpose of carrying on their fishing industry. They may make on these coasts the necessary repairs to their boats and nets, haul the latter on land and land their fish and aquatic products, and salt, dry, prepare, and store their fish and other hauls there. For these purposes they shall be at liberty to construct thereon buildings, stores, cabins, and drying houses, or to remove them.

Article IV. Japanese subjects and Russian subjects who have acquired fishing tracts in the regions specified in Article I of the present convention shall be treated on an equal footing in everything regarding imposts or taxes, which are or shall be levied on the right to fish and to prepare fishing products, or on the movable or immovable property necessary in this industry.

Article V. The Imperial Russian Government shall not collect any duty on fish and aquatic products, cut or taken in the provinces of the coast and of the Amour. . . .

Article VI. No restriction shall be established regarding the nationality of persons employed by Japanese subjects in fishing or in the preparation, etc.

Article VII. With regard to the mode of preparation of fish and aquatic products, the Imperial Russian Government agrees not to impose on Japanese subjects any special restrictions from which Russian subjects are exempt, etc.

* * * * * * * * *

Article IX. Japanese and Russian subjects who have acquired fishing tracts in the regions specified in Article I of the present convention shall be placed on a footing of equality with regard to the laws, regulations, and ordinances at present in force or which may be enacted in future concerning fish culture and the protection of fish and aquatic products, the supervision of the industry connected therewith, and any other matter relating to fisheries.

The Japanese Government shall be notified of newly enacted laws and regulations at least six months before their enforcement.

With regard to newly enacted ordinances, notice shall be given thereof to the Japanese consul at Vladivostok at least two months before they go into effect.

Article X. With regard to matters not specially designated in the present convention, but which relate to the fishing industry in the regions specified in Article I of the said convention, Japanese subjects shall be treated on the same footing as Russian subjects who have acquired fishing tracts in the aforementioned regions.

That is an example of rights of fishing in common, and a recognition of both sides of the common right. They are to be expressly subject to the laws and regulations, and they are to be expressly entitled to all the privileges and opportunities of Russian subjects.

If the Tribunal should be of the opinion that the British contention is correct, I submit that the logical and necessary consequence of their contention as to the legal effect of making this fishing in common is that it carries common opportunity as well as common liability; and the restrictions and exclusions and differentiations between the exercise of a common right by Newfoundlanders and inhabitants of the United States must be wiped out. You cannot have one without having the other.

I now pass to the alleged implication of a right to restrict or modify the exercise of this grant by analogy to the grants of trade and travel rights in treaties generally; and shall seek to fulfill my promise upon the question asked by the president of the Tribunal this morning upon that subject.

From what does the idea arise that trade and travel rights granted by treaty to a foreign country for the benefit of its citizens are to be exercised subject to the laws and regulations of the country in which they are to be exercised? Counsel for Great Britain have placed great stress upon this, and Sir Robert Finlay put it as being a matter of common understanding that such rights are subject to regulation. The Attorney-General went farther and said [p. 1001]:

> The United States would not suggest that the captain of the ship would be entitled to say: Oh, my right to come here is territorial, you have not given me a mere ordinary trading obligation, you have given me a right to enter your gates, to stop on your soil, or in the water that covers your soil, and because it is territorial I am a specially privileged person.
>
> Such a contention as that would never be dreamed of, nor would it be dreamed of on the part of the commercial traveler who comes also under treaty. He comes there to compete with our own tradesmen and manu-

facturers in the sale of goods. He has a right to enter the gates of our territory, a right to remain there, a right to claim the protection of our laws, and he also would be entitled to say, You have put no restriction upon my right, look at your treaty. There are hundreds of these treaties passing continually under the observation of the lawyers who have to advise governments in trading countries — hundreds of such treaties. We do not find any restriction saying, for instance, that a trader is only to trade on six days a week. The commercial traveler might say, I am not a Sabbatarian, I do not want a day's rest, your population may want a day's rest, I do not, and my treaty says I am to trade. Everybody knows that the commercial traveler, putting up such a claim, would be derided. Nobody would suggest for a moment that such an obligation as that fails to carry with it all the laws which will attach to the exercise of local jurisdiction.

That is a full statement of the view. My observation does not agree with that of the Attorney-General regarding the interpretation of treaties. To begin with, under the condition of international law and practice as it was in 1818, the general, practically the universal, rule, in treaties granting trade and travel rights, was to include an express reservation of the right of municipal regulation and control.

If we turn to the treaties in our own record here — the Jay Treaty (British Case Appendix, p. 20), the treaty between Great Britain and the United States of 1794. It begins on p. 16. I read from the last paragraph in Article 13, in which trading rights in the East Indies are given. That paragraph is:

And the citizens of the United States, whenever they arrive in any port or harbor in the said territories, or if they should be permitted in manner aforesaid, to go to any place therein, shall always be subject to the laws, government, and jurisdiction of what nature established in such harbor, port, or place, according as the same may be.

And in Article 14, which gives generally trading rights, the last clause on p. 21 is:

but subject always as to what respects this article to the laws and statutes of the two countries respectively.

The men who made that treaty understood that when governments granted even the temporary and reciprocal right of residence and travel, entry for ships, residence and travel for citizens, there should be an express reservation of subordination to the municipal laws and regulations. The unratified treaty of 1806 between the United States and Great Britain, in the American Counter-Case Appendix, at p. 19, grants trading rights and provides (in the next to the last sentence in Article 3):

And the citizens of the United States, whenever they arrive in any port or harbor in the said territories, or if they should be permitted in manner aforesaid to go to any other place therein, shall always be subject to the laws, government, and jurisdiction of whatever nature, established in such harbor, port, or place, according as the same may be.

The commercial treaty of 1815 between Great Britain and the United States, found in the British Case Appendix at p. 29, in Article 1, confers rights stated thus:

The inhabitants of the two countries, respectively, shall have liberty freely and securely to come with their ships and cargoes to all such places, ports, and rivers in the territories aforesaid, to which other foreigners are permitted to come, to enter into the same, and to remain and reside in any parts of the said territories, respectively; also to hire and occupy houses and warehouses for the purposes of their commerce; and, generally, the merchants and traders of each nation, respectively, shall enjoy the most complete protection and security for their commerce, but subject always to the laws and statutes of the two countries, respectively.

And in Article 3, the provision regarding outlying dominions of the British Empire (reading from the last paragraph):

The vessels of the United States may also touch for refreshment, but not for commerce, in the course of their voyage to or from the British territories in India, or to or from the dominions of the Emperor of China, at the Cape of Good Hope, the Island of St. Helena, or such other places as may be in the possession of Great Britain, in the African or Indian Seas; it being well understood that, in all that regards this article, the citizens of the United States shall be subject in all respects to the laws and regulations of the British Government from time to time established.

I will hand to the court and to counsel on the other side a paper containing printed copies of the articles containing the trade grants in a long series of treaties made between Great Britain and other countries, and between the United States and other countries prior to or in the approximate neighborhood of the year 1818; and in all of them are express reservations of the right of the country in which trade and travel privileges are to be enjoyed by the citizens of the other nation to the exercise of that country's full right of regulation and the requirement of subjection to its laws.

The United States treaties, which are taken from the volume of treaties and conventions that is available in every library, are with the Netherlands in 1782, with Prussia in 1785, with Prussia in 1799, with Great Britain in 1815, with Sweden and Norway in 1816, with Colombia in 1824, with Central America in 1825, with Denmark in 1826, with Sweden and Norway in 1827, with the Hanseatic republics in 1827, with Brazil in 1828, with Prussia in 1828, with Austria-Hungary in 1829, with Greece in 1837, with Sardinia in 1838, with Portugal in 1840, with Hanover in 1840, with the Argentine Confederation in 1853, with the two Sicilies in 1855, and with Great Britain in 1794 — the treaty I have already referred to.

The treaties of Great Britain with other countries which contain similar express reservations: treaty with Portugal, 1642; with Portugal, 1654; with Sweden, 1654; with Denmark, 1660; with Sweden, 1661; with Spain, 1669; with Denmark, 1670; with France, 1786; with Portugal, 1810; with the Netherlands, 1815; with France, 1815; with the two Sicilies, 1816; with the Netherlands, 1824; with Buenos Ayres, 1825; with Colombia, 1825; with Sweden, 1826; with Mexico, 1826; with Austria, 1829; with Frankfort, 1832; with Austria, 1838.

It is plain to see where the idea originated that trade and travel rights are to be exercised subject to the municipal right of regulation and control; because it was the general practice of the world, in the treaties that granted these rights, during this formative period of the new régime of international intercourse and trade; it was the general practice to include in the treaties that limited the sovereign right of exclusion express provision for the application of the laws of the country that had limited its right of exclusion.

There are some treaties, a very small number, coming within these limits which had already begun to follow the modern practice, instead of making an express reservation, of establishing a standard by reference to the rights and privileges of the citizens of the state, or the most favored nation. But the Tribunal will see that equally establishes a standard. The exercise of the right of the foreigner who comes in is to be measured by the exercise of the right by the citizen, or by the citizen of the most favored nation; and nothing in the way of law or regulation affecting the exercise of his right can be objected to by him which is not in contravention of the standard of regulation of citizens, or the standard of regulation or control which is applied to the most favored nation; and that is the common practice now, to put these treaty rights on the most favored nation basis. And I venture to say that if the Attorney-General will look over again these hundreds of treaties, he will find that to be the case. If he goes back to this period regarding which we are treating, he will find the origin of the idea in express reservations, and coming down he will find the general rule, the establishment of a standard of treatment.

THE PRESIDENT: May I ask, Mr. Senator Root, if this disposition were not inserted, would the citizens of both parties have been exterritorial? Was it the practice before the conclusion of these treaties that a citizen of one state, say of one European state who comes to any other European state, or a citizen of the United States who comes to one of the European states, was exterritorial? Was it necessary to exclude exterritoriality by a specific provision?

SENATOR ROOT: Not so far as the application of the ordinary jurisdiction was concerned, but so far as the treatment of the very right which he was exercising in the period concerning which we are dealing, it would have been, because there had not then developed what has been developed now, a universal recognition of a right — an imperfect right, to be sure; a right subject to the power of exception and withdrawal — but a universal right on the part of all mankind, to free intercourse, travel, and trade. The growth of the principle of free intercourse and universal trade is a thing of recent years; and now there are two things to be considered regarding the exercise of such rights, though incorporated in a treaty. One is that the enjoyment of the rights is practically necessarily subordinate to municipal regulation, because the enjoyment is through the instrumentality of private persons. When one comes to reside, he must get a place to reside. He gets a private title, he buys a house or hires a house; he secures a room in a hotel, and what he gets is the private title, and that of course is a title subordinate to all the laws and regulations of the country. When he trades he makes contracts, and the person with whom he makes the contract is of course subordinate, and the making of the contract must be in accordance with the laws of the country within which the trading is done. So that practically the substantial enjoyment of rights of trade and travel is necessarily subordinate to laws and regulations. And there is no really practical subject-matter upon which the question that we are considering can arise. The other thing to be said is that now these treaties are merely a recognition of an existing rule and right which is accorded without treaty to all mankind. We none of us produced any passports coming here. We go at large through the civilized world, and except it be some particular country which has a special principle of exclusion for some class, and which wishes always to scrutinize for the purpose of determining whether we belong to that class, we are exercising the general right of modern civilization, which is recognized generally as being for the benefit of all nations, and which no nation can afford to deny, because the principle of commercial intercourse has taken the place of the principle of isolation. And, really, putting such a right into a treaty now is nothing more than practically a recognition of the fact, a formal recognition of the fact, that the two countries are on terms of peace and amity, which the inhabitants may freely enjoy, and that there is no barrier to their exercise of the general rights which obtain in all civilized countries. Such a treaty does serve, perhaps I should say in addition, to negative special grounds of exclusion which sometimes exist. For instance, both the United States and Canada, while extending the freest possible hospitality to travel and residence and trade on the part of all the people of the earth, do make an exception based upon a special ground regarding the coolies, the laborers from the Orient; and that is based upon a special ground which is recognized by the Oriental nations. It is that immigration *en masse*, which amounts to peaceful invasion of a country by a great body of people who would take possession of, and occupy a portion of the territory to the exclusion of the natives, is different in kind from the exercise of ordinary travel and trade rights; and upon that principle is recognized a specific right of exclusion not inconsistent with the according of the general rights of trade and travel. But as that custom of the civilized world which gradually crystallizes into the law of nations grows, more and more, it is necessary for a nation, for its own self-respect, for the preservation of its standing among the nations of the earth, for the preservation of its own interests, for the continuance of those relations of intercourse, of trade, which are necessary to its existence in the family of nations, to give a reason for such an exception. The whole burden of proof has changed. Instead of giving a reason for admitting, if we exclude now we must give reasons for the exclusion. The strict right of exclusion remains, but it is a right that no nation can justify itself in exercising unless it has a specific reason. And the necessity of expressing a reservation of the right of municipal control over the privilege which is thus exercised freely by all the people of the earth, when an expression of the imperfect right of intercourse is put into a treaty, in my judgment no longer exists; but it did exist in 1818, because this general principle of free and universal intercourse and trade had not then reached its development; and it was through the rule, it was through the great range and practically universal custom of putting into treaties granting such rights, the express reservation of the right of municipal control that this general rule of intercourse among states grew up, and the people of the world became accustomed to it; and the custom, with all its incidents, grew out of this great range of conventions.

THE PRESIDENT: Could it not be said, Mr. Senator Root, that the very general recurrence of a disposition like this one — I have myself looked over these treaties of this period, and I have found none which does not contain a similar disposition — is rather the enactment of a recognized rule or a recognized principle of international law than the establishment of a new principle? Is not that one of the ways in which international law is developed — that generally recognized principles are put into treaties, are enacted in the written dispositions of treaties?

SENATOR ROOT: Certainly.

THE PRESIDENT: Was not that, perhaps, one of these developments of international law, that the principle which was already recognized became expressed now in treaties?

SENATOR ROOT: I should put it rather the other way — that the general recognition of the principle followed the practice dictated by convenience of including the provision in the treaties, than that the treaties arose from the recognition of the practice; because I do not think that the practice existed at the time when the series of treaties began to put the provision in. I think the world had not yet passed out of the period of isolation into the period of commercial free intercourse at that time. And I should say that the practice which we now enjoy was rather the result of the gradual adoption of the rule and putting it into this great number of treaties, so that the world became accustomed to that arrangement of the rights of trade, and finally it became the universal custom.

Sir Robert Finlay also instances, as furnishing an analogy upon which we are to assume that the right of regulation existed, rivers and canals; and he asked, who would say, when the right to navigate a river or a canal is given, that it is not to be under the rules and regulations of the country in which the river or canal is. What rivers and canals? It is better to answer such a question as that with reference to the rights that are granted. Is there any universal custom under which rights to navigate rivers granted by one nation to another by treaty without any express reservation of the right to regulate the navigation, imply such a reservation? Is there any general custom to that effect? I know of none. Where will my learned friend find the rivers? The rivers of Europe are open to navigation under the provisions of the Congress of Vienna of 1815 — that great landmark. And in that treaty there was a special and most elaborate series of provisions for the joint regulation of these rivers, with special reference to the convenience and the rights of the riparian states.

You will find quite readily in the rivers of Europe the basis for a supposition that the rights of a state navigating a river which passes through the territory of another state are subject to regulations; but it is the regulation specifically provided by treaty, and by the commissioners provided for by treaty, as established by the Congress of Vienna.

In North America are there any such rivers? We have here in the record a reference to some. In the treaty of 1871, which is in the British Case Appendix, p. 39, in Article 26, a provision as to the navigation of the River St. Lawrence, and of the Rivers Yukon, Porcupine, and Stikine, and those are with express reservations of the laws and regulations of either country within its own territory, not inconsistent with the privilege of free navigation. In South America does he find any such rivers? I know of none. The Argentine Republic has made treaties under which she has thrown open the Parana and the Uruguay to navigation, but she expressly reserves the right of regulation, and the navigation is subject to the "regulations sanctioned or which may hereafter be sanctioned by the national authority of the Confederation." The Amazon is open to traffic not by treaty, but by decree of Brazil and of Peru; and of course those decrees afford unlimited opportunity for amendment, alteration, and repeal by the country in whose territory the river is. Bolivia expressly reserves the right of regulation on her water. The Orinoco is thrown open by decree on the part of Venezuela. Where does my learned friend find the rivers the navigation of which being subject to regulation otherwise than by the navigating state furnishes an analogy upon which he may say that in this grant of a right to use this specific territory of Great Britain for the benefit of the United States there is to be implied a right of limitation and modification by the municipal regulation of Great Britain?

So about canals. It is difficult to see how any one can navigate a canal except under the rules of the canal, any more than one can travel on a railroad except under the rules of the railroad. But the canals which we have reference to here in this treaty of 1871 are subject to an express reservation.

Article 27 of the treaty of 1871 is the only one to which we have been referred, and the only one that we know of, about the international use of the canals by the United States — the only one which we have in this record at all events:

> The Government of Her Britannic Majesty engages to urge upon the Government of the Dominion of Canada to secure to the citizens of the United States the use of the Welland, St. Lawrence, and other canals in the Dominion on terms of equality with the inhabitants of the Dominion.

And the reciprocal undertaking of the United States for the enjoyment of the use of the St. Clair Flats Canal is to be on terms of equality with the inhabitants of the United States. And the provision regarding the several state canals is that the use is to be on terms of equality with the inhabitants, and so on.

Now observe that postulates the making of terms which, of course, must be made with regard to the navigation of a canal; those terms are to be made, and the standard is that the terms are to be on equality with the citizens of the United States or of the Dominion.

An entirely different provision, you will perceive, in this treaty, which is not that the inhabitants of the United States shall use this territory for fishing purposes on terms of equality with the subjects of Great Britain, but that they shall have the " liberty " in common. It is a common right which they are to exercise, with no provision or stipulation whatever regarding the terms on which it is to be exercised, and no reservation which directly or indirectly in any way whatever points towards the imposing of any regulations or terms whatever on the exercise of the right.

There is a treaty, to which I referred yesterday — a fishing treaty — which illustrates the way in which such a reserved right of modification may properly be secured — the treaty between Austria-Hungary and Italy of October, 1878.

That treaty provides as follows:

Maintaining expressly in principle for the subjects of the country the exclusive right of fishing along the coasts, there shall be reciprocally accorded as an exception thereto and for the duration of this Treaty (regard being had to particular local circumstances, and, on the part of Austria-Hungary, regard being had in addition to the concessions made in return by Italy) to Austro-Hungarian inhabitants and the Italians of the shores of the Adriatic the right to fish along the coasts of the other state, reserving therefrom, however, the coral and sponge fishery as well as the fishery within a marine mile of the coast, which is reserved exclusively to the inhabitants of the coast.

It is understood that the Regulations for maritime fishery in force in the respective states must be strictly observed, and especially those which forbid the fishery carried on in a manner injurious to the propagation of the species.

There is a real reservation, a reservation made as it would have been made in this treaty of 1818 if the makers of the treaty had intended that there should be a reservation of the right of control over the liberty to fish such as it was universal to express in the treaties of the time granting trading privileges to the citizens of one country in territory of another.

I now pass to my proposition that the makers of this treaty of 1818 understood the treaty in accordance with the American contention; that they had no idea whatever that the grant which they were making was subject to any power or authority of Great Britain to restrict, limit, modify, or affect it by subsequent legislation.

And the first circumstance which shows that is the circumstance to which I have just been referring in dealing with the subject of the analogy of trading treaties; that is, that these gentlemen who made this treaty in 1818 refrained from inserting in it the customary reservation of the time — the reservation which it was the practically universal rule of the time to put in when to one country was granted a right for its citizens to enter into and obtain benefit within the territory of another country.

You will have observed that I have quoted these express reservations in three treaties between the United States and Great Britain made prior to 1818 — the treaty of 1794, the Jay Treaty, the treaty of 1806, and the treaty of 1815; that is, all the treaties that had ever been made between Great Britain and the United States granting rights to the citizens of one country to enter into and be relieved from the power of exclusion on the part of the government of the other country. Those are the three commercial treaties, three treaties granting trade and travel rights between the two countries, and they are all.

Now, would it not be extraordinary if these gentlemen who made the treaty of 1818, coming to grant these rights and intending that there should be a right of municipal regulation over the exercise of the right, should not put in the provision that was in every other treaty that had been made? They must have known of this great list of treaties I have detailed. They were not ignorant persons. They knew something about the business in which they were engaged. They were not simple, dull-witted English squires, as the counsel for Great Britain might seem to have you think. They were men of exceptional ability and eminence. Mr. Goulburn was Peel's Chancellor of the Exchequer. He was the negotiator, not merely of the treaty of 1818, but of the treaty of 1815, one of the negotiators of the treaty of

1814, and the negotiator of the treaty between Great Britain and Spain of 1818 — accomplished, able, eminent.

Mr. Robinson was of long experience in the diplomatic life of Great Britain. He had been secretary to the British Embassy at Constantinople in 1807. He accompanied Lord Castlereagh to Paris in 1814 when Europe was rearranged diplomatically; he remained there with him until after the conclusion of the Treaty of Paris in 1815; he was Prime Minister of England as Viscount Goderich, and became Earl of Ripon.

Three of the men who made the treaty of 1818 made the treaty of 1815, in which this express reservation occurs: Robinson, Goulburn, both the British negotiators, and Gallatin of the American negotiators. They could not have forgotten that. We know they could not have forgotten that, because this treaty of 1818 reënacts and carries into its provisions the treaty of 1815. The fourth article of the treaty of 1818 is:

> All the provisions of the convention "to regulate the commerce between the territories of the United States and of His Britannic Majesty," concluded at London on the third day of July, in the year of our Lord one thousand eight hundred and fifteen, with the exception of the clause which limited its duration to four years, and excepting, also, so far as the same was affected by the declaration of His Majesty respecting the Island of St. Helena, are hereby extended and continued in force for the term of ten years from the date of the signature of the present convention, in the same manner as if all the provisions of the said convention were herein specially recited.

This reference to the declaration regarding the island of St. Helena refers to the very clause of the treaty of 1815 from which I have read to you the express reservation of the right of municipal regulation.

So here you have in this treaty the same men who made the treaty of 1815 and who put into it the express reservation of the right of municipal regulation, reënacting it here with that clause, and at the same time granting this right to the United States for its inhabitants to enter upon the territory of Great Britain and subject it to their use — this right which Lord Bathurst has already called in the letter which was the corner stone of the negotiation resulting in the treaty, the right of an independent nation to enter and use at its discretion the territory of Great Britain, and they do not apply any reservation to that right.

I say it is quite incredible that they should have refrained from following the custom — following their own custom — following the custom that obtained between the two countries employing the same familiar expression which they themselves had employed in the treaty they were reënacting in regard to trade and travel rights, if they intended or dreamed of the idea that this right in the territory of Great Britain conveyed in Article 1 was to be subject to such regulation.

The President: Please, sir, was it not necessary to make, in the Treaty of Commerce for instance in 1815, a distinct disposition concerning the exception of foreigners? Was it not at that time, and I believe still in some of the states of the United States and, if I am not wrong, in Great Britain also, the rule that foreigners cannot acquire landed property, and was it not necessary to make this exception? If this exception had not been made, then foreigners could have claimed the right to be proprietors of land. I believe, if I am not quite wrong, in the year 1815 neither the laws of Great Britain nor the laws of the United States admitted in general foreigners to be proprietors of land, or there were at least some dispositions discriminating between foreigners and citizens.

Sir William Robson: In 1871 there was a statute permitting aliens to hold land in Great Britain; prior to that time aliens had no such right.

THE PRESIDENT: And for saving this discriminatory disposition, and probably other discriminatory dispositions between the rights of foreigners and citizens, it was perhaps necessary to insert in the Treaty of Commerce of 1815 a disposition like this, whereas, as to the exercising of the fishing industry, the subjects of both states should be treated on the principle of equality, in common, so that such a disposition was not necessary ?

SENATOR ROOT: There undoubtedly may have been a variety of reasons for subjecting foreigners to the laws of Great Britain on the one side and of the United States on the other; one of them may have had reference to the laws regarding alienage and title to property; but it remains, nevertheless, that the method employed to bring about the subjection to the laws was this express reservation, and if it had been intended that the fishermen should be subjected to laws of Great Britain respecting their right, the same method would have been adopted.

I shall draw an inference from the observation of the president in favor of the position which I am taking, and that is, that they saw no reason why American inhabitants going upon the treaty coasts to exercise their liberty should, in respect of that liberty, be subjected to the laws of Great Britain. However many reasons there may have been for subjecting the travelers and traders here, whatever the reasons were, they knew how to subject them, and the fact that they did not subject them on the fishing coast shows that they saw no reason to subject them.

THE PRESIDENT: But was there not one difference ? Concerning the general right of aliens to enter foreign territory, to live in foreign territory, to exercise certain industries, there was the general intention of upholding certain discriminatory dispositions, whereas, as to the exercise of the fishing industry, there was the intention of making no discrimination between foreigners and citizens, as they had the right in common.

SENATOR ROOT: It may have been that the intentions upon the treaty coast were much more benevolent than they were in regard to the holding of real estate. Nevertheless, the fact that it was deemed necessary in the one case to expressly subject the foreign citizens coming into the territory to the laws holds good in the other. Whatever may have been the reasons for subjecting or not subjecting, the very object of subjecting was plain. And if they did not employ that recognized, customary, effective way of subjecting the foreign citizen to the laws and regulations of the country — whatever the reasons may have been — if they did not employ it, we are bound to infer that they did not intend to subject them.

The next consideration tending to show, tending very powerfully to show, that the makers of the treaty had no idea of subjecting the inhabitants of the United States to any restriction or modification of their rights, was that the negotiators had before them the example of the French rights. They knew (the evidence is here in this record) all about the French rights. Of course no one negotiating a treaty regarding the fisheries could have failed to know, to be familiar with, the French right. Mr. Gallatin, minister to Paris, Swiss by birth, French his native language, one of the most acute and able men among the many whom the continent of Europe furnished to the formative period of the young republic across the Atlantic, he knew, of course. Mr. Rush, a man who, as minister to England, stood against Castlereagh for the rights of South America, and collaborated with Canning that arrangement or understanding between Great Britain and the United States that brought forth Canning's famous remark that he had redressed the balance of power of the old world by bringing the new world into life; and the still more famous declaration of Monroe, of which our old friend John Quincy Adams really was the true author, no one can doubt Richard Rush's competency or knowledge of the subject with which he was dealing, and all these gentlemen of course knew, and these negotiators had before them the fact that for more than a hundred years, on this very coast, the French had exercised the right of fishing granted in the same words, and never subject to regulation by the laws of Great Britain; never.

And, with that before them, is it credible that they conceived that there would be an implication of such a right on the part of Great Britain ? With that before them is it credible that, if they had intended or supposed that there was to be such a reservation, they would not have expressed it ? Would they not have followed this universal custom and expressed it ?

Now I beg you to observe, regarding the French right, that for seventy years before the treaty of 1783 France exercised this right. Before any declaration of 1783 France exercised the right, first under the Treaty of Utrecht, which said the French citizens shall be allowed, and then under the Treaty of Paris of 1763, which said the "subjects of France shall have the liberty of fishing."

Everybody knew, these negotiators knew, the question during that seventy years was not whether Great Britain could regulate France, but whether Great Britain had any right at all on the coast, whether France could not exclude Great Britain. Of course they knew that. The treaty of 1778 between the United States and France treats the French right as exclusive.

It is suggested here that these gentlemen had forgotten it. Forgotten the great event of the French Alliance ! Forgotten that compact which alone enabled the United States to secure its independence! The two great facts that stood out in

American history for every one who approached the subject of diplomacy were the treaty of 1778 with France and the treaty of peace of 1783 with Great Britain.

The whole history of the French right is very fully displayed in the letter of Lord Salisbury, of 9th July, 1889, which appears in the United States Case Appendix, p. 1083. In that letter Lord Salisbury argues to M. Waddington, not for the British right to control the French fishery, but for the British right to participate in it. He says, in the third paragraph on p. 1083:

> In my note of the 24th August, 1887, relative to this claim, I had stated that the right of fishery conferred on the French citizens by the Treaty of Utrecht did not take away, but only restricted during a certain portion of the year and on certain parts of the coast, the British right of fishery inherent in the sovereignty of the island. And in my subsequent note of the 28th July last I observed that the right of British subjects to fish concurrently with French citizens has never been surrendered, though the British fishermen are prohibited by the second paragraph of the Declaration of Versailles from interrupting in any manner by their competition the fishery of the French during the temporary exercise of it which is granted to them.

That is a specimen of the numerous contentions which are to be found throughout this long historical document, all of which go to the assertion that Great Britain had a right to participate as against the French assertion of their right to exclude British subjects. You remember Lord Derby's letter of the 12th June, 1884, in which he says that the grant of the French rights impressed upon the waters of Newfoundland something of the character of a common sea for the purpose of fishery. In the correspondence in 1886 we have a very illuminating exposition of what the real character of the French and English right was considered to be by Great Britain. I refer to the United States Counter-Case Appendix, p. 316, where will be found a letter from Count d'Aubigny to the Earl of Iddesleigh. It is dated 20th September, 1886:

My Lord: A decree of the Newfoundland Government dated the 9th August last, has prohibited lobster fishing for three years, from the 30th September next, in Rocky Harbor (Bonne Bay, " French Shore ").

I am instructed to inform your Excellency that, in view of the fishery right conferred on France by the treaties in the part of the island to which the Decree applies, a right which can evidently not be restricted in its exercise, it is impossible for my Government to recognize in any way the validity of the measure taken by the Newfoundland authorities.

On p. 317 we have another from the French Captain LeClerc to Captain Hamond, a British captain, and in the last paragraph, p. 318, Captain LeClerc says:

I think it right to let you know that I am giving orders to vessels of my division to take no notice of a Decree which regulates a fishery the enjoyment of which belongs only to France.

On p. 319 there is a letter from the Governor of Newfoundland to Mr. Stanhope, of the Colonial Office, in which he says:

Sir: In accordance with your instructions,

this is dated 24th November, 1886 —

I have communicated to my Ministers your despatch of the 30th October, 1886, with reference to the lobster fishery on that part of the coast of Newfoundland where the French have fishing rights. . . . Though I have as yet had no communication from my Ministers on the subject, I may mention at once that there was never any intention of enforcing this Order against French subjects.

On the 12th February, 1887, there is a letter, p. 320 of the United States Counter-Case Appendix, in which the Colonial Office of Great Britain, writing to the Foreign Office, says:

Count d'Aubigny appears to found his complaint on the fact that the French right of fishery cannot be limited by a Colonial Decree; but the position taken by Captain LeClerc is tantamount to a denial of the right of the Colonial authorities to issue any Decree binding upon British subjects on matters concerning the fisheries on that part of the coast.

The Marquis of Salisbury writes M. Waddington on the 5th July, 1887, communicating the fact that he has received a formal assurance from the Government of Newfoundland that the prohibition is not to be enforced against French citizens.

Another question arose between the French and British which brought out some further correspondence, and, on the 23d November, 1888, Lord Salisbury, writing to M. Waddington, in the letter which appears at p. 324, states the view of Great Britain regarding the French rights. He says, in the paragraph at the foot of the page:

> Her Majesty's Government are unable to assent to the claim advanced by your Excellency that the French Government must be *sole judge* as to what constitutes such interference within the terms of the British Declaration of 1783.
>
> That is a question on which *both governments have an equal right* to form any opinion, and as to which Her Majesty's Government have always endeavored to meet the views of the French Government as far as was possible consistently with the just claims of the Colony.

That is the British view of the French rights, and that is the description of the rights as they existed, and as they were exercised prior to the making of the treaty of 1818. The limit of Great Britain's contention regarding them was not that she could regulate the French rights — that she repudiated — but that France was not the sole judge regarding the exercise of her rights, and that both nations had an equal right to form an opinion as to what constituted interference. These letters are long subsequent to the treaty of 1818, but they furnish an authentic statement of what the rights were, and a statement by the head of the British Foreign Office, who had made the most complete and exhaustive study of the subject of any of the statesmen of Great Britain.

It was well understood that the American rights, granted in the same terms, were, in effect, the same rights. Perhaps I should here call attention to the relation of the British declaration of 1783 to the rights granted under the treaties of 1713 and 1763. I have already said that the terms of the treaty of 1763 were the same as the terms which contained the grant of the American right — "shall have the liberty" and so forth. The treaty with France of 1783 granted no new right, made no change in the right. It changed the limits slightly, cutting off at one end and extending at the other. On p. 11 of the British Appendix, in Article 5 of the French treaty of the 3d September, 1783, is the provision:

His Majesty the Most Christian King, in order to prevent the quarrels which have hitherto arisen between the two nations of England and France, consents to renounce the right of fishing, which belongs to him in virtue of the aforesaid article of the Treaty of Utrecht from Cape Bonavista to Cape St. John, situated on the eastern coast of Newfoundland, . . . and His Majesty the King of Great Britain consents, on his part, that the fishery assigned to the subjects of His Most Christian Majesty, beginning at the said Cape St. John, passing to the north, and descending by the western coast of the Island of Newfoundland, shall extend to the place called Cape Ray. . . . The French fishermen shall enjoy the fishery which is assigned to them by the present article, as they had the right to enjoy that which was assigned to them by the Treaty of Utrecht.

The right in all that great part of the coast which was not affected by this renunciation on one end and addition on the other remained untouched, and the addition was to be upon the same basis as that which remained untouched; that is to say, it was the same right which was granted by the treaty of 1763.

Then, in the declaration, which Mr. Turner has very justly characterized as a modality, there is no additional right given to France — none whatever. The seventy years of exercise of this French right had developed quarrels and controversies between the French and the English. The French were claiming that their right was exclusive. The British were refusing to assent to that, but what Great Britain did do was to say:

The King, having entirely agreed with His Most Christian Majesty upon the articles of the definitive treaty, will seek every means which shall not only insure the execution thereof, with his accustomed good faith and punctuality, but will besides give, on his part, all possible efficacy to the principles which shall prevent even the least foundation of dispute for the future.

It was the execution of the existing treaty, and

To this end, —

that is, to the end of executing that treaty, —

and in order that the fishermen of the two nations may not give cause for daily quarrels, His Britannic Majesty will take the most positive measures for preventing his subjects from interrupting, in any manner, by their competition, the fishery of the French, during the temporary exercise of it which is granted to them upon the coasts of the Island of Newfoundland; and he will, for this purpose, cause the fixed settlements, which shall be formed there, to be removed.

JUDGE GRAY: That language, "by their competition", is not in the treaty? —

SENATOR ROOT: No, sir, it is in that declaration; and, of course, that language implies necessarily that there is competition, and that there is a right of competition. There is no surrender of the right. There is an agreement to do, for the purpose of executing the treaty, precisely what Great Britain, in fact, did by the Act and Order-in-Council of 1819 for the execution of the treaty of 1818, expressly ordering her people in Newfoundland not to interrupt the exercise of the treaty right by Americans. There is there on the part of France no right whatever except the right granted in the same words as the grant to the United States of 1783 and 1818, with a promise on the part of the King of Great Britain to make that right effective by prohibiting his subjects from interrupting the exercise by their competition.

They were quite well understood to be the same rights. I find, on p. 229 of the Appendix to the Counter-Case of the United States, that the Governor of Newfoundland, writing to Sir John Pakington, says, in the fourth paragraph:

> The very terms of the Declaration in question whilst forbidding the English fishermen to interrupt by their competition, or to injure the Stages, etc., of the French, recognize their presence, and the whole question would appear to be settled by the concession on the part of our Government, to the citizens of the United States in the treaty of 1818, of the same rights which had been conceded to the French in that of 1783.

The Newfoundland Legislature, in resolutions adopted in 1876, appearing on p. 276 and following pages of the United States Counter-Case Appendix, said, in the paragraph which begins towards the bottom of p. 277:

> That the rights of fishing involved in the absurd claims of an exclusive fishery by the French are not limited to the residents of Newfoundland; they are the rights of the other provinces of British North America, and also those of the United States, to the latter granted them under their Treaty with Great Britain in the year 1818. England could not and would not have granted to the United States that which she had no right to grant, and much less would she deprive the inhabitants of the soil of rights she had granted to non-residents and to aliens.

This French right was well understood to be the same as the American right before the exigencies of the situation led to refinement and subtlety, before lawyers began to argue about it and try to find fine distinctions between the two. Great Britain had conceded this right, expressed in the treaty of 1783, which was part of the same transaction with the American treaty of 1783, and relating to the same coast of Newfoundland, with confessedly no thought of regulation on the part of Great Britain, confessedly no idea that there was any possible right of regulation on the part of Great Britain, and these negotiators, knowing it all, proved by the record to have discussed it in their negotiations, to have discussed the whole subject of the fisheries, including the French rights, going on and repeating the language of the treaty of 1763, in making the grant to the United States, put in no reservation of a right of regulation and control.

Is it open to us then to decide rights upon the assumption that these negotiators supposed that the grant to the United States would carry an implied right, an implied reservation of the right to do what never had been thought of with regard to the French right? Nor are we to suppose that the negotiators ever dreamed that Great Britain would want to regulate the fisheries. She was not regulating the French fisheries. Why should it be supposed that she would expect to regulate the American fisheries upon the same coast? There stands that great concrete fact which the negotiators could not ignore, and we cannot ignore, excluding any possible idea of an implied reservation or of an intention that there should be a reservation of the right to regulate.

THE PRESIDENT: May I ask one question, Mr. Senator Root, concerning the British conception of the French right? Was it necessary for the British Government to make any regulation concerning the exercise of the French right? In fact, they had recognized the exclusiveness of the French right. May I draw your attention to the last few words of section 1 of the British statute of 1788, which is the statute concerning the treaty with France, British Case Appendix, p. 561? I read four lines from the top of p. 563:

> also all ships, vessels, and boats, belonging to His Majesty's subjects, which shall be found within the limits aforesaid, and also, in case of refusal to depart from within the limits aforesaid, to compel any of His Majesty's subjects to depart from thence; any law, usage, or custom, to the contrary notwithstanding.

Does it not follow from this statute that the British Government considered that British subjects had no right on that coast at all, and that, therefore, they had no reason to make regulations concerning that coast; whereas, with respect to the American fishery right, which was to be exercised in common by American and British subjects, there might be reason for the British Government to regulate?

SENATOR ROOT: That strengthens my argument, Mr. President, which is, that having before them the example of the French right, under which they had been compelled to abandon the practical concurrent use, or common use, and under which the effect of the grant had been wholly to exclude them from applying their laws and regulations to the French right, if they did not want such a result to happen under the grant to the Americans the British would, of course, have put in an express provision to prevent it from happening. My proposition is that the presence of this great French right and the annoyance, difficulty, turmoil, embarrassment which Great Britain had suffered from her exclusion from all practical control over this very coast was a most cogent reason why, if the negotiators had any idea of preserving the right of control, they would have put it in the treaty, instead of leaving the right to be expressed in the very terms which had been used in the grant to the French. That finishes what I was proposing to say regarding the inference to be drawn from the French right.

THE PRESIDENT: Have you finished what you intended saying concerning that point?

SENATOR ROOT: Yes; but may I say one further thing, not part of the argument? On the 20th June, the Tribunal requested the agents and counsel, *in camera*, to designate experts to be appointed as members of the commission pursuant to the third article of the Special Agreement. The agent for the United States immediately cabled to the United States to have an expert come. He came some little time ago and we have been waiting for some action to be taken to employ him. As so long a time has elapsed it seems to me appropriate that I should bring the matter to the attention of the Tribunal and say that the United States nominates for a member of the Expert Commission under Article 3 of the treaty, Mr. Hugh M. Smith, deputy commissioner of fisheries of the United States, who is here present and ready to perform his duties.

THE PRESIDENT: Thank you, sir. The court adjourns until Monday at 10 o'clock.[1]

THE PRESIDENT: Will you kindly continue, Mr. Root?[2]

SENATOR ROOT (resuming): I wish to add to what I was saying about the example of the French fishing rights on the Newfoundland coast, as affecting the minds of the negotiators of the treaty of 1818, a reference to the observation of Sir Robert Finlay in his opening argument, which appears at p. 1204 of the typewritten report [p. 207 *supra*]. He said:

> It is perfectly true that Great Britain did not frame regulations for the exercise by French fishermen of their rights upon the French shore of Newfoundland, and she did not do it for this reason. France throughout claimed that her rights upon these shores were exclusive. She asserted that in the strongest way. And, although that right was never admitted by Great Britain, it is perfectly obvious that Great Britain could not have undertaken the framing of regulations for the exercise by the French fishermen of their privileges upon the coast of Newfoundland, without producing most serious friction with France.

That I believe to have been a just statement of the condition which existed from very early times, practically from the time of the Treaty of Utrecht of 1713 down to the making of the treaty of 1904, which so radically changed the relations between Great Britain and France upon that shore.

But the fact that Great Britain found in her relations with France a reason for not framing regulations, whatever it may have been, whatever may have been the secret spring of policy which moved the Government of Great Britain, still leaves the fact standing that in 1818, when these nego-

[1] Thereupon, at 4.15 o'clock P.M., the court adjourned until Monday, 8th August, 1910, at 10 o'clock A.M.

[2] Monday, August 8, 1910. The Tribunal met at 10 A.M.

tiators were regranting to the United States the right that its inhabitants should have the liberty to take fish upon that coast, they had before them the example of a grant by Great Britain to France in those very words of a "liberty" to take fish upon those shores, and for one hundred and five years that "liberty" had been exercised by France without possibility of regulation by Great Britain. And if the negotiators intended that the right that they were granting to the United States should be different in respect of regulation from the right which had been granted to France, they should have said so then and there, and they would have said so then and there in the treaty in which they made the grant.

I now pass, Mr. President, to the practice under the treaty of 1783 between Great Britain and the United States.

A schedule has been presented by the Attorney-General containing a reference to a great number of statutes upon which it is asserted on behalf of Great Britain that the rights of the United States to fish upon the treaty coast under the treaty of 1783 were subjected to regulation by Great Britain. That proposition I controvert, and I affirm upon the record that is here that the exercise of fishing right by the inhabitants of the United States upon the treaty coast under the treaty of 1783 never was subjected to regulation by Great Britain.

These statutes in the British Memorandum are arranged in order of date, without special reference to the countries, or without any complete separation in respect of the countries or colonies in which the statutes were enacted.

Let me first refer to the statutes which are said to have been passed in certain of the colonies now forming part of the United States, and which did in 1818 form part of the United States.

I do not consider that those statutes are relevant to the question whether American rights on the treaty coast were regulated under the treaty of 1783. Manifestly they are not. Their materiality is, I suppose, considered to be that their existence would naturally have suggested to the negotiators the fact that fishing was a thing appropriate and proper to be regulated; a suggestion which we are not disposed materially to controvert; indeed, I intend hereafter to show that they did have specifically in mind the subject of regulation, and that they acted specifically upon it, and that there was a perfectly distinct understanding with regard to regulation. Nevertheless, I will make some remarks upon these American statutes.

They did not contain any general scheme of regulation or suggest any general scheme of regulation. The first referred to are the statutes of Massachusetts and New Hampshire. They appear upon p. 4 of the British Memorandum. And they constitute a series of statutes which upon examination are designed to control the trade in fish, rather than the taking of fish.

There was one in 1668 that provided that no cod-fish should be killed or dried for sale in December or January; no mackerel to be caught except for spending while fresh before the 1st June. This was amended in 1692, or rather reënacted in 1692, and in that form it has a preamble which is:

> Upon consideration of great damage and scandal that hath happened upon the account of pickled fish, although afterwards closed and hardly discoverable, to the great loss of money, and also the ill-reputation on this province and the fishery of it.
>
> No mackerel to be caught while fresh before first of July

and so on. That is to say, they were endeavoring to keep up the standard of this great article of commerce by preventing fish being taken at such time that when it was put up or preserved to be kept and dealt with as an article of commerce it would be a bad article, and would destroy the reputation of the commercial article of the country.

JUDGE GRAY: I did not quite understand one word. The object was to prevent the fish after being taken from being prepared for sale?

SENATOR ROOT: The object was to prevent fish from being taken at such a time that it would not be a prime article of commerce. It was to prevent its being taken in the spawning season, because the fish is not a good article then. It was a kind of pure food act rather than a fishery regulation.

Massachusetts was engaged in trade, and her great stock-in-trade was fish. The fish were caught and they were cured, dried, salted, pickled, put up in such form that they became an article of commerce.

Now, if the fish were taken when they were spawning they were a bad article of commerce, and when they were sold they destroyed the reputation of the pickled fish of Massachusetts; and for the preservation of that reputation, and keeping up the standard of this great article of commerce, these statutes were passed.

Then there is the same sort of statute in New Hampshire, 1687. Here is the preamble:

> Whereas much Damage hath been sustained and the Credit of the fishing Trade is greatly impaired by the bad making of fish, and disorderly acting of fishermen, etc.

and the act goes on to provide for the inspecting of catches and the curing of all fish. Then that has the same words, "No mackerel to be caught except for spending while fresh before 1st July; no mackerel to be caught with seines." And so that was with the same purpose.

Then there is a statute, a series of statutes, of New Plymouth, which is now part of Massachusetts, one of the original colonies that entered into the constitution of the colony of Massachusetts. The statutes of 1668, 1670, 1672, 1677 are statutes regulating fishing, only by either excluding outsiders from fishing or letting them in to fish.

Then there is a statute, or two successive statutes in New York, relating to fishing in the county of Suffolk.

Now those are fish regulations. They are shore regulations of the most obnoxious kind. They are designed to prevent any market fishing at all; anybody coming from outside to interfere with the natives in taking fish.

Perhaps it is a little clearer to me than it would be to some other readers, because I think I have fished over every bay, and every cove, and creek, and inlet in Suffolk County. It is the east end of Long Island, a place by itself, which, in those days, before there was any railroad, was almost self-governing under the sovereignty of the state of New York. And they got the legislature of New York to pass a law which would keep their fishing for themselves; the natives on the shore practically barred everybody else out. No person to draw any seine or net of any length, or set any seine or net more than six fathoms long, with meshes not less than three inches square, from the 15th November to the 15th April, in the bays, rivers, or creeks of the county of Suffolk.

Now, the observation I have to make about that is this: If these negotiators had ever heard of these little local regulations down at the east end of Long Island, far to the south, they would have undertaken not to permit that kind of regulation, but to prevent it. But there was no general system of fish regulation of any kind.

Then there are, over on p. 13 of the Memorandum, three statutes cited: one of New Jersey in 1826, that is eight years after the treaty of 1818, which limited fishing to the citizens of New Jersey; one of Delaware in 1871, fifty odd years after the treaty, and I do not think we need trouble about that; and one of Maryland in 1896, nearly eighty years after the treaty. Those are all of the American statutes.

Now, as to the statutes of Great Britain and her colonies: In the first place there were proclamations in this Memorandum. Proclamations were succeeded by statutes and were superseded by statutes and had been superseded by statutes long years before these treaties were made; and in the printed Memorandum which the United States has handed in your honors will see that we have arranged these statutes and proclamations under the heads of the colonies to which they relate: Newfoundland by itself; Nova Scotia by itself; New Brunswick by itself; Lower Canada by itself.

JUDGE GRAY: That is the arrangement of the British Memorandum, is it not?

SENATOR ROOT: No, they put all before 1783 in a series, containing all the countries, and then they put all between 1783 and 1818 in a series, and then all after that in a series, so when you come to read them there is a confusion of statutes with reference to their territorial application.

As an appendix to this paper we insert an extract from a decision of the Supreme Court of Newfoundland in the year 1820, passing upon the validity and effectiveness of one of these proclamations which is printed in the British Case Appendix, and deciding that the proclamations had not the force and effect of law. They are gone. They are disposed of, as would naturally be the case. They are in their nature but preliminaries to the establishment of government, and when a governor has made a proclamation, and afterwards the legislative body comes and covers the subject by its enactment, of course that takes the place of the previous proclamation.

Many of these proclamations were made during the intervals of possession, which was afterwards given up by Great Britain to France, and of course sovereignty or possession changing, the proclamation in the previous occupation went by the board.

SIR CHARLES FITZPATRICK: That would not apply to proclamations issued under statute, by authority of statute.

SENATOR ROOT: No, it would not.

Now, I will refer to the regulation of fishing in Newfoundland. I will not detain you by going into all these details, because you have them in print. I will state merely the conclusions which I draw from them, and I hope you will not find that I have been unduly influenced by the attitude of counsel in drawing those conclusions, and that what I say is sustained by the facts that are pointed out.

I draw the conclusion first, that there was not, either in 1783 or in 1818, any regulation as to the time and manner of fishing on the coasts of Newfoundland or Labrador.

There had been in an act of 15 Charles II, 1663, away back before France ceded Newfoundland to Great Britain by the Treaty of Utrecht, a curious provision about catching the spawn or young fry of Poor John. It has been read several times. Poor John, I believe, is a small variety of cod-fish.

That provision, however, was superseded by the Order-in-Council of 1670, which is in the Appendix to the British Case and is cited here in this paper, which provided:

> That all the subjects of His Majesty's kingdom of England shall and may forever hereafter peaceably hold and enjoy the freedom of taking bait and fishing in any of the rivers, lakes, creeks, harbors, or roads in or about Newfoundland.

If it had not been superseded by that, it would have been superseded by the statute of 1699, which gives the same freedom to " all His Majesty's subjects residing within his realm of England or the dominions thereunto belonging." That Poor John clause of 1663 was part of the restrictive policy of Great Britain in respect of the island of Newfoundland. It was when she was trying to keep anybody from settling in Newfoundland, trying to preserve the fishing and the use of Newfoundland for fishing purposes, entirely for her own subjects dwelling in England, Wales, and Berwick-on-Tweed, and this was a provision that any planter or other person or persons remaining in Newfoundland should not do thus and so. When England abandoned that extreme restrictive policy and began to permit people to go to Newfoundland the statutes wiped out that among other restrictions. There had been also a provision in the Act of 1699 which was read here by Mr. Turner and commented upon, and which provided against the bounty fishermen.

THE PRESIDENT: Will you permit me, Mr. Senator Root, to draw your attention to the proviso that is contained in the Order-in-Council of 1670, p. 519, of the British Appendix? The second clause of this Order-in-Council seems to contradict the disposition concerning the taking of young fry in the statute of 1663, because there it is said:

> That all the subjects of His Majesty's kingdom of England shall and may forever hereafter peaceably hold and enjoy the freedom of taking bait, etc.

In a subsequent clause of the Order-in-Council of 1670 there is the following proviso:

> Provided always that they submit unto, and observe all such rules and orders as now are, or hereafter shall be established, by His Majesty, his heirs, or successors, for the government of the said fishery in Newfoundland.

Does not the proviso, "Provided always that they submit unto, and observe all such rules" as are now or may hereafter be in force, apply to the statute of 1663, and is not this disposition, under the head of No. 7 of the statute of 1663, maintained by this disposition of 1670?

SENATOR ROOT: I do not read it so. I read it in this way: such rules and orders as now are or hereafter shall be established; and then they proceed to establish them. You can see that it is immediately followed by a long series of orders.

THE PRESIDENT: Yes.

SENATOR ROOT: In that way you make consistency. In 1663 there had been a prohibition against —

THE PRESIDENT: Against a special kind of fishing.

SENATOR ROOT: That; and there is a prohibition against any kind of fishing as well. It is broad prohibition against fishing. Now, here comes a broad declaration of freedom of fishing. It cannot be that the proviso was intended to repeal the main enactment, but you are perfectly consistent when you say that they refer to the rules and orders which they are now establishing in this order-in-council. Therefore they call them rules and orders and do not call them statutes. Thus it says that there shall be general freedom of fishing "provided always that they submit unto, and observe all such rules and orders as now are, or hereafter shall be established." Then they proceed in this very order-in-council to establish this series of rules and orders.

THE PRESIDENT: If the statute of 1663, No. 7, would be an entire prohibition of fishing in Newfoundland, then there would certainly be the contradiction you are alluding to, Mr. Senator Root; but does it not rather seem that the disposition of No. 7 of 1663 is not a complete prohibition of fishing, but only a prohibition of taking spawn or the young fry of Poor John except for bait? It does not seem to be a total prohibition of fishing, but a prohibition of fishing within very restricted limits, and this prohibition within restricted limits might well be the one to which the proviso of the Order-in-Council of 1670 refers. It seems to be the same as the provision already existing, except the proviso that they must always submit to such rules as now are or may hereafter be in force.

SENATOR ROOT: I tried to work out an understanding of this curious Poor John provision along that line and, if that be the case, counsel for the United States need not concern themselves any more about it, for if it merely relates to spawn or the young fry of Poor John, it is not a regulation of the industrial enterprise of fishing. That is not the kind of regulation with which we are dealing. It is the sort of regulation which applies to a small boy with his trousers rolled up paddling along the shore and taking the spawn or the little small fry of the fish.

THE PRESIDENT: Perhaps it is not of great importance, but this disposition seems to be a prohibition of a certain kind of fishing, and this proviso may be understood in the sense that this prohibition of a particular, and perhaps not very important, mode of fishing is to be continued.

SENATOR ROOT: May it not be put in this way — that this provision No. 7 of the statute of 1663 either is limited to the taking of spawn and the young fry of Poor John — and the words which follow all qualify that — that is, the taking of spawn or the young fry of Poor John "for any other use or uses, except for the taking of bait only" — and in that case we need not concern ourselves with No. 7 because it was not a regulation of the industrial enterprise of fishing; or it means to prohibit the taking of spawn or the young fry of Poor John, the casting or laying of "any seine or other net in or near any harbor in Newfoundland, whereby to take the spawn or young fry of the Poor John, or for any other use or uses, except for the taking of bait only"? In that case it would be so complete a prohibition of fishing that it would be repealed by this Order-in-Council. I am quite indifferent which construction is adopted.

But when we come to the Act of 1699 we find that if the Order-in-Council did not supersede this old Poor John provision, the first article of the Act of 1699, I am quite clear, would have superseded it:

That from henceforth it shall and may be lawful for all His Majesty's subjects residing within this realm of England, or the dominions thereunto belonging, trading or that shall trade to Newfoundland, and the seas, rivers, lakes, creeks, harbors in or about Newfoundland, or any of the islands adjoining or adjacent thereunto, to have, use, and enjoy the free trade and traffic, and art of merchandise and fishery, to and from Newfoundland, and peaceably to have, use, and enjoy the freedom of taking bait and fishing in any of the rivers, lakes, creeks, harbors, or roads in or about Newfoundland.

It covers the entire ground and plainly supersedes the provision of the statute of 1663, if it had not been already superseded. That is all I can find here which seems to have any characteristic as limiting or restricting the exercise of the liberty of fishing down to 1783. After 1783 there was the Act of 1786 which, as you will remember, was a bounty act, providing for the payment of bounty to vessels that went to the Grand Banks for the purpose of the cod-fishery, and it provided in detail for the vessels taking cod going to the south coast of Newfoundland to dry and cure them. It is quite specific in its provisions, and in it there is a provision against fishermen " engaged in the said fishery ", that is, the bounty-fed fishery on the Grand Banks, taking fish on the coast of Newfoundland, and limited strictly to them, that is all. There were provisions in these statutes which prohibited the throwing of ballast over into the harbors; which prohibited the throwing of gurry, or the offal of fish, overboard; which prohibited the casting or dropping of anchors; not fishing limitations, in so far as anchors and ballast are concerned, but harbor protection regulations as to all ships of all kinds everywhere, coming for whatever purpose, and provision against net interference and theft of nets invariably associated in the same sentence. All of these are police regulations, and they constituted all there was in the way of regulation in Newfoundland either in 1783 or in 1818, or at any time between those dates and for many years after.

Sir Charles Fitzpatrick: There was the prohibition of fishing on Sunday contained in clause 16 of the Act of 1699.

Senator Root: That was repealed in 1775, as stated by Lord Elgin, in the letter which he wrote to Governor MacGregor at the time we were talking about the *modus vivendi*, so that did not exist. Lord Elgin, in that letter, states very clearly what the situation was after the treaty of 1818 was made. The Tribunal will remember that in 1855 there was a call made for a statement of all the regulations there were, for the purpose of presenting them to the United States for its consideration with respect to the application of the treaty of 1854, and that the Attorney-General reported that there were none. My learned friend the Attorney-General fell into an error in regard to that report, he following, I think, Mr. Ewart, in supposing that the report was erroneous, or that the report was limited only to local regulations. The report was quite accurate. Senator Turner calls my attention, with reference to my answer to Chief Justice Fitzpatrick on the question of the Sunday prohibition of 1699, to the fact, and it does appear to be the case, that it was a Sunday observance provision which had no particular reference to fishing.

Sir Charles Fitzpatrick: The words are "shall strictly and decently observe every Lord's Day, commonly called Sunday." It depends on what that means.

Senator Root: I have known of one fishing club where observance of the Sabbath was enforced by a rule against playing cards, but they fished, and another where the observance was enforced by a rule against fishing, but they played cards. I do not know what the construction of that would be, but at all events the subsequent statute of 1775 disposed of it in so far as fishing was concerned at least.

The President: But does the statute of 1775 relate to fishing on the coast of Newfoundland, or does it not rather only refer to fishing on the banks? If one reads the preamble to the statute of 1775, p. 543 of the British Case Appendix, it seems to refer only to the fishery on the banks. It is, perhaps, not clear, but they speak only about fishing on the banks:

Now, in order to promote these great and important purposes, and with a view, in the first place, to induce His Majesty's subjects to proceed early from the ports of Great Britain to the banks of Newfoundland, and thereby to prosecute the fishery on the said banks to the greatest advantage, may it please Your Majesty that it may be enacted.

Then again:

for eleven years, for a certain number of ships or vessels employed in the British fishery on the banks of Newfoundland.

They speak only of the fishery on the banks. Then, a little below the middle of the page, after having referred to the Act of King William III, they say:

and shall be fitted and cleared out from some port in Great Britain after the first Day of January, one thousand seven hundred and seventy-six, and after that day in each succeeding year, and shall proceed to the banks of Newfoundland; and having catched a cargo of fish upon those banks.

Then again, some lines below:

Before the said fifteenth Day of July in each year, at the said island, with a like cargo, and shall proceed again to the said banks.

In the next line you again find the word "banks", and two lines below again the word "banks." In the whole of that statute they speak only of the fishery on the banks.

SENATOR ROOT: It was the same fishery. It was then, as it is now, all the same fishery. The fishery on the banks was the great object of the use of Newfoundland, and this statute of 1775, like all the previous statutes, in fact, treats them as a whole because the successful prosecution of the bank fishery required the use of the proximate shores, and I cannot doubt that the general provisions of the statute did operate to cover all persons such as were the British themselves and as were the Americans themselves, and as were all the British and Americans in 1783 and from 1783 to 1818 — all those engaged in that fishery, the object of which was to take fish from the banks, and which employed and involved the use of the shores and waters of Newfoundland as an adjunct to its successful prosecution. Lord Elgin correctly gives, as we conceive, the opinion of the Government of Great Britain regarding this statute. His letter will be found at p. 986 of the United States Case Appendix, and it bears date the 8th August, 1906. He says at the top of p. 987:

> Light dues were presumably not levied in 1818, seines were apparently in use, the prohibition of Sunday fishing had been abolished in 1776 —

that is a misprint for 1775, because it goes on to say " (see 15 George III, cap. 31)," which is the Act of 1775 —

> and fishing-ships were exempted from entry at Custom-house, and required only to make a report on first arrival and on clearing.

I think it is fairly reasonably to be said that when we came to the making of the treaty in 1783 there was a free hand for the prosecution of the industry such as was contemplated on the part of the American fishermen.

SIR CHARLES FITZPATRICK: May I ask you if you can tell me whether or not the new charter referred to at p. 529 of the British Case Appendix, relating to trade and fishery in Newfoundland, is printed anywhere? Referring to the passage about the middle of the page, I see the following:

> And on the 27th of January, 1675, His said Majesty, after due consideration had of the best ways and means of regulating, securing and improving the Fishing Trade in Newfoundland passed the New Charter which recited and confirmed all the old Laws, and several others were added for the better government of the Fishery.

I have not been able to find it myself.

SENATOR ROOT: I have not found the record.

SIR CHARLES FITZPATRICK: I do not think it is printed.

SENATOR ROOT: Unless it refers to one of these statutes.

SIR CHARLES FITZPATRICK: It is dated 1718.

SENATOR ROOT: No, Mr. Anderson tells me there is nothing in the record to which that corresponds. I was observing that my learned friends on the other side had fallen into an error in supposing that the attorney-general of

Newfoundland, in 1855, when he reported that there were no regulations as to fishing, was mistaken. The whole subject of Newfoundland appears to have been covered and codified in the Act of 1824, which you will remember, I presume — British Case Appendix, p. 567. This is:

> An Act to repeal several Laws relating to the Fisheries carried on upon the Banks and Shores of Newfoundland, and to make Provision for the better Conduct of the said Fisheries for Five Years, and from thence to the End of the then next Session of Parliament.

It goes on in the first article and repeals 10 and 11 William III, 15 George III, 26 George III, and 29 George III, and then covers the ground pretty fully. It reproduces the provisions of the old Act of 1688 regarding the French claims, the Act of 1819, and the Order-in-Council of 1819, all in one paragraph (12) bunching them together as being subject to the same general provision:

> That it shall and may be lawful for His Majesty, His Heirs and Successors, by Advice of His or their Council, from time to time to give such Orders and Instructions to the Governor of Newfoundland, or to any Officer or Officers on that Station, as he or they shall deem proper and necessary to fulfill the Purposes of any Treaty or Treaties now in force between His Majesty and any Foreign State or Power.

It reproduces the various prohibitions against the casting of ballast overboard, against the casting of anchor at places where it would hinder the drawing of nets, against net interference, or stealing or purloining of nets or fish. All these are reproduced, but the statute wiped out all other provisions and laws applying to fishing. The statute, as you will see by the last article, at the top of page 570, is to be in force only for five years and thence to the end of the next session of Parliament. So that everything that there had been, in so far as it continued in the year 1818, was gathered together in this Act of 1824, and a five-year limit was put upon it. The reason was quite plain. They evidently then had come to the conclusion to give Newfoundland a legislative body of its own, and were making this statute so as to carry it over until there should be a legislature for Newfoundland itself.

At p. 329 of the United States Counter-Case Appendix, Sir W. V. Whiteway made an explanation in the House of Lords on the 23d April, 1891, upon this subject. The Tribunal will find that in the last paragraph on p. 329 Sir William Whiteway refers to this Act of 1824, and says that in 1824 an act entitled "An Act to repeal several laws", etc., contained two sections, 12 and 13, almost literally the same as those above quoted; that is, the sections which I have referred to as being in Article 12 of the Act of 1824. Then he goes on, in the first paragraph on p. 330, to tell what happened to this act, and says:

> An Act was passed in 1829 to continue the Act 5 George IV, chap. 51, last referred to, until the 31st of December, 1832.

That is, this 1824 act was a five-year act; when it was about to expire, Parliament passed another act to extend it until the 31st December, 1832; and in 1832 the Act 5 George IV, chapter 51, was further extended until 1834, and no longer.

> In 1832 a legislature was granted to Newfoundland. . . .

a great year, 1832, for England — legislature to Newfoundland; Reform Bill; new ideas were germinating, and bringing forth fruit there. I continue reading:

> its first assembling taking place in 1833; and Parliament did not in 1834 further continue in force the law enacted in 1824, leaving to the Legislature of the Colony the task of passing laws and enforcing regulations to carry out the treaties and declarations.

So there we have the end of British legislation regarding Newfoundland. And until 1862 there was no act passed by the Legislature of Newfoundland which in any way whatever could be deemed to touch this subject, except that in 1838 they passed a law prohibiting ballast being thrown overboard in the harbor. So that during all that period Newfoundland and Labrador were free from regulation or suspicion of regulation.

Now, as to Nova Scotia: In 1770 it appears by this Memorandum and by the Appendix to the British Case that there was a law passed prohibiting the throwing of gurry overboard for three leagues from the coast of Nova Scotia — a police regulation, and of course not applicable to anybody but the citizens of Nova Scotia, by the settled principles of English law. A statute of that description, which in terms extends beyond the territory of Great Britain, applies only to the subjects of Great Britain. I will not stop to cite authorities upon it. You will find the rule referred to by, I think, several of the judges in the case of the Queen *vs.* Keyn, which has been so often cited here, in the Law Reports, 2 Exchequer Division, p. 63. It is of no particular consequence. It was a police regulation. That is all there was in Nova Scotia in 1783.

Then there was, in 1786, a law passed to amend an old act against obstructing the passage of fish in the rivers, an act which by its terms was to last but one year, and which in the preamble said that it was an act in addition to and amendment of an act made in the third year of the reign of his present Majesty George III, entitled "An Act to prevent nuisances by hedges, weirs, and other incumbrances obstructing the passage of fish in the rivers of this province."

That act undertook to remedy this interference with the run of fish up the rivers by authorizing the local justices to make regulations regarding the manner of placing nets and seines in rivers, creeks, and so on. As I say, it lasted but one year; and there is no indication or evidence whatever that any such regulations were ever made, or if they were ever made that they were applied, or if they were ever applied that they were ever applied to any American.

So, when we come down to 1818, there never had been a statute in Nova Scotia which in any way affected the exercise of the liberty granted to the United States by the treaty of 1783.

Now, as to Prince Edward Island: There were no statutes of any kind. There are none cited in the Memorandum.

Lower Canada: Covering this great stretch of the Labrador coast from the banks of the St. Lawrence (indicating on map). In 1783 there had been no statute whatever. In 1785 there was a statute which related strictly to the regulation of the rights of the people who landed and used the beach, the shore of the Bay of Chaleur; and it did also contain a ballast provision against throwing offal into the sea within two leagues of the shore — extra-territorial. Of course that was because the shore people did not want the offal to be washed up on their shore, to be driven in, where it would become offensive. I say this statute relates specifically to the people who came to use the beach, the shore, on the north shore of the Bay of Chaleur, within the Canadian limits, and does not extend itself out to sea at all, except by this ballast provision. That is all for Lower Canada.

So there was not, in 1783 or in 1818, or at any time between them, any provision in Lower Canada which in any degree regulated or affected the time and manner in which American fishermen might exercise their liberty.

There was in New Brunswick a series of statutes, that is, a statute with amendments, relating to the river and harbor of St. John, passed in 1793, a statute for the protection of river fishing, with clauses in it apparently for the protection of the harbor channels in the Bay of St. John, into which the river runs. The tides in the Bay of Fundy, the Tribunal will remember — and we are very proud of the fact — are the highest in the world; and the water rushes in and out with tremendous violence. This statute prohibited the running of nets out from the shore more than a certain distance. A careful examination of the statute will show that it relates to nets running out from the shore. They are to be not nearer together than so much, measured by a line parallel to the shore, and only so many lengths of net out from the shore. So that it is purely a river shore regulation. Nevertheless, there is a very interesting circumstance affecting this river regulation, to which I shall call attention before very long, and I will ask the Tribunal to recall the description that I have given, both of that Nova Scotia authorization for one year to magistrates to make rules for the protection of the run of fish in the rivers and this St. John River protection. The negotiators heard of the subject in the course of their negotiations, as I shall presently show.

Then there was in New Brunswick a statute containing a local regulation of the shore rights in Northumberland County, in the Bay of Miramichi, and authorizing local magistrates to make regulations. And there was in two of this series of statutes a Sunday regulation. Those laws were 1793, 1799, and 1810. I think I have fairly described them.

So the Tribunal will perceive that here, over this whole extent of coast, all of Newfoundland, east and south and west, all of Labrador, both the Newfoundland Labrador and the Canadian Labrador, all of Nova Scotia and Prince Edward Island, all of the south coast of this part of the Gulf of St. Lawrence which joins the River St. Lawrence — over all this tremendous stretch there was no regulation of the exercise of the American liberty of fishing, and there never had been any when this treaty was made in 1818. There was a river protection statute, up here in New Brunswick (indicating on map), up the bay, and there was in here, in New Brunswick (indicating on map), a Sunday regulation.

Of course, there is no evidence whatever that any American fisherman ever was subjected to that river regulation or ever was subjected to that Sunday regulation. On the contrary, the evidence is full and satisfactory the other way. In the first place, the Tribunal will remember the very able and cogent argument of Sir Robert Finlay, to the effect that the Americans did not fish in the bays at all prior to 1838. I think he brought down the absence of fishing in the bays to too late a date. He put it at 1838, in quoting Mr. Tuck; when Mr. Tuck had spoken of the time when the mackerel fishing was transferred from our coasts to the south up to the coast of the British possessions in North America, he had referred to a statute of 1828, and Sir Robert thought that that was a mistake for 1838. I do not think so. I think the beginning is marked by that statute that Mr. Tuck referred to of 1828. But there is no question whatever that back in 1818, and prior to 1818, Sir Robert's statements are perfectly correct. They practically were not fishing in the bays. What they were doing was fishing for cod-fish on the banks — all these banks running along here (indicating on map) outside the coast of Nova Scotia, along Sable Island and Banquereau, which the fishermen up there now call Quero, and up on all this series of banks clear up to the Grand Bank of Newfoundland. There was a bounty paid for cod-fish. They were cod fishermen. Herring fishery was unknown. Mackerel fishing had not moved up to these regions at all. There were plenty of mackerel down on the southern American coast below. And then their sole use for these coasts, aside from curing and drying, was to get bait for their cod-fishing, which earned them their bounty and which furnished them with their great article of food and of trade. And they would come along these coasts to the banks, and run up to the nearest point where they could get bait to go back to the cod-fishery, and they would never run up into these bays. There was nothing to take them up there. They were fishing for cod, and all along these coasts which bore any relation at all to their voyages to the banks, or any of the banks for cod-fish, there was no regulation of American fishing whatever.

We have the evidence that Sir Robert Finlay has been good enough to furnish to us here to establish that fact, and the negative evidence that out of fifty-one cases, I think, of seizures of American vessels for all causes — a few of them before 1818 — never one was in New Brunswick. There was never a seizure or a complaint or a suggestion of any regulation or of any contact between an American fisherman and the Sunday provision in New Brunswick up the bay, or over six hundred miles around from their course to the banks in Miramichi.

We have still further evidence. The Tribunal will remember that in the report of the American commissioners for the negotiation of the treaty of 1818 they give an account of the renunciation clause and its effect. Permit me to read one paragraph of their report, from p. 323 of the United States Case Appendix. They say:

> It was by *our* act that the United States *renounced* the right to the fisheries not guaranteed to them by the convention. That clause did not find a place in the British counter-projet. We deemed it proper under a threefold view: 1, to exclude the implication of the fisheries secured to us being a new grant; 2, to place the rights secured and renounced, on the same footing of permanence; 3, that it might expressly appear, that our renunciation was limited to three miles from the coasts. This last point we deemed of the more consequence from our fishermen having informed us, that the whole fishing ground on the coast of Nova Scotia, extended to a greater distance than three miles from land; whereas, along the coasts of Labrador it was almost universally close in with the shore.

That was the situation. That means all of this coast along on the way up to the fishing banks (indicating on map).

We had in 1855, the Tribunal will remember, a consideration of regulations which led to the Marcy circular. And there are some things rather interesting there, in the account of the correspondence and interviews regarding those regulations. On the 5th May, 1855, Manners Sutton, the Lieutenant-Governor of New Brunswick, wrote to the British Colonial Secretary a letter which appears at p. 204 of the British Case Appendix. Lieutenant-Governor Sutton says that the time is approaching when the United States fishermen will come into the waters of New Brunswick to take fish, and he thinks it is desirable that they should be made acquainted with the laws and regulations which existed at the time the treaty was made; and he tells in general what they are. He says, after referring to such and such provisions of the revised statutes of New Brunswick, that by a certain provision of the revised statutes the justices in sessions of each county in the province "are invested with the power to make regulations," etc. And then he says:

> I am not as yet in a position to furnish your Lordship with the particulars of all these Regulations, but I hope to be able by the next mail to send to your Lordship a complete set of all the Laws, Bye-Laws and Regulations, respecting the fisheries of this Province.
>
> It is impossible to expect that either the fishermen or even the Government of the United States should be aware of the nature of the local Regulations on this subject, even if they are cognizant of the provisions of Provincial Statutes.

Then he submits whether it is not desirable that he should receive instructions to forward to Her Majesty's minister in Washington copies of the laws and regulations. That is approved by the Colonial Office, in a letter which appears at the top of the next page, from Lord John Russell to the Lieutenant-Governor of New Brunswick; and Lord John Russell transmits, in that letter to the Lieutenant-Governor, five copies of the laws and regulations in force in the British North American provinces with reference to the fisheries. Then Mr. Manners Sutton, when he gets these five copies, writes to the British minister at Washington a letter, dated the 16th June, 1855, on the same page, 205, of the British Case Appendix, and in that he says:

> The statutory regulations are contained in one Act: ch: 101 — title 22: of the Revised Statutes of New Brunswick.
>
> The local regulations, are of two different kinds — 1stly those, which, under the provisions of the 6th secn of the Act: referred to, have been made by the Governor in Council; & 2ly those which the Justices in Session of the respective counties are empowered, by the Provincial Act — ch: 64 title 8: of the Revised Statutes to make for the govt of fisheries within the rivers of the several counties.
>
> The local regulations of the last mentioned description, altho' issued in many counties, & having the force of law were not included in the collection, published from H. M.'s Stationery Office in 1853, because, as appears from a despatch from Sir E. Head to the Duke of Newcastle, which is printed in page 37 of that paper, — of which yr Ex no doubt has a copy, — these regulations were at the time considered to be immaterial, inasmuch as they do not affect the outside fisheries.

Then he goes on to say he thinks that they ought to be included and made known. This paper, which he sent on, is what Lord John Russell sent him from the Colonial Office. So the Tribunal will perceive that if these magistrates made any local regulations, they were of such a character that they did not affect outside fishermen, and they were not printed, so that anybody could ever know what they were. They were not included in the printed copy of laws relating to fishing.

Still further: Mr. Crampton, the British minister at Washington, transmits the laws which Mr. Manners Sutton had —

JUDGE GRAY: Pardon me, Mr. Root. Do I understand, in the middle of the next to the last paragraph of that letter from which you read on p. 205 of the British Appendix, that the language

> these regulations were at the time considered to be immaterial, inasmuch as they do not affect the outside fisheries

referred to the bank fisheries?

SENATOR ROOT: I should suppose not. I should suppose that they did not affect any fisheries except those of the inhabitants; the fishery as carried on from the shore.

JUDGE GRAY: They do not affect the outside fisheries?

SENATOR ROOT: They do not affect the fisheries by outsiders.

JUDGE GRAY: That is just what I wanted to get at — what the meaning of it was: as to whether it was fisheries by outsiders, or fisheries that were outside of these waters.

SENATOR ROOT: That is what I suppose to be the reason. At all events, the point is that they were not published; they were not included in the publications of the fishery laws relating to the provinces, and the reason is that they did not affect the outside fisheries. Whether that means the bank fisheries, or whether it means the fisheries by outsiders, I do not know. I should think that the latter would be the more complete reason for not publishing them.

SIR CHARLES FITZPATRICK: It means they are not published from Her Majesty's Stationery Office, I think; that is all that is contained in this letter.

SENATOR ROOT: That is where he sent to get them.

SIR CHARLES FITZPATRICK: Yes. Her Majesty's Stationery Office, of course, is in England. Local regulations are not usually published.

THE PRESIDENT: Perhaps "outside fisheries" is used in contradistinction to river fisheries. The following sentence leads me to that supposition:

> But your Excellency will observe that they do, in some instances at least, affect the fisheries in the harbors of this province, which are now thrown open to the fishermen of the United States as well as the river fisheries, which are reserved to Her Majesty's subjects.

SENATOR ROOT: Yes, I think that does have a bearing upon it; that is, that they did, in some respects, protecting the rivers, run the provisions into the harbors.

THE PRESIDENT: At first he considers them as not important because principally they had referred only to river fisheries; but in some respects they might also affect the harbor fisheries, and therefore he considers them also, now, as material. That seems to be the meaning.

SIR CHARLES FITZPATRICK: The very first paragraph makes the distinction: "the outside fisheries" and "the fisheries in the harbors."

SENATOR ROOT: Well, he sent the statutes to the British minister at Washington, who sent them to Mr. Marcy, and Mr. Marcy examined them and approved them. And what were they? There is only one that can be deemed to be a reënactment or representative in these revised statutes of any of these laws prior to 1818. There is no Sunday provision. At the foot of p. 207 of the British Case Appendix, the Tribunal will find them attached to Mr. Marcy's first circular. There is a gurry ground provision; there is a spawning ground provision on the Grand Menan; and there is a provision relating to river protection in certain parishes of New Brunswick.

That is all down to 1855. That is, all the provisions which were deemed worthy to be brought to the attention of the government of the United States as bearing upon the exercise of the liberty granted by the treaty of 1854 on those coasts: two provisions passed after 1818; and the one which we find a trace of before 1818, and which I dare say came down in the revised statutes, was a provision for river protection.

THE PRESIDENT: Is not that No. 15 for the establishment of a close season? "No herring shall be taken between the 15th of July and the 15th of October in any year."

SENATOR ROOT: On the spawning grounds.

THE PRESIDENT: Yes. It was a close season.

SENATOR ROOT: Yes, on the spawning grounds. And it was approved, and properly approved, by Mr. Marcy when presented to him. And the Tribunal will observe it was presented to him with this understanding, which appears in Mr. Crampton's letter of 27th June, 1853, to Mr. Manners Sutton, which will be found on pp. 205 and 206 of the British Case Appendix. The Tribunal will observe in that letter, at the top of p. 206 of the British Case Appendix, that Mr. Crampton says:

Mr. Marcy entirely concurs with me in the opinion that such a measure would be calculated to prevent the occurrence of any misunderstanding on the part of American fishermen, who may now resort to New Brunswick for the purpose of exercising their newly acquired rights under the Treaty of Reciprocity, and proposes that, after the documents — with which Your Excellency is about to furnish me — shall have been examined by him, and shall have been found, as he doubts not will be the case, *to contain no provisions inconsistent with the full enjoyment of the American citizens of the rights of fishing* secured them by the Treaty, and to direct the "Collectors of the United States Customs" to furnish copies of the same to the masters of all the vessels clearing from American ports to the British fisheries.

That is the proposition on which these laws were presented to Mr. Marcy for his consideration and approval: the proposition that their provisions were not inconsistent with the full enjoyment of the American citizens' rights of fishing secured to them by the treaty. And, indeed, a provision might well be approved which prevented the throwing of gurry overboard except at a particular place, and which protected the spawning ground, and which protected the rivers of New Brunswick in which we had no right to fish.

But the paucity of regulation twenty-seven years after the treaty of 1818 was made is what I call the attention of the Tribunal to now, as tending to support the statements which I have made regarding the existence of any system of regulation in 1818 or at any time prior to that time.

One other thing is to be observed. Mr. Crampton, in his letter of June, 1855, which appears on p. 206 of the British Case Appendix, says:

I have thought it right to bring this matter under the immediate attention of the Governor-General of Canada, and the Lieutenant-Governors of Nova Scotia and Prince Edward Island, with a view to the adoption of a similar arrangement in regard to the fisheries of those provinces, to that now proposed, in regard to the fisheries of New Brunswick; — I have the honor to enclose herewith the copy of a letter which I have addressed to their Excellencies for that purpose.

Then follows the letter of the 28th June, 1855, on pp. 206 and 207 of the British Case Appendix, from Mr. Crampton to all these governors; but that produced no regulations whatever.

So that down to 1855, in all this stretch of coast of Nova Scotia, Prince Edward Island, Newfoundland, Labrador, and Lower Canada, there were no regulations whatever that were worthy to be brought to the attention of the American fishermen, who were about to resume fishing upon all that coast under the provisions of the treaty of 1854. And you come down to a clear case of no regulation which could by any possibility affect the exercise by American fishermen of their liberty under the treaty of 1783, — evidence affirmatively establishing that fact — although it was unnecessary to affirmatively establish it, because there has been no evidence produced whatever that any regulation was brought into contact in any way whatever with any American fisherman exercising his liberty.

But we are not left entirely to the absence of regulation. There is affirmative evidence, perfectly clear evidence, that the negotiators did have regulations in mind. What they had in mind were not regulations which were determined upon by Great Britain, or any of its colonies, in the exercise of its sole judgment; but they were regulations established by the concurrence, the accord of the judgment both of Great Britain and the United States regarding the exercise of the common liberty.

I will ask the attention of the Tribunal again to a letter which I have so often referred to, and shall again, the letter from Lord Bathurst to Mr. Adams of the 30th October, 1815, in the United States Case Appendix, p. 278. I begin at the last paragraph on p. 277. Mr. Adams and Lord Bathurst had been arguing out the question, the Tribunal will remember, as to whether the liberty granted in 1783 survived the War of 1812, and had been stating their reasons; and in this letter Lord Bathurst had stated his ground for insisting that the liberty fell with the war. Then he goes on:

Although His Majesty's Government cannot admit that the claim of the American fishermen to fish within British jurisdiction, *and* to use the British territory for purposes connected with their fishery, is analogous to the indulgence which has been granted to enemy's subjects engaged in fishing on the high seas, for the purpose of conveying fresh fish to market, yet they do feel that the enjoyment of the liberties, formerly used by the inhabitants of the United States, may be very conducive to their national and individual prosperity, though they should be placed under some modifications, and this feeling operates most forcibly in favor of concession. But Great Britain can only offer the concession in a way which shall effectually protect her own subjects from such obstructions to their lawful enterprises as they too frequently experienced immediately previous to the late war, and which are, from their very nature, calculated to produce collision and disunion between the two states.

It was not of fair competition that His Majesty's Government had reason to complain, but of the preoccupation of British harbors and creeks, in North America, by the fishing vessels of the United States, and the forcible exclusion of British vessels from places where the fishery might be most advantageously conducted. They had, likewise, reason to complain of the clandestine introduction of prohibited goods into the British colonies by American vessels ostensibly engaged in the fishing trade, to the great injury of the British revenue.

The undersigned has felt it encumbent on him thus generally to notice these obstructions, in the hope that the attention of the Government of the United States will be directed to the subject; and that they may be induced, amicably and cordially, to co-operate with His Majesty's Government in devising such regulations as shall prevent the recurrence of similar inconveniences.

His Majesty's Government are willing to enter into negotiations with the Government of the United States for the modified renewal of the liberties in question.

The Tribunal will perceive that Lord Bathurst there, while denying the right of the United States to claim a continuance of the liberties granted in 1783, and notwithstanding the war, was willing to continue those liberties, regrant them, provided the United States " would co-operate with His Majesty's Government in devising such regulations as shall prevent the recurrence of inconveniences similar to those " which he has recounted. That is joint regulation. That is not bringing to bear upon the exercise of the liberties of the Americans the sole and uncontrolled judgment of Great Britain. It is a distinct proposal, in the letter that formed the basis and corner stone of the negotiations of 1818, that this renewal should be on the basis of joint regulation.

Mr. Adams, on p. 286 of the United States Case Appendix, in his reply to Lord Bathurst, closes his letter with an acceptance, as full as a minister dealing with a new proposition, without having had time to consult with his Government, could well make it, of this proposal for joint regulation. I read the last paragraph on p. 286 of the United States Case Appendix, where Mr. Adams says:

> The collision of particular interests which heretofore may have produced altercations between the fishermen of the two nations, and the clandestine introduction of prohibited goods by means of American fishing vessels, may be obviated by arrangements duly concerted between the two Governments. That of the United States, he is persuaded, will readily co-operate in any measure to secure those ends compatible with the enjoyment by the people of the United States of the liberties to which they consider their title as unimpaired, inasmuch as it has never been renounced by themselves.

Mr. Adams reported this correspondence to Washington, and thereupon Mr. Monroe, who was then Secretary of State, replied, acknowledging the receipt of the correspondence, in a letter dated the 27th February, 1816, which appears on p. 287 of the United States Case Appendix. Mr. Monroe says:

It appears by these communications that, although the British Government denies our right of taking, curing, and drying fish within their jurisdiction, and on the coast of the British provinces in North America, it is willing to secure to our citizens the liberty stipulated by the treaty of 1783, under such regulations as will secure the benefit to both parties, and will likewise prevent the smuggling of goods into the British provinces by our vessels engaged in the fisheries.

Then he goes on to say that he encloses a power authorizing Mr. Adams to negotiate a convention providing for the objects contemplated.

And on p. 288 of the United States Case Appendix, the very next page, the Tribunal will find a power from Mr. Monroe to Mr. Adams, dated the 27th February, 1816, the same day as the letter which I have just read:

Sir: It being represented, by your letter of the 8th of November, that the British Government was disposed to regulate, in concert with the United States, the taking of fish on the coasts, bays, and creeks of all His Britannic Majesty's dominions in America, and the curing and drying of fish by their citizens on the unsettled bays, harbors, and creeks of Nova Scotia, Magdalen islands, and Labrador, in such manner as to promote the interest of both nations, you will consider this letter an authority and instruction to negotiate a convention for these purposes.

The negotiation went on with a long period of offer and refusal and new offers, and give-and-take bargaining regarding the extent of territory, until finally it brought up with these negotiators at London making the treaty of 1818, and with these letters in their hands — both parties; and there the British negotiators proposed express joint regulations. In the articles presented by the British negotiators at the fifth conference, appearing at p. 312 of the United States Case Appendix, the Tribunal will see that they proposed express joint regulations to govern the protection of rivers — the very subject on which this power of local regulations had been given to the local magistrates, and to which this New Brunswick statute about the River St. John referred, and to which the revised statutes of New Brunswick referred.

They do not depend upon any power of Great Britain or of any British colony to pass laws which shall carry river protection into the bays or harbors to which the Americans may come. They do not rely upon any power of any British legislative body to draw the line between the river and the bay, to draw the line where they may go with their protection of their exclusive river fishing, or to say that for common benefit the exercise of the American liberty shall be limited and restricted thus and so; but following the proposal that was in Lord Bathurst's letter that formed the basis for the negotiations accepted by Mr. Adams and ratified by the formal action of the American Government, they proceed to propose a joint regulation upon that question. They further propose a joint regulation with regard to smuggling — very stringent in its character.

JUDGE GRAY: I was looking for the joint regulation to which you are referring — the proposal for joint regulation.

SENATOR ROOT: The one to which I have been referring?

JUDGE GRAY: Yes.

SENATOR ROOT: That is on p. 312, in Article A, the second paragraph of Article A, the article as proposed by the British negotiators.

THE PRESIDENT (reading):

> And it is further agreed that nothing contained in this article —

SIR CHARLES FITZPATRICK: The last part of it: "And it is agreed on the part of the United States that the fishermen of the United States," etc.

THE PRESIDENT: Yes.

> and it is agreed on the part of the fishermen of the United States resorting to the mouth of such rivers . . . shall not obstruct the navigation thereof. . . .

SIR CHARLES FITZPATRICK (reading):

> nor willfully injure nor destroy the fish within the same, etc.

THE PRESIDENT: Is that a joint regulation?

JUDGE GRAY: Yes; in the treaty itself.

SENATOR ROOT: Yes.

JUDGE GRAY: It is a provision in the treaty itself for a regulation.

SENATOR ROOT: Yes; it is putting a regulation into the treaty.

SIR CHARLES FITZPATRICK: It is putting an obligation on the United States to impose certain restrictions on its citizens. That is what it is.

SENATOR ROOT: Putting an obligation on the United States to impose certain restrictions?

SIR CHARLES FITZPATRICK: Yes; putting an obligation on its own citizens. That is what it is.

SENATOR ROOT: Yes, I quite agree to that proposition.

JUDGE GRAY: That is a regulation.

SIR CHARLES FITZPATRICK: Yes.

SENATOR ROOT: Then in the last paragraph of this Article A, on p. 313 of the United States Case Appendix, is another regulation:

> And in order the more effectually to guard against smuggling, it shall not be lawful for the vessels of the United States engaged in the said fishery to have on board any goods, wares, or merchandise whatever, except such as may be necessary for the prosecution of the fishery, or the support of the fishermen whilst engaged therein or in the prosecution of their voyages to and from the said fishing grounds. And any vessel of the United States which shall contravene this regulation may be seized, condemned, and confiscated, together with her cargo.

That is putting the enforcement directly into the hands, I suppose, of the —

SIR CHARLES FITZPATRICK: That is a customs regulation.

SENATOR ROOT: Yes.

SIR CHARLES FITZPATRICK: That is a customs regulation, not a fishery regulation.

JUDGE GRAY: It regulates fishing vessels.

SENATOR ROOT: It regulates fishing vessels and subjects fishing vessels to the supervision and judgment of local officers; for of course somebody has to determine whether the "goods, wares, or merchandise on board of the fishing vessel" are necessary for the transaction of their fishery or the support of the fishermen. Somebody has to say that; and this regulation, I apprehend, was objected to because it put the decision of that question in the hands of the local officer, who, if he did not feel very kindly toward foreigners that were coming there to take his neighbors' fish away, would be apt to find that they had things on board which they did not need, just as in Canada there was for a time applied the rule that a vessel under the renunciatory clause could not go to the non-treaty coast for shelter, wood, and water, unless she was actually in distress, and unless she brought wood and water with her sufficient for her voyage, and had been unexpectedly deprived of her store; that is to say, they held that a vessel could not come up to the coast with an insufficient supply of wood or water and rely upon getting it there. It had got to be a case of real distress, arising without premeditation, in order to justify it. Of course that did not last for many years. I think that was disposed of by the opinion of the law officers of the Crown in 1839.

These two were rejected by the United States, and the ground of the objection is stated at p. 314 of the United States Case Appendix, in a formal memorandum given by the United States commissioners to the British commissioners. I read from the second paragraph on p. 314. The American commissioners say, regarding these proposals:

The liberty of taking fish within rivers is not asked. A positive clause to except them is unnecessary, unless it be intended to comprehend under that name waters which might otherwise be considered as bays or creeks. Whatever extent of fishing ground may be secured to American fishermen, the American plenipotentiaries are not prepared to accept it on a tenure or on conditions different from those on which the whole has heretofore been held. Their instructions did not anticipate that any new terms or restrictions would be annexed, as none were suggested in the proposals made by Mr. Bagot to the American Government. The clauses forbidding the spreading of nets, and making vessels liable to confiscation in case any articles not wanted for carrying on the fishery should be found on board, are of that description, and would expose the fishermen to endless vexations.

And that was assented to by the British commissioners upon the ground not that there was a right of legislation to cover these points, but upon the ground that it was not important. The letter from the British negotiators, or from Mr. Robinson for the British negotiators, of the 10th October, 1818, appears in the British Case Appendix at p. 92. Mr. Robinson writes Viscount Castlereagh, and says:

I then proceeded to state to them that upon the fishery article, we were not disposed to insist upon the exclusion of those points, the introduction of which they had at our last conference represented to be a *sine qua non;* and after some discussion it was also agreed on our part not to insist upon the two provisions contained in our proposed article respecting the fishing in rivers and smuggling, to which they felt very considerable objections, and which did not appear to me to be of such importance as to require to be urged in a way that might prevent an arrangement upon the fisheries taking place.

Now, the reason why these provisions were unimportant, the reason why they did not go to work to redraft them and put them in such shape that they would be unobjectionable as joint regulations, appears in the correspondence which had taken place during this period of bargaining as to the extent of the new grant. Remember that Lord Bathurst's language, in his letter which I first quoted upon this subject, appeared to contemplate a renewal of the entire liberty of 1783. It appeared to, although not binding him specifically, and it was evidently so understood by Mr. Adams and by Mr. Monroe. But when they came to get down to details, the British negotiators cut down the grant, and if they ever did have such generous intention as would appear to have been contemplated by Lord Bathurst, they abandoned it; for the first step in that process of bargaining that I have referred to, intermediate the arrangement for joint regulation and the actual making of the treaty, was by Mr. Bagot, in Washington. to Mr. Monroe, on the 27th November, 1816, (in the United States Case Appendix, p. 289).

He begins the bartering by an offer of the coast of Labrador alone, and he begins by saying to Mr. Monroe:

In the conversation which I had with you a few days ago, upon the subject of the negotiation into which the British Government is willing to enter, for the purpose of affording to the citizens of the United States such accommodation for their fishery, within the British jurisdiction, as may be *consistent with the proper administration* of His Majesty's dominions you appeared to apprehend that neither of the propositions which I had had the honor to make to you upon this subject would be considered as affording in a sufficient degree the advantages which were deemed requisite.

I ask you to observe that phrase —

such accommodation . . . as may be consistent with the proper administration of His Majesty's dominions.

And you will see, as we go on with this correspondence, that what dwelt in the minds of the British negotiators was that it was not consistent with proper administration and control on the part of His Majesty's Government to have the United States granted access to these coasts. It was an interference with due administration; and so they proposed to shove them off to the coast of Labrador, where there was not anybody but cod-fish and whales and icebergs — or this little strip of the south coast of Newfoundland.

Over on the next page, 290, Mr. Bagot goes on to say:

It is not necessary for me to advert to the discussion which has taken place between Earl Bathurst and Mr. Adams. In the correspondence was a full exposition of the grounds upon which the liberty of drying and fishing within the British limits, as granted to the citizens of the United States by the treaty of 1783, was considered to have ceased with the war, and not to have been revived by the late treaty of peace.

You will also have seen therein detailed the serious considerations affecting not only the prosperity of the British fishery, but the general interests of the British dominions, in matters of revenue as well as government, which made it incumbent upon His Majesty's Government to oppose the renewal of so extensive and injurious a concession, within the British sovereignty, to a foreign state, founded upon no principle of reciprocity or adequate compensation whatever.

Then, towards the foot of that page, he refers to his offer of the coast of Labrador; and then he refers to an alternative offer that he had made of the south coast of Newfoundland from Cape Ray to Ramea Islands — this same one which is now included in the treaty, as an alternative to the Labrador coast — either one or the other. And he goes on to say in the last paragraph of this letter:

The advantages of this portion of coast are accurately known to the British Government; and, in consenting to assign it to the uses of the American fishermen, it was certainly conceived that an accommodation was afforded as ample as it was possible to concede, *without abandoning that control within the entire of His Majesty's own harbors and coasts which the essential interests of His Majesty's dominions required.*

You will see there carried on the idea that the admission of Americans was an interference with administration and an abandonment of control. For that reason they wanted to shove them off to these unfrequented and practically unsettled coasts.

Mr. Monroe declined each of these offers, and Mr. Bagot came back with a letter on the 31st December, 1816, in which he offered both of these stretches which he had formerly offered in the alternative. The letter is on p. 292 of the United States Case Appendix, and in it he says:

The object of His Majesty's Government, in framing these propositions, was to endeavor to assign to the American fishermen, in the prosecution of their employment, as large a participation of the conveniences afforded by the neighboring coasts of His Majesty's settlements as might be reconcilable with the just rights and interests of His Majesty's own subjects, and the due administration of His Majesty's dominions.

Mr. Monroe declined that proposition, and when the negotiators came together (the negotiations having been kept open by expressions of good intentions of both parties) the American negotiators presented a third proposition, which is the one now in the treaty, which took in both the Labrador coast and the south coast of Newfoundland, that had been offered, first, alternatively, and, second, collectively; and also the west coast of Newfoundland. They presented that on the 17th September, 1818, and on that same day Messrs. Robinson and Goulburn, the British negotiators, reported to their Government the reasons given by the Americans for the action which they took; and that appears at p. 86 of the British Case Appendix. I shall be very glad to have your honor's attention to that letter. This is the letter, not dated, except September, but which I have already observed, is located as of the 17th by reference to the protocols of that day. Reading about one-third down, the third paragraph on p. 86, the writers say:

With respect to the fisheries they observed —

that is, the American commissioners observed —

that in consideration of the different opinions known to be entertained by the Governments of the two countries, as to the right of the United States to a participation in the fisheries within the British jurisdiction, and to the use for those purposes of British territory, they had been induced to forego a statement of their views of this right in the article which they had proposed; but they desired to be understood, as in no degree abandoning the ground upon which the right to the fishery had been claimed by the Government of the United States, and only waiving discussion of it, upon the principle that that right was not to be limited in any way, which should exclude the United States from a fair participation in the advantages of the fishery: They added that while they could not but regard the propositions made to the Government of the United States by Mr. Bagot as altogether inadmissible, inasmuch as they restricted the American fishing to a line of coast so limited as to exclude them from this fair participation, they had nevertheless been anxious in securing to themselves an adequate extent of coast, to guard against the inconveniences which they understood to constitute the leading objection to the unlimited exercise of their fishing. With this view they had contented themselves with requiring a further extent of coast in those very quarters which Great Britain had pointed out, because it appeared to them that the very small population established in that quarter, and the unfitness of the soil for cultivation, rendered it improbable that any conduct of the American fishermen in that quarter could either give rise to disputes with the inhabitants, or to injuries to the revenue.

So you will see that the proposal for joint regulation, made and accepted, under which these joint regulations were proposed to be put into the treaty, was laid aside in favor of a plan which involved pushing the United States right off on to a wild and uninhabited coast, where it was not necessary to have any regulations; where there could not be any collisions, for there was nobody to collide with; where there could not be any smuggling, for there was nobody there to smuggle to, as indeed all these coasts were uninhabited in the year 1818; and where, the soil being unfit for cultivation, there was no probability that in the future there would be any such population as to make it necessary for the negotiators at that time, in 1818, to bother their heads about joint regulations.

THE ATTORNEY-GENERAL: May I detain the Tribunal for one moment ? I should like to draw attention to one point raised by Mr.Root. I think I should do it at once, instead of waiting until the end of his speech and then asking permission to lay it before the Tribunal.

Mr. Root thought I had been mistaken in saying that the opinion expressed by the law officers of Newfoundland in 1854, I think, as to the absence of local regulation at that time, was a correct opinion; and he pointed out that the earlier legislation of Newfoundland had already been consolidated and repealed, reënacted as to part, in a statute of 1824, which was a five-year statute, continued until 1829, continued again until 1832, and then dropped.

Now, Mr. Root argued that —

SIR CHARLES FITZPATRICK: It was continued until 1834, and then dropped.

THE ATTORNEY-GENERAL: Continued until 1834 and then dropped. Yes.

Mr. Root argued that the repeal was permanent, although the statute itself was temporary; and that, therefore, when the statute expired there was no regulation. It is a matter of English law, which the Tribunal will find in *Maxwell on Statutes*, under the heading of " Repeals ", that if a statute repealed an antecedent statute at that stage in our history — it is not so now — and the repealing statute itself determined or was repealed, all the statutes that it had repealed revived. So that when the statute of 1824 expired, all the repealed statutes therein contained revived. Otherwise Newfoundland would have been left without regulation at all.

SIR CHARLES FITZPATRICK: Without legislation at all — without anything ?

THE ATTORNEY-GENERAL: Without legislation, yes. But, in fact, of course, all these statutes continued, and the law officers of Newfoundland were all right when they said there were no local regulations; because there had been no local regulations since 1834. But the whole of the antecedent imperial legislation continued and was in full force.

I hope Mr. Root will forgive me for making this statement at this time. I did not wish to interrupt him while he was speaking, and I thought I had better mention it now, so that if he wishes to deal with it at a later period in his argument he will have an opportunity to do so.[1]

THE PRESIDENT: Will you please to continue, Mr. Senator Root ?[2]

[1] Thereupon, at 12.15 o'clock P.M., the Tribunal took a recess until 2.15 o'clock P.M.

[2] Afternoon session, Monday, August 8, 1910, 2.15 P.M.

Senator Root: Regarding the subject of which the Attorney-General spoke just at the time of adjournment, my remarks were addressed solely to the question of the continuance of the statute of 1824, and the question as to whether the expiration of that statute in the year 1834 resulted in reviving the statutes which it had repealed, was one that I did not address myself to, and it does not seem to be a matter of any particular consequence upon the issues in this case, because those statutes contained no regulation of fisheries in Newfoundland. The situation as it existed when the Act of 1824 was passed was that there were no regulations in respect of the time and manner of taking fish in Newfoundland.

It may be an interesting question, although not material to this controversy, as to whether the limitation of the statute applies to the repeal; the statute of 1824 is an act to repeal several laws relating to the fisheries carried on upon the banks and shores of Newfoundland, and to make provision for the better conduct of the said fisheries for five years. That is the title. It recites:

> Whereas it is expedient to repeal and amend divers statutes and laws relating to the fisheries,

and so on. Now, whether the limitation of time would operate as a limitation upon that apparently executed provision of the statute so as to revive the others, may be an interesting question, but as I say, not especially material to this controversy.

It is evident that in Newfoundland they did not consider that anything had been revived, for the letter of the governor of Newfoundland to the Colonial Office, which appears on p. 250 of the United States Counter-Case Appendix under date the 29th September, 1855, says:

> I have the honor to transmit herewith a copy of the Report from the Law Officers of the Crown, which has been furnished in fulfilment of the

instructions conveyed by your despatch of the 3d ulto., No. 6, and which I shall take care to communicate to the British Minister at Washington, with whom I have already been in correspondence on the subject to which it relates.

2. You will perceive by this Report, which is entirely accordant with that of the late Attorney-General, Mr. Archibald, dated July 5th, 1853, copy of which was transmitted with my predecessor's despatch, No. 46, July 12th, 1853, that there are in fact no Laws or Regulations whatever relating to the Fisheries practically in force in this Colony.

THE PRESIDENT: The attorney-general in the enclosed letter says:

apart from the common law of England, which is in operation here . . . there are no special enactments of the Local Legislature in operation here for the regulation of the fisheries.

SIR CHARLES FITZPATRICK: What would be the common law of England under these circumstances?

SENATOR ROOT: I should not like to answer that question.

SIR CHARLES FITZPATRICK: Would the statutes in force at the time in England, applicable to Newfoundland, be part of the common law of England at that time?

SENATOR ROOT: I do not know what he meant, but it is evident what the governor thought he meant.

THE PRESIDENT: And what would be the consequence of the repealing, by the Act of 1824, of the part of statute of 1775, by which it was enacted that fishermen on the Newfoundland banks, or, perhaps, on the Newfoundland shores, are not liable to restraint concerning the hours and days of working?

SENATOR ROOT: I do not suppose that would impose a restraint.

THE PRESIDENT: Would it impose a restraint, because the repealing act had been repealed? That is a very complicated question.

SENATOR ROOT: It is evident it was not considered there was any practical restriction, and that is all we really have to do with.

If the expiration of the Act of 1824 wiped out the repeal, it reinstated that provision, and there were no restrictions to be reinstated.

Now I wish to ask your attention to the express provisions regarding restriction which the negotiators did put into the treaty of 1818.

When they came to deal with the rights granted by the first article of the treaty, there were three. There was the fishing right, there was the drying and curing right on shore, and there was the right to enter the bays and harbors of that part of the coast to which the renunciation applied, for shelter, repairs, wood, and water; and upon that one of the three rights granted relating to the shore, they imposed an express restriction. That " so soon as the same [that is bays, harbors, and creeks on the southern part of the coast] or any portion thereof, shall be settled, it shall not be lawful for the said fishermen to dry or cure fish at such portion so settled without previous agreement for such purpose with the inhabitants, proprietors, or possessors of the ground." And they did that in face of the fact that in the letter of Mr. Adams, which is a part of the correspondence forming the basis of the negotiation and in the hands of the negotiators for both countries, there had been a discussion of that restriction as it stood in the treaty of 1783, and a declaration by Mr. Adams that the inclusion of that express restriction under the doctrine *expressio unius est exclusio alterius* was an exclusion of any implied restriction.

On p. 283 of the United States Case Appendix, in Mr. Adams's letter of the 22d January, 1816, to Lord Castlereagh, at the foot of the page, is the observation to which I have referred. Mr. Adams says:

Among them [that is among the benefits coming to the inhabitants of the United States] was the liberty of drying and curing fish on the shores, then uninhabited, adjoining certain bays, harbors, and creeks. But, when those shores should become settled, and thereby become private and individual property, it was obvious that the liberty of drying and curing fish upon them must be conciliated with the proprietary rights of the owners of the soil. The same restriction would apply to British fishermen; and it was precisely because no grant of a new right was intended, but merely the continuance of what had been previously enjoyed, that the restriction must have been assented to on the part of the United States. But, upon the common and equitable rule of construction for treaties, the expression of one restriction implies the exclusion of all others not expressed; and thus the very limitation which looks forward to the time when the unsettled deserts should become inhabited, to modify the enjoyment of the same liberty conformably to the change of circumstances, corroborates the conclusion that the whole purport of the compact was permanent and not temporary — not experimental, but definitive.

Now, I say, in that letter, which was one of the series of letters forming the basis of this negotiation and in the hands of the negotiators upon both sides, there was the argument with respect to the expression of that restriction, that it excluded any possible implication of other restrictions, however circumstances might change, and, in the face of that, the negotiators included in their treaty that express restriction without any saving as against the application of the doctrine *expressio unius*.

THE PRESIDENT: Could it not be said, Mr. Root, that for this reservation there was quite a special reason and a special necessity in the word "forever", because if this reservation had not been made, then the use of the shore for drying purposes would also be a permanent use without any regard to its becoming inhabited on the shores?

SENATOR ROOT: Yes, Mr. President, that may be said. That furnishes a reason for putting in the express restriction, but emphasizes the inference inevitably to be drawn from the fact that in the face of the argument which Mr. Adams had used as to the well-known implication that from the expression of one restriction, the absence of power to impose any others has to be drawn. In the face of that they did put it in.

However good the reason may have been, doubtless there was a reason, evidently there was a reason, but the fact that there was a reason does not interfere at all with the inference we are bound to draw from the fact that with fair notice that that rule would be applied to them, was being applied to them, they chose to put it in without any saving clause to negative the application of the rule.

THE PRESIDENT: This reservation was to express that the right to fish was a permanent right, and that the right to dry and cure was not a permanent right, but depended upon the circumstance whether the shore remained unsettled, as at that time it was, or became afterwards settled.

SENATOR ROOT: Precisely. There was a good reason for putting it in, and there was not, manifestly, in the minds of the negotiators, any occasion for negativing the inference that would be drawn from the fact that they did put one restriction in.

Then they proceed in dealing with the third branch of the treaty right, that which relates to the entrance of the American fishermen into bays or harbors on what we call the non-treaty coast, although one of my friends on the other side has justly remarked it was all treaty coast, for the purpose of shelter and repairing damage, purchasing wood and obtaining water, to impose there an express reservation of the power of restriction:

> They shall be under such restriction as may be necessary to prevent their taking, drying, or curing fish therein or in any other manner whatever abusing the privileges hereby reserved to them.

That is an express reservation of the power of future restriction by regulation limited to the specific purposes that are designated here.

So these negotiators did not merely refrain from imposing upon the grant of right to have the inhabitants of the United

States enter this territory, and exercise the liberty of taking fish, those restrictions which they themselves put upon the ordinary rights of trade and travel and residence in the treaty which they reproduced in the fourth article of this convention of 1818 — they did not merely refrain from attaching to this grant the reservation of the right of municipal legislation which they attached to that grant, but as to the two of the three branches of the rights they granted, they dealt with the subject of restriction. As to one they included an express restriction; as to the other they included an express reservation of the power of future restriction, limited to a specific purpose.

Now, what must be the inference ? Why is it — I put the question with great earnestness to your honors — why is it that these negotiators treated the two different kinds of rights, the kind of right which was described in the treaty of 1815 that they reproduce in Article 4, and the kind of right which was the subject of this specific grant, so differently ?

Let me answer first, narrowly, out of the mouths of the men who were concerned in the transaction, and then I will answer broadly according to my general view of the underlying basis of the different treatment.

First, the narrow answer, from the report of Mr. Gallatin, British Case Appendix, p. 97. He is reporting to Mr. Adams, his secretary of state at home, the reason why Great Britain was unwilling to continue the broad grant of 1783, and insisting upon the narrow limitations which were finally imposed upon the extent to which the renewal of the grant should apply. And he says, just below the middle of p. 97:

> That right of taking and drying fish in harbors within the exclusive jurisdiction of Great Britain, particularly on coasts now inhabited, was extremely obnoxious to her, and was considered as what the French civilians call a servitude.

It is appropriate to consider here what it was that the French civilians called a "servitude" and I refer you to the

Code Civil of France of 1804, that had been in force for fourteen years before the making of the treaty of 1818. That code, in Article 637, says:

A servitude is a burden imposed upon an estate for the use and utility of an estate belonging to another owner.

Article 686:

It is permitted to owners to establish on their property or in favor of their property such servitudes as appear to them proper, provided, nevertheless, that the use established shall not be imposed either upon a person nor in favor of a person, but only upon an estate, and for an estate, and provided that these burdens shall moreover contain nothing contrary to public order. The use and extent of the servitudes thus established are regulated by the grant which constitutes them. In default of such provision by the following rules.

And, among those rules, Article 697:

He to whom a servitude is granted has the right of doing everything necessary to make use of it and preserve it.

Article 701:

The owner of the servient domain can do nothing which tends to diminish the use of it or render its use more inconvenient.

Now, that is what we may reasonably assume was what the French civilians called a servitude. And that, according to the report of Mr. Gallatin, is what the British negotiators considered this right to be, and because they considered it to be that, it was obnoxious, and they were unwilling to continue it upon coasts, especially upon coasts that were inhabited. That is the meaning of these letters from Mr. Bagot, in which he explains that Great Britain is unwilling to give a wider extent of fishing rights, to give an extent of fishing right anywhere but upon these wild and unfrequented coasts, because it would interfere with the due administration of His Majesty's Government, and the control which His Majesty exercised over his own territory.

This report is produced and printed by Great Britain. It is a statement by Mr. Gallatin, whose eminence, whose penetrating intelligence, and whose historical position make it impossible to doubt for a moment the genuineness and the veracity of the statement. And by what is it met ?

Where are the reports of the negotiators of Great Britain which might meet it, which might explain it ? I do not complain of their absence. Great Britain is not obliged to produce any papers. She produces what she pleases, and she is under no obligation to furnish evidence unless it helps her case; but I should be unwilling to have this case close, and leave the counsel of the United States open to the imputation hereafter if these reports should ever appear, should ever become public, and they should appear to have matter in them relevant and important to the determination of this case, that counsel of the United States had overlooked the fact that there were probably such reports, and that they had not been produced, or that we had neglected to say to the court that we must insist upon having the inferences drawn which are natural to be drawn when evidence within the control of a party which might lead to one result or another is not produced.

It appears with great circumstantiality that there must have been reports, for on the 17th September, 1818, we have printed in the British Case Appendix a formal report of the British negotiators to Lord Castlereagh at the head of the Foreign Office (p. 86, British Case Appendix):

MY LORD,

We have the honor to report to your Lordship, that we had yesterday agreeably to appointment a further conference with the commissioners of the United States.

And then it proceeds to give in great detail what happened at the conference. And on the 10th October there was a letter from Mr. Robinson, one of the negotiators, to Viscount

Castlereagh, which appears on p. 92 of the British Case Appendix, an extract, in which he states what had happened in the conference of the 6th October, and a postscript at the foot in which he says:

> Although from Mr. Goulburn's absence I am not yet enabled to send to your Lordship a detailed account of what passed at our preceding conference (the fifth) on the 6th of October, I think it right to enclose for your information, copies of four articles which we then produced as *contre-projets* to articles upon similar points, previously submitted by the American plenipotentiaries.

After the 6th October, to which this informal letter of Mr. Robinson applies, there is a blank.

Of course the British plenipotentiaries went on with their reports. Whatever light their reports would have thrown upon these negotiations, whatever light they would have thrown upon the way the words " in common " came in, the reasons why they came in, whatever light they would have thrown upon the views of the negotiators as to the character of the right that was being granted, and the reasons why there were reservations as to trading privileges, imported from former treaties, and a special reservation of the right of restriction regarding the entry of ships on the non-treaty coast, and no mention of any reservation as to the right of fishing, we cannot tell, but we are entitled to draw the inference that those reports contain nothing which in the slightest degree would shake or mitigate or detract from the statement of Mr. Gallatin in the report that he made.

So the British negotiators naturally refrained from providing that the grant of the fishing right should be subject to the authority of Great Britain to limit or restrict it by municipal legislation, because that would have been inconsistent with the nature of the right as they understood it.

Another answer from the British negotiators — that is, from their superior officer — is the letter of Lord Bathurst, which I have already referred to as the corner stone of this negotiation. I call the attention of the Tribunal to a paragraph of that letter to which I have already referred for another purpose, p. 274 of the Appendix to the Case of the United States. In this letter Lord Bathurst states the position which Great Britain took and upon which she stood before the world to justify herself for refusing to America the further exercise of the rights granted by the treaty of 1783. It is essential to his purpose that in arguing, in stating, and in maintaining that position upon that all-important subject, he should state the nature of the right, for the question whether it survived or perished with the war depended upon what the nature of the right was, and in this paragraph that I will now read he states that. I have read it once before for another purpose, but I beg you to bear with me if I read it again in order that I may bring to your minds the effect of it upon the argument which I am now endeavoring to make. He says:

> The Minister of the United States appears, by his letter, to be well aware that Great Britain has always considered the liberty formerly enjoyed by the United States of fishing within British limits, and using British territory, as derived from the third article of the treaty of 1783, and from that alone, —

Upon that his whole argument rested. He proceeds:

> and that the claim of an independent state to occupy and use *at its discretion* any portion of the territory of another, without compensation or corresponding indulgence cannot rest on any other foundation than conventional stipulation.

There is the authentic and unimpeachable declaration of the Government of Great Britain as to the character of the right that they conceived themselves to have granted to the United States under the treaty of 1783, and that they authorized these negotiators to regrant in the treaty of 1818. It was the right of an independent state to occupy and use *at its dis-*

cretion a portion of the territory of Great Britain. Of course, they would not for a moment think of imposing upon such a right a reservation of the right of municipal legislation. That is why Lord Bathurst, in this very letter complaining of the difficulties that had arisen in the exercise of the right under the treaty of 1783, proposed not to pass laws to remedy the injury, but proposed joint regulations with the United States to remedy it. It is because the United States so understood it that it accepted his proposition, and power was sent to the American minister in London to negotiate for joint regulations.

SIR CHARLES FITZPATRICK: May I ask you whether or not the claim of an independent state, which you have just referred to, has reference to the first paragraph of the same letter on p. 273 ?

SENATOR ROOT: Undoubtedly.

SIR CHARLES FITZPATRICK: He is answering the grounds advanced in the letter of the United States minister. Let me carry you back further, to p. 272, and ask you whether or not you think that the claim spoken of by Lord Bathurst is that set forth by Mr. John Quincy Adams in these words:

> Upon this foundation, my lord, the Government of the United States consider the people thereof as fully entitled, of right to all the liberties in the North American fisheries which have always belonged to them; which in the treaty of 1783 were, by Great Britain, recognized as belonging to them; and which they never have, by any act of theirs, consented to renounce.

Would that be the claim that he speaks of ?

SENATOR ROOT: Very likely. What he says of it is not that that is not what the United States has, but that that right can rest only upon a conventional stipulation. He accepts the view of the right, he denies the origin of the right, and he ascribes to the right, which he describes in these words, an origin which is the basis of his argument.

JUDGE GRAY: It was conventional.

SENATOR ROOT: It was conventional. Now, a view not so narrow as these specific utterances, but which does furnish the reason for them; there is an inherent, essential, ineradicable, generic difference between the two kinds of right, the kind of right which was granted in the treaty of 1815, that treaty which was continued by the treaty of 1818, and which, I may observe, was again continued in 1827, and is the treaty under which we live today, to travel and reside, and upon which these British negotiators had imposed the express reservation of the right of municipal legislation, and the kind of right which was granted under this treaty with respect to fishery. I have to acknowledge hospitality and courtesy from the people of Newfoundland, because I have been there, and, with them, have shot caribou in their wilderness and killed salmon in their streams, accompanied by Newfoundlanders. We were exercising privileges in common and with no limitation upon one that was not upon the other. We could fish together, buy and sell, borrow and lend, give and take without restriction; we could have fished from the same boat, could have drawn the seine upon the same strand, we could have employed one or another in each other's service. I was mingling with the people of Newfoundland as an individual because I was going there under the privilege of a general right of intercourse which obtains among all civilized nations, declared and expressed in the treaty of 1815 and in this treaty of 1818.

But how different would have been the situation had I gone as an American fisherman upon an American ship! Then I would have been a member of a class set apart by itself, not sharing in any of the common opportunities, or advantages, or privileges of the people of Newfoundland. If I had fished from the same boat as a Newfoundlander he would have been arrested, tried, and convicted. If we drew a seine together upon the same strand, punishment would follow to him, or confiscation to my vessel. If I say that I want bait or the implements of fishing, I cannot obtain them but at the risk of criminality on his part.

One right is a right in which the individual mingles with the community subject to the same laws and entitled to the same opportunities. There are millions of people, natives of one country, who are living so in peace in the other countries of the earth today; but under the other right there is a special class set apart with none of these opportunities, to be held down narrowly and rigidly to the precise right that is found within the four corners of the treaty. Laws and regulations which are bound to operate equally upon individuals are bound, in the working of human nature, to operate unequally when established by one class as against another class. There is a radical and perpetual distinction between the two, and for months here counsel for Great Britain have been seeking to drive into your minds an impression which would lead you to read into the treaty of 1818, as to the fishing grant, considerations appropriate only to the exercise of the other kind of right which can be enjoyed by individuals and not by a class bound closely to the specific rights of a treaty.

These two kinds of right demand and receive entirely different treatment. The principles applicable to one are inapplicable to the other as a matter of justice, equity, convenience, the reason of the thing, which is Mansfield's definition of international law. The counsel for Great Britain have been urging upon you that you shall read into this provision the reservation of the right in Great Britain to treat this grant as if it were a general grant to be enjoyed by individuals in common with the natives of the country, while they treat their laws upon the other and irreconcilable theory. They treat their laws as laws not bound in any respect to give to the persons enjoying the privilege of this fishery grant an opportunity as if they were, in fact, exercising the privileges in common with the people of Newfoundland. They wish to read their right into the treaty and to preserve their right against their own theory of the treaty. The treaty must be read either in one way or the other. If the treaty is a treaty to be considered as subject to those rights of municipal legislation that arise from the intermingling of individuals and foreigners in common opportunity, common privilege, and the common exercise of a common right, then their laws should give that to us. If, on the other hand, this treaty is to be read as a treaty in the exercise of which we, as a class, coming from a foreign shore, under a foreign flag, fishing in competition with the people of Newfoundland, are to be rigidly restrained to the letter of our treaty grant, they must not read into the treaty right that it imposes upon us regulations which are appropriate, natural, and reasonable to the exercise of the other kind of right.

That is what Lord Bathurst had in his mind; that is what the negotiators, as reported by Mr. Gallatin, had in their minds; that is why they imposed an express reservation of the right of regulation upon the treaty grant of 1815, and why, when they came to deal with this fishery right, they imposed no such reservation; and why, as to one of the three rights, they made an express regulation; as to another they expressed a limited right of restriction, and as to the third they were silent.

I call your honors' attention to the fact that the propositions which I am now making depend not at all upon the essential character of this grant which I argued the other day. They are as applicable, as effective, as peremptory and imperative, if this be a contract — a mere obligatory contract — as they are if this be a conveyance of a real right, for the limitation of the contract obligation rests upon Great Britain so long as the contract remains. It may not survive war as an obligation, it may not survive a change of sovereignty as an obligation, but so long as it subsists, so long as it limits either the power or the exercise of the power of Great Britain, so long will this Tribunal see it as being the law and the guide to its award.

The President: Concerning the proviso at the foot of Article 1, I should like to ask a question: To whom does the restriction apply that they are not allowed to enter except for these four purposes? It says, "provided, however, that the American fishermen shall be admitted to enter such bays," etc. Does this restriction apply only to American fishermen, or does it apply to British subjects? Is it limited to American fishermen?

Senator Root: Yes.

The President: Do the regulations which Great Britain claims to have the right to make concerning the exercise of the fishery apply to American and British fishermen?

Senator Root: They may and they may not, so long as they are two separate classes. One class is what Mr. Evarts calls the strand fishermen, and the other class is what he calls the vessel fishermen. They are precluded from mingling, they cannot fish on the same boat and cannot deal with each other in the ordinary intercourse of life. The vessel fishermen cannot use the strand for any of the numerous purposes for which it is desirable so long as they do constitute a separate and distinct class. One prosecuting this industry under its common right in one way and under one set of conditions, and the other prosecuting its industry under its common right under another set of conditions, it is impossible that regulations imposed upon one set of fishermen should be reasonable and adequate, when they are applicable to the other. The claim of Great Britain necessarily is that she, being representative of one distinct class, is entitled to restrict and modify by her sole will, which she intends to exercise reasonably, but by her sole will, with all the prepossessions and prejudices of one class, the exercise of the right of the other class. I say it is an entirely different situation, governed by different principles, from the situation created where individuals go in and commingle as they are doing all over the world with all the privileges and all the opportunities of the people of the country into which they go. That distinction is clearly pointed out and put beyond reasonable question by these very statements of the men of the time who made this treaty.

JUDGE GRAY: Does not the proviso necessarily refer to American fishermen?

SENATOR ROOT: Necessarily so.

JUDGE GRAY: It is that they are permitted to enter for the four purposes?

SENATOR ROOT: Yes, precisely. They constitute a separate class by themselves, differing from the other class. We have other questions which really touch upon the same line as to whether, for example, the customs law regarding entry, manifests, and all the cumbersome machinery of a customs tariff and its enforcement with reference to the vessels of the Canadians is applicable to this different and distinct class which comes in to exercise a special right as a special and separate class under this treaty.

THE PRESIDENT: This proviso is a discriminating provision, for if it has any reason for existence it must have been put in the treaty as being a discriminating provision.

SENATOR ROOT: Well, still you have the inference from the fact that it is put in, and as I have intended to make clear, the fact of the distinction between the situations of the two competing classes makes it impossible that provisions properly governing them should not be discriminating, just as many of these statutes that I have been referring to, in words apparently covering everybody, operate to produce a distinct discrimination against the foreign class that comes in.

THE PRESIDENT: Under different circumstances; they are working in different ways ?

SENATOR ROOT: Precisely, so that the idea of non-discrimination is an illusion, it is a form, it is not a reality in any sense whatever. As opposed to all this evidence, there is not one word coming from these negotiators during the entire course of this negotiation to show that any one having anything to do with the negotiation for a moment conceived the idea that there was reason to imply a right of municipal legislation to limit and restrict the exercise of this treaty right.

I now pass to the construction placed upon this treaty by the parties when the treaty has been made. I shall, I think, show that for sixty years after the making of the treaty both Governments treated it in accordance with the view which I have imputed to the negotiators of the treaty. The first thing done under the treaty was the passing of the Act of 1819, which appears in the United States Case Appendix at p. 112. I need not dwell very long upon that, further than to say what, I think, has already been said, that the act neither provides for nor contemplates any regulation of the right of fishing. It does expressly provide that His Majesty, with the advice of the Privy Council, may

Make such Regulations, and give such Directions, Orders and Instructions to the Governor of Newfoundland, or to any Officer or Officers on that Station, or to any other person or persons whomsoever, as shall or may be from time to time deemed proper and necessary for the carrying into Effect the Purposes of the said Convention.

Of course, the other person or persons are persons to whom it is competent for the king in council to give orders, persons whose position would enable them to exercise an influence on giving effect to the treaty provisions. On the other hand, the act vests in His Majesty in council and in the governor or person exercising the office of governor, in such parts of His Majesty's dominions in America as are covered by the renunciatory clause, the power to make regulations under that clause.

The first step taken by the British Government after the treaty is a step which does not contemplate regulating the American exercise of the American right of fishing, but does contemplate giving effect to that right and regulating the right of vessels on the non-treaty coasts. The next step was the Order-in-Council of the 19th June, 1819, which appears at p. 114 of the United States Case Appendix.

THE PRESIDENT: May I ask your comment, Mr. Senator Root, concerning a disposition in no. 4 of the act, where it is said, about the middle of the article:

> if any Person or Persons shall refuse or neglect to conform to any Regulations or Directions which shall be made or given for the Execution of any of the Purposes of this Act, every such Person, so refusing or otherwise offending against this Act shall forfeit the Sum of Two hundred Pounds.

Does that refer to the non-treaty coast only, or does it refer also to the treaty coast ? And what are the regulations which are meant in this part of the act ?

SENATOR ROOT: I understand it to be, although this is rather a first impression on the president's question, a reference to the " directions, orders, and instructions to the Governor of Newfoundland, or to any officer or officers on that station, or to any other person or persons whomsoever," and a refusal or neglect " to conform to any regulations or directions which shall be made or given for the execution of any of the purposes of this Act," although it may include both. It would require more careful examination and consideration than I have given to the question for me to determine in my own mind. But the act seems to contemplate two quite different proceedings. One is the giving of orders for carrying into effect the purposes of the said Convention with relation to the taking, drying, and curing of fish by inhabitants of the United States of America

and the other is the making of regulations containing

such restrictions as may be necessary to prevent such fishermen of the said United States from taking, drying, or curing fish in the said bays or harbors

of the non-treaty coast

or in any other manner whatever abusing the said privileges by the said treaty and this Act reserved to them.

And that function may be performed either by an order or orders to be made by His Majesty in council or by regulations issued by the governor or person exercising the office of governor in the colony.

Article 4 provides:

That if any Person or Persons, upon the Requisition made by the Governor of Newfoundland, or the Person exercising the Office of Governor, or by any Governor or Person exercising the Office of Governor, in any other Parts of His Majesty's Dominions in America as aforesaid, or by any Officer or Officers acting under such Governor or Person exercising the Office of Governor, in the Execution of any Orders or Instructions from His Majesty in Council, shall refuse to depart from such Bays or Harbors; or if any Person or Persons shall refuse or neglect to conform to any Regulations or Directions which shall be made or given

then he shall be punished. I should think it applied to both.

JUDGE GRAY: And to British subjects as well, who may presume to interfere with treaty rights ?

SENATOR ROOT: Certainly; it applies to everybody. I think it is a general clause, giving sanction to the execution of both of these powers; the power in the king in council to give orders for carrying out and giving effect to the treaty, and the power in the king in council and the governors of the provinces for restricting the abuse of the treaty rights on the non-treaty coast.

The Order-in-Council of the 19th June, 1819, appears at p. 114, and I begin to read at middle of p. 115 of the United States Case Appendix. It provides, after a recital of the treaty and the statute:

> It is ordered by His Royal Highness the Prince Regent, in the name and on the behalf of His Majesty, and by and with the advice of His Majesty's Privy Council, in pursuance of the powers vested in His Majesty by the said Act, that the Governor of Newfoundland do give notice to all His Majesty's subjects being in or resorting to the said ports that they are not to interrupt in any manner the aforesaid fishery so as aforesaid allowed to be carried on by the inhabitants of the said United States in common with His Majesty's subjects on the said coasts, within the limits assigned to them by the said Treaty: and that the Governor of Newfoundland do conform himself to the said Treaty, and to such instructions as he shall from time to time receive thereon in conformity to the said Treaty.

That, as the Tribunal will see, contemplates no regulation of the exercise of this right by the inhabitants of the United States.

The next step was the letter from Lord Bathurst communicating this order-in-council to the governor of Newfoundland. That is in the British Case Appendix, p. 99, dated the 21st June, 1819, and says he encloses a copy of the act, and that the inhabitants of the United States will undoubtedly proceed without delay to exercise the privilege granted to them under that convention, and proceeds:

> His Royal Highness has commanded me to call your special attention to some points upon which it is probable that in regulating your conduct under the convention you may desire to receive instructions.
>
> You will in the first place observe that the privilege granted to the citizens of the United States is one purely of fishery and of drying and curing fish within the limits severally specified in the convention. It is the pleasure of His Royal Highness that this privilege as limited by the convention should be freely enjoyed by them without any hindrance or interference.

Then he goes on to say:

> But you will at the same time remark that all attempts to carry on trade or to introduce articles for sale or barter into His Majesty's possessions under the pretense of exercising the rights conferred by the conven-

tion is in every respect at variance with its stipulations. You will therefore promulgate as publicly as possible the nature of the indulgence which you are under the convention instructed to allow to them, and in case any of the inhabitants of the United States should be found attempting to carry on a trade not authorized by the convention you will in the first instance warn them

and then take legal proceedings.

The Tribunal will see that that indicates no idea on the part of Great Britain at that time that there was to be any limitation, modification, supervision, or regulation of our right; but that that was to be fully and freely enjoyed without any hindrance or interference.

And so the matter went on, with no act whatever in contravention of this letter of Lord Bathurst transmitting the order-in-council, without any attempt at interfering with the exercise of the fishing liberty by the inhabitants of the United States in their discretion or in the discretion of the United States, at such times and in such manner and by such means as they saw fit, until 1852, when there was a letter from Lord Malmesbury to Mr. Crampton dated the 10th August, 1852, and which appears in the United States Case Appendix at p. 519. Lord Malmesbury, the secretary of state for foreign affairs of Great Britain, writes to Mr. Crampton, the British minister in Washington, in regard to the circular or proclamation or public notice which the Tribunal will remember came from Mr. Webster at the time that the controversy about bays was at its height. Lord Malmesbury states for Mr. Crampton's benefit the views of the British Government regarding the rights laid down in the treaty of 1818. Beginning at the middle of p. 519, I read:

The rights are laid down in the treaty of 1818, as quoted by Mr. Webster; that is, undoubted and unlimited privileges of fishing in certain places were thereby given by Great Britain to the inhabitants of the United States; and the government of the United States, on their part, renounced forever any liberty previously enjoyed or claimed by its citizens to fish within three marine miles of any other of the coasts, bays, creeks, or harbors of the British dominions.

The Tribunal will perceive that it is quite plain that the Foreign Office of Great Britain at that time took the same view regarding the American right that I am taking here. The secretary says:

That is, undoubted and unlimited privileges of fishing . . . were given.

That is in contrast to what he goes on to say about the bays, and seems to leave no doubt as to what the view of Great Britain then was.

The following year, on the 28th September, 1853, the Governor of Newfoundland wrote to Lord Newcastle a letter, which appears in the United States Counter-Case Appendix at p. 247. This letter is discussing the history of the fishery with reference both to French and American rights, and it appears that the making of a treaty which ultimately resulted in the convention of 1854 was mooted; and he says to the Colonial Office:

In any new convention that may be made, —

that is, with France —

it should be a *sine qua non*, if the Sale of Bait is made a stipulation, that the right of purchase must be subject to such regulations as may be made by the Local Legislature for the protection of the breeding and the preservation of the bait; regulations that are now imperatively demanded, and without which the Bait in our Southern Bays will in time be exterminated. As regards the effect upon this part of the question of embracing Newfoundland in any Treaty of Reciprocity between the North American Colonies and the United States, by which the Americans may be admitted to a participation in our fisheries, it should, as I have no doubt it will, be provided that the citizens of the United States shall, equally with British subjects, be subject to such Legislative Regulations as may be established for the protection and preservation of Bait. Regulations of this nature would, under such circumstances, be obviously matters of common interest to all.

It is apparent that the Governor of Newfoundland did not consider that the American Government was subject to the right of legislative regulations, and he wanted provision to that effect in case a new treaty was made.

The Tribunal is familiar with the report of 1855, to which reference has just been made, that down to that time there was no regulation of any kind in practical effect; so that, of course, the Americans could not have been regulated. Then, in 1862, the first Newfoundland act regulating fishing was passed, and in that act was included the saving clause that

nothing in this Act contained shall in any way affect or interfere with the rights and privileges granted by treaty to the subjects or citizens of any state or power in amity with Her Majesty.

I shall presently show the Tribunal that that was understood in Newfoundland to except Americans from the purview of the act. That clause is continued in most of the statutes of Newfoundland which follow. There are a few short statutes in which it does not appear, but I think it may fairly be considered that those were regarded as amendments of acts in which it did appear, so that it would be operative. I do not know when the idea of Newfoundlanders changed about the effect of that saving clause. There is evidence which I shall present to the Tribunal that in 1862 they considered that the law they were passing did not apply to Americans. In 1905 they considered that their law did apply to Americans. Just where the change occurred I do not know. But the saving clause appears in their statutes of 1862, consolidated statutes of 1872, in their statutes of 1887, 1889, 1892, consolidated statutes, their "Foreign Fishing-Vessels Act of 1893," their act establishing the department of marine and fisheries in 1898, and "The Foreign Fishing-Vessels Act of 1905." The act establishing the department of marine and fisheries in 1898 provides:

Nothing in this Act or any rules and regulations to be made hereunder shall be construed to affect the rights and privileges granted by treaty to the subjects of any state or power in amity with Her Majesty.

So that it covered all regulations made under that statute by the department which is the department still in operation.

I say I do not know when the change occurred, but I do know that there was a considerable period during which Newfoundland did not consider that her fishery regulation statutes applied to Americans; and the first bit of evidence upon that point is in a letter from the Duke of Newcastle to Governor Bannerman of the 3d August, 1863, which appears in the United States Case Appendix at p. 1082. This is headed: "Copy of a despatch from the Secretary of State for the Colonies in reply to a request from the Governor that a copy of a draft bill for regulating the fisheries may be looked over, and any parts pointed out, such as probably might not be sanctioned by the Crown."

This is the year after the Act of 1862 was passed — that first act regulating the fisheries.

Sir Charles Fitzpatrick: Are these words in italics on the original document?

Senator Root: Well, I really do not know. Mr. Anderson can tell. Mr. Anderson calls attention to the fact that there is a preceding line: "Extracts from the journal of the Legislative Assembly of Newfoundland, 1864." That is where we got it.

Sir Charles Fitzpatrick: Yes.

Senator Root: And these words that I have read appear in that journal. I suppose they are the description of the despatch by the clerk or secretary, or whoever made up the journal; but it appears to be a correct description or syllabus of the letter.

The Duke acknowledges the letter of the Governor, and the copy of the proceedings of the committee appointed to inquire into the state of the fisheries, together with a draft bill, and says:

I apprehend that it is not your expectation that I should express an opinion respecting the practical modes of conducting those fisheries.

And then he says:

The observations which suggest themselves to me, however, on the perusal of the draft bill are —

1st. That if any misconception exists in Newfoundland respecting the limits of the colonial jurisdiction, it would be desirable that it should be put at rest by embodying in the act a distinct settlement that the regulations contained in it are of no force except within three miles of the shore of the colony.

I would stop on that if I were arguing Question 5 now; but I am not.

2d. That no act can be allowed which prohibits expressly, or is calculated by a circuitous method to prevent, the sale of bait.

3d. That all fishing acts should expressly declare that their provisions do not extend or interfere with any existing treaties with any foreign nation in amity with Great Britain.

4th. That, in any part of the colonial waters, it would be highly unjust and inconvenient to impose upon British fishermen restrictions which could not, without violating existing treaties, be imposed upon foreigners using the same fisheries. On this point, however, I would refer you to my despatch, marked " confidential," of the 2d of February.

That we have not.

The Tribunal will perceive there that the Colonial Office considered that the saving clause, which was made peremptory, precluded non-discriminating legislation affecting foreigners using fisheries under treaties:

it would be highly unjust and inconvenient to impose upon British fishermen restrictions which could not, without violating existing treaties, be imposed upon foreigners using the same fisheries.

That is non-discriminatory. The Duke of Newcastle's observation is that there should not be any regulation imposed upon British fishermen which could not extend to and cover foreign fishermen. And he manifestly understood that the fishermen under these treaties were outside the power of regulation, and that that fact was good reason for not imposing a regulation which would apply to the British fishermen and could not apply to them.

The next circumstance is the correspondence and action in regard to the Newfoundland treaty legislation of 1873 and 1874. I have referred to that for a specific purpose, and I am going to ask the members of the Tribunal to bring their minds back to it in order to indicate another aspect of the correspondence and legislation which bears upon the proposition that I am now arguing. That is, that the two Governments did not consider that there was any right of municipal legislation to restrict the exercise of the American liberty.

The Tribunal will remember that the first law passed by Newfoundland to put the treaty of 1871 into effect, to make it apply to Newfoundland, contained a provision:

> Provided that such laws, rules and regulations *relating to the time and manner* of prosecuting the fisheries on the coast of this island shall not be in any way affected by such suspension.

That is the suspension of statutes. On the 19th June, 1873, Mr. Thornton wrote a letter which appears in the United States Counter-Case Appendix at p. 195, in which he proposes to Mr. Fish, the American secretary of state, a protocol to supplement the treaty, relating to this proviso of the Newfoundland statute. I read from the paragraph in the middle of p. 195:

> I am, therefore, instructed to propose to you to sign a protocol with regard to Newfoundland similar to that which I had the honor to sign with you on the 7th instant, with the addition of a clause following as nearly as possible the proviso at the end of the first article of the Newfoundland act, namely, that the laws, rules and regulations of the colony *relating to the time and manner of prosecuting the fisheries* on the coast of the island shall not in any way be affected by the suspension of the laws of the colony which operate to prevent Articles 18 to 25 of the Treaty of Washington from taking full effect during the period mentioned in the 33d article of the treaty.

On the next day, Mr. Thornton wrote to Mr. Fish a letter which appears on p. 196, dated the 20th June, 1873, and I ask the particular attention of the Tribunal to this letter. It says:

> With reference to my note of yesterday's date and to our conversation upon the subject of the Act passed by the Legislature of Newfoundland for carrying into effect Articles 18 to 25 of the Treaty of May 8, 1871, I have the honor to state that from a report made by the Attorney-General of Newfoundland to the Governor it would appear that the Proviso at the end of Section 1 of that Act has reference to *the time for the prosecution of the Herring fishery on the Western Coast of the Island* —

that is, the treaty coast under the Act of 1818 —

> *and was merely intended to place citizens of the United States on the same footing with Her Majesty's subjects in that particular so that the rules and regulations imposed upon the Newfoundland Fishermen with regard to that fishery might also be observed by American Fishermen.*

The Tribunal will see the force of that. The treaty of 1871 would, during its operation, supersede, take the place of the treaty of 1818. It applied to all the coasts of Newfoundland, and in so far as it varied or enlarged or changed in any way the rights under the treaty of 1818 it would, during the period of its operation, take the place of the treaty of 1818, as the law for the parties engaged in fishing on that coast. Newfoundland had this law of 1862 and her consolidated statutes of 1872, although I do not know whether they should be regarded as included; at all events, she had this law of 1862, and she wanted to have its provisions extended over American fishermen. She knew they did not apply to American fishermen. She knew that the provision in that act that it should not extend to or affect the rights of other powers under treaty prevented its applying to American fishermen; that under the treaty there was no right on the part of Newfoundland to make that statute apply to American fishermen. And she proposed to put this proviso into her Act of 1873, in accordance with this statement, excepting from suspension laws relating to the time and manner of fishing, in order that when the treaty of 1871 came in, that statute should be extended over American fishermen on the west coast. Well, that was met by Mr. Fish's refusal.

There was one further representation made by Mr. Thornton, based upon information that he received from Newfoundland, I suppose. He says in his letter of the 30th July, 1873, to Mr. Davis, the assistant secretary of state:

> These laws —

that is, the laws to which this correspondence referred; the laws referred to in the proviso, relating to the time and manner of fishing —

> are already in existence, and the proviso does not refer to any further restrictions; I have now the honor to inclose copies of the laws themselves. It does not appear therefore that these laws need form an obstacle to the admission of Newfoundland to the participation of benefits arising from the action of a Treaty stipulation, the operation of which is still prospective as far as Newfoundland is concerned.

That is to say, Newfoundland, even then, did not understand that a proviso to her suspension of statutes, during the life of the treaty of 1871 —

> provided that such laws, rules, and regulations relating to the time and manner of prosecuting the fisheries on the coasts of this island shall not be in any way affected by such suspension —

would apply to subsequent legislation. She seeks to get the treaty of 1871 supplemented by a protocol so as to permit this proviso to take effect, upon the ground that it does not apply to subsequent legislation, but only applies to past legislation, and that the sole object of it is to bring the Americans on the west coast in under the operations of the provisions of the Act of 1862, which did not then apply to them.

I hope my references to the Act of 1862 are intelligible to the Tribunal.

JUDGE GRAY: The Newfoundland Act of 1862 ?

Senator Root: Yes; the Newfoundland Act of 1862.

The treaty of 1871, which was for its life to supersede the operation of the treaty of 1818, required an act by Newfoundland to make it applicable. Newfoundland passed the act, suspending all laws inconsistent with the treaty, with a proviso that the suspension should not operate upon laws or regulations relating to the time and manner of fishing. And she asked for a protocol supplementing the treaty by the acceptance of that proviso, upon the ground that it would not apply to any subsequent legislation, and that its only object was to bring the American fishermen on the west coast in under the operation of the already existing statutes of Newfoundland, which, *a fortiori*, did not apply to the American fishermen at all; that is, statutes relating to the time and manner of fishing. Nothing can be clearer than that this authentic, authoritative position of the Government of Newfoundland, indicated through the British minister at Washington, was in accordance with the view which I have been pressing upon the Tribunal.

I shall not detain the Tribunal by going over again the question about the Halifax case, further than to make the single observation that in that case the computation by the British counsel of the profits, the benefits which would be derived by the United States from the exercise of the treaty privileges conferred, were based upon the full exercise of the treaty rights, without any limitation as to time or manner, and upon a consideration of the use in that exercise of the very methods of taking fish which are denounced by the laws of Newfoundland. So that the award, based upon those computations, must necessarily have been based upon an error of law if it had turned out that Great Britain was contending that the American fishermen, under the treaty of 1871, could not use methods or exercise that full scope of their industry which would appear to be possible under the terms of the treaty, and which was counted upon and made the basis of the computation. As Mr. Evarts pointed out, the very law of Newfoundland which prohibits the winter fishery, that is, this Act of 1862 prohibiting seining from the 20th October to April, would, if applied, exclude our people from the winter fishery, which was one of the principal things that entered into the computation of the counsel for Great Britain before the Halifax Commission. They were put in the position, by Lord Salisbury's first view, that they had got an award based upon the right to carry on a profitable industry in Newfoundland, and then, before the award was made, came the proposition that, by the law of Newfoundland, American fishermen were prevented from doing that very thing.

I must now trouble your honors by returning again to the Fortune Bay correspondence, because my former reference to it was only for a specific purpose, and it has an important bearing upon the matter that I am now presenting.

The Tribunal will remember that American fishermen in 1878, some twenty odd vessels, went into Fortune Bay for the purpose of catching fish. They went ashore and were drawing their seines, and the inhabitants came and interfered with them, and there was a good deal of disturbance, and finally some of the nets were cut and the fish already taken were let out, and there was a claim for damages by the United States. To that claim for damages Lord Salisbury replied with a refusal, saying that the fishermen were violating three distinct laws of the colony. Thereupon Mr. Evarts, who was smarting a little under what we regarded in the United States as being a very excessive award on the part of the Halifax Commission, an award of 5,500,000 dollars that the United States was called upon to pay for the privileges under the treaty of 1871, wrote very promptly regarding the observation by Lord Salisbury about the three distinct violations of law, and I now read this from p. 655 of the United States Case Appendix, because it is the matter to which Lord Salisbury makes answer in his subsequent letter. Mr. Evarts says, beginning with the third paragraph on this p. 655:

In this observation of Lord Salisbury, this Government cannot fail to see a necessary implication that Her Majesty's Government conceives that in the prosecution of the right of fishing accorded to the United States by Article XVIII of the treaty *our fishermen are subject to the local regulations which govern the coast population of Newfoundland in their prosecution of their fishing industry,* whatever those regulations may be, and whether enacted before or since the Treaty of Washington.

The three particulars in which our fishermen are supposed to be constrained by actual legislation of the province cover in principle every degree of regulation of our fishing industry within the three-mile line which can well be conceived. But they are, in themselves, so important and so serious a limitation of the rights secured by the treaty as practically to exclude our fishermen from any profitable pursuit of the right, which, I need not add, is equivalent to annulling or canceling by the Provincial Government of the privilege accorded by the treaty with the British Government.

If our fishing-fleet is subject to the Sunday laws of Newfoundland, made for the coast population; if it is excluded from the fishing grounds for half the year, from October to April; if our "seines and other contrivances" for catching fish are subject to the regulations of the legislature of Newfoundland, it is not easy to see what firm or valuable measure for the privilege of Article XVIII, as conceded to the United States, this Government can promise to its citizens under the guaranty of the treaty.

It would not, under any circumstances, be admissible for one government to subject the persons, the property, and the interests of its fishermen to the unregulated regulation of another government upon the suggestion that such authority will not be oppressively or capriciously exercised, nor would any government accept as an adequate guaranty of the proper exercise of such authority over its citizens by a foreign government, that, presumptively, regulations would be uniform in their operation upon the subjects of both governments in similar case. If there are to be regulations of a common enjoyment, they must be authenticated by a common or joint authority.

That is a clear, definite, and unequivocal statement of Mr. Evarts' view. In closing the letter, in the last paragraph on page 657, he says:

In the opinion of this Government, it is essential that we should at once invite the attention of Lord Salisbury *to the question of provincial control over the fishermen of the United States* in their prosecution of the privilege secured to them by the treaty. So grave a question, in its bearing upon the obligations of this Government under the treaty, makes it necessary that the President should ask from Her Majesty's Government a frank *avowal or disavowal of the paramount authority of Provincial legislation to regulate the enjoyment by our people of the inshore fishery,* which seems to be intimated, if not asserted, in Lord Salisbury's note.

Before the receipt of a reply from Her Majesty's Government, it would be premature to consider what should be the course of this Government should this limitation upon the treaty privileges of the United States be insisted upon by the British Government as their construction of the treaty.

And it is in answer to that demand that Lord Salisbury immediately responds in his letter of the 7th November, 1878. It is in this answer that, after stating his view that he hardly believes Mr. Evarts would consider that no British authority has any right to pass any kind of laws binding upon Americans, he proceeds to say on p. 658:

On the other hand, Her Majesty's Government will readily admit — what is, indeed, self-evident — that British sovereignty, as regards those waters, is limited in its scope by the engagements of the Treaty of Washington, which cannot be modified or affected by any municipal legislation.

I think the world knows enough of this great statesman, one of the best representatives of the English people who ever took part in international affairs — a great foreign secretary, a great prime minister — I think the world knows enough of him to know that he would repudiate with indignation the idea that he was in that answer attempting an evasion of the question of Mr. Evarts. The question was: "an avowal or disavowal of the paramount authority of provincial legislation to regulate the enjoyment by our people of the inshore fishery"; and the answer was: "that British sovereignty, as regards those waters, is limited in its scope by the engagements of the Treaty of Washington, which cannot be modified or affected by any municipal legislation."

The answer must be read with the question to which it is an answer. And upon that the Government of Great Britain stands today, by the declaration of her counsel, including her Attorney-General.

In this letter Lord Salisbury, after saying that if there had been inadvertent trespass upon the line, the limits, by any laws which contravened treaties, the matter should be taken up by the governments, proceeds to say that Mr. Evarts has not specified any recent legislation which is supposed to pass the limits of the American right. Thereupon Mr. Evarts proceeds to specify, in his letter in reply, of the 1st August, 1879. He specifies [p. 671] the prohibition against " taking herring by the seine or other such contrivance between the 20th of October and the 12th of April," and the prohibition against "taking herring between the 20th of December and the 1st of April with seines of less than " a certain mesh, and the prohibition against taking herring between the 10th May and the 20th October — that is, the bank fishing season — within a mile of any settlement on the south coast, and the Sunday prohibition. And he advises Lord Salisbury that the rights of the United States, the treaty rights, are both " seriously modified and injuriously affected ", using Lord Salisbury's words, by municipal legislation " which closes such fishery absolutely for seven months of the year, prescribes a special method of exercise, forbids exportation for five months, and, in certain localities, absolutely limits the three-mile area which it was the express purpose of the treaty to open."

Thereupon Lord Salisbury makes another reply, in which he supplements and leaves no possibility of doubt as to the meaning and scope and effect of his previous declarations. That is in his letter of the 3d April, 1880, which begins on

p. 683 of the United States Case Appendix. He says in the second paragraph of the letter, on p. 683:

> In considering whether compensation can properly be demanded and paid in this case, regard must be had to the facts as established, and to the intent and effect of the articles of the Treaty of Washington and the convention of 1818 which are applicable to those facts.

And he proceeds to a careful consideration of those instruments and their effect.

I shall ask the Tribunal also to observe that in the first paragraph he explains the delay in sending this letter by saying that it has been occasioned by the necessity of instituting a very careful inquiry, and the fullest consideration, and that the inquiry has now been completed. So this is a very deliberate, matured, and fully considered communication.

Over on p. 684, at the top of the page, he says:

> Such being the facts, the following two questions arise:
>
> 1. Have United States fishermen the right to use the strand for purposes of actual fishing?
>
> 2. Have they the right to take herrings with a seine at the season of the year in question, or to use a seine at any season of the year for the purpose of barring herrings on the coast of Newfoundland?

And he proceeds to answer both questions in the negative. The first question he answers in the negative upon an examination of the nature of the right conferred by the treaty of 1818 and the Treaty of Washington. And he describes the right. He says, at the beginning of the paragraph in the middle of p. 684:

> Articles XVIII and XXXII of the Treaty of Washington superadded to the above-mentioned privileges —

that is, the privileges which he had just recited from the treaty of 1818 —

> the right for United States fishermen to take fish of every kind (with certain exceptions not relevant to the present case) on all portions of the coast, etc.

Then he says:

Thus, *whilst absolute freedom in the matter of fishing in territorial waters is granted,* the right to use the shore for four specified purposes alone is mentioned in the treaty articles, from which United States fishermen derive their privileges, namely, to purchase wood, to obtain water, to dry nets, and cure fish.

The citizens of the United States are thus by clear implication absolutely precluded from the use of the shore in the direct act of catching fish.

The Tribunal will observe that, examining the treaty of 1818 and the treaty of 1871, he declares that *absolute freedom in the matter of fishing in territorial waters is granted,* and the right to use the shore for only specified purposes, and not in general. He finds, as a matter of fact, that the American fishermen went on shore; and therefore, he says, they were exceeding their treaty right.

He next proceeds to the second question, and upon that he says:

But it cannot be claimed, consistently with this right of participation in common with the British fishermen, that the United States fishermen have any *other*, and still less that they have *greater* rights than the British fishermen had at the *date* of the treaty.

I am now reading about two-thirds of the way down p. 685:

If, then, at the *date* of the signature of the Treaty of Washington, certain restraints were, by the municipal law, imposed upon the *British fishermen,* the United States fishermen were, by the *express terms* of the treaty, equally subjected to those restraints, and the obligation to observe in common with the British the then existing local laws and regulations, which is implied by the words "*in common*", attached to the United States citizens as soon as they claimed the benefit of the treaty.

He then cites Mr. Marcy's circular as expressing that view, the circular which related to laws which were in force at the time the treaty of 1854 took effect. Then he says, on p. 686:

I have the honor to enclose a copy of an act passed by the Colonial Legislature of Newfoundland, on the 27th March, 1862 . . . and a copy of . . . the consolidated statutes of Newfoundland, passed in 1872.

Then he says:

These regulations, which were in force at the date of the Treaty of Washington, were not abolished, but confirmed by the subsequent statutes, and are binding under the treaty upon the citizens of the United States in common with British subjects.

He abandons the Sunday regulation passed in 1876 after the treaty of 1871 took effect, and which was really the only thing in the minds of the Newfoundland fishermen, and plants himself strictly upon the proposition, not that the United States was subject to any subsequent legislation, but that the treaty made it subject to regulations which existed at the time the treaty was made; and in order to leave no doubt whatever of what he means and the limit and force of it, he proceeds in the last paragraph of his letter on p. 687 to say:

Mr. Evarts will not require to be assured that Her Majesty's Government, while unable to admit the contention of the United States Government on the present occasion, are fully sensible of the evils arising from any difference of opinion between the two governments in regard to the fishery rights of their respective subjects. They have always admitted *the incompetence of the colonial or the imperial legislature to limit by subsequent legislation* the advantages secured by treaty to the subjects of another power.

There you have the full question and answer and specification and reply; a demand by Mr. Evarts for an explicit avowal as to whether Great Britain claims paramount authority of her legislation over the exercise of the treaty right; a response by Lord Salisbury that Great Britain concedes that " British sovereignty is limited in its scope by the engagements of the treaty, which cannot be modified or affected by municipal legislation "; a call by Lord Salisbury upon Mr. Evarts to specify what recent legislation he considers contravenes the treaty; a specification by Mr. Evarts of statutes, some within the life of the treaty and some prior to the life of the treaty; a reply by Lord Salisbury that the effect of the treaty, which conferred a right in common with Newfoundland fishermen, was to impose upon American fishermen regulations and limitations of the statutes existing at the time that treaty was made, but that they recognized the incompetence of Great Britain to limit by subsequent regulation the advantages secured by the treaty.

This answers to the definition finely drawn by the Attorney-General between mere admissions on the part of government officers and the acts of the government itself. This was the formal and the authentic action of the Government of Great Britain denying the claim for compensation on the part of the United States, and doing it in the face of the grave declarations made by Mr. Evarts regarding the course which it would be the duty of the Government of the United States to take if it should find that the claim of Great Britain to paramount authority over the exercise of the American right so far destroyed that right as to make it worthless.

JUDGE GRAY: The Sunday law had been enacted after 1871 ?

SENATOR ROOT: After 1871, yes; and it is abandoned by Lord Salisbury.

If there ever was a case in which the evidence was clear and incontrovertible of the positive position taken by one government towards another, it appears here in this record; and we are none of us at liberty to ignore it or to make a decision against it.[1]

THE PRESIDENT: Will you kindly continue, Mr. Senator Root ?[2]

SENATOR ROOT: There have been some transactions mentioned by counsel for Great Britain as constituting admissions on the part of the United States to the contrary view which has been maintained by Great Britain; that is, admis-

[1] Thereupon, at 4.15 o'clock P.M., the Tribunal adjourned until August 9th, 1910, at 10 o'clock A.M.

[2] Tuesday, August 9, 1910. The Tribunal met at 10 o'clock A.M.

sions on the part of the United States that there was a right, under the first article of the treaty of 1818, for Great Britain to limit and control the exercise of the liberty by municipal legislation.

Upon examination those alleged admissions disappear entirely. I have already given an account of the Marcy circular for another purpose, sufficient, I think, to show that the general proposition I have just made applies to that.

It is apparent, if the Tribunal will recall the circumstances, that there was nothing to the Marcy circular transaction except this: that when the provisions of the temporary and reciprocal treaty of 1854 were about to be put into effect, the governor of New Brunswick suggested to the British minister, and he to Mr. Marcy, the American secretary of state, that the American fishermen would naturally be bound by the statutes which existed in New Brunswick. The statutes already existing in New Brunswick provided, he said, nothing inconsistent with the full exercise of the treaty right. Mr. Marcy looked at the statutes and found that they were statutes which were, in fact, beneficial to both, and he approved them, and sent out his circular, in which he enjoined upon the American fishermen observance of them. And in the circular, by common arrangement, he put the duty of observing the laws just as strongly as he could, to prevent the fishermen from being recalcitrant and taking matters into their own hands.

But what he said was that all laws not inconsistent with the treaty were binding. Of course there was no admission of any kind there. It was what we all agree to on both sides. It was the fair statement, in the most general terms, of an incontrovertible proposition, without the expression of any opinion, and without any study or consideration as to what would be inconsistent with the treaty, or where the line was to be drawn.

Judge Gray: Was there or not an implication in that circular, and in the correspondence that preceded and followed it, that the only regulations that were necessary to be considered and that would be applicable were those that existed at the date of the new treaty of 1871 ?

Senator Root: That was the clear implication, and that was the fact which Lord Salisbury mentioned when he quoted that circular in his letter to Mr. Evarts to which I have already referred. He quoted that circular in support of his proposition that laws in existence at the time the treaty was made were binding, although subsequent laws would not be. He quoted that circular saying such was the view taken by Mr. Marcy, and that is clearly the only subject that Mr. Marcy had under consideration.

The next transaction to which is ascribed some element of injurious admission on the part of the United States is the Cardwell letter. On the 12th April, 1866, Mr. Cardwell wrote a letter — Mr. Cardwell being the colonial secretary of Great Britain — and the letter being to the Lords of the Admiralty, with reference to the conduct of British naval vessels. In that letter, which is quite long and contains a great variety of observations calculated to govern the conduct of naval vessels of Great Britain, he states the limits of the treaty grant, that Americans are entitled to take fish in such and such limits, cure them within such and such limits on the shore, and he includes a statement of what he apparently assumes as a matter of course, that naval officers should be aware that Americans who exercise their right of fishing in colonial waters —

Dr. Savornin Lohman: From what page are you reading?

Senator Root: Page 601 of the United States Case Appendix. I will read the full paragraph, just below the middle of the page:

On the other hand, naval officers should be aware that Americans who exercise their right of fishing in Colonial waters in common with subjects of Her Majesty, are also bound in common with those subjects, to obey the law of the country, including such Colonial laws as have been passed to insure the peaceable and profitable enjoyment of the fisheries by all persons entitled thereto.

That letter, with that general observation embosomed in it, rested for four years without being communicated to any one except to the persons to whom it was addressed and the officers, very probably, who were under them. But four years afterwards, on the 3d June, 1870, the difficulties which led to the making of the treaty of 1871 being active, an active controversy on the bay question having arisen again, there was a correspondence on that subject between the British and the American authorities, and on p. 597 of the United States Case Appendix, at the top of the page, the Tribunal will find a letter from the British minister (Mr. Thornton) to the American secretary of state (Mr. Fish), dated 3d June, 1870, in which he transmits a letter relating to the enforcement of the British view regarding the limits of American fishing in the bays. Mr. Thornton says, at the top of p. 597:

In compliance with instructions which I have received from the Earl of Clarendon, I have the honor to transmit for your information copy of a letter addressed by the Admiralty to the Foreign Office inclosing copy of one received from Vice-Admiral Wellesley, commanding Her Majesty's naval forces on this Station, in which he states the names of the vessels to be employed in maintaining order at the Canadian Fisheries and forwarding a copy of the instructions which were to be issued to the commanders of those vessels.

"Maintaining order at the Canadian Fisheries" was something which had nothing whatever to do with the treaty coast, or the exercise of the fishing right, or drying and curing under the treaty of 1818. It related solely to maintaining the line of demarcation between the waters which were renounced and the waters which were not renounced upon the non-treaty coast. The Tribunal will see that very readily, by reference to the instructions which are enclosed in this letter of Mr. Thornton's. There were a series of enclosures. The first enclosure in that letter on p. 597 is the enclosure marked No. 1, a letter from Mr. Vernon Lushington, from the British Admiralty, saying:

> I am commanded by my Lords Commissioners of the Admiralty to transmit, for the information of the Earl of Clarendon, a copy of a letter from Vice-Admiral Wellesley, dated April 27th, No. 151, stating that the *Plover*, *Royalist*, and *Britomart* —

the names of British vessels —

> are about to be despatched to the Bay of Fundy, and the Coasts of Nova Scotia and Prince Edward Island for the protection of the Canadian Fisheries.
>
> Enclosed is a copy of the special instructions furnished to these ships.

Enclosure No. 2 is a letter from Vice-Admiral Wellesley to the Admiralty telling when these vessels are to leave for the coast of Nova Scotia and Prince Edward Island, and enclosing a copy of the instructions which will be given to the ships by the Admiral.

Enclosure No. 3 consists of the instructions of the Vice-Admiral to the commanding officers of these ships that were on the way to Nova Scotia. And over on p. 600 the Tribunal will see that, as an annex to this third enclosure of Mr. Thornton's letter to Mr. Fish, is to be found this four-year-old Cardwell letter. The subject then under discussion was the old question of bays. That was the only subject under discussion. The subject to which Mr. Thornton's letter referred was that. The enclosures in his letter to Mr. Fish related to that. The question up was: What were British naval vessels going to do ? What might they rightfully do in arresting, preventing, seizing American vessels in the great bays of Nova Scotia and Prince Edward Island — the non-treaty coast ? Mr. Thornton did not send this Cardwell letter to Mr. Fish as a subject to which he called his attention.

It was an annex to one of the enclosures in the letter relating to the bay subject, and in this annex to one of the series of papers relating to the bay question there was this letter; and in this letter a single sentence which referred to an entirely different subject, a subject which was not under discussion at all.

Mr. Fish on the 8th June acknowledged Mr. Thornton's letter and properly and naturally expressed some views regarding the subject-matter to which the letter related regarding the controversy about which the letter was written, regarding the practical question which was then before the two Governments. Upon that he points out a discrepancy between the terms of the instructions which Mr. Thornton had sent to him and of certain other instructions which had been given; the difference being the difference between employing the 10-mile and the 6-mile limit, that is, applying the 3-mile or the 5-mile zone limit. That was relevant to the subject they were discussing. That was relevant to the subject that was up before the two Governments. Then he says (United States Case Appendix, p. 610):

> Without entering into any consideration of questions which might be suggested by the letter referred to, which I understand to be superseded by later instructions, I think it best to call your attention to the inconsistencies referred to, in order to guard against misunderstandings and complications. . . .

Surely no one ever more effectively guarded himself against being understood to have made admissions and to be bound by irrelevant matter in the exhibits or appendices, annexes which happened to be in the mass of papers that had been sent him because they contained matter which was relevant to a subject under discussion, than Mr. Fish did here. Of course, in the practical conduct of government, as in the ordinary affairs of life, many subjects become mingled in the same paper, many papers have to be communicated, communicated because of their relevancy and materiality upon some subject which is under discussion. It is a matter of every-day experience that papers are sent to be examined with reference to their bearing upon a particular subject which is under discussion, and there may be a hundred matters in them which are not relevant or not important. Is the person who receives them obliged to sit down and construct elaborate arguments upon every subject that is touched upon in those letters, or is he to treat merely what is relevant and material, but as to matters which have nothing to do with the subject under discussion save himself by some general expression of this kind? It needed no general expression to save him; but he did include in this letter this clear and distinct statement, "without entering into any consideration of questions which might be suggested by the letter." It is a pretty slender case that has to rest upon such a reed as that.

Another circumstance to which reference is made is what we have got in the habit of calling the Boutwell circular. The Boutwell circular was a circular sent by the secretary of the treasury in pursuance of a letter from the secretary of state, Mr. Fish, in 1870, to the collectors of customs, in order that they might communicate with the American fishing vessels as they went out. The circular related exclusively and solely to the non-treaty coast, and it had no relation whatever, nor did a word in it have any relation whatever, to the conduct of American fishermen, the obligations or duties or rights of American fishermen on the treaty coast, except as that might be contained in the fact that there was a quotation from the first article of the treaty of 1818, by way of stating an exception from the subject-matter. The circular was sent by Mr. Boutwell upon the request of the secretary of state, contained in a letter of the 23d April, 1870, which appears at p. 187 of the

American Counter-Case Appendix. Of course, the secretary of state is the minister of foreign affairs of the United States, and it is his business to express the views of the Government of the United States upon international questions, and not the business of the secretary of the treasury. Therefore the secretary of the treasury, in issuing a circular to his collectors of customs, in order to reach the fishermen, upon international questions, on the request of the secretary of state, cannot be supposed to have intended to set up for himself an inconsistent position, or to do anything other than that which the secretary of state had requested him to do. There is the strongest kind of presumption that he was, in following the secretary of state, undertaking to do what the secretary of state requested. I will ask the Tribunal to kindly consider that letter of Mr. Fish, the secretary of state:

HON. GEORGE S. BOUTWELL,
Secretary of the Treasury

SIR, April 23, 1870.

I have the honor to enclose a copy of House of Representatives Ex. Doc. No. 239, 2d session, 41st Congress, and of a communication of the 14th instant, from the British Minister, relating to the measures adopted, and proposed to be adopted, by the Authorities of the Dominion of Canada, *for the exclusion from certain of the inshore fisheries within the jurisdiction thereof, of foreign fishermen.* I beg leave to suggest, that with a view to fully acquainting citizens of the United States interested in the fishing business in waters adjacent to the Dominion of Canada, with these facts that a circular be issued at your earliest convenience to Collectors of the Customs at the ports of the United States in which fishing vessels are fitted out or to which they resort, enclosing to each of them, a sufficient number of copies of a printed notification for distribution among the fishermen and the business firms interested in the subject, setting forth *the material facts presented in the enclosed papers, and putting them on their guard against committing acts which would render them liable to the penalties prescribed by Canadian Laws, respecting inshore fisheries not open to the fishermen of the United States under the 1st Article of the treaty between the United States and Great Britain of 1818.*

I hope the Tribunal will observe the perfectly clear and distinct limitation:

> putting them on their guard against committing acts which would render them liable to the penalties prescribed by Canadian Laws, respecting in-shore fisheries not open to the fishermen of the United States under the 1st Article of the treaty between the United States and Great Britain of 1818.

That was Mr. Boutwell's warrant for issuing the circular, and that was his sole warrant for expressing any opinion regarding the international relations of the United States. Outside of that he had no more power and authority to express the views of the United States upon this subject than any man in the street.

But we are not left without definite information as to what led Mr. Fish to request this circular, and the limitations which he put upon the request; for it appears by the circular that the law to which it referred was a Canadian law of 1868. The circular appears in the British Appendix, p. 235. This is the first circular, I think, issued by Mr. Boutwell. He sends this out, under date of 16th May, 1870, and I read from the bottom of the page:

> In compliance with the request of the Secretary of State, you are hereby authorized and directed to inform all masters of fishing vessels, at the time of clearance from your port, that the authorities of the Dominion of Canada have terminated the system of granting fishing licenses to foreign vessels, under which they have heretofore been permitted to fish within the maritime jurisdiction of the said Dominion, that is to say, within three marine miles of the shores thereof; and that all fishermen of the United States are prohibited from the use of such in-shore fisheries *except* so far as stipulated in the first Article of the Treaty of October 20, 1818.

Then he quotes the article and proceeds:

> The Canadian Law of the 22d of May, 1868, . . . entitled " An Act respecting Fishing by Foreign Vessels," among other things, enacts, etc.

And then follows a statement of the provisions of the Canadian law of May, 1868. That law had been communicated to Mr. Fish and it was the origin of the letter from Mr. Fish requesting Mr. Boutwell to issue the circular. In the British Case Appendix, p. 628, is the law of 1868. That law begins with a provision that:

> The Governor may, from time to time, grant to any foreign ship, vessel or boat, or to any ship, vessel or boat not navigated according to the laws of the United Kingdom, or of Canada, at such rate, and for such period not exceeding one year, as he may deem expedient, a license to fish for or take, dry or cure any fish of any kind whatever, in British waters, within three marine miles of any of the coasts, bays, creeks, or harbors whatever, of Canada, *not included within the limits specified and described in the first article of the convention between* His late Majesty King George the Third and the United States of America, made and signed at London on the 20th day of October, 1818.

That is to say, the law which it was the purpose of Mr. Boutwell's circular to call to the attention of American fishermen and merchants, which it was the object of Mr. Fish in writing to Mr. Boutwell, and of Mr. Boutwell in issuing the circular to bring to the attention of Americans, in order that they might guard against incurring its penalties, was a law that by its express terms excluded the treaty coast. It applied to the waters of Canada

> *not included* within the limits specified and described in the first article of the Convention between His late Majesty King George the Third and the United States of America made and signed at London on the 20th day of October, 1818.

So it did not apply to the Magdalen Islands, or to this strip of wilderness coast called Canadian Labrador. Practically those places were negligible in Canadian legislation until the most recent times. They were not thinking about them. There is not much law in Labrador. People get on by the law of common sense and good nature. As to the Magdalen Islands, I do not know how it is now, but back in the treaty days they were the property of a single individual. At all events, this law to which this whole transaction related, was a law which specifically excluded from its purview the treaty coast — that small portion of the treaty coast which was within the Dominion of Canada.

But there was an order-in-council issued, giving effect to the law, and that order-in-council appears at pp. 230 and 231 of the British Appendix. Perhaps I should not have described it as an order-in-council. It was in the form of a report of a committee of the Privy Council, approved by the Governor-General. I do not know whether that should properly be called an order-in-council or not.

SIR CHARLES FITZPATRICK: When it is once approved, it becomes an order-in-council.

SENATOR ROOT: Very well, then; I will revert to my description.

At the end of p. 230 of the British Case Appendix, I read:

> The Committee having had under consideration the reports of the Minister of Marine and Fisheries, dated respectively the 15th and 20th ult., in connection with certain despatches from Lord Granville, on the subject of protecting the fisheries of Canada, beg to recommend:
>
> That the system of granting fishing licenses to foreign vessels, under the Act 31 Vic., c. 61, be discontinued, and that, henceforth, foreign fishermen be not permitted to fish in the waters of Canada.

The Tribunal will perceive that in that order-in-council they omitted the limitation which the statute contained; and when this statute was sent to the Government of the United States, it was sent with the order-in-council. The correspondence appears at pp. 580 and 581 of the American Appendix.

Mr. Thornton — Sir Edward Thornton by that time, I think — sends to Mr. Fish, in a note of the 14th April, 1870, a copy of a despatch from the Governor-General of Canada, at the top of p. 580 of the American Appendix. In that despatch is a statement of the provisions of the Act of 1868 to which I have referred, and also a statement of the order-in-council to which I have referred, quoting the terms of the order-in-council — not quoting the limitation in the act, but quoting the words of the order: " that henceforth all foreign fishermen shall be prevented from fishing in the waters of Canada." And thereupon Mr. Fish writes back to Mr. Thornton a letter which appears on p. 581, dated the 21st April, 1870, acknowledges the receipt of this statute and this order-in-council, and calls attention to the fact that the language of the order-in-council would appear to be broad enough to cover the treaty coast.

JUDGE GRAY: The treaty coasts of Canada?

SENATOR ROOT: The treaty coasts of Canada. Mr. Fish says, after acknowledging the receipt of the note of Mr. Thornton:

> I must invite your attention and that of Her Majesty's authorities to the first paragraph of the order-in-council of the 8th of January last, as quoted in the memorandum of the Prime Minister of the Dominion of Canada, accompanying the despatch of His Excellency the Governor-General, which paragraph is in the following language, to wit:
>
> That the system of granting fishing license to foreign vessels, under the Act 31 Vic., cap. 61, be discontinued, *and that henceforth all foreign fishermen be prevented from fishing in the waters of Canada.*
>
> The words underscored seem to contemplate an interference with rights guaranteed to the United States under the first article of the treaty of 1818, which secures to American fishermen the right of fishing in certain waters which are understood to be claimed at present as belonging to Canada.

Mr. Thornton writes back to Mr. Fish a letter on the same page (581 of the United States Case Appendix), acknowledging Mr. Fish's note and saying:

> I am forwarding a copy of your note to the Governor-General of Canada; but, in the meantime, I beg you will allow me to express my conviction that there was not the slightest intention in issuing the above-mentioned order, to abridge citizens of the United States of any of the rights to which they are entitled by the treaty of October 20, 1818, and which are tacitly acknowledged in the Canadian law of May 22, 1868, a copy of which I had the honor to forward to you in my note of the 14th instant.

Subsequently these were sent, and on pp. 587 and 588 may be found communications which straighten out the whole question in accordance with Mr. Thornton's assurance.

On p. 587 is a further letter from Mr. Thornton to Mr. Davis, the assistant secretary of state, enclosing a copy of a despatch from the Governor-General of Canada, to whose attention this question raised by Mr. Fish had been brought; and the Governor-General of Canada, it appears on this same p. 587, had sent to Mr. Thornton a report of the Minister of Marine of Canada, and that report appears on p. 588, together with a report of a committee of the Privy Council of Canada.

The Minister of Marine says in his report of 28th April, which was thus passed on to Mr. Fish, and which appears on p. 588:

> that the wording of the minute of council referred to clearly shows, by providing for the prevention of "*illegal* encroachment by foreigners" on the in-shore fisheries of Canada, that the Canadian Government never contemplated any interference with rights secured to United States citizens by the treaty in question between the British and American Governments.

And towards the foot of that report, on p. 589, he says of the terms

> in any case they could apply only to those waters within which our "in-shore fisheries" are situated, and in which neither American nor other foreign subjects have any legal right to fish.

So it appears that the broad words of the order-in-council were inadvertent in extending beyond the carefully limited terms of the treaty under which the order was issued; and we have here the most explicit and binding assurance to Mr. Fish that the statute and the order-in-council were both confined — or perhaps I should say that the order-in-council was subject to the same limits that the statute expressed, confining the operation of both to the waters of Canada not included within the grant of fishing rights by the treaty of 1818.

Then it is, after receiving this assurance, having this question resolved, that Mr. Fish sent to Mr. Boutwell a letter requesting him to issue a circular calling attention to this statute and order, and guarding against penalties respecting in-shore fisheries not open to fishermen of the United States under the fishing grant of the treaty of 1818.

Under that, Mr. Boutwell issued the circular to which I have referred. And it so happened that along about that time there was an amendment passed by the Canadian Parliament to this Act of 1868. On the 20th of May, 1870, Mr. Thornton sent a little note to Mr. Fish, which appears on page 589 of the United States Case Appendix, saying:

> With reference to my note of the 14th ultimo to the Secretary of State, in which I forwarded to him a copy of the Canadian act respecting fishing by foreign vessels, of the 22d of May, 1868, I have now the honor to enclose a further law of the 12th instant, repealing the third section of the above-mentioned act.

The act to which Mr. Thornton refers appears on p. 136 of the American Appendix, and the language which it repeals is:

> Any one of such officers or persons as aie above-mentioned, may bring any ship, vessel or boat, being within any harbor in Canada, or hovering (in British waters) within three marine miles of any of the coasts, bays, etc.

JUDGE GRAY: It does not repeal that, does it, Mr. Root? That is a substitute.

SENATOR ROOT: Yes, that is the substitute. The section which it repeals runs:

> If such ship, vessel or boat be bound elsewhere, and shall continue within such harbor or so hovering for twenty-four hours after the Master shall have been required to depart, any one of such officers, or persons, as are above-mentioned may bring such ship, vessel or boat into port, etc.

That appears on p. 133 of the American Appendix.

JUDGE GRAY: Yes.

The President: The change is that the requisite that the master was required to depart has been left out?

Senator Root: Yes.

The President: That is the difference between the two acts?

Senator Root: Yes; it is a little more stringent.

The President: A little more stringent?

Senator Root: It is a little more stringent, and does not give them quite so much opportunity for notice.

The President: It is much more stringent, yes.

Senator Root: That having been received from Mr. Thornton, and, of course, being an amendment of the original statute, subject to all the limitations of the original statute, it was handed over to Mr. Boutwell, and Mr. Boutwell issued a new circular which included a reference to that amendatory statute, together with the original statute of 1868. That new circular is to be found in the British Case Appendix at p. 237 and in that new circular he included this sentence:

> Fishermen of the United States are bound to respect the British laws and regulations for the regulation and preservation of the fisheries to the same extent to which they are applicable to British or Canadian fishermen.

Then he goes on to recite the Act of 1868 again, and the Act of May, 1870, which amended it, by making the third section more stringent; and he also inserts this clause, which is in italics in the copy in the British Case Appendix on p. 238:

> It will be observed, that the warning formerly given is not required under the amended Act, but that vessels are liable to seizure without such warning.

Well, now is it not plain that the whole subject-matter to which the circular related was the non-treaty coast, and that it had no reference whatever to the treaty coast? That the regulations for the preservation of the Canadian fisheries, which the fishermen of the United States were said by Mr.

Boutwell to be bound to respect to the same extent to which they are applicable to British or Canadian fishermen, are the regulations in force and effect prescribed by these statutes for the preservation of the fisheries on the non-treaty coast to which the circular related, and in which he desired to warn American fishermen against incurring the penalties of these statutes which related to the non-treaty coast, and only to the non-treaty coast. These statutes were statutes for the preservation of their fisheries. They were statutes to prevent American fishing vessels coming in under the color of the right of shelter and repairs, and wood and water, and taking without leave or license, by device and deceit, the benefit of the Canadian fisheries away from the Canadians. Those statutes were binding upon our fishermen.

Judge Gray: Would they or would they not have been binding if they had not referred to the preservation of the fisheries? If they had been merely acts of exclusion?

Senator Root: Unless they excluded in contravention of the four purposes; except within the limits of the treaty right to enter for those four purposes on what we call the non-treaty coast, all those laws were binding upon the Americans who went in there, of course.

Now, to take a circular issued with express reference to one thing, limited in express terms to one thing, take the language of it and carry it over and apply it to something else, cannot add much strength to a case.

The President: And American fishermen fishing in these waters without violating any of these regulations for the preservation of the fisheries would be punishable for the act of fishing itself, without having violated any of the acts concerning the preservation of the fisheries? Would the boat of an American fisherman have been forfeited if he had fished in non-treaty waters, without having violated any one of these regulations?

SENATOR ROOT: He could not fish in non-treaty waters without violating.

THE PRESIDENT: Yes, but if he did ?

SENATOR ROOT: Fishing would be a violation.

THE PRESIDENT: Fishing would be a violation, yes. Without violation of regulations and with violation would be slightly different, I think, in that case. The principal offense would be the fishing.

SENATOR ROOT: Yes, but that of itself would be a violation.

THE PRESIDENT: That of itself would have been a violation. Therefore it would not have been necessary to have a penalty attached to fishing, under certain circumstances, because the fishing itself would have been punishable.

SENATOR ROOT: Certainly, fishing itself would be punishable. There were provisions relating to boats "preparing to fish" as leading so directly to the act itself as to amount to a substantive offense in itself. We may readily conceive quite appropriate regulations to prevent the privilege of shelter, repair, wood, and water, from being abused by fishing; regulations quite consistent with those, but necessary to prevent the abuse, and designed for that purpose; regulations not in themselves pointing to fishing. So that there might well be regulations which might be violated by American fishermen on the non-treaty coast — regulations appropriate and necessary to prevent an abuse, and designed for the protection of the fisheries, and by which they would be bound.

I do not suppose Mr. Boutwell refined about it as much as we may in discussing it, but what he was talking about was regulation on that non-treaty coast. That is perfectly clear. And it is perfectly clear there were provisions designed for the preservation of the fisheries answering to this description:

Fishermen of the United States are bound to respect the British laws and regulations for the preservation of the fisheries to the same extent as they are applicable to Canadian fishermen.

Speaking only of the non-treaty coast. That is quite a reasonable proposition, and not anything inapplicable to the non-treaty coast.

So that I think the Boutwell circular goes with the Marcy circular and the Cardwell letter, and there is nothing left at all of the Boutwell circular, for nowhere on either side in any transaction, letter, or reported interview, or written or printed matter, is there any expression of opinion of any kind regarding the rights and powers of the respective parties, or their subjects or inhabitants upon the treaty coast.

As to the Marcy circular and as to the Cardwell letter there is nothing to be said, except that in each case a British official, not of the Foreign Office and not charged with interpreting the position of the Government of Great Britain upon an international question, expressed an opinion involving the natural assumption that British law was supreme in British territory, without adverting to any question of distinction between the general jurisdiction and jurisdiction over fishery, and without any consideration or study or discussion of the subject of the scope or the power and authority under the treaty of 1818. One of those opinions was expressed by Mr. Cardwell in 1866; another was expressed by the British Minister and Lord Clarendon in 1855. They were both completely disposed of when the governments themselves, through their authorized representatives, their foreign offices, took up and considered and dealt formally and authoritatively with the question of the rights and powers created by the treaty of 1818, both in the correspondence and action regarding the Newfoundland legislation of 1873 and 1874, and in the Evarts-Salisbury correspondence of 1878, 1879, and 1880.

So it rests, that for sixty-two years after this treaty of 1818 was made, there was no position taken by the Government of Great Britain that involved the assertion of a right to alter, or modify, or limit, or restrain the discretion of the United States in determining the time and manner in which the liberty to fish should be exercised.

On the contrary, time after time the Government of Great Britain, by its authorized representatives, assented to and asserted and based its argument and position upon the non-existence of any such right on the part of Great Britain and the existence of a discretion on the part of the United States; and it rests, that for thirty-seven years after the treaty was made, no British official, however casually, ever expressed a doubt or question regarding the right of the United States to exercise its own discretion in determining the implements it should use in taking fish on the treaty coast, and the times when it should take the fish.

Now, I want to group together four expressions upon this subject which have occurred in the transactions which I have been detailing, but which have necessarily been presented at widely separated points in my argument.

First, Lord Bathurst, in the paper which formed the basis of the negotiation in 1815, described the American right under the treaty of 1783 as the claim of an independent state to occupy and use at its discretion any portion of the territory of another.

Sir Charles Fitzpatrick: Just for convenience, will you give the page ?

Senator Root: Page 274 of the American Appendix. And, I will observe there, that while it is true, as Chief Justice Fitzpatrick observed yesterday, that Lord Bathurst is speaking with reference to the prior letter to Mr. Adams, which he is answering, it is not Mr. Adams' characterizing of the right which is expressed here, it is Lord Bathurst's characterizing of the right. Mr. Adams had claimed that the rights of the United States under the treaty of 1783 — which they have been enjoying since the treaty of 1783

— were rights of original possession, rights which they had independently of the treaty, and for the purpose of controverting that claim. Lord Bathurst states what the right is, declaring that it can rest only in conventional stipulation:

> The claim of an independent state to occupy and use at its discretion any portion of the territory of another,

and he says:

> It is unnecessary to inquire into the motives which might have originally influenced Great Britain in conceding such liberties to the United States.

Those are the liberties that were conceded, according to Lord Bathurst, the liberties he has described, the liberty of an independent state to occupy and use at its discretion a portion of the territory. He says: It is unnecessary to inquire what influenced Great Britain in conceding such liberties, and whether the other articles of the treaty did or did not in fact afford an equivalent for them, describing what was in fact done. This liberty is a liberty which was conceded, and it is unnecessary to inquire whether the treaty contained adequate compensation for it, and the liberty is that of an independent state to occupy and use at its discretion the territory of another.

Second, the description by Lord Malmesbury, in 1852, where he, secretary of state of Great Britain, as Lord Bathurst was at the time of his letter (p. 519, American Appendix), describes our right in these words:

> The rights are laid down in the treaty of 1818, as quoted by Mr. Webster; that is, undoubted and unlimited privileges of fishing in certain places were thereby given by Great Britain to the inhabitants of the United States.

Undoubted and unlimited privileges of fishing.

The expression of the Legislature of Newfoundland in the request for a supplementary protocol which should make the proviso of the Newfoundland Act of 1873 operative, upon the acceptance of the treaty of 1871, when Sir Edward

Thornton, the British minister, speaking at the instance of the Government of Newfoundland, in his letter of the 20th June, 1873 (p. 196 of the American Counter-Case Appendix), declares that that proviso, which in terms reserves to Newfoundland the right of regulating the time and manner of prosecuting the fisheries, had reference to the time for the prosecution of the herring fishery on the west coast of Newfoundland, and was merely intended to place citizens of the United States on the same footing with Her Majesty's subjects in that particular, so that the same rules and regulations imposed upon Newfoundland fishermen with regard to that fishery might also be observed by American fishermen.

The expression of Lord Salisbury, another great secretary of state for foreign affairs, appears in the United States Case Appendix at p. 684, in his often-quoted letter of the 3d April, 1880, where he bases his argument for the rejection of the American claim for damages upon this proposition as to the treaty of 1818 and the treaty of 1871. I read his words:

> Thus, whilst absolute freedom in the matter of fishing in territorial waters is granted, the right to use the shore for four specified purposes alone is mentioned in the treaty articles.

" The right of an independent nation to use the territory of Great Britain at its discretion," " the unlimited right of fishing," " absolute freedom in the matter of fishing." Those are the words of three great British secretaries of state for foreign affairs, used in describing the American right for the purpose of passing upon the character of the right, and stating the position that Great Britain was taking in controversies with the United States.

And those descriptions of the character of the American right are in consonance with the rules of construction that obtain in England and America, and I believe obtain throughout the civilized world, for it is the law, and it was then the law, that where by grant or by deed or contract a right is given by one to another to do a thing which involves the exercise of discretion as to time when and manner in which it shall be done, and there is silence as to who shall exercise the discretion, the discretion is vested in the person who has to do the thing. And this is the law of England and the law of America and, while I speak with the greatest diffidence in the presence of gentlemen who have wide experience of the systems of law under which I have not lived, I believe it to be the universal law, for it was the law of Rome. The grant of an *iter* or a *via* under the Roman law gave to the grantee the right to say where he should lay out his path or his road; subject always to the rule of common sense, that he must not exercise his discretion in a way unnecessarily and burdensomely to injure.

These great and authorized representatives of Great Britain were without question applying to the construction of this grant the ordinary and natural rule of construction. They might well have added, and to support the view they took, the view the British Government took for sixty-two years after this treaty was made, the view the makers of the treaty took, and we may add another principle of construction which is binding upon us; that we must construe the grant of a deed or a contract in such a way as to make it effective, and we are not at liberty to construe it in such a way as to destroy the grant; and to construe this grant now upon this new and latter-day theory, to construe this grant in such a way as to reverse the ordinary application of the canon of construction, and to carry the discretion, not to the person who has to do the act, but to the person who has granted the right to do the act, and make the exercise of the right subject to the power of the grantor of the right, in its uncontrolled judgment, to limit and restrain, is making it bear in its own breast the seeds of its own destruction.

We may add to the support of the British position in all that long period before the pressure of the Newfoundland trader began to warp the expression and the action of British statesmen — we may add in support of that earlier position the rule that the words of a grant by deed or contract are to be construed in the sense in which the grantor had reason to believe the grantee understood them, a rule of morality, a rule of good faith and honor; and here, without contradiction, is the evidence as to how the grantee of 1818 understood this grant in the statement of Mr. Gallatin, which stated that the right was regarded as what the French civilians call a servitude.

When we attempt to read into this grant, contrary to the accepted principles of construction, contrary to the construction of the makers and the construction of the two countries, a right of the grantor to modify and change, to what do we appeal? To nothing but the fact that Great Britain is sovereign there, and that from the fact of sovereignty must be implied the right to control.

Did any one ever hear of applying such a rule to the powers of ownership? If an owner of land grant to another the right to make use of the land, to the extent of the use granted he excludes the exercise of his powers of ownership. Did any one ever hear of a claim that he could regulate, modify, or restrict the exercise of the right granted because he was the owner? He may think it is for the common benefit that the right that he has granted may be restricted and modified; but did any one ever hear that because he was the owner he alone was entitled to judge? Common sense says that when a nation grants to another nation a right to be exercised in its territory the grant puts a limitation upon the sovereignty, which limitation goes as far as the grant does, and there is no room within the limit of the grant for an implication arising from the fact of sovereignty.

Now, I have argued Question No. 1 in the main upon the proposition that the grant of the treaty of 1818, being a grant to an independent nation, there was, by the controlling, or one of the controlling features of the grant, carried into it by the use of the word " forever " the conveyance of a real right. I have argued that the Tribunal was bound to give effect to that dominant feature of the grant, and could give effect to it only by treating it as a real right, because mere obligatory rights end with war and end with a change of sovereignty. But that position, while, in the judgment of counsel for the United States, it is a true and sound position, is not necessary to reach the result with which the Tribunal has to deal now and here. So long as the contract exists, whether it be a real right that is created or an obligation, as I have already observed incidentally, the Tribunal must treat it as binding and enforce the limitations which it imposes upon the exercise of sovereignty of Great Britain.

There is this difference between the results which would follow from treating this right that passed to the United States by the ratification of the treaty of 1818 as a real right, on the one hand, and treating it as an obligation in terms perpetual on the part of Great Britain on the other hand. The first difference in the nature of the right is that in the first view the treaty would be deemed to take out from Great Britain a fragment of her sovereignty itself, and from that it would follow as a logical conclusion that Great Britain could not order, regulate, control, limit, or restrict the right that had passed to us because it was not hers.

SIR CHARLES FITZPATRICK: The property had passed from her?

SENATOR ROOT: It had passed. She had no more right to do that than one would have the right to continue ordering any piece of property that he had conveyed away. On the other hand, if this is to be regarded as not creating a real right, but as creating an obligation, Great Britain is prevented from exercising control, limitation, or restriction over the right which passed by her obligation, and therefore the obligation is such that it excludes her from doing that thing. We are all agreed that the contract, whether creating a real or an obligatory right, did limit British sovereignty. Great Britain, by her attorney-general, quotes the words of Lord Salisbury, in which he says that:

> British sovereignty, as regards those waters, is limited in its scope by the engagements of the Treaty of Washington, which cannot be modified or affected by any municipal legislation.

And the Attorney-General says:

> That is the position we take today.

He further says:

> I cannot anticipate that with regard to these principles any difference will be found to exist between the views of the two Governments.

The Attorney-General says further in his argument that:

> That right of exclusion is a sovereign right, and the right is limited, in fact quoad particular persons it is abandoned; I limit my sovereignty to the extent of saying I will not exclude you.
>
> JUDGE GRAY: Then it becomes, in that view of it, confining yourself to what you have just said, a question of the extent of the limitation upon sovereign power?
>
> SIR WILLIAM ROBSON: Yes. Of course every contract is a limitation as I have so frequently said.

He says further:

> They —

the United States —

> want something more than mere restriction of sovereignty. They want to have it established that when a United States inhabitant comes in, not merely is the sovereign right of Great Britain restricted to the extent that it cannot put him out, but they say it cannot govern him when he is there in the exercise of his right.

So, we are all agreed and it is to be taken as a law of this case that this contract, whether it be a real right, in our view, or whether it be obligatory, in the view of Great Britain, does restrict the sovereignty of Great Britain.

Now, there is a restriction of sovereignty, and from that restriction follows a binding obligation which limits the power of Great Britain to deal with the right which she has contracted away.

There is a second difference — this one as to result. If this be a real right, as we think it is, the United States would have a right of control over the conduct of its citizens in the exercise of the real right in this territory, and laws made to govern the time and manner in which they exercise that right would be laws which, for their validity, required the assent of the United States. They would be invalid, as affecting its citizens, but for the assent of the United States. The law-making power of Great Britain would not be " competent ", to use Lord Salisbury's language, to make what would be a law binding upon the citizens of the United States without the assent of the United States, as an element in the law making.

On the other hand, if the treaty creates an obligatory limit upon Great Britain, if the limitation of her sovereignty is a limitation created by perpetual obligation, and if the exercise of the sovereign power of Great Britain in that territory makes a law which oversteps the limit of her obligation, which she was bound in the contract not to make, that is a wrongful exercise of her sovereignty, from which this Tribunal is bound, if it can see it, to restrain her, because this Tribunal is to enforce the obligation wherever the obligation is. I hope I make the distinction clear.

The President: Very clear.

Senator Root: The practical result would be that if you say this is an obligation which prevents Great Britain from rightfully making certain laws, then, while Great Britain would have the sovereign power to make the laws, she would be precluded by your award from making them, or putting them into force, until she had got the concurrence of the United States in their being reasonable, fair, necessary, and proper for the regulation of the common right. But so long as no war has intervened to put an end to this right, so long as no change of sovereignty has come, while Great Britain is sovereign, the parties stand as they stood when the treaty was made, and you reach the same practical result, with the exception of the distinction which I have just made.

SIR CHARLES FITZPATRICK: The difficulty, Mr. Root, with regard to assent is that I cannot understand how, constitutionally, the assent of the Government of the United States could give effect to British legislation. As to your second proposition, I think there is a great deal to be said in favor of it, at all events; but as to the other question, I do not quite understand how your assent could give effect to British legislation. I think your theory would drive you necessarily to the conclusion that if the United States were to exercise its right, on the assumption that sovereignty had been parted with, you would be the sole arbiter, the sole judge of the action of your own citizens with respect to the exercise of the treaty right in British waters. I think that is the logical conclusion, and in the Constitution of the United States you might find some difficulties.

SENATOR ROOT: I see that very probably there will be constitutional difficulties, but we have to treat this case upon the theory that this treaty is a valid treaty, and that it is constitutionally valid.

SIR CHARLES FITZPATRICK: It is not as to the constitutional validity of the treaty, but it is as to the constitutional exercise of your assent.

SENATOR ROOT: Perhaps I do not quite catch your meaning.

SIR CHARLES FITZPATRICK: However, I do not think it is very important, in view of your second position. In view of your second position, I do not think we need trouble ourselves about assent.

SENATOR ROOT: The practical result you reach now would be the same, although you would reach it by a little different process of reasoning. I do not think we need trouble ourselves where this *iter* or *via* goes.

SIR CHARLES FITZPATRICK: Except that the *iter* and *viator* must go where the grantor stipulates—with all due deference.

SENATOR ROOT: They must go to a point, if a point is prescribed. They must go where the grantor stipulates, if the grantor settles it in the grant. They must go where the contract provides, if the contractor settles it in the contract.

SIR CHARLES FITZPATRICK: Yes.

SENATOR ROOT: If he does not say anything about it, then they must go where the person who is to do the going settles it in the exercise of his discretion.

SIR CHARLES FITZPATRICK: And it is not to be settled by the person who is to suffer the burden?

SENATOR ROOT: No. You cannot drive your ox-team along the *via* through a man's house; you must not make the burden unnecessarily grievous, but the discretion is in the person who does the thing unless there is a limit put in the contract.

THE PRESIDENT: In that respect is there an analogy between the position of the private proprietor and the sovereign of a state in dealing with such a real right? The private proprietor cannot decide the question how the entitled may use his right because he consults only his personal interest, whereas the sovereign of a state has to consider not only his personal interest, but the interest of a large community. Is the position, therefore, of the private proprietor, in that respect, strictly analogous with the position of the sovereign of the state?

Senator Root: The private proprietor may have a large family.

The President: Of course, but he has only enlarged individual interests.

Senator Root: The sovereign of the state is the community, and the interests of this particular kind of grant are diverse interests, as I pointed out yesterday. There is no such common interest that the proprietor could be deemed to be invested with a trust to be exercised impartially and judically for the benefit of both of the competing classes.

Now, under this theory of obligation, as I have said, it is agreed equally, as upon the theory of perpetual right, that the sovereignty of Great Britain is limited; and it remains that there can be no implied reservation of the rightful exercise of the sovereign power of Great Britain within the field covered by the grant, because the very essential purpose of the grant being to limit the rightful exercise of British sovereignty as to that subject-matter, the exercise of the sovereignty is excluded just so far as the grant goes, and when the terms of the grant have been read no limitation can be imposed upon them derived from the existence of the sovereignty, or the nature of the sovereignty, which it was the purpose of the grant to limit and exclude from rightful exercise.

In this case of obligation, as in the case of real right, the terms of the contract control, and those terms cannot, consistently with the contract, be subjected to the exercise of any power not found in the terms of the contract, or of any power which is imported into the contract from the fact of the sovereignty which it was the object of the contract to limit and exclude.

In this case, as in the other, the terms of the contract assure to the United States, for its inhabitants, the right, in common with British subjects, to take fish without expressing any limitation upon the exercise of that right, without expressing or suggesting any authority in the grantor of the contract right to say that the right shall not be exercised at any time or in any manner which the grantee of the right deems proper to the exercise thereof.

In this case, as in the other, we are precluded from considering that the grantor nation, which had by the grant excluded itself from the rightful exercise of its sovereignty, within the field covered by the grant, should assume to exercise over the subject-matter of the grant an authority which, in its nature, would make it possible for the grantor practically to destroy the value of the grant.

In this case, as in the other, we are precluded from considering that it was within the contemplation of the parties that the grantor should continue to exercise an authority in respect of the subject-matter of the grant which, when applied to the grant in terms perpetual, would, in the ordinary course of human affairs, ultimately lead to the desire coupled with the power to destroy the value of the grant.

We are precluded from considering that the right vested in the grantee by the contract is to be treated by the grantor as being of a lower degree of sanctity and inviolability than the common right declared by the contract to remain in the subjects of the grantor.

We are precluded from considering that it was the intention of the parties that the common right of the grantee should be subject in its exercise to the control of the grantor, while the equal common right of the grantor was not to be subject to control by the grantee.

In this case, as in the other, the principle of equality of right resting upon the contract remains as inviolable as the principle of equality of right resting upon the ownership of a right by an independent nation to which it has been conveyed, according to the American view.

There is no principle of law or reason which justifies one party to a contract in limiting or modifying the exercise of the other party to the contract in accordance with the first party's own judgment as to what is for the common interest irrespective of the judgment of the other party to the contract. There is no warrant for assuming in this case, more than in the other, that in the absence of express provision in the contract the parties intended that one party to the contract should exercise such a power over the rights of the other party.

When Great Britain concedes, as she does in the statement of Question 1, that regulations of the common right must be reasonable, necessary, fair, etc., she concedes a limitation upon her sovereignty which precludes the exercise of her sole judgment to impose restrictions in her sole will. When Great Britain argues, as she does here, that there was an implied reservation of the sovereignty which enables, justifies, or authorizes her to be the sole judge of what is reasonable, necessary, and fair, she reinstates in her conception of her rights the very principle that she abjured when she put into the statement of her contention in Question 1 the principle of reasonableness, necessity, and fairness. She is not at liberty to abjure it. She has precluded herself from it by the contention of Question 1, which puts the test of reasonableness, fairness, and necessity into the exercise of the liberty, and she is not at liberty to make that test an illusion, to destroy it, to withdraw it by saying: My will, my judgment alone, shall be sovereign — as she does say when she arrogates to herself the sole right to decide; and there is no more right to destroy the test under the theory of obligatory relation than under the theory of a real right. Great Britain is not at liberty to stand, on the position she asserts here, upon either theory, that her judgment and her will, or the judgment that she has handed over to the Legislature of

Newfoundland in its will, shall make and put into force a law which shall bind our fishermen in the exercise of our right, under which our vessels shall be seized and forfeited, under which men shall be arrested, under which our fishermen shall be kept off the coast and shall be prevented from following their industry and exercising it profitably, on the faith that at some future day we will carry an appeal to the Government of Great Britain, then an appeal to a tribunal to be created in the future, and all the time suffering the slow process of diplomatic correspondence pending the framing of the submission, pending the framing of the questions, the selection of the arbitrators, and the creation of such a feeling on the part of both countries as to justify their governments in making an appeal, while all that time the judgment — the uncontrolled, sole judgment — of the Legislature of Newfoundland is, according to the British theory, to be in effect and operation.

It requires a long, long period of accumulated grievances to move two great nations to an arbitration. Many a fisherman has worn out his life waiting upon that slow process. I know men working for day's wages now who ten, fifteen, or twenty years ago were masters of ships, and who have a claim that never yet has reached final decision and fruition. It is not one grievance, or two, or a dozen, but through the long process of years an accumulation of grievances must occur before the humble fishermen of the United States can move two great countries to an arbitration.

Now, I say against the exercise of the uncontrolled power of the legislature of Great Britain or the legislature of Newfoundland to make and put into force provisions relating to the time and manner of the exercise of this treaty right, under the obligatory view, as under the real view, the concession of Great Britain, in the statement of Question 1, stands as a barrier; and under the obligatory view, as under the real view, against that position, stands always the definition of international law by the great Mansfield — justice, equity, convenience, the reason of the thing. I care little by what pathway you reach your conclusion, because I am so optimistic as to believe that this great empire of Britain will continue so long as cod-fish swim around the shores of Newfoundland, and that never, during all these long ages, will there be another war between Great Britain and the United States.

When I made a statement regarding the Roman law to the effect that if a man grants an *iter* or a *via* over his land to another, the discretion to determine where to lay out the *iter* or the *via* was in the person to whom it was granted, I think there were some symptoms of doubt or dissent.

SIR CHARLES FITZPATRICK: Yes, I think you can attribute that to me; I will take the responsibility for that.

SENATOR ROOT: My own authority as a civilian is too little to let that statement stand by itself, and I beg to cite as authority a section of the Digest of Justinian from Mr. Munro's translation. The work was produced at Cambridge by a Fellow of Gonville and Caius College, Cambridge, and published in 1909, second volume, 65th page, 9th paragraph of the first title of the book. Digest 5:

> If a via over anyone's land is conveyed or bequeathed to a man without more [a note says the Latin word here is "simpliciter." If a via over anyone's land is conveyed or bequeathed to a man "simpliciter"], he will be at liberty to walk or drive without restriction, that is to say, over any part of the land that he likes; only, however, in a reasonable way, as the language which people use is always subject to some tacit reservation. The party cannot be allowed to walk or drive through the house itself, or straight across the vineyards, when he might have gone some other way with equal convenience and with less damage to the servient land.

You will see that sustains the same proposition which is stated in section of the Code Civil of 1804 to which I referred as elucidating Mr. Gallatin's reference to the French civilians.

And there is another authority running along a cognate line of contract which was so great an authority at the time when this treaty of 1818 was made that I think it may be interesting for the Tribunal to have it. It is in Hargrave and Butler's *Coke upon Lyttleton.*

In 1818 this was a book of very great authority. It had been published and republished in many editions, and this particular book which I read is an American edition published in Philadelphia in 1827, from the last London edition which was published in 1818, the very year of the negotiation of the treaty. Lord Coke says:

> Fourthly, in case an election be given of two several things, always he which is the first agent, and which ought to do the first act, shall have the election. As if a man granteth a rent of twenty shillings, or a robe to one of his heirs, the grantor shall have the election; for he is the first agent, by the payment of the one, or delivery of the other. So if a man maketh a lease, rendering a rent or a robe, the lessee shall have the election *causa qua supra.* And with this agree the books in the margent. But if I give unto you one of my horses in my stable, there you shall have the election; for you shall be the first agent by taking or seisure of one of them. And if one grant to another twenty loads of hazle or twenty loads of maple to be taken in his wood of D., there the grantee shall have election; for he ought to do the first act, *scil.* to fell and take the same.

You see, Lord Coke there is referring to the rule in the transactions of every-day life in England, and this book, and the customary law which it records, so entered into the life of the English people that very well-informed gentlemen like these negotiators on the part of Great Britain must have known of the rule which it records — very well-informed gentlemen belonging to the class from which Great Britain took her chancellors of the exchequer, like Mr. Goulburn, and her prime ministers, like Mr. Robinson.

THE PRESIDENT: The court will adjourn until 2 o'clock.[1]

[1] Thereupon, at 12.05 o'clock P.M., the Tribunal took a recess until 2 o'clock P.M.

THE PRESIDENT: Will you kindly continue, Mr. Senator Root?[1]

SENATOR ROOT: Before leaving the subject upon which I was speaking, before noon, I wish to cite another rule of construction which, with acknowledgment to the Attorney-General, I will take from his argument. I read from p. 5819 of the typewritten copy [p. 989, *supra*]. Says the Attorney-General:

It is scarcely necessary, but I will read here just one passage from Oppenheim, upon the question of interpretation, in order that I may not appear to be submitting these facts as merely my own ideas, but to fortify myself with the name of some authority; though, in truth, I do not think any authority is needed by the Tribunal for such a proposition. Oppenheim says, at page 559:

> It must be emphasized that interpretation of treaties is in the first instance a matter of consent between the contracting parties. If they choose a certain interpretation, no other has any basis. It is only when they disagree that an interpretation based on scientific grounds can ask for a hearing; and these scientific grounds can be no other than those provided by jurisprudence.

I read that because it is not quite the same as most municipal laws. I have very little knowledge of the laws of any country except my own, but I can well imagine that municipal law might provide that the construction of a contract was to turn simply upon the language of the contract itself; that you would not be at liberty, as of course in English law you would not be at liberty, to look at all these letters and this correspondence. They would all be completely and absolutely excluded, and we should have to try to derive what knowledge we could of the intention of the parties (which is the aim of all construction) from the contract itself, together with any custom which might be supposed to form the basis of the contract. But Oppenheim lays down as a rule in international law, and it seems an extremely good rule, that after all, international tribunals, in dealing with such documents, must first consider: How have the parties interpreted the contract? Because a great Tribunal like this is free, as I have already said, from many of the technical rules that hamper judicial bodies under national laws; and that certainly is an equitable and sound rule. No matter what the contract says, under a technical construction if the parties have agreed and themselves stated what it is to be taken to mean, that is to be its meaning.

[1] Tuesday, August 9, 1910, 2 P.M.

Both the quotation from Oppenheim and the observations of the Attorney-General seem to be very apposite to the interpretation placed upon this treaty by the parties, to which I have devoted so long a period of explanation and exposition during the past two days. There is a very sound basis for the rule. There is this defect in all human reasoning: that no human reasoner has ever collected, or can ever collect in his premises, all the facts which may go to form the basis of a just logical deduction. It is impossible for us, at a distance of almost a century, to reproduce for ourselves all those conditions and circumstances which the people of the period when the treaty was made and of the generation which followed, felt, knew without finding them stated in documents or expressed in terms. We might, looking at the language of a treaty with our knowledge, interpreting the words in the light of what we know, come to one conclusion; but our knowledge is necessarily imperfect. We cannot completely put ourselves in the position of the earlier time; and the interpretation which was put upon this treaty at the time when it was made, and for many years succeeding, is the product of a knowledge more complete than ours can possibly be; and the absence of one single word in any document or conversation during all that period which points to the existence of an idea in the minds of the parties that Great Britain was to say what limitations there might be, or should be, upon our right is, in the view of this rule presented by the Attorney-General, of the greatest cogency.

There is another subject to which I must briefly call the attention of the Tribunal. Other nations have granted rights having the same generic qualities and characteristics as the right which we have here under consideration. Other nations have had their questions regarding them, have discussed them, have reached conclusions, and have fallen into a course of settled practice regarding them. Other publicists have reasoned about them, have examined them, analyzed them, considered their nature, the legal effect and rules of construction which are to be applied; and the results of these processes have been to give in the international law of the past two centuries a wide field of accepted rules, following upon thorough consideration. We cannot ignore this; but it is not my purpose to weary the Tribunal by going over the subject which was so learnedly and clearly presented by Senator Turner. The Tribunal has the authorities which he presented, the exposition of the international law relating to rights belonging to this class, and I shall not trouble the members of the Tribunal further with them. Yet I cannot ignore it, because the Tribunal cannot ignore it. A great international tribunal owes a duty not merely to the parties, but, if we are ever to have a system of international law which justifies the existence of a great permanent court, a tribunal like this owes a duty to mankind, a duty to the nations, in reaching such a conclusion regarding such a matter as is presented here as shall tend not to break down, to disintegrate, but to build up, to perfect, to strengthen a system of settled and accepted rules which shall furnish a guide to such a permanent court in applying principles and rules of law to the peaceful settlement of international disputes.

So I do not feel at liberty to pass the subject by, to close my discussion of the first question submitted, without making some observations regarding the application of the conclusions reached and the evidence presented by the writers who are cited by Senator Turner, and the relation of those conclusions to the evidence and the question which is here.

The effect of a rule of international law, if such a rule there be, which may be relevant in any degree to the consideration of a treaty between two independent nations is rather that of a rule of construction than of a statute upon which rights are based. Again I am indebted to the learned Attorney-General for the very just exposition of that relation. He says [p. 1073, *supra*]:

> Of course in dealing with international law in relation to treaties, — a subject with which I have already dealt at such length, — I admitted that international law, when well established and clearly proved, like municipal law, may be taken as the basis of a contract, and may be read into a contract on those matters as to which the contract is silent because, no doubt, the parties were contracting with knowledge of the law.

In that statement, with which I fully agree, my learned friend demolishes with one blow the ingenious and subtle argument which he had made upon Question 1 in regard to the futility of the United States undertaking to base any claim of right here against Great Britain upon a rule of international law. The argument had been that international law can be established only by proof of custom; that a servitude can be established only by proof of a convention; and that therefore it is impossible that a servitude, necessarily based upon convention, can be maintained by proof of international law. He has stated the right view in the observation which I have cited. The bearing of whatever there is in this wide field of consideration and exposition by the publicists who have dealt with international law, upon the question before this Tribunal, is that it affords a guide to the construction of the instrument, to the interpretation of the instrument. Indeed, it is an inversion of the truth to suppose that rights such as we are presenting here are based upon rules of international law. They are based upon the treaty. It is an inversion to suppose that all these gentlemen who have written about servitudes are establishing a basis for servitudes by their references to the analogy of the civil law, of the Roman law. The process is precisely the contrary. In international law, as in the customary law of municipalities, the internal private law of states, a right is discerned; men by contract, or nations by treaties, create a right; natural and necessary consequences are seen to flow from that right; and in international law a series of consequences flowing from the creation of a particular class of rights has been explained by publicists by a reference to the analogy of servitudes under the Roman law. The rights are not made to depend upon the analogy; they are explained by the analogy. That is all that an analogy can ever do — to elucidate, make clear, carry home to the mind the true nature of the subject to which the analogy is applied. We are not here, and we never have been here claiming that we are entitled to have our treaty right here held inviolable because it is a right founded upon an analogy to the Roman law of servitudes. We are here saying that this is a right which may be understood under a treaty which must be interpreted in the light of the explanations of this and similar rights during a long series of years, and explanations accepted by the nations of the world, so that they have become a rule of construction for conventions which create similar rights. How are we to find, how are we to prove, in the words of the Attorney-General, what the rule of international law is which is to be applied to the construction of this convention? We are not without an exposition of the method of proof by a very great English judge, and a very great authority in international law. In the case of the Queen *vs.* Keyn, so often cited here, in L. R. 2 Exchequer Division, p. 63, Sir Robert Phillimore, in his very able opinion, in which he based his construction of the statutes of Great Britain and his view of the legal effect of those statutes very largely upon an application of the rules of construction which had been built up in this way by the common consent of nations, cites a number of authorities which are very pertinent to the question as to the way to prove the rule of construction to which the Attorney-General appeals.

He cites Mr. Wheaton as saying:

"Text writers of authority, showing what is the approved usage of nations, or the general opinion respecting their mutual conduct, with the definitions and modifications introduced by general consent, are placed as the second branch of international law."

Lord Mansfield, deciding a case in which ambassadorial privileges were concerned, said that he remembered a case before Lord Talbot, in which he

"Had declared a clear opinion that the law of nations was to be collected from the practice of different nations and the authority of writers. Accordingly he argued and determined from such instances and the authority of Grotius, Barbeyrac, Bynkershoek, Wiquefort, etc., there being no English writer of eminence upon the subject."

This deliverance of Lord Mansfield was some years before the making of our treaty, and I believe there was no English writer of eminence on the subject of international law for quite a number of years after the year 1818, although continental treatises upon international law had been translated into English and were available for the use and guidance of England.

THE PRESIDENT: Rutherforth was perhaps prior. I think Rutherforth was in the eighteenth century.

SENATOR ROOT: I do not remember his date.

THE PRESIDENT: I am not quite sure, but I think he would have been prior; but he was, perhaps, the only one.

SENATOR ROOT: That might have been; yes. Sir Robert Phillimore cites Chancellor Kent as saying:

In cases where the principal jurists agree the presumption will be very greatly in favor of the solidity of their maxims, and no civilized nation that does not arrogantly set all ordinary law and justice at defiance will venture to disregard the uniform sense of the established writers of international law.

He cites von Holtzendorf as saying

that the usage and practice of international law is in great measure founded upon the tardy recognition of principles which have been long before taught and recommended by the voice of the wise and discerning men, and that thus the fabric of international jurisprudence has been built up.

He says himself (Sir Robert Phillimore) that:

> Of course the value of these responsa prudentum is affected by various circumstances; for instance, the period at which the particular work was written, the general reputation of the writer, the reception which his work has met with from the authorities of civilized states, are circumstances which, though in no case rendering his opinion a substitute of reason, may enhance or derogate from the consideration due to it.

We have produced here a very great array of evidence as to the existence of an accepted custom among the nations of the earth to consider rights of the kind conferred in this treaty as constituting a special class with certain special incidents. I am not concerned now with the processes of reasoning by which these writers reach the conclusion. I am not concerned with the name that they gave to the right. I should agree with the Attorney-General that it is an unfortunate name, because it seems to connote a condition of inferiority on the part of one to another, which is rather repulsive to the proud spirit of an independent nation. What I am concerned with, and what I wish to impress upon the Tribunal, is that there is, by approved evidence of a great array of the recognized and most highly respected authorities, and has been since long before the treaty of 1818 was made, a rule among the nations of the earth to treat this kind of right as having certain special incidents — incidents derived from the nature of the right, the nature of the parties to the right, the necessities of the continued existence of the right; therefore the necessities of effectuating the grant of the right. Whether it be that the conclusion was reached by a process which treated the right as real; whether by a process which treated it as obligatory — I am not concerned with that. I do maintain that, giving full effect to such rights, giving them the full effect of perpetuity, it is necessary to treat them as real rights. But the existence of the rule does not depend upon that; nor does the existence of the rule depend upon a transfer of sovereignty. The essential features of the right which is the subject-matter of the rule here are that it shall, in favor of one independent nation, limit the sovereignty of another independent nation in respect of the use of its territory. The majority of writers consider that it must be perpetual; some consider that it need not be. We are not concerned with that here, because this is perpetual, and there are none who place a right which has the basis of perpetuity below a right which has but a temporary continuance. I say that the essential features, and the only essential features of a right which have been universally accepted by the nations as constituting a special class of rights, with certain special incidents, are the features that exist here: that one nation conveys or assures by conventional stipulation to another independent nation the right to make a use for its own benefit or the benefit of its citizens of the territory of the first nation, limiting the sovereignty — and I care not whether it be power or rightful exercise — limiting the scope of sovereignty of the nation that has conferred the right. I conceive, and humbly submit to the Tribunal, that it would be a very great misfortune, not merely to the interests of these litigants here, both of whom are deeply concerned in having a consistent system of international law maintained and built up, but a very great misfortune to the world if a conclusion were to be reached here which ignores, which sets at naught, which rejects the almost universal testimony of the approved witnesses as to the existence of rules of international law. It would be a misfortune if the judgment here should disappoint the just expectations with which the civilized world looks to the decision of a great international tribunal engaged in that administration of justice which should always be not merely a disposal of the rights of the litigants, but a constructive force in the building up of a system to assure justice in future times and in future disputes between nations.

We cannot shuffle off the relation of the rule to which I have referred to the construction of this instrument by treating the great founders and expounders of international law as freaks in a museum of antiquities.

I have said that the essential quality of this special class of rights, granted by convention between two independent nations and having a perpetual quality in the right granted, is the restriction of sovereignty. Let me give a few of the brief expressions of that idea by the witnesses whom we have called:

Bluntschli says:

> The name of international servitudes is given to every conventional and perpetual restriction affecting the territorial sovereignty of a state in favor of another state.

Bonfils says;

> The servitudes called *conventional* alone constitute veritable restrictions upon the free exercise of internal sovereignty for the benefit of other states.

I beg the Tribunal, while I read these expressions, to receive them free from any prejudice arising from the fact that these gentlemen used the term "international servitudes." They are merely using a name which they have chosen to apply to a special class of rights, and under which some of them group other characteristics and some do not. This is the one essential characteristic, and the all-sufficient characteristic:

Calvo says:

> International servitudes are every restriction confining the territorial sovereignty of a state in favor of another state.

Chrétien:

> A state may have renounced for the benefit of one or several others the exercise of a right conferred by its sovereignty. . . . If this is permanent an international servitude results.

Clauss:

State servitudes are permanent limitations of territorial sovereignty of one state in regard to another state, created by special agreements or by possession from time immemorial.

Despagnet:

These (international servitudes) consist essentially in a limitation affecting the internal or external sovereignty of a state, which is constrained not to do, or to allow another state to do for its benefit, that which it could normally accomplish or prevent.

Diena:

A state obligates itself . . . to allow another state to perform certain acts on its own territory which it might prevent, or else it obligates itself to abstain from doing certain acts which it would have a right to perform; such restrictions, *when they are of a permanent character*, give rise to the so-called international servitudes.

Fabre:

From a juridical point of view it matters little whether the servitudes burden the state or the territory; they are all real rights, those burdening the state effecting a diminution of ruling and juridical right, and those burdening the territory effecting a diminution of the right of exclusive use over the territory.

Fiore:

An international servitude consists in a territorial right constituted in favor of one state upon the territory of another state.

Hall:

Servitudes are derogations from the full enforcement of sovereignty over parts of the national territory.

Hartmann:

If the territorial sovereignty of a state is so permanently limited for the benefit of another state that the international personality of the limited state is not destroyed, there arises an international servitude.

Heffter:

The servitudes here discussed have for their exclusive object sovereign rights or royal prerogatives and generally the public domain. . . .

The effects of public servitudes consist sometimes in investing a foreign state with the enjoyment of certain sovereign rights within a territory; at other times in forbidding it the exercise of a like right upon its own territory.

Heilborn:

International *jura in re aliena* exist when one nation has a right to require all other nations to refrain from certain acts on foreign territory.

Hollatz:

State servitude is a real limitation of foreign territorial sovereignty.

Holtzendorff:

An international servitude exists when the rights of territorial sovereignty of a sovereign nation are permanently restricted in favor of one or more other nations so that otherwise permissible acts of governmental control . . . become impermissible within the servient territory, or otherwise impermissible acts of control by a foreign government become permissible.

Klüber:

A public servitude is a right founded upon a special title which restrains . . . the liberty of another state.

Lomonaco:

A servitude is a conventional restriction placed upon the sovereignty of one nation in favor of another.

G. F. de Martens:

A servitude of public international law is a perfect right within the territory of another by virtue of which the latter obligates itself to do, to tolerate, or to refrain from doing for the advantage of the other state, that which it would not naturally be bound to do and which it cannot ask in return.

Neumann:

State servitudes are limitations of the sovereign rights of a state. . . . It is immaterial whether the state is directly entitled as such, or whether it possesses the right on behalf of its subjects.

H. B. Oppenheim:

All international servitudes are determined and well-defined restrictions of territorial sovereignty.

L. Oppenheim:

State servitudes are those exceptional and conventional restrictions on the territorial supremacy of a state by which a part or a whole of its territory is in a limited way made to perpetually serve a certain purpose or interest of another state.

Phillimore:

> A state may *voluntarily* subject herself to obligations in favor of another state, both with respect to persons and things which would not *naturally* be binding upon her. These are *servitudes juris gentium voluntarial.*
>
> The servitudes *juris gentium* must, however, be almost always the result either of certain prescriptive customs or of positive conventions.

Rivier:

> International servitudes are relations of state to state . . . as a real right burdening the territory of a state for the benefit of . . . another state, the international servitude passes with the territory. . . . The servitude is a permanent restriction of territorial sovereignty and not of independence in general.

Ullmann:

> International servitudes can only be established between independent nations and constitute a restriction of the territorial sovereignty of the servient nation. . . . In substance, international servitudes constitute a tolerance, when the dominant nation is allowed to perform acts of territorial sovereignty, in the territory of the servient nation, by its own authority and independently of the servient nation; or a forbearance, when the servient nation refrains from performing acts of territorial sovereignty on its own territory for the benefit of the dominant nation.

The Tribunal will perceive that the essential quality of the class of rights regarding which all these writers have spoken is the very thing that is here: an independent state limiting its sovereignty, the power or rightful exercise, so as to permit, and permanently permit, another state itself, or through its citizens, to have the beneficial use of the territory of the state that limits its sovereignty.

It is with regard to the situation thus created that a rule has grown up; and I repeat that the rule is independent of any process of reasoning that any of these gentlemen go through in explaining it. It is there. It is the custom of nations. It has the consent of nations, by unimpeachable and overwhelming evidence, and must be applied to the construction of this treaty, which confessedly creates just such a right as the rule applies to.

Since long before this treaty was made, the accepted rule of international law has been that the kind of right, or the class of rights which I have been discussing, unlike general trading, and travel, and residence rights, the class of rights which constitute a permanent burden in favor of one state upon the territory of another, protected by a limitation of the sovereignty of the burdened state, protected by a solemn conventional limitation keeping away from the right the exercise of that sovereignty, protected by a stipulation which protects the right that constitutes the burden fromthe exercise of the sovereignty, are not subject to the unrestrained exercise of that sovereignty, are not subject to that exercise of its discretion resting in its own will, which is the necessary incident of all sovereignty, and which is claimed here.

Artopæus, in 1689, speaking of this kind of right, says:

> The general principles are the following: The servient territory shall not hamper the dominant one in the exercise of the servitude, or lessen the right by various dispositions.

That was 129 years before this treaty of 1818 was made. He proceeds:

> The right created by the servitude shall not be extended beyond the compass explicitly granted; this does not impede the dominant party from taking the measures necessary for the exercise of its right. For when a certain right is granted, the measures necessary for its exercise must also be given.

I would rather put here a different use of words, because I sympathize with the Attorney-General's antipathy to the use of the word "servitude." I would rather say: "The sovereign of the burdened territory shall not hamper the possessor of the right that constitutes the burden in the exercise of that right, or lessen the right by various dispositions."

There is no doubt about what it means. There is no doubt but that it applies directly to the right which, a hundred and odd years after, these gentlemen made in the treaty of 1818.

In 1749, Wolf, who I need not tell this Tribunal was one of the great founders of modern international law, accepted as the highest authority, one of those few men whose work in an inconspicuous field, without any of the glamour of those bloody controversies which characterized the day in which he lived, survives the generations and the centuries in the judgment of men whose estimate is worth having — Wolf says, of the nation which has the kind of right we confessedly have here:

Since anybody can grant any right he chooses to a third party concerning this thing, so has each nation a right to grant another nation a certain right in its territory. . . . It belongs even to the mutual duties of nations for the one to create certain rights in his territory for the advantage of the other, in so far as no abuse of the territory takes place. Examples of such rights are the following: Fishing rights in foreign rivers or occupied parts of the sea, rights of fortification on alien soil, right of garrisoning a foreign fortified place, jurisdiction in certain localities of a foreign territory or for certain legal actions or over certain persons, etc. The constitution of rights in foreign territories is not of interest to neighboring nations alone, but also to those living at a distance . . . for the exercise of his right is absolutely independent of the will of the sovereign of the territory, he not being subject to the laws of the land with regard to acts connected with the exercise of his right; but as to other acts cannot be regarded otherwise than as a foreigner residing in a foreign territory.

There is great authority, not expressing his own opinion, but stating what the law of nations was seventy years before this treaty was made — authority of the highest character, stating what the law of nations was in regard to the grant of precisely such a right as we have here.

The great Vattel, in 1758, just five years before the treaty of 1763 assured to France that her subjects should have the liberty to take fish on the shore of Newfoundland, and just sixty years before the treaty of 1818 was made, says:

There exists no reason why a nation, or a sovereign, if authorized by the laws, may not grant various privileges in their territories to another nation, or to foreigners in general, since everyone may dispose of his own property as he thinks fit. Thus, several sovereigns in the Indies have granted to the trading nations of Europe the privilege of having factories, ports, and even fortresses and garrisons in certain places within their dominions. We may in the same manner grant the right of fishing in a river, or on the coast, that of hunting in the forests, etc., and, when once these rights have been validly ceded, they constitute a part of the possessions of him who has acquired them, and ought to be respected in the same manner as his former possessions.

To come to later witnesses, and without wearying the Tribunal by going all through the long list — witnesses not telling what the law is at the time they write, but telling what the law long has been — I will testify to my confidence in the accuracy of Mr. Clauss. He says, after describing what he calls the servitude, what I have been calling a burden, in the words which I have already cited:

From this it follows that the entitled state cannot be hindered in the exercise of the authority belonging to it, or even have such exercise rendered difficult for it by certain measures; just as, on the other hand, it is also the duty of the entitled state not to go beyond the rights granted to it. Within the limits created by treaty, however, the dominant state is entirely free and independent of the sovereignty of the servient state. The legislation of the servient state must yield to the servitude right of the foreign state.

That is not Mr. Clauss's opinion about what ought to be; that is the evidence of one of the best, if not the best, and most approved statements of recent time regarding what the law of nations has been and is.

Klüber says:

It is likewise essential that the state to which the right belongs shall be, as to its exercise, independent of the state burdened with the servitude.

Heilborn cites as being correct the words of Clauss which I have just read.

I will not multiply these citations, they are to be found in the copious extracts presented by Mr. Turner. I select them from different periods, from most approved writers, showing illustrations of the testimony regarding the nature of this rule, and I care not whether you say that this is a real right or an obligatory right, it is proved beyond peradventure that the nations have confirmed by usage, and regard as a matter of rule, that this kind of right is a right which in limiting sovereignty excludes the sovereignty of the burdened state from diminishing, modifying, or restricting the right that constitutes the burden.

JUDGE GRAY: You do not depend on that, Mr. Root, do you, for the contention that there was no right to modify or limit? It does not depend upon its classification as a technical servitude?

SENATOR ROOT: Certainly not.

JUDGE GRAY: You do not suppose Lord Salisbury had that in mind, or that any of the negotiators (unless Mr. Gallatin, who alluded to a servitude) had in mind any relation to this definition by the writers up to that time?

SENATOR ROOT: I suppose the negotiators understood the way in which rights of that character were generally regarded. I suppose that the testimony of these writers whom I have been reading shows what the general view of nations was before 1818, and I suppose the trained diplomats of Great Britain and of the United States who were there participated in that general view regarding those rights. I do not suppose that they considered that they were acting under a technical rule of servitudes. But I am citing the evidence which sustains this view of this particular kind of right; first, because it confirms the reasoning which has been presented to the Tribunal through the poor efforts of counsel for the United States, by similar reasoning, reaching similar conclusions, on the part of many of the greatest, the ablest, and the wisest of mankind; and second, because it is evidence that the nations before the treaty was made took the same view of these rights that we are taking now. I am not basing our position upon any technical rule of servitudes, but supporting it by the evidence that similar conclusions had been reached by wiser and abler men than we at this bar, and that those conclusions had entered into the way of regarding this kind of right on the part of the nations of the earth.

This particular specific kind of right which these gentlemen call "economic servitudes" has been recognized as constituting a class by itself, so freely, so generally, that I submit the Tribunal cannot ignore the fact that it is a class by itself, and a class which has the incident that I have been contending for.

I say we produce evidence that the conclusion which we have been urging upon the Tribunal, whether on the basis of real right or on the basis of the limitation created by an obligatory stipulation — the conclusions we have been urging upon you, have been reached by substantially all the writers upon International Law, and accepted by the nations of the earth, and constitute a rule of construction to be applied to this treaty, powerfully supporting our reasoning and making it impossible to ignore that, because of the insignificance and incompetency of the men who presented it.

That these rights which are called "economic servitudes", and which I should prefer to call burdens upon the territory of one state for the benefit of the inhabitants or citizens of another, constitute a class by themselves, appears in the writings which we have presented, and from Vattel, Chrétien, Despagnet, Diena, Fabre, Fiore, Hartmann, Heffter, Hollatz, Rivier, Ullmann, Wharton, Wolf, Wilson, and Tucker, Holtzendorff, Merignhac, Olivart, Oppenheim, and Pradier-Fodéré.

Now, they support us, they have reached the same conclusions we have, and they testify that the nations, whose consent makes international law, have accepted the conclusion, however reached, by whatever process of reasoning, the conclusion that such a right as this is a thing by itself, and, from the necessity of its existence, independent of the kind of control which Great Britain claims to read into this treaty as a matter of implication. And I submit that our reasoning cannot be rejected without at the the same time rejecting the general opinion of the world of international law.

I should modify that — it is not our reasoning, but our conclusion that cannot be rejected, without rejecting the opinion of the world of international law which has reached that same conclusion, by various routes and on various grounds, but all coming to the same conclusion, accepted and confirmed by usage.

These very rights regarding which we have been arguing (the French and American fishing rights on the Newfoundland coast) have generally been regarded, have been specified, as examples of the class of right standing by itself, protected from the exercise of the sovereign power of the burdened state, and that use of them as examples is found in Bonfils, Chrétien, Clauss, Despagnet, Diena, Fabre, Hollatz, Holtzendorff, Merignhac, Olivart, Oppenheim, Rivier, Ullmann, Wharton, and some others I dare say, but those I have noted.

Now, if it is possible for any one to support argument by authority, if it is possible for any one to give dignity and consideration to the process of his own reasoning by showing that others have reached the same conclusion, we certainly have given substance, and weight, and authority to the conclusion which we have been deducing here from the record and from the nature of this grant.

There is one matter to which I must call attention before leaving the subject. Counsel for Great Britain have cited a number of decisions in the United States in regard to the exercise of rights of fishing by the people of one state in the territory of another, and some cases in the British colonies. I shall not detain you by any extended consideration of those cases. In the British colonies they were a matter of the internal polity of the British Empire. All these laws had to receive the approval of the sovereign, they became laws by the authority of the sovereign law, and present purely a matter of internal polity. These laws, statutes, and cases in the United States also are entirely a matter of internal polity, the internal distribution of power within our own country, and can have no relation whatever to an international question of this description.

There was, however, one case which was referred to as indicating that the courts of the United States took a rather inconsistent position with regard to the rights conferred upon an Indian tribe by what we call a treaty. That comes pretty nearly being a matter of internal polity, for our Indian tribes are rather dependent sovereigns; nevertheless the case is worthy of attention because it involves a charge of inconsistency.

It was the case of the United States against the Alaska Packers Association, 79 Federal Reporter. That case decided against certain rights which were secured to Indians by treaty, to be exercised in common with the citizens of Washington territory generally, upon the northwestern coast. The case was decided upon the authority of certain previous decisions, and the judge who wrote the opinion says, "I have given the same interpretation to similar treaties with other tribes of Indians in Washington territory", citing United States *vs.* James G. Swan, 50 Federal Reporter, and United States *vs.* Winans, 73 Federal Reporter, p. 72, and he says up to the present time these decisions have not been reversed.

They have now been reversed by the Supreme Court of the United States in the case of the United States *vs.* Winans. That is the case which is mentioned there as decided by the same judge and followed by him in his decision.

The case is reported in 198 United States Reports, p. 371, and was decided at the October term, 1904. I cannot ask anything better from the Tribunal than the decision of this case would lead to inevitably. The syllabus begins:

This court will construe a treaty with Indians as they understood it and as justice and reason demand.

The right of taking fish at all usual and accustomed places in common with the citizens of the Territory of Washington and the right of erecting temporary buildings for curing them, reserved to the Yakima Indians in the treaty of 1859, was not a grant of right to the Indians but a reservation by the Indians of the rights already possessed and not granted away by them. The rights so reserved imposed a servitude on the entire land relinquished to the United States under the treaty and which, as was intended to be, was continuing against the United States and its grantees as well as against the state and its grantees.

And accordingly upon that ground they reversed the decision cited by my learned friend on the other side.

The Court says (p. 379):

The pivot of the controversy is the construction of the second paragraph. Respondents contend that the words " the right of taking fish at all usual and accustomed places *in common* with the citizens of the Territory " confer only such rights as a white man would have under the conditions of ownership of the lands bordering on the river, and under the laws of the state, and, such being the rights conferred, the respondents further contend that they have the power to exclude the Indians from the river by reason of such ownership.

And upon that proposition the Court says (p. 381):

The reservations were in large areas of territory and the negotiations were with the tribe. They reserved rights, however, to every individual Indian, as though named therein. They imposed a servitude upon every piece of land as though described therein. There was an exclusive right of fishing reserved within certain boundaries. There was a right outside of those boundaries reserved " in common with citizens of the Territory." As a mere right, it was not exclusive in the Indians. Citizens might share it, but the Indians were secured in its enjoyment by a special provision of means for its exercise. They were given " the right of taking fish at all usual and accustomed places," and the right " of erecting temporary buildings for curing them." The contingency of the future ownership of the lands, therefore, was foreseen and provided for — in other words, the Indians were given a right in the land — the right of crossing it to the river — the right to occupy it to the extent and for the purpose mentioned. No other conclusion would give effect to the treaty. And the right was intended to be continuing against the United States and its grantees as well as against the state and its grantees.

A question was asked during the discussion upon the French treaty rights, as to what reference there was in the correspondence, and Mr. Turner said that an examination would be made.

We have made such examination as was practicable, although under great difficulty, the only papers accessible to us being two or three French Yellow Books and the British Blue Books. There were no such publications covering the early history of transactions between Great Britain and France, and the French Yellow Books began in the sixties. There are only three. We have them here. We have printed some extracts from them which we will hand to our friends on the other side, and hand up to the court. There is one extract here from the British Blue Book which Mr. Turner read in court, and which we have reproduced here for your convenience.

They serve, taken together with the correspondence which is already in the record, particularly the correspondence between Lord Salisbury and M. Waddington, to exhibit in a very clear light the attitudes of the two countries in respect of these rights, and I think they show the relative attitudes of the two countries, not only at the precise time when the letters were written, but historically; they show what it had been from the beginning; and without detaining you to read these letters, I will hand them in, with your permission.

Now, I wish to say a word about the practical application of the American view of the right conferred upon us by this treaty, and of the way in which the line should be drawn.

Our view is, I need hardly say, that the terms of the treaty itself, which give to the inhabitants of the United States the liberty to take fish of every kind, and reserve no right on the part of the sovereign, whose sovereignty is limited, to prohibit taking at such time as the United States chooses, or in such manner as it chooses, furnished the line which is to be drawn, with the entire field of general sovereignty open and covered by Great Britain. We say that in either view, either the view of a real right or the view of a binding obligation, when Great Britain comes to the subject-matter of the right, she must stop; that furnishes the line. When she comes to the subject-matter of the right, she is prohibited by her contract, by her grant to us (and it is a part of the limitation of her sovereignty), that she must not say this right shall not cover the taking of fish except at such time as she thinks desirable, or it shall not cover the taking of fish except in such manner as she thinks desirable. If she does think it is desirable to restrict and modify the exercise of that right, because it is a right that she has given to us, she must say to us it is desirable, and we must agree upon the limitations upon our right. It is our view that this furnishes a practicable, convenient, equitable, and beneficent guide for the conduct of this business hereafter by the two nations. That if we cannot agree, then under Article 4 either party can appeal to the Tribunal which is constituted under this new treaty, or under Article 4 either party can appeal to the method which I hope your honors may be able to prescribe to the satisfaction of both parties for perhaps a simpler and less expensive proceeding. And, from this point of view, I want to repeat what I said the other day, bearing upon our view, that the best thing for all parties is to have a definite line, the definite line that the treaty itself establishes, instead of reading into the treaty this perfectly vague and indefinite idea that Great Britain can go just as far as she thinks reasonable, just as far as Newfoundland thinks reasonable, which is no line at all; which would put always upon Great Britain the necessity of either assenting to the always extreme position that Newfoundland must take, which the conditions, the nature of things, the fact that they are burdened, the fact that we are their competitor, would compel them to take; or of overruling Newfoundland without any definite line of right on which to overrule her, and of course creating resentment and trouble.

It is better for all parties as a practical matter to have a clear line drawn, so that the position of Great Britain will be one of a relation to her colony upon a line of right, instead of a most invidious and difficult position of being compelled to be a judge deciding for or against her own child in a matter of uncontrolled discretion.

I want to submit to you that the history of our relations with Great Britain indicates that there will not be any trouble about agreement. There may be some specific and definite question that we will have to leave out to somebody, that we will have to get an opinion upon, but rather for the purpose of backing us up in making an agreement than for any other reason. There is no reason why, if we had this line of right settled, we should not take up the subject of general regulations just where Lord Bathurst and Mr. Adams left off. When Lord Bathurst proposed and our Government accepted the proposition that there should be joint regulations it was, as you will remember, pushed aside by the alternative of pushing us aside to the wild and unsettled coast, where there was not any real use of going on with the subject of joint regulations. There is no reason why we should not take it up but for this difficulty of Great Britain in dealing with a colony that is sure to be extreme, without having any definite line of right upon which to deal with it.

That there is no obstacle to regulations if both parties know what they are entitled to is quite clear from the way in which countries about this sea live under the joint regulations of the North Sea Fishery. There is no reason why this should not be done as well as Great Britain and France, for so many years bitter enemies, have been able to make their regulations under the treaty of 1839, to make joint regulations in so far as they were concerned between each other under the treaty of 1857, which contained an elaborate scheme of joint regulation for the Newfoundland coast, but which was rejected by Newfoundland, and as at last they have done under their treaty of 1904, which was finally accepted by Newfoundland.

You will remember that in 1889 Lord Knutsford wrote to Governor O'Brien, of Newfoundland, when the colony had been particularly insistent upon its very extreme views of its own rights and convenience:

> There is no reasonable ground on which the Government of Newfoundland can object to the introduction into that colony of Regulations similar to those which the Governments interested in the North Sea fisheries have agreed upon as best calculated to insure proper police and to prevent the occurrence of disputes among rival fishermen.

That is dated the 31st May, 1889, and is found in the United States Counter-Case Appendix, p. 325. He says that there is no reasonable ground. The only obstacle lies in the fact that Great Britain has no measure of control over Newfoundland except her own will, and Newfoundland would naturally resent any restraint on what she believes to be necessary for her prosperity at the mere uncontrolled will of the mother-country. If you give a clear, definite line of right, such as we are contending for, all that difficulty is obviated.

There would be no trouble with the United States. We have here, and I have already referred to it, an act of the Congress of the United States, passed on the 15th March, 1862, and presented in the British Case Appendix, at p. 787, authorizing the appointment by the President of a representative of the United States to take part in a joint commission with France and Great Britain for the regulation of the fisheries. I think that it probably referred to the outside bank fisheries, but my purpose in referring to it now is to show the spirit and the ease with which such a matter can be arranged if people know what their rights are. The practical adaptation is comparatively simple. The Chamberlain-Bayard treaty of 1888 contains a series of agreed regulations regarding the enforcement of Canadian laws and regulations for the preservation of their fishery. That treaty failed of confirmation not because of these features at all, but because of other features, and the treaty illustrates how easy it is for two friendly nations, who are familiar with the case and adopt a moderate attitude with respect to international intercourse, to get on with each other, make modalities and agree upon the best way for the industry to be profitably pursued, provided that they are allowed to.

A very good illustration of what I am now saying is to be found in the history of the so-called *modus* of 1888. Somebody spoke of it here the other day as being still in force in Canada. Well, it was an informal agreement dealing with a lot of these subjects that we are agonizing about here, binding for only two years. Twenty years ago its binding force ended. The two countries have gone on under it ever since because common sense ruled them, and under it each country finds that its interests are better served by the friendly intercourse that it provides than they would be by breaking up again and going to quarreling. The debates upon it in the Canadian Parliament — active and exciting debates — have developed argument as to whether it should continue, but the common sense of Canada has prevailed. Canada has become a nation with a sense of national responsibility, of a national future, and of the value and importance of commercial relations, and it is her own will that she continues them and she is not concerned by any narrow and limited view of the people of a particular locality.

Sir Charles Fitzpatrick: And it is practically not her only industry ?

Senator Root: Well, it is not; that is true. It is not practically her only industry, and that makes it easier for her. The same thing is illustrated by the way in which we have got on under the *modus vivendi* of 1906 and the *modus* of 1907 regarding this same Newfoundland matter. Sir Edward Grey, the American Secretary of State, the American Ambassador to Great Britain, the British Ambassador to Washington — none of them had any trouble about it except that Newfoundland screamed loudly over Great Britain undertaking to make an agreement which Newfoundland considered to be overriding her constitutional rights, and it was only because it was a necessity to the prosecution of the idea of having an arbitration that the *modus* was made. It was only because of such a necessity that Great Britain was able to stand up and insist upon it against the violent protests of Newfoundland.

I want to impress upon your minds what Governor MacGregor said about the way in which they got along under those moduses. The Governor made a report to Lord Elgin, to be found on pp. 360 and 361 of the American Counter-Case Appendix. He says:

> I have had personal interview with Inspector O'Reilly who has arrived from Bay of Islands at St. John's, Newfoundland.

This is a report on the working of the *modus* of 1906, and is dated the 22d November, 1906.

> No ill-feeling towards American ships on the part of Newfoundland fishermen, and no interference with American ships.
>
> About forty American ships, about twenty Canadian ships, about fourteen Newfoundland vessels, Bay of Islands; three vessels loaded, sailed for Gloucester

and so on.

> Alexander has been on friendly terms with Newfoundland officers; American ships consult with Alexander on all points raised, and are guided

by his careful advice; Alexander understands position, and endeavors to prevent trouble.

Neither master nor owner American ships offered any opposition to legal proceedings against Dubois and Crane, but rather facilitated matters advised by Alexander.

Legal proceedings produced no result. There is no excitement; fishermen are at work as if nothing had happened.

All American ships have entered Customs House and Light Dues have been paid without any trouble.

American ships have observed in good faith the conditions laid down in *modus vivendi*.

No trouble expected if matters remain the same as at the present time, but enforcement of Bait Act in general might produce disturbance.

You can get on all right under an arrangement with Great Britain and the fishermen can get on all right together, but for this disturbing influence for which I cannot blame Newfoundland, because it is quite inevitable. At p. 366 he makes another report, dated the 29th December, 1906. He says:

Relations of fishermen on friendly terms.

There was considerable cutting of fishing nets and gear, principally American ships, against each other, but Newfoundland fishermen have suffered from this.

Potomac did good service for Newfoundland fishermen during the ice blockade about the middle of this month in releasing fishing nets and fishing smacks when blocked by ice; *Potomac* broke the ice for fishermen without distinction (of) nationality.

Captain Anstruther, in his report of the 4th December, 1906 (p. 366), says:

The ice was from four to six inches thick and the fishermen were powerless to recover their property. The *Potomac* spent all Saturday and Sunday ice-breaking, which enabled many of the nets to be recovered, but I fear a large number will be lost. This work, though of course beneficial to American fishermen, was also of material assistance to Newfoundland, so I took upon myself to thank Lieutenant Hinds on behalf of the Newfoundland fishermen for his co-operation.

The " Potomac " was an American vessel, and I should observe that she was not a man-of-war. There was no man-of-war there. She was there as a white-winged messenger of peace. She was a revenue vessel of the United States sent up to help make the *modus* work, and apparently she did. If you will give us a clear line to work on, Great Britain and the United States will get on all right, and the fishermen of Newfoundland and of the United States will get on all right; but so long as the traders of Newfoundland really believe that the American right is under the uncontrolled control of Great Britain, they will, by the necessity of human nature, insist that Great Britain shall exercise that control to the farthest limit. That brings me to the close of what I have to say regarding Question 1. Is it the wish of the Tribunal that I shall take up another question ?

THE PRESIDENT: Do you desire to continue ?

SENATOR ROOT: It is hardly worth while unless you are going to sit after 4 o'clock.

THE PRESIDENT: Then the court will adjourn until Thursday at 10 o'clock.[1]

THE PRESIDENT: Will you please continue, Mr. Senator Root ? [2]

SENATOR ROOT (resuming): I shall ask your further consideration for a time of the fifth question: " From where must be measured the ' three marine miles of any of the coasts, bays, creeks, or harbors ' referred to in the said article?" This, of course, is equivalent to calling for a decision as to the scope of the renunciation clause in the first article:

> And the United States hereby renounce forever any liberty heretofore enjoyed or claimed by the inhabitants thereof to take, dry, or cure fish on or within three marine miles of any of the coasts, bays, creeks, or harbors of His Britannic Majesty's dominions in America, not included within the above-mentioned limits.

[1] Thereupon, at 3.50 o'clock P.M., the Tribunal adjourned until Thursday, the 11th August, 1910, at 10 o'clock A.M.

[2] Thursday, August 11, 1910. The Tribunal met at 10 A.M.

" The above-mentioned limits " were, of course, the limits of what we call the treaty coast, the west coast of Newfoundland, a portion of the south coast of Newfoundland, and the coast of Labrador, and the Magdalen Islands.

The question as to the scope of this renunciation appears to turn upon the meaning to be given to the word " bays." The inhabitants are not to take, dry, or cure fish on or within three marine miles of any of the coasts, bays, creeks, or harbors.

It is not suggested that there can be any question about the meaning or scope to be given to the word " creeks " or to the word " harbors " but the word "bays" is, by our friends on the other side, taken out of the category in which it was placed and has a meaning ascribed to it making it cover all these great indentations dividing the coasts of New Brunswick, Nova Scotia, and Cape Breton, Prince Edward Island, and indenting the shores of New Brunswick and of Newfoundland.

On the other hand, the United States contend that the " bays " contemplated are the " bays " which are naturally to be classified with creeks and harbors, occurring along the coast, and separating different coasts, different portions of the coasts, and which are to be found along the different coasts of these great indentations. That is to say, that the " bays " referred to there are these smaller bays running off, to be found all along these different coasts; and that the word had not in the minds of the negotiators, the makers of the treaty, any reference to these great bodies of water.

I should add a statement as to the British contention. It is that the word " bays " is used in a geographical sense, so that all these great bays are included, because they were known to the world as "bays", appeared on maps as "bays", and were what everybody knew to be " bays."

The question is not a negligible one, it is serious, and cannot be decided as a matter of first impression by saying that " bays " means " bays." If it could be decided in that way we should have been spared this long discussion.

The more it has been studied, the more the history of the time and of the negotiation has been studied, the more cause the student has found to question that simple and easy surface disposition of the matter.

That the contention of the United States is entitled to very careful consideration before it is dismissed is made manifest by the fact that the Government of Great Britain once reached the same conclusion which the United States now present to the Tribunal, and stated the fact that it had reached it in the letter from Lord Stanley to Viscount Falkland of the 19th May, 1845, appearing in the British Case Appendix, pp. 145 and 146.

As that contains an admirable statement of the American side of the case, I beg the liberty of calling your attention to it. Lord Stanley says:

My Lord,

H. M. Govt having frequently had before them the complaints of the Minister of the U. States in this country on account of the capture of vessels belonging to fishermen of the U. States by the provincial cruisers of Nova Scotia and N. Brunswick for alleged infractions of the Convention of the 20th Oct. 1818 between G. Britain and the U. States, I have to acquaint your Lordship that, after mature deliberation, H. M. Govt deem it advisable for the interests of both countries to relax the strict rule of exclusion exercised by G. Britain over the fishing vessels of the U. States entering the bays of the sea on the B.N. American coasts. H.M. Govt therefore henceforward propose to regard as bays, in the sense of the treaty —

You will perceive that this letter is upon the subject of the construction, of the meaning of the treaty, not of granting a favor nor of refraining from enforcing the treaty in accordance with its construction, but it relates to a determination upon what the treaty means —

H. M. Govt therefore henceforward propose to regard as bays, in the sense of the treaty, only those inlets of the sea which measure from headland to headland at their entrance the double of the distance of 3 miles, within which it will still be prohibited to the fishing vessels of the United States to approach the coast for the purpose of fishing. I transmit to your Lordship herewith the copy of a letter, together with its enclosures, which I have received from the Foreign Office upon this subject, from which you will learn the general views entertained by H. M. Govt as to the expediency of extending to the whole of the coasts of the British possessions in N. America, the same liberality with respect to U. States fishing boats as H.M. Govt have recently thought fit to apply to the Bay of Fundy; and I have to request that your Lordship would inform me whether you have any objections to offer, on provincial or other grounds, to the proposed relaxation of the construction of the Treaty of 1818 between this country and the U. States.

I have, etc.

STANLEY

The complaints referred to by the Minister of the United States on account of the capture of vessels belonging to fishermen of the United States by the provincial cruisers of Nova Scotia or New Brunswick are doubtless the complaints relating to the capture of the "Washington" and the "Argus," which were the only vessels ever captured outside of the three-mile limit, and which were taken by provincial cruisers, and not by the vessels of Great Britain.

This letter shows that, having brought sharply before it the assertion of Nova Scotia that the treaty covered by its renunciation clause the great bodies of water geographically known as bays, and being faced with the demand of the United States for reparation for the acts which the United States deemed to be unwarranted and injurious, of seizing the "Argus" and the "Washington," the British Government reëxamined the subject; plainly they then discovered, or had already discovered, the error in the former opinion of the law officers of the Crown, who had based an expression of opinion that the renunciation clause of the treaty did cover these "bays" upon the supposed use of the word "headlands" in the treaty. Plainly the Government of Great Britain had discovered that that opinion was built on sand,

and the opinion had fallen in the estimation of the Foreign Office; and we have here a statement that the Foreign Office had prepared and communicated to the Colonial Office, at the head of which Lord Stanley was, an examination and exposition of the subject. He says:

> I transmit to your Lordship herewith a copy of a letter which I have received from the Foreign Office on the subject.

That is to say, having the matter sharply presented by the demand for reparation for the seizure of the "Washington" and the "Argus," the Foreign Office took the subject up in earnest, examined it, found that the opinion of the law officers of the Crown, upon which Nova Scotia had been proceeding, was not worth the paper it was written on, because it was based upon an erroneous assumption as to the terms of the treaty, came to the conclusion that the construction which is now contended for by the United States was the correct construction of the treaty, communicated that fact, with the reasons, to the Colonial Office, and the Colonial Office advised the Governor of Nova Scotia in this letter that the Government of Great Britain had determined to regard as bays, in the sense of the treaty, only those inlets of the sea which measure from headland to headland, at their entrance, double the distance of three miles.

The Government of Great Britain was driven back from giving effect to that conclusion by the protest that came from Nova Scotia, based upon the interests of the colony.

Nevertheless, we have of record that deliberate, reasoned, matured decision of the Government of Great Britain as to the meaning of the renunciation clause in this treaty.

Motives of policy affecting their colony prevented them from giving effect to their decision, but the decision remains as authority for us in our consideration of the question.

There are two or three other communications from Great Britain which serve to mark the outlines of the subject and define the question, which I should be very glad to have you consider — a letter from Lord Kimberley to Lord Lisgar of the 16th February, 1871, p. 636 of the American Appendix.

THE PRESIDENT: The letter from the Minister of Foreign Affairs to Lord Stanley, with its enclosure, has not been published ?

SENATOR ROOT: We have not been favored with that. No; I should like to see it. Of course we have it not, and it is not here. The knowledge of its existence serves merely the purpose of certifying to us that this conclusion announced by Lord Stanley was a conclusion upon grounds of reason.

The Earl of Kimberley, writing from the Foreign Office to Lord Lisgar in 1871, the time when the making of the new treaty was proposed (Lord Lisgar was governor-general of Canada), says, reading from the third paragraph on p. 636:

> As at present advised, Her Majesty's Government are of opinion that the right of Canada to exclude Americans from fishing in the waters within the limits of three marine miles of the coast, is beyond dispute, and can only be ceded for an adequate consideration.

Then the third paragraph below:

> With respect to the question, what is a Bay or Creek, within the meaning of the first Article of the Treaty of 1818, Her Majesty's Government adhere to the interpretation which they have hitherto maintained of that Article, but they consider that the difference which has arisen with the United States on this point might be a fit subject for compromise.

I cite this for two purposes. One is, the terms in which the question is stated; the right of Canada to exclude Americans from fishing in the waters within the limits of *three marine miles from the coast* is what is said to be beyond dispute. The question, what is a bay or creek within the meaning of the first article of the treaty, is a matter on which Her Majesty's Government adhere to the interpretation they hitherto maintained, but they consider it a fair subject for compromise.

Another statement of the question is to be found at p. 629 of the American Appendix, and that is a memorandum made for the Foreign Office, and sent by the Earl of Kimberley, the minister of foreign affairs, to Sir John Young, who was then governor-general of Canada, on the 10th October, 1870. That is, it was a memorandum made for the Foreign Office, I do not know where, but adopted by the Foreign Office, and transmitted by the Minister of Foreign Affairs to the Governor-General of Canada.

This memorandum recites the convention of 1818, quotes the renunciation clause, and proceeds:

> The right of Great Britain to exclude American fishermen from waters within three miles of the coast is unambiguous, and it is believed, uncontested. But there appears to be some doubt what are the waters described as within three miles of bays, creeks, and harbors. When a bay is less than six miles broad, its waters are within the three miles limit, and therefore clearly within the meaning of the Treaty; but when it is more than that breadth, the question arises whether it is a bay of Her Britannic Majesty's Dominions.
>
> This is a question which has to be considered in each particular case with regard to International Law and usage. When such a bay, etc., is not a bay of Her Majesty's Dominions, the American fishermen will be entitled to fish in it, except within three miles of the "coast"; "when it is a bay of Her Majesty's Dominions" they will not be entitled to fish within three miles of it, that is to say (it is presumed), within three miles of a line drawn from headland to headland.

Both of these communications you will perceive in stating this question use as the test the question: the limit of three marine miles of the coast; their description of the territorial zone is of a zone within the limit of three marine miles of the coast; as to that there is no question; as to "bays" which may be outside of that limit there is serious doubt.

They use the expression very much as it was used by Lord Aberdeen in a letter to which I will now call your attention, which appears on p. 488 of the American Appendix. It was written to Mr. Everett, the 10th March, 1845, from the

Foreign Office. That is the letter in which the British Government relaxed, even before this determination evinced in Lord Stanley's letter of the 19th May, 1845, the application of the rule based upon the Nova Scotian construction of the renunciation clause, and relieved the Bay of Fundy from the application of it. In that letter Lord Aberdeen says, reading from the next to the last paragraph on p. 489:

> The undersigned has accordingly much pleasure in announcing to Mr. Everett, the determination to which Her Majesty's Government have come to relax in favor of the United States fishermen that right which Great Britain has hitherto exercised, of excluding those fishermen from the British portion of the Bay of Fundy, and they are prepared to direct their colonial authorities to allow henceforward the United States fishermen to pursue their avocations in any part of the Bay of Fundy, provided they do not approach except in the cases specified in the Treaty of 1818, within three miles of the entrance of any bay on the coast of Nova Scotia or New Brunswick.

That is to say, American fishermen may pursue their avocation in any part of the Bay of Fundy provided they do not approach within three miles of the entrance of any bay on the coast of Nova Scotia, or on the coast of New Brunswick.

Now, insensibly Lord Aberdeen is using the term there, exactly as we say it was used in the treaty.

My learned friend Mr. Ewart told us that we might substitute for this general distributive use of the word coasts, on any of the coasts, bays, and so forth — that we might substitute on the coasts of Nova Scotia, and the coasts of New Brunswick, and the coasts of Prince Edward Island, and the coasts of Newfoundland; and that is exactly what Lord Aberdeen does here; and the necessary result is that which you get here in this description by Lord Aberdeen, that the coasts meant in the treaty are the coasts of Nova Scotia, the coasts of New Brunswick, the coasts of Newfoundland, and the bays are the bays of those coasts.

It is the kind of view which one naturally falls into in dealing with a fisherman's subject, looking at the subject from the point of view of the exercise of the fisherman's avocation, as Lord Aberdeen was here, as the treaty-makers were — the fisherman who crawls along the coast, to whom this (indicating on map) is one coast, and that is another, looking at it from the interior point of view, and not the point of view of the great merchant ship that comes sailing across the sea from the coast of Europe, and that looks at the western coast of the ocean as a whole. That is the occasion of this distributive form, and I shall presently show that it had an origin in a still more distributive and separative use of the word.

Now, this question depends, as a matter of reasoning, in the view of the United States, upon this fundamental proposition that the terms of the renunciation clause are to be limited, as a matter of construction, to the matter which was in controversy. As to that I do not understand that there is any dispute. The article recites that

> differences have arisen respecting the liberty, claimed by the United States for the inhabitants thereof, to take, dry, and cure fish on certain coasts, bays, harbors, and creeks.

Therefore, it is agreed, first, that the inhabitants of the United States shall have the liberty to take, dry, and cure fish within certain limits; and next, the United States, for its inhabitants, renounces all the liberty that it has had or claimed upon all coasts not included within the limits. It is a clear-cut, compact settlement of the matter in controversy between the parties by one of the parties keeping one part and giving up the other part. We are confined in our construction of the meaning of the words to such meaning as applies to the matter in controversy, and does not carry them outside to other matters. If there are two possible meanings, one which is within and one which is without, we must reject the one which is without and take the meaning that is within the subject-matter.

The second proposition upon which we are fortunately removed from the necessity of long discussion is that the matter in controversy was limited to those waters which were within the territorial jurisdiction, the maritime jurisdiction, the maritime limits, the limits of British sovereignty, using a variety of expressions which we find in these negotiations and correspondence, all referring to the same thing. The subject-matter in controversy is limited to the exercise of the liberties within the territorial waters of Great Britain. That follows necessarily from a great number of expressions which were used in the negotiations, and which were authoritative statements of the position of Great Britain which the United States had to meet, and which were statements of the subject-matter which was to be settled. An expression of this is to be found in Lord Bathurst's letter of instructions to the commissioners at Ghent, which appears in this pamphlet, p. 9. He says to the commissioners, at the foot of the first paragraph:

> You are instructed to state, that the three material points which remain for consideration are the following:

Then, at the foot of the page:

> Secondly, the fisheries. You are to state that Great Britain admits the right of the United States to fish on the high seas without the *maritime jurisdiction* of the territorial possessions of Great Britain in North America.

Then he goes on to say something, which I shall refer to hereafter, regarding the extent of that, and continues:

> But they cannot agree to renew the privilege, granted in the Treaty of 1783, of allowing the Americans to land and dry their fish on the unsettled shores belonging to his Britannic Majesty, etc.

As to everything *without the maritime jurisdiction* of the territorial possessions of Great Britain there was no controversy, there was agreement. As to the area of water *within the martime jurisdiction*, within the limits of British sovereignty, there was controversy, and to that controversy this statement related.

THE PRESIDENT: As to the waters without, there was no controversy; whereas, as to the waters within, there was controversy ?

SENATOR ROOT: Precisely.

THE PRESIDENT: How am I to understand that ? I should think that if, concerning the waters within, there was controversy, this controversy would extend each way, and would, therefore, also extend to the waters without, because what is not within is without and what is not without is within.

SENATOR ROOT: You will see that they would be quite different controversies. The controversy to which I refer was a controversy as to whether, within those limits, whatever they were, we had the right to fish or not. We said that within them we had the right to fish because we had it before, that it was granted in 1783 and still continued, notwithstanding the war. Great Britain said: Within those limits you have no right to fish; you have the right outside of them, but within them you have not, because your treaty grant of 1783 is ended by the war. If there were a controversy about where the limits were that would be quite a different controversy, dependent upon facts and different rules of law. All I am addressing myself to now is the proposition that the words of the renunciation clause must be construed as applying solely to the matter which was in controversy then, and that that controversy was solely about the right to be exercised or not exercised within the territorial limits, whatever those limits were, and I am about to proceed to the further proposition that it follows that if we can ascertain what those limits were, the limits of sovereignty, of jurisdiction, the maritime limits, the territorial limits, whatever those varying expressions may be, we have an infallible guide to ascertain the meaning of the word " bays " in this renunciation. We can put a limit to them. We have drawn a line around the field to which it is possible to apply the word " bays " or " harbors " or " creeks." The proposition I am now engaged upon is that the matter in controversy was, in fact, limited to the territorial waters, to the maritime limits, whatever they were, and that that is what the negotiators had in mind when they were settling rights about those particular waters.

Mr. Ewart has been very frank and clear upon that; he regarded it as a step in his own argument. He said [p. 756]:

> Then I come to one that bulked very largely in Mr. Warren's argument: That the negotiators understood that they were dealing with waters " within the maritime jurisdiction of Great Britain," " within British sovereignty," and so on. I had made a collection of excerpts for the purpose of proving that to be true, but my list is not nearly so long or so full as Mr. Warren's, and I therefore do not trouble the Tribunal with it. If, however, there is any way in which I can emphasize what he said, I should like to do so. It seems to me important. It seems to me, Sirs, that when the negotiators went to negotiate about this treaty, even if they had had no instructions at all, they would have known that they were going to deal with waters in British sovereignty. Nor would the British imagine that the Americans were going to renounce parts of the high seas.

Further down he repeats the same proposition.

JUDGE GRAY: I was very much interested in that point of Mr. Ewart's argument. Mr. Ewart further said in that connection, if I recollect his argument, that the treaty is a convention between Great Britain and the United States, and that by the fact of its being a convention it established between them the conventional territoriality of all bays.

SENATOR ROOT: I remember that Mr. Ewart did subsequently —

JUDGE GRAY: He said that it was a conventional establishment of the territoriality of bays. I merely call it to your attention.

SENATOR ROOT: That proposition of Mr. Ewart has the fatal vice of depending entirely on ascribing to the word "bays" his own meaning — a meaning which is in question here. If the word "bays" in the treaty means what Mr. Ewart says it does, that is true; if it means what we say it does, precisely the contrary result is accomplished. We are now engaged in trying to find what it means, and you must give some other evidence as to what the extent of the territorial jurisdiction was in order to ascertain the meaning of "bays." You, by assuming a meaning and putting it into the treaty, cannot ascertain the meaning. That is a perfect *petitio principii.*

JUDGE GRAY: The proposition was made by him in connection with Mr. Warren's argument that, in order that "bays" might be considered territorial — exceptionally so — there must have been some assertion by the Power claiming them and recognition by some other Powers of their territoriality, and so he said that the convention itself was a recognition of bays. But you contend that that is something of a circle.

SENATOR ROOT: Plainly so. It was a recognition only if you assume, first, the meaning which British counsel give to "bays", for we have already reached a point now upon this agreement of Mr. Ewart and Mr. Warren, which shows that these gentlemen were dealing solely with territorial waters; that the renunciation applied solely to territorial waters; that they had nothing else in mind; that they were not settling anything except in regard to territorial waters. We have already reached a point where you have excluded a geographical bay as a geographical bay. In order to bring "bay" within the meaning of the treaty, you have to regard it as a territorial bay. It must be within the territorial limits of Great Britain. It cannot be without, whatever it may be, geographical or otherwise, and whatever any map may say about it. We have reached a point where we know now that these gentlemen were not thinking about a map. Incidentally, I may remark that there is no evidence that they used any map. Mitchell's map was used in 1783 when they were fixing a boundary between the two countries at the original separation, but there is no evidence that I know of that in 1818 they had any map at all. But we know now that they were not making an agreement with reference to any map; they were making an agreement regarding the disposition of certain waters which were within the territorial jurisdiction of Great Britain, and they were dealing with nothing else. Indeed, that conclusion would follow almost inevitably from the mere words of the renunciation clause. The United States renounced

> Any liberty . . . to take, dry, or cure fish on or within three marine miles of any of the coasts, bays, creeks, or harbors of His Britannic Majesty's dominions.

On or within. That three miles is not an arbitrary expression or measurement. It is a reference to the recognized territorial zone. We must ascribe that force to it. Lord Stowell had already so described it in the "Twee Gebroeders" case, and the treaty of 1806 had already fixed the normal zone at three marine miles. Lord Bathurst, in his instructions to the Ghent commissioners, had already said that a limit of three marine miles must be observed. Then by 1818 all those vague, old claims which nobody was quite sure about and everybody was very insistent upon or against, had disappeared, and they had come down to the three-mile limit. The zone of jurisdiction which, as a matter of course and without any assertion, is accorded to every country for the protection of its coast, and this "three marine miles" plainly refers to that three-mile territorial zone. You must suppose that the bays which are talked about here are bays which are within the territorial zone wherever it lies, and the renunciation is of the right to take fish, etc., on coasts, bays, creeks, and harbors that are within this territorial zone. I say that there is a natural conclusion to be drawn from these words perfectly in accord with the conclusion that, by another line of reasoning, another route, Mr. Warren and Mr. Ewart reached — the agreement as to the proposition that the subject-matter in controversy, the matter to which the words " bays, creeks, harbors " apply, is the territory within, and not additional to, the territorial limit, the territorial jurisdiction of Great Britain.

THE PRESIDENT: Would it not then have been more natural to have expressed it as you have expressed it just now by putting in the words, " within three marine miles " behind " coasts, bays, creeks, and harbors ", instead of before? You said, " coasts, bays, creeks, or harbors within three marine miles "; would it not have been natural to have expressed it in the treaty in the same way as you now express it in your argument?

SENATOR ROOT: I do not think any more natural than this. I think it is merely a matter of style. It would have involved the use of one more word.

SIR CHARLES FITZPATRICK: Style and meaning.

SENATOR ROOT: I cannot see that there would be any difference in the meaning.

> The United States hereby renounce, forever, any liberty heretofore enjoyed or claimed by the inhabitants thereof to take, dry, or cure fish on the coasts, bays, creeks, or harbors of His Britannic Majesty's dominions in America, or within three marine miles thereof

would be the president's suggestion. That is a very good way to express it, but I think it is merely a question of style as to whether you make an additional clause or incorporate the words in the same line.

THE PRESIDENT: It would certainly express your idea in a clearer way, I should think.

SENATOR ROOT: That would probably result from the fact that the style of the president of the Tribunal is superior.

THE PRESIDENT: I make no pretensions at all as to style.

SENATOR ROOT: Whatever inference is to be drawn here, there is no dispute — and I take it there can be none — that the bays, harbors, and creeks referred to were within the territorial limits of Great Britain, and were not something additional to those territorial limits. As I said a few minutes ago, in answer to a question, if we can ascertain what those territorial limits are, we have an infallible guide to show us what bays, harbors, and creeks were referred to.

The first proposition which I wish to make in the effort to ascertain what the negotiators understood these limits to be, for, after all, that is the great question — we are not so much concerned about what some arguments might have established them to be as with what the makers of the treaty considered them to be — is that there is now, there was then, and there always has been, ever since the old vague claims to great areas of the sea were dispelled and abandoned, a rule, which is a rule of common sense, almost of necessity, that if any nation wishes to extend its jurisdiction over a bit of water extending beyond the limit of its accepted and accorded territorial zone, it must claim it. It must assert its right. There was not in 1818, and there is not now, any rule of law or any custom of nations under which the large bodies of water indenting the coast of a country are regarded as being within the jurisdiction of the country unless the country asserts her jurisdiction over them, unless the country claims them.

The general rule of law accords to every country a territorial zone over which it has rights of sovereignty based upon the necessity and the reasonableness of protection. The most general view is that the reasonable width of such a zone is three miles. Some countries take a different view; Norway, I think, claiming four miles. In the treaty of 1806, to which I shall have to refer again presently, Great Britain and the United States agreed upon three miles as the width of such a zone as all the world was bound to recognize, and upon five miles that they would recognize as between themselves for the peculiar and special circumstances treated of in that treaty. The Institute of International Law, at its meeting in 1894, expressed the view that six miles would be reasonable. But the width is immaterial to my present argument. Whatever it be, the world accords to every country, as a matter of course, and without its making any assertion of it, or claim to it, a right of sovereignty over the strip of water which surrounds its coast. It was originally fixed by the distance of cannon-shot, and, of course, fixed by measurement from the solid land, because you do not take cannon out in the water and fire them off; you shoot them from the land, and the three miles, the four miles, the six miles, whatever it is to be, is a computation of the old idea of cannon-shot. Great Britain and the United States agreed, as between themselves, that the cannon-shot should be conventionally treated as being three miles in length. As the cannon-shot grows longer there is a tendency to increase the width of this zone, for two reasons — because the country can defend itself over a wider zone, and because the country is liable to attack across a wider zone, and therefore it has to keep ships of war farther away. It all comes back to the principle of protection, and, for the purposes of protection without assertion, without claim as a matter of course, to every country the law of nations accords the right of sovereignty over a strip of water measured from her solid soil. Originally they had this width determined by the competency of cannon, going as far as explosives would send a shot, and more recently measured by an agreed computation as to the length of cannon-shot — three miles, four miles, six miles, whatever it may be.

But there is no such right accorded by the law of nations to any country outside of that zone, whatever its width may be, measured by cannon-shot or a computation of the length of cannon-shot from the solid land. There is no such sovereignty accorded over any bay, or creek, or inlet, or harbor that does not come within that normal zone, unless the nation has affirmatively elected to take the bay, creek, or harbor into its jurisdiction, and asserted its right to take it into its jurisdiction, upon facts which, when analyzed, will be found always to go back to the same doctrine of protection.

The United States had no rights over Delaware Bay unless she elected to appropriate Delaware Bay, as she did. Great Britain had no rights and could have no rights over the Bay of Fundy, over Chaleur, Miramichi, Conception, Placentia, White Bay, unless she elected to appropriate them. The writers say these bays, more than double the width of the territorial zone, may be prescribed for. That is what Stowell says in the "Twee Gebroeders" case. He says an area of sea outside of the limits may be prescribed for. Phillimore says:

> Besides the right of property and jurisdiction within the limit of cannon-shot from the shore, there are certain portions of the sea which, though they exceed this verge, may, under special circumstances, *be prescribed for.*

The Attorney-General here in his argument says [p. 1103]:

> If you want to be acknowledged as the possessor of a bay, you must claim it.

Very just.

Chitty speaks of appropriating gulfs and straits, in a quotation my friends have read on the other side.

De Martens speaks, in a quotation read by the British counsel, in these words:

> A nation may occupy and extend its dominion beyond

this recognized limit.

To prescribe for a thing is to claim it upon the ground of possession. We cannot have a better statement of the precise situation than was made by the British negotiators of the treaty of 1806, Lords Holland and Auckland, at p. 61 of the British Appendix. In the second paragraph of their report to the British Foreign Office of the 14th November, 1806, they condense a statement of the law and the existing conditions in the world at that time most admirably. Let me read the first two paragraphs, for they both are apposite. They say:

My Lord,

In elucidation of the subject of our public despatch we beg leave to lay before you the following observations on the nature of the extension of jurisdiction suggested by the American commissioners, on the real value of such a concession compared with that which they seem to set upon it as well as the reasons which in our opinion induce them to urge it so strenuously.

The distance of a cannon-shot from shore is as far as we have been able to ascertain the general limit of maritime jurisdiction and that distance is for the sake of convenience practically construed into three miles or a league. All independent nations possess such jurisdiction on their coasts; and the right to it is not only generally contained in the acknowledgment of the independence of the United States, but seems to have been specifically alluded to in the 25th article of the treaty of 1794. Particular circumstances resulting from immemorial usage, geographical position or stipulations of treaty have sometimes led to an extension of jurisdiction, and may therefore, when applicable, be urged as a justification of such a pretension.

That is the precise situation in which Great Britain and the United States stood.

The President: Does this passage refer to bays, or does it refer only to an extension of the distance on the open coast?

Senator Root: I shall show you, sir, that it refers to bays. It refers to any extension beyond the three-mile limit.

The President: The fourth paragraph in this despatch begins with the words "the space between headlands is more generally laid down, and admitted by Grotius himself, as subject to the exclusive jurisdiction of the power to whom the land belongs." That is in the fourth paragraph of the same despatch.

SENATOR ROOT: Yes. They go on to discuss the proposition of the Americans, which related to the subject of bays. I will take that up. I intend to return to this letter in a few minutes.

THE PRESIDENT: Yes.

SENATOR ROOT: I was reading this portion only as a statement of what I conceive to be the actual condition of law under which these gentlemen stood at the time they were making this treaty. I shall return to it for another purpose.

Upon attentive consideration of this long and voluminous record I have become satisfied, and I think that the Tribunal must become satisfied, that

First, Great Britain never, down to the final conclusion of the treaty of 1818, claimed or asserted a right to the extension of her jurisdiction beyond the cannon-shot, and over the waters of any of these bays that exceeded double the cannon-shot distance, or its computed length of three miles. That may be qualified, and as to that I shall say something particularly, but my general statement should be qualified by a reference to the fact that it may be that there were certain municipal statutes which related to Chaleur and Miramichi that are open to discussion as to whether they did not amount to an assertion of jurisdiction. It is claimed by Great Britain that they did amount to an assertion of jurisdiction. We say they did not. But as to all these others, laying aside Chaleur and Miramichi, to which these municipal statutes related — as to all these others, Fundy, St. George, Fortune, Placentia, Notre Dame, White — as to all of them, so far as I can ascertain upon the most painstaking examination, there never was an election by Great Britain to regard them as being within her jurisdiction, there never was any prescribing for them, there never was any claim to them. That is the first thing that I think will be established.

The second is, that the United States insistently urged upon Great Britain the inclusion within the conventional limits of the maritime jurisdiction of both countries of bays, chambers within headlands; and Great Britain refused to permit it, expressly.

The third is, that Great Britain not merely refrained from making any claim, not merely refused to permit the United States to get into the treaties a statement of jurisdiction over these large bays, but she industriously and expressly excluded it.

Of course, when I say Great Britain made no claim, I have to depend upon a negative. There is none here that I can find, and the only way I can prove that is by reading all these documents, from which I am sure the court will excuse me.

JUDGE GRAY: I think, Mr. Root, it was with reference to that absence that you speak of in evidence of the assertion or recognition of these other large bays that Mr. Ewart seemed to depend upon for what he called the conventional recognition or agreement between the two parties.

SENATOR ROOT: Yes. The sole suggestion that he had to make of any assertion or claim was by ascribing his meaning to the word " bays " in this treaty.

I have said that the United States sought to include these large bodies of water within jurisdiction, and that Great Britain refused it. That appears from the correspondence which begins on p. 60 of the British Appendix, a letter from Mr. Madison to Messrs. Monroe and Pinckney, who were the plenipotentiaries engaged in London in negotiating the treaty of 1806. The third paragraph, just below the middle of the page, contains the following statement from Mr. Madison, who was then secretary of state:

With this example, and with a view to what is suggested by our own experience, it may be expected that the British Government will not refuse to concur in an article to the following effect:

"It is agreed that all armed vessels belonging to either of the parties engaged in war, shall be effectually restrained by positive orders, and penal provisions, from seizing, searching, or otherwise interrupting or disturbing vessels to whomsoever belonging, whether outward or inward bound, within the harbors or the chambers formed by headlands, or anywhere at sea, within the distance of four leagues from the shore, or from a right line from one headland to another; it is further agreed, that, by like orders and provisions, all armed vessels shall be effectually restrained by the party to which they respectively belong, from stationing themselves, or from roving or hovering so near the entry of any of the harbors or coasts of the other, as that merchantmen shall apprehend their passage to be unsafe, or in danger of being set upon and surprised."

That is a clear proposal, is it not, to include by convention within the jurisdiction of the two parties chambers formed by headlands, and a territorial zone which extends for four leagues from a line drawn from headland to headland?

SIR CHARLES FITZPATRICK: You would include bays in "chambers formed by headlands"?

SENATOR ROOT: I should say so; yes. I should say so.

SIR CHARLES FITZPATRICK: It is curious they do not use the word "bays", is it not?

SENATOR ROOT: "Chambers formed by headlands" is a much more comprehensive expression I should say; and it was, you will recall, the expression that had been used in the controversy about the king's chambers that had been going on; and it included in the British assertion of jurisdiction very large bodies of water.

JUDGE GRAY: The "Argus" was claimed within a line drawn from headlands a hundred miles apart — those curvatures or convexities of the coast.

SENATOR ROOT: Yes. Now let us see what reception that proposal of Mr. Madison's met with on the part of Great Britain. I will ask the Tribunal to turn to the Counter-Case Appendix of the United States at p. 95, where there is a report from Mr. Monroe and Mr. Pinckney, who are the negotiators of the treaty of 1806. Just below the middle of the page, after speaking of some other things, in this report dated the 11th November, 1806, they say:

> The question of blockade, and others connected with it, may, we think, be satisfactorily arranged. They will agree also to acknowledge our jurisdiction to the extent of a league from our coasts; we have claimed that acknowledgment to the extent of three leagues.

So much for that letter. The next letter is the Holland and Auckland letter on p. 61 of the British Appendix, to which I have already referred. And I beg the Tribunal to consider that letter now with reference to that proposal of Mr. Madison, which was the thing that the American negotiators were urging, and that the British negotiators were considering; and the Tribunal will see that that is the reason why, in the fourth paragraph to which the president refers, he discusses the subject of the space between headlands. That is why after defining the limit of maritime jurisdiction at three miles — the general limit of maritime jurisdiction — they go on to speak of particular circumstances resulting from immemorial usage, geographical position or stipulations of treaty leading to an extension of jurisdiction, which "may therefore, when applicable, be urged as a justification of such a pretension." They are writing about this proposal of Mr. Madison's, which is a proposal embracing not merely the width of the territorial zone, but the inclusion in the jurisdiction of the two countries of the chambers between headlands, and carrying the zone outward a long distance beyond a line drawn from headland to headland.

Now I beg the Tribunal to go on to the part of this letter at the foot of p. 61 of the British Appendix, and consider what the British negotiators say further:

> If your Lordship should deem it expedient on other grounds to concede any extension of jurisdiction to the United States beyond that which their

independence necessarily implies, the American commissioners have more than once assured us that they are ready in the article itself to acknowledge it as an exception to the general rule arising from the particular circumstances of their situation and peculiar nature of their coast. We shall also observe that their utmost expectation after our conversations on the subject is two marines leagues.

The Tribunal will perceive that what their independence necessarily implies has already been stated in the second paragraph of the letter. They proceed:

The disadvantages of such a stipulation to us would be the additional protection of a league to our enemies and to our deserters in the American service, and a fear has also been expressed by a very intelligent sea officer, that the difficulty of ascertaining the distance would add to the frequency of the disputes, . . .

We might on the other hand derive some little advantage from the claim it would justify of an extended jurisdiction and consequent protection of revenue and commerce on the coasts of our colonial possessions.

There is squarely the question: Shall Great Britain assent to the insistence of the United States upon this extension of jurisdiction, which includes chambers between headlands, and a broader zone than three miles, in view of the disadvantage which would come from additional protection to enemies and in view of the advantage which might be derived from the claim it would justify of an extended jurisdiction, and consequent protection of revenue and commerce on the coasts of the colonial possessions?

The President: Do you think, Mr. Senator Root, that the circumstances of the time — it was in the height of the power of Napoleon that these transactions took place, 1806 — might be of some influence concerning the decision of Great Britain whether the benefits for revenue and commerce ought to be considered, or the difficulties which in this great struggle between maritime power and land power and continental power would strengthen the force of the enemy?

Senator Root: I am sure those circumstances had a very great weight, and I shall, in a very few minutes, state what

I think their relation was, and what the effect of these circumstances was. In the meantime, however, let me ask the Tribunal to look at the Monroe and Pinckney report of the 3d January, 1807, which appears in the Counter-Case Appendix of the United States at p. 96. They are transmitting the treaty itself, and they say under date of the 3d January, 1807:

> The twelfth article establishes the *maritime jurisdiction* of the United States to the distance of five marine miles from their coast, in favor of their own vessels and the unarmed vessels of all other Powers who may acknowledge the same limit. This government (Great Britain) contended that three marine miles was the greatest extent to which the pretension could be carried by the law of nations, and resisted, at the instance of the Admiralty and the law officers of the Crown, in Doctors' Commons, the concession, which was supposed to be made by this arrangement, with great earnestness. The ministry seemed to view our claim in the light of an innovation of dangerous tendency, whose admission, especially at the present time, might be deemed an act unworthy of the Government. The outrages lately committed on our coast, which made some provision of the kind necessary as a useful lesson to the commanders of their squadrons, and a reparation for the insults offered to our Government, increased the difficulty of obtaining any accommodation whatever.

The treaty of 1806, which is at p. 22 of the same Counter-Case Appendix, shows the result of this negotiation, which began with the proposal of the United States to take into the maritime jurisdiction of both countries an extended belt or territorial zone and the chambers between headlands and to draw the territorial zone outside of a line extending from headland to headland.

SIR CHARLES FITZPATRICK: At that time England had acquiesced in the claim of the United States with respect to Delaware and Chesapeake?

SENATOR ROOT: With respect to Delaware, yes. Chesapeake had not arisen yet.

SIR CHARLES FITZPATRICK: No.

SENATOR ROOT: It was in 1793 that the Delaware Bay question came up.

SIR CHARLES FITZPATRICK: What year was the Chesapeake Bay question ?

JUDGE GRAY: It was after the Civil War.

SENATOR ROOT: 1885; yes, long after.

In view of what the negotiation had been, what the American position had been, and the attitude exhibited by Great Britain according to these letters, the questions as stated by the British negotiators in their report — Lord Holland and Lord Auckland — I ask for a reconsideration of the terms of the treaty of 1806. It says, in Article 12, on p. 22 of the American Counter-Case Appendix:

> And whereas it is expedient to make special provisions respecting the *maritime jurisdiction* of the high contracting parties on the coast of their respective possessions in North America on account of peculiar circumstances belonging to those coasts, it is agreed that in all cases where one of the said high contracting parties shall be engaged in war, and the other shall be at peace, the belligerent Power shall not stop except for the purpose hereafter mentioned, the vessels of the neutral Power, or the unarmed vessels of other nations, within *five marine miles from the shore* belonging to the said neutral Power on the American seas.

You will perceive that they are not fixing the *width of the territorial zone merely*. They are making a rule for the "American seas" alone, and the rule is a *rule of maritime jurisdiction*. They are covering the entire ground for the exercise of sovereignty beyond the limits of the solid earth:

> *Provided*, That the said stipulation shall not take effect in favor of the ships of any nation or nations which shall not have agreed to respect the limits aforesaid, *as the line of maritime jurisdiction* of the said neutral state. And it is further stipulated, that if either of the high contracting parties shall be at war with any nation or nations which shall not have agreed to respect the said special limit *or line of maritime jurisdiction* herein agreed upon, such contracting party shall have the right to stop or search any vessel beyond the limit of a cannon-shot, *or three marine miles* from the said coast of the neutral Power, for the purpose of ascertaining the nation to which such vessel shall belong; and with respect to the ships and property of the nation or nations not having agreed to respect the

aforesaid *line of jurisdiction*, the belligerent Power shall exercise the same rights as if this article did not exist.

That covers the whole ground on the balance of interests exhibited in the letters of the negotiators, Lords Holland and Auckland, as the result of the resistance of Great Britain under all the circumstances that existed at the time, to the urgency of the Americans. As a result, they agreed upon the line of maritime jurisdiction which is stated here, and that expressly excludes from the maritime jurisdiction of the two Powers the chambers between headlands.

THE PRESIDENT: In the text of Article 12 it is stated that this disposition has been agreed upon "on account of the peculiar circumstances belonging to those coasts."

SENATOR ROOT: Yes.

THE PRESIDENT: Is it not possible that this passage "on account of the peculiar circumstances belonging to the coasts" is evidence that this is a specific provision concerning the open coast, and not referring to the bays?

SENATOR ROOT: I could not think of any circumstances more peculiar, as belonging to coasts, than the number, size, and character of the bays which indent them.

THE ATTORNEY-GENERAL: The shelving nature of the coast.

THE PRESIDENT: In the letter from Lord Holland and Lord Auckland to Lord Howick, of the 14th November, 1806 (British Case Appendix, p. 61), the fifth paragraph seems perhaps to have some connection with Article 12:

The circumstance however on which the American commissioners have chiefly relied is the *shelving nature of their coast;* and though from the east end of Long Island northwards it does not deserve such a description they allege that it is so broken with rocks as to oblige coasting vessels to keep at a considerable distance from the land.

Could it not be said that in consequence of this mention here of this shelving nature of the coast and of the reference to the peculiar circumstances belonging to the coasts, this Article 12 refers only to the coast — to the open coast, in contradistinction to the bays ?

SENATOR ROOT: But Article 12 cannot refer only to the coasts, because it *in ipsissimis verbis* fixes the maritime jurisdiction, and maritime jurisdiction is an all-comprehensive term. Great Britain cannot have any jurisdiction beyond its maritime jurisdiction. Of course, you cannot disassociate the shelving nature of the coasts from the conformation of them, from the bays and from the islands which are referred to here by Lords Holland and Auckland.

SIR CHARLES FITZPATRICK: Your theory is that "coasts" in Article 12 includes bays and harbors: "peculiar circumstances belonging to these coasts" would mean peculiar circumstances belong to these coasts, bays, and harbors ?

SENATOR ROOT: Of course on the coasts of their respective possessions; that is an all-embracing term.

SIR CHARLES FITZPATRICK: Yes. You notice on p. 97 of the American Counter-Case Appendix, Messrs. Monroe and Pinckney in their report made a very sharp distinction between coasts, bays, and harbors — the concluding words of the second last sentence:

> It is fair to presume, that the sentiment of respect which Great Britain has shown by this measure for the United States, will be felt and observed in future by her squadrons in their conduct on our coast, and in our bays and harbors.

SENATOR ROOT: Yes. I see that. Frequently the word is used most comprehensively; and frequently it is used in a narrower sense.

SIR CHARLES FITZPATRICK: Yes.

SENATOR ROOT: As distinguished from bays and harbors.

SIR CHARLES FITZPATRICK: Except that the letter has reference to the treaty.

SENATOR ROOT: My proposition here is not based on any inference from the use of the word "coast" or any other particular word. It is that this treaty is declared to be for the purpose of *establishing the limit of maritime jurisdiction.* And when you have got that limit of maritime jurisdiction you have your infallible guide to what "bays" means in the treaty of 1818, if the same view continued. The limit of maritime jurisdiction is fixed here in this treaty as being five miles from the shore, or three miles in the alternative.

The reason for this is perfectly plain; it is one which has already been referred to by the president. The Prussian decree, made at the instance and under the compulsion of Bonaparte, which declared these coasts here of the North Sea closed against Great Britain, was on the 28th March, 1806. And the first order-in-council by Great Britain retaliating for that decree, which declared the blockade of the Ems, the Weser, the Elbe, and the Travz, was on the 8th April, 1806. On the 16th May, 1806, came the order-in-council declaring the blockade of the whole coast of the Continent from the Elbe to the port of Brest. On the 14th October, 1806, came the famous Berlin decree, which put a ban upon all commerce with England. On the 7th January, 1807, came the retaliatory order-in-council, which declared all neutral trading with France, or from port to port in any possession of France, or of any of the allies of France anywhere in the world, to be cause for condemnation. And on the 17th December, 1807, came the Milan decree, which outlawed England and English ships everywhere. The two countries were in the throes of that titanic conflict which bore very hard upon the United States. England had the greatest navy of the world; the United States had no navy, but she had a great neutral commerce that had grown up. It was for the interest of England to extend the radius of the operations of her naval vessels clear to the verge of every coast and into every bay in the known world, to free them from all shackles in action; and it was for the interests of the United States to push away from her coasts these hovering warships that frightened and drove away the commerce upon which she was growing rich.

I join most heartily in the expression of a kindlier judgment upon the actions which were brought about by the exigencies of that terrible struggle; but in those days they were bitter for the people of the United States. The United States was urging relief, and Great Britain was insisting upon full and unfettered opportunity for her policy.

It is a mistake to look upon the questions that we have here in the light only of Canadian or Nova Scotian or Newfoundland interests. They were part of a great world-wide empire, and the policy that Great Britain followed was the policy of the empire. My learned friend has drawn a picture of the inconvenience, the danger, the alarm which would be created by permitting the shelter of a fleet of war-ships in Chaleur or Miramichi — in any of the bays of these dominions. True, that is the Canadian view; a natural view for the inhabitants of these colonies. But how convenient for the war-ships! How necessary, perhaps, to their operations, on which the fate of empire might depend. That is the British view. Great Britain was needing sheltering bays on every sea, and therefore the policy of empire required that Great Britain should resist the urgency of the United States to withdraw from the general use of the navies of the world, and appropriate to special jurisdiction the chambers within headlands, and a broad strip of territorial zone. That is why England made no claim and acceded to no proposal for the appropriation of these bodies of water. Justice requires me to assert that in those early days Great Britain never neglected the duty of claiming what she wanted. She refrained from claiming jurisdiction over Fundy and Chaleur and

Miramichi and Placentia and Fortune Bays because, more than she wanted that jurisdiction, she wanted to be free from the jurisdiction of other nations upon other bays all over the world.

I now pass to the proposition that Great Britain has always maintained the same policy and does to this day.

SIR CHARLES FITZPATRICK: Was not the doctrine of the King's Chambers essentially an English doctrine?

SENATOR ROOT: Ah, yes, it was essentially an English doctrine. In the early times, when nations were isolated and protecting themselves against the others, then arose the doctrine of the King's Chambers; then arose these claims to sovereignty over closed seas. But, with the new era of commercial freedom, which began in that wonderful period when, within the space of a few years, Columbus discovered America, and Vasco da Gama rounded the Cape, in the era when Grotius wrote the *Mare Liberum*; when great commercial nations arose, and England became the greatest; then the old basis of the doctrine of King's Chambers became of little consequence compared with the doctrine of freedom upon all other coasts. The importance of that principle of the widest possible extent of freedom, for naval operations, developed by these compelling causes to which I have referred, marks the difference between the Jay Treaty of 1794 and this treaty of 1806. In 1794 — the head of Louis XVI had just fallen by the guillotine in the preceding year — a disorderly and tumultuous strife was going on in which all Europe was against republican and communistic France. No powers were tested and no dangers were apprehended. While in 1806 the great genius Napoleon had taken control and was frightening the world, and Great Britain realized that she must fight for her life and for civilization, the position she assumed then I say she never departed from.

It is very interesting to observe that Great Britain never has made any general claim to sovereignty over the bays that indent her dominions since the passing away of her old, wide, vague claims. The treaty of 1839 with France is an exclusion of such claims. That adopted the three-mile limit, and it adopted a line of maritime jurisdiction at a point where a bay becomes ten miles wide. What became of all the rest? That shows that in 1839 Great Britain was not asserting any general jurisdiction over chambers between headlands, bays indenting her territory, merely because they were between headlands, and merely because they indented her territory; but that, as to all the generality of bays, she was willing to fix the limit of her maritime jurisdiction at the point where they became ten miles wide. The North Sea Treaty of 1882 shows, upon a wider scale, the same disposition.

It is a most interesting fact that nowhere in the long discussions which have occurred between Great Britain and the United States regarding the right of Great Britain to exclude American fishermen from these great bays — nowhere, at no time, has Great Britain ever planted herself upon the proposition that those bays were territorial waters of Great Britain. I confess to some surprise when an examination of this correspondence for the purpose of ascertaining whether that was, or was not, so revealed to me the fact that Great Britain had never planted herself upon that position. She has always stood narrowly upon the construction of the renunciation clause. Canada asserted the territorial right, Nova Scotia asserted it, but Great Britain never. There was an express assertion of a right to exclude Americans from the waters of these bays on the part of Canada, in a formal communication to Great Britain. It occurs in the letter from Lord Falkland to Lord John Russell of the 8th May, 1841, which appears in the British Appendix at p. 127. Over on

p. 128, in stating the views of the law officers of the colony of Nova Scotia, in the third paragraph, Lord Falkland says:

> On this point the law officers of the Crown in the colony express themselves *very strongly* both on the general principle of international law and the letter and direct spirit of the Convention. They deem it to be a settled rule, that the shore of a state lying on the sea is determined by a line drawn from the projecting headlands and *not* by following the indentations of the coast —

referring to Chitty:

> (*vide* Chitty — vol. 1st, pages 99 and 100, an extract from which is contained in the paper marked No. 2 herewith transmitted) and therefore think it a necessary consequence that the three miles fixed upon by the Convention should always be measured from such a line.

But they also say that the words of the convention would put an end to the question, if any could be raised on the general rule.

Great Britain never adopted or mentioned that first proposition of the law officers of the colony. She has always stood solely upon the construction of the renunciatory clause. And the Tribunal will observe that she has been admitting from time to time that it was exceedingly doubtful — the construction of the renunciation clause. I began by reading to the Tribunal letters in which they said it is exceedingly doubtful, it is a matter for compromise, and they went so far as to say, among themselves, that we were right; but never did they support themselves by saying: " These are territorial waters of Great Britain." It would have ended the question if they could have established that. What a powerful support that would have brought to the contention based upon the doubtful construction of the renunciation clause, if they had been able to say: " You have renounced this; but also, this is the territorial water of Great Britain, and you have no business here, anyway." But they never did — never. That is what makes important the fact that never, in all this long history, has Great Britain given an instruction to a naval officer, and never has a British naval officer made a seizure of an American vessel outside a line measured three miles from the shore. Two seizures were made, the "Washington" and the "Argus," based upon this theory of the colonial law officers — made by colonial vessels, under the command of colonial officers; and upon those two going to arbitration, both of them were decided in favor of the United States and against Great Britain.

THE PRESIDENT: If you please, Mr. Senator Root, is there any treaty, or any act of Parliament, or any other public act, in which the limits of British territorial waters have been fixed for every purpose, in a general way — not only for fishing purposes as in some treaties, or for the purpose of detaining neutral vessels as in other treaties, or for criminal jurisdiction as in the Territorial Waters Jurisdiction Act? Is there any public act in which these limits of British maritime sovereignty have been regulated in a general way?

SENATOR ROOT: The only information I can give your honor on that subject is derived from two communications which appear in the record. One is a report of the Committee of the Privy Council for Canada in June, 1886. I think the report was actually made by Mr. Foster, minister of marine and fisheries of Canada. It is on p. 812 of the American Appendix. Near the foot of the page occurs the first of a series of statements of fact which he makes, and I will read it:

> In the first place the undersigned would ask it to be remembered that the extent of the jurisdiction of the Parliament of Canada is not limited (nor was that of the Provinces before the union) to the sea-coast, but extends for three marine miles from the shore as to all matters over which any legislative authority can in any country be exercised within that space.

It goes on to say:

> The legislation which has been adopted on this subject by the Parliament of Canada (and previously to confederation by the Provinces) does not reach beyond that limit.

It is quite true the Nova Scotia Act of 1836, under which they made seizures, merely reproduced the language of the treaty, and contained no assertion of jurisdiction outside of the three-mile limit, unless it were involved in a construction of the language of the treaty.

Then, at p. 1083 of the same Appendix, there is a statement about Newfoundland, in the letter from the Duke of Newcastle to Governor Bannerman, of the 3d August, 1863, which I have already cited upon another question. In that letter this occurs:

> The observations which suggest themselves to me, however, on the perusal of the draft bill are —

the draft bill was to regulate fisheries —

> 1st. That if any misconception exists in Newfoundland respecting the limits of the colonial jurisdiction, it would be desirable that it should be put at rest by embodying in the act a distinct settlement —

that may mean " statement " —

> that the regulations contained in it are of no force except within three miles of the shore of the colony.

That was the position taken by the Government of Great Britain down so late as 1863.

THE PRESIDENT: But there seems to be no law or no treaty in which the limits of British territorial waters were exactly fixed for all purposes. These laws, or these treaties, fix the limits, as it seems, only for specific purposes: one for the purpose of fishery, the others for the purpose of limiting the activity of war-ships in time of war, and others for criminal jurisdiction, as is the case in the Territorial Waters Jurisdiction Act.

SENATOR ROOT: The broadest is that statement by Mr. Foster regarding the jurisdiction of Canada; but I do not know of any single instrument which undertakes to lay down any theoretical rule. They were dealing with practical questions as they came up. I may say, in passing, that the same limitation exists in the United States. Reference has been made to a Delaware statute. The jurisdiction of Delaware does not go beyond three miles. There was a letter of Mr. Jefferson, speaking about the states having passed laws regarding the subject that he was speaking of. The laws are limited to three miles.

THE PRESIDENT: Then may I ask: Is it to be ascertained when the pretensions of Great Britain concerning the King's Chambers have been abandoned? Is the year to be fixed? I do not know whether the year is to be fixed when these pretensions have been abandoned, or approximately fixed.

SENATOR ROOT: I should think, Mr. President, that the best view of that subject to be obtained would be in the opinions of the judges in the case of the Queen *vs.* Keyn, in L. R. 2 Exchequer Division, p. 63.

THE ATTORNEY-GENERAL: They have never been abandoned. The claims of Great Britain to the King's Chambers stand perfectly good. There was nothing in the case of the Queen *vs.* Keyn to diminish or retract those claims.

I hope before Mr. Root leaves this subject I may be permitted to draw attention to one paragraph of one of the letters, which has not yet been read, which I think it is fair I should read before he leaves the subject. It is the fourth paragraph in Lord Holland's letter (British Case Appendix, p. 61). In the earlier part of the letter Lord Holland spoke of the maritime jurisdiction as being limited to a league. Now, says Mr. Root, that fixes the extent of the maritime jurisdiction. But in the other paragraph, relating to the space between headlands, Lord Holland there first mentions bays. He says that they, even at ninety miles' distance between headlands, are "necessarily dependent on and belonging to the adjoining territory"; showing that he distinguishes between territorial jurisdiction over bays which are in the body of the country, and the maritime jurisdiction which he limited to the three-mile zone around the coast. Mr. Root has treated maritime jurisdiction, which is an expression applicable solely to the maritime zone around the coast, as though it covered bays. Lord Holland and Lord Auckland, and everybody else, treat bays as being something independent of that. Waters ninety miles between headlands they claim for bays, though they only claim three miles on a shelving coast along the open coast.

THE PRESIDENT: I understood, Mr. Root, that you will discuss this passage afterwards? I took the liberty of drawing the attention of Mr. Root to this passage, and he had the kindness to say that he will afterwards discuss this matter in another connection.

SENATOR ROOT: Before we separate, let me say: I have never said that Lord Holland and Lord Auckland had fixed the limit of maritime jurisdiction in this second paragraph of their letter, or that what they say fixes the limit of maritime jurisdiction. I say that they point to two areas of maritime jurisdiction: one the general limit of maritime jurisdiction, and the other the extension of jurisdiction which may be based upon particular circumstances urged as a justification for the extension.

JUDGE GRAY: For the extension?

SENATOR ROOT: For the extension, yes; and that when you have got both of them, the general limit which is accorded by all countries to all countries, and the particular extensions based upon the circumstances of each particular case justifying the pretension, when you have got them both, then you have got the limits of maritime jurisdiction, and there cannot be a bay or a harbor or a creek or an inlet or a roadstead or a coast outside of those limits over which a country has any sovereignty whatever.[1]

[1] Thereupon, at 12.15 o'clock P.M., the Tribunal adjourned until 2.15 o'clock P.M.

THE PRESIDENT: Will you kindly continue, Mr. Senator Root ?[1]

SENATOR ROOT (resuming): Mr. President, I had been pursuing the ascertainment of what was considered to be the maritime jurisdiction of Great Britain upon the American coasts in the year 1818, and I had shown that in the negotiation of the treaty of 1806 the American proposal was, in regard to the maritime jurisdiction of both countries on those coasts (and the chambers formed by headlands), to have the territorial zone pass outside of those, but that had been rejected by Great Britain, and that the two countries had agreed upon an extent of maritime jurisdiction which was measured from the shore, and which was limited to five miles from the shore.

I had been stating, too, a series of circumstances which showed that the policy of Great Britain which led her to reject the American proposal to include chambers formed by headlands within maritime jurisdiction of the two countries, and which led her to refrain from asserting any general jurisdiction over bays, was the continuous policy of the empire, and continued throughout all this period of discussion.

That leads me to the statement made by Lord Fitzmaurice of the position of the British Government in the House of Lords, on the 21st February, 1907, during the debate regarding a question that had arisen upon the waters of the Moray Firth.

You will recall that Lord Fitzmaurice, in response to a question, said there:

> I pass to the position of the Foreign Office. The jurisdiction which is exercised by a state over its merchant or trading vessels upon the high seas is conceded to it in virtue of its ownership of them as property in a place where no local jurisdiction exists. Therefore, the first thing that, in these cases, the Foreign Office has to ask is, Was there or was there not, territorial jurisdiction in the place where the alleged events occurred ?

[1] Thursday, August 11, 1910, 2.15 P.M.

In regard to that I can certainly say that according to the views hitherto accepted by all the Departments of the Government chiefly concerned — the Foreign Office, the Admiralty, the Colonial Office, the Board of Trade, and the Board of Agriculture and Fisheries — and apart from the provisions of special treaties, such as, for instance, the North Sea Convention, within the limits to which that instrument applies, territorial waters are: — First, the waters which extend from the coastline of any part of the territory of a state to three miles from the low-water mark of such coastline; secondly, the waters of bays the entrance to which is not more than six miles in width, and of which the entire land boundary forms part of the territory of a state. By custom, however, and by Treaty and in special convention the six-mile limit has frequently been extended to more than six miles.

As, for example, it had been in the North Sea Convention and the treaty of 1839 with France.

Now, that is no idle remark, it is no indifferent admission or expression: it is a formal and authoritative statement by the under-secretary of foreign affairs of the position of the Foreign Office and the Colonial Office, and of the other branches of the British Government which have any relation to the subject-matter in regard to the policy of the empire. It was not a statement made with regard to the particular interests of Canada to a particular bay, or of Newfoundland to a particular bay. It was a statement of the policy of the great empire which had interests all over the world, and which had a great navy going out to every sea. And the statement was a declaration of the same policy which was exhibited by Great Britain in refraining from making any claim to territorial jurisdiction over these Canadian bays generally. It was the same policy which was exhibited by Great Britain in refusing to accept the proposal of the United States to include chambers within headlands in the maritime jurisdiction in 1806, and to pass the territorial zone outside of the line drawn from headland to headland. It was the same policy which led Great Britain to refrain always, during all these discussions, from ever asserting that the fishermen of the United States were to be excluded from these bays because they were territorial waters, or within the maritime jurisdiction of Great Britain, and to stand always narrowly upon the construction of the renunciation clause.

There was a subsequent reference to this subject in the course of the same debate which is contained in a pamphlet that has already been brought to the attention of the Tribunal, containing the report of the debate for Wednesday, the 11th November, 1907. In that Lord Fitzmaurice explained that in particular places, where what may be called the facts of nature have made difficulties in applying that principle, there are some slight modifications in practice. This does not affect the general principle or the general policy which was stated. It is in strict accordance with the proposal I started with, that in each case where the necessities of protection make the possession of a particular sheet of water seem to a nation desirable and necessary, she may assert the particular circumstances which make it reasonable that she should appropriate to herself that particular place.

That is quite a different thing, you will perceive, from a general principle that bays indenting the coasts of a country are to be regarded as being within the jurisdiction of the country, because they are indentations running into the territory between headlands.

That special principle would apply to the Bay of Miramichi and the Bay of Chaleur, if the significance is to be ascribed to these local statutes which my learned friends on the other side ascribe to them. That is the assertion of particular reasons for appropriating and asserting jurisdiction, prescribing, and claiming, in the particular case, the right of sovereignty over a particular area of water; but it brings out in clearer relief the general policy, not to regard these indentations as coming within maritime jurisdiction, unless a specific cause is given, and a specific claim made.

Such was the claim made by the United States over Delaware Bay. It, at the instance of Great Britain, and against France, asserted reasons why the principle of protection made it just and necessary that in that particular place the United States should exercise jurisdiction. It did not apply to bays generally, and so, when the agreement was made upon the five-mile limit, measured from the shore, as the limit of maritime jurisdiction, it was quite consistent with the claim to Delaware Bay, and was an expression of the same policy of Great Britain, thus authoritatively stated by Lord Fitzmaurice in the House of Lords.

And, while I have stated as an inference from general knowledge of the condition of the times and the history of Great Britain that there was a reason in British policy for the adoption and the maintenance of this unvarying course of conduct, I find very powerful support for it in an observation of Lord Lansdowne in this same debate, p. 225 of this same pamphlet of November 11th, 1907.

Lord Lansdowne, whom you will recall as the honored and highly respected minister of foreign affairs under the last administration of Great Britain, a colleague of our friend Sir Robert Finlay in the Cabinet of which Mr. Balfour was premier, says:

> From whatever authority they proceed, I am bound to point out that it is not always very easy to determine where the open sea ends and territorial waters begin; and anyone who has had anything to do with these questions knows that there have been interminable negotiations upon the subject of the right of fishing within bays in different parts of the world, and that if you open the question as between this country and foreign countries in regard to a particular bay in which we are interested, they will desire to have it opened in regard to other bays and enclosed waters in other parts of the world.

There is the key to the position of Great Britain. That is why she did not make a general claim. She could not make a general claim without laying it open to all of the countries, all over the world, to make similar claims, and the great policy of the empire overbore and put aside what might have been the particular interest of this comparatively small part of the British Empire. The greater interest controlled.

One further observation I should make about this debate. The debate arose upon the arrest of certain Norwegian fishermen in the waters of the Moray Firth, a great indentation which runs into the coast of Scotland, very much as the Bay of Fundy runs into the coast of the British possessions in North America. There was a statute which in terms prohibited certain kinds of fishing in the waters of that firth; and Norway protested against the arrest of her citizens in that water, which Norway claimed to be the free sea.

Under the old doctrine of the King's Chambers it would have been the territorial water of Great Britain; but the doctrine of the King's Chambers, as it has survived that old period of wide and vague claims, is now a doctrine based upon the circumstance of each case in regard to each area of water, and Moray Firth must depend upon the question whether there were circumstances to be asserted by Great Britain justifying an appropriation by her of the waters of that indentation, and the exercise of sovereignty by her over it.

Upon this debate the Foreign Office of Great Britain allowed the protest of Norway, and released the Norwegian citizens who had been arrested for violating this statute upon that water; and accepted the situation that this statute, which in terms covered this water, was to be construed as the courts in England have always construed statutes, that by their terms extend beyond the limits of British jurisdiction, as applying only to British subjects, and not applying to Norwegian subjects.

I now have to state what seems to me a very interesting fact, that this proposal of the Americans, which was the basis of the negotiation of 1806, to include the chambers within headlands in the maritime jurisdiction of the two countries, and to construe the territorial zone as passing outside of a line drawn from headland to headland, was repeated in the negotiation of 1818.

The proposal was included in the same paper, which included the proposal by the Americans of the fishery article. That is a paper which was submitted by the American plenipotentiaries at the conference of the 17th September, 1818. It is included in Article G of that paper, which is not printed in the appendices. Both countries have the paper, and both have printed extracts from the paper, but neither printed this particular part of it. In that proposition which the Americans submitted, Article A referred to fisheries, Article B related to boundaries, Article C related to imports and exports, Article D related to slaves, Article F related to the general system of impressments, and Article G related to limits within which or out of which certain acts of sovereignty by the two countries in respect of the treatment of vessels should be exercised.

Paragraph (*d*) of Article G provided, as proposed by the Americans:

> (*d*) In all cases where one of the high contracting parties shall be at war, the armed vessels belonging to such party shall not station themselves, nor rove or hover, nor stop, search, or disturb the vessels of the other party, or the unarmed vessels of other nations, within the chambers formed by headlands, or within five marine miles from the shore belonging to the other party, or from a right line from one headland to another.

You will see that is a substantial repetition of the proposal of 1806, which was rejected, and in place of which the maritime jurisdiction was fixed as not extending beyond five marine miles from the shore. This also was rejected in the negotiation of 1818.

So Great Britain not merely refrained from asserting jurisdiction over bays generally, however large, however small, unless they came within the territorial zone measured from the shore; but she refused, both in the negotiations of 1806 and in the negotiations of 1818, to accept the proposal of the Americans which would include chambers between headlands within the limits of the maritime jurisdiction of Great Britain.

SIR CHARLES FITZPATRICK: What have you just read from? I do not think you gave a note of it.

SENATOR ROOT: I read this extract from the American proposal of the 17th September, 1818, from American State Papers, vol. IV, Foreign Relations, p. 337. That is the same book which is referred to as the source of the extracts from these papers which were printed.

I conjecture that this policy of Great Britain, which I have said accounted for a series of facts to which I have called attention, also accounts for the very curious form of the British Case, Counter-Case, and British Argument before this Tribunal.

The position taken by Great Britain certainly was a curious one: the position that the word " bays " related entirely to geographical bays. Although in argument counsel have claimed that all of these bays were in fact territorial, the position of Great Britain, the authoritative position taken in her pleading, was not that they were territorial, it was that they were geographical, and you will recall that this led to a question by the court. The court asked counsel of both parties to tell them whether they understood " the position of Great Britain to be that under the renunciation clause of the treaty of 1818 the United States fishermen have renounced the right to enter bays that are non-territorial as well as those that are territorial. That is to say, bays in the geographical sense of the word without referring to their territoriality."

And in answer, on behalf of the counsel for the United States, I read a series of excerpts from the British Case, Counter-Case, and printed argument:

> His Majesty's Government contend that the negotiators of the treaty, meant by " bays," all those waters which, at the time, everyone knew as bays.

In the British Case, p. 103:

> His Majesty's Government contends that the term " bays " as used in the renunciation clause of Article one, includes all tracts of water on the non-treaty coasts which were known under the name of bays in 1818, and that the 3 marine miles must be measured from a line drawn between the headlands of those waters.

They are concentrated at pp. 3900 and 3901 of the type-written copy of the argument [pp. 642–643, *supra*].

That to me was a rather curious position. It seems to reject as the basis of the British case, the case on which they stand, the case on which they can be held internationally — to reject from that any planting of Great Britain on the territorial character of these waters. It is quite in accord with the unvarying conduct of Great Britain. She never had planted herself; the Foreign Office of Great Britain never did plant itself in any discussion with the United States upon the proposal that these bays were territorial waters of Great Britain, and she did not do so here in this case.

Counsel may argue what they please, but the record is a record in which Great Britain has scrupulously refrained from taking that position, and it is reasonable to infer that Great Britain was unwilling to take that position, because she felt the weakness of her position in regard to the construction of the renunciation clause. If we could ever see that reasoned exposition that went from the Foreign Office to the Colonial Office, and is referred to by Lord Stanley in his announcement of the decision of Great Britain in 1845 — if we could see that, we should know; but circumstantial evidence of what that contained is clear enough. Observe, I am not seeking to hold Great Britain to that decision. We do not base anything upon that decision, because she withdrew from it upon the objection of her colony. Her colony objected that it would be a bitter stroke at the policy and the interests of the colony, and Great Britain withdrew from it; but it remains that that is what she thought about the merits of this question.

There is the evidence that that is what she thought. She thought that our construction was right. If she had been willing to say this is "within our territorial waters", she would have thought that, no matter whether our construction was right or wrong, it was her duty to exclude our fishermen from those waters in the interest of her colony.

But, there is a further step to be taken in my argument. Not only had Great Britain always refrained from asserting any jurisdiction over those bays, refrained from conferring it upon her colonies, refrained from planting herself upon it, refused to permit jurisdiction to be created by convention with the United States, but she expressly excluded those waters from the limits of her maritime or territorial jurisdiction in the negotiation of the treaty of 1818. She expressly put a limit upon the maritime jurisdiction from which she proposed to exclude American fishermen, exactly as she put a limit upon territorial jurisdiction, or maritime jurisdiction, under the terms of the treaty of 1806, and it was a limit which excluded from that jurisdiction those sheets of water.

The first paper to which I turn in support of that proposition is the Baker letter, so often referred to, the letter of Lord Bathurst to Mr. Baker — Mr. Anthony St. John Baker, who was chargé d'affaires at Washington — dated 7th September

1815, British Case Appendix, p. 64. You will remember that the negotiators of 1814, after making the treaty of peace of that year, separated without having included in the treaty any stipulation regarding the fisheries, and that some little time after that, the master of a British naval vessel, the "Jaseur", seized an American vessel some sixty miles off the coast of the British possessions. There was an immediate protest and an immediate disavowal of the act of this officer. In disavowing his act in seizing a vessel sixty miles off the shore, it became necessary, or practically necessary, for Great Britain to put a limit upon her disavowal, to show how far it went. The United States was claiming to have the right to fish clear up to the shore. She claimed that the right survived from the treaty of 1783, which carried her fishermen clear to the shore and into every bay, harbor, creek, and inlet. So when Great Britain made a disavowal of this act of her officer in command of the "Jaseur", it was incumbent upon her to show how far the disavowal went, to guard herself against having it apply to the whole American claim; and in the performance of that duty Lord Bathurst, who then held the seals of the Foreign Office, wrote this letter of the 7th September, 1815, and I will ask you to bear with me while I read it. It is very brief:

FOREIGN OFFICE,
September 7, 1815.

SIR,

Your several despatches to No. 25 inclusive have been received and laid before the Prince Regent.

The necessity of immediately dispatching this messenger with my preceding numbers prevents my replying to the various topics which your more recent communications embrace. I shall therefore confine myself to conveying to you the sentiments of His Majesty's Government on the one requiring the most immediate explanation with the Government of the United States, namely, the fisheries, premising the instructions I have to give to you on the subject, with informing you that the line which you have taken in the discussion on that point, as explained in your No. 24, has met with the approbation of His Majesty's Government.

You will take an early opportunity of assuring Mr. Monroe that, as, on the one hand, the British Government cannot acknowledge the right of the United States to use the British territory for the purpose connected with the fishery, and that their fishing vessels will be excluded from the bays, harbors, rivers, creeks, and inlets of all His Majesty's possessions; so, on the other hand the British Government does not pretend to interfere with the fishery in which the subjects of the United States may be engaged, either on the Grand Bank of Newfoundland, the Gulf of St. Lawrence, or other places in the sea, without the jurisdiction of the maritime league from the coasts under the dominion of Great Britain.

You will perceive that here he draws a line between, on the one hand, all the waters from which it is the purpose of the Government of Great Britain to exclude American fishermen, and, on the other hand, all the waters from which it is the purpose of the Government of Great Britain not to exclude American fishermen. Those waters from which it is the purpose to exclude are described as " bays, harbors, rivers, creeks, and inlets " specifically. They are all within the jurisdiction of the maritime league from the coasts under the dominion of Great Britain, for it is the purpose not to exclude American fishermen from any waters without the jurisdiction of the maritime league from the coasts. My learned friends on the other side, reading this letter and giving their own meaning to the word " bays ", say that it shows the intention of Great Britain to exclude from bays. But here we have a certain and positive proof of the meaning which the negotiators of the treaty of 1818 and which the Government of Great Britain ascribe to the word " bays " when used in the phrase " bays, harbors, rivers, creeks, and inlets." To a demonstration the bays from which they propose to exclude the fishermen of the United States were bays within the maritime league of the coast.

Can anything be clearer than that ? On the one hand, the area of exclusion, of prevention, of prohibition, covering bays rivers, harbors, creeks, and inlets *within* the jurisdiction of the maritime league from the coasts; on the other hand, the area of freedom *without* the jurisdiction of the maritime league from the coast.

THE PRESIDENT: Was not the expression "places without the jurisdiction of the maritime league" used in the correspondence as designating the places corresponding with the first branch of Article 3 of the treaty of 1783? The controversy was whether the whole of Article 3 survived the war, or only the first part of it. The British contention was that the second branch of Article 3 had been superseded by the war, and was not the language of this correspondence based upon the contradistinction between the places designated in the first and second branches of Article 3?

SENATOR ROOT: Doubtless, and this draws an accurate and authoritative line between the two. Those areas which, in this year 1815, the British Government regarded as covered by the first branch, are those outside of the marine league from the coasts. That is the very thing that they are defining. They are drawing a line between the first branch and the second branch of the treaty of 1783 and they are declaring that everything *without* the jurisdiction of the maritime league from the coasts is to be admitted to continue to the United States, under the first branch of the treaty of 1783, and that only such areas of water as are *within* the jurisdiction of the marine league from the coasts are to be treated as being lost by the United States, because under the second branch of the treaty of 1783.

Now, I might call attention, for a more complete understanding of this letter, to the letters which I read at the opening of my argument this morning. I would refer first to the letter of the Earl of Kimberley to Lord Lisgar, p. 636 of the American Case Appendix, in which the Earl of Kimberley says:

As at present advised, Her Majesty's Government are of opinion that the right of Canada to exclude Americans from fishing in the waters within the limits of three marine miles of the coast, is beyond dispute, and can only be ceded for an adequate consideration.

That, you will see, is the same phrase that is used in the letter by Lord Bathurst. Of course, in this letter, Lord Kimberley is using the expression " limits of three marine miles of the coast " in the same sense as " three marine miles of the shore." The memorandum, sent by the Foreign Office to the Governor-General of Canada, which appears at p. 629 of the American Appendix, in the third paragraph, says:

The right of Great Britain to exclude American fishermen from waters within three miles of the coast is unambiguous, and it is believed, uncontested.

They use the same expression as the letter from Lord Bathurst to Mr. Baker, and they use the expression " within three miles of the coast " as the equivalent of " within three miles of the shore." The further development of the subject in the memorandum leaves no doubt whatever of that.

Now, will you go back to the treaty of 1818 and read the renunciation clause in the light of this letter of Lord Bathurst to Mr. Baker:

The United States hereby renounce, forever, any liberty heretofore enjoyed or claimed by the inhabitants thereof to take, dry, or cure fish on or within three marine miles of any of the coasts, bays, creeks, or harbors of His Britannic Majesty's dominions in America

and apply to that the declaration of the letter to Mr. Baker that bays, creeks, and harbors are bays, creeks, and harbors within three marine miles of the coast, are within the jurisdiction of the maritime league from the coasts, and are not without the jurisdiction of the maritime league from the coasts. If we had had that authoritative clause in the language of the renunciation clause, would there have been any question to discuss here? Is there any room left, with this letter, which my honorable friends have proved here within a few days was read to the President of the United States by Mr. Baker, for the contention that the negotiators of the treaty of 1818 considered, or for a moment supposed, that the maritime jurisdiction of Great Britain, from which they proposed to exclude American fishermen, extended beyond three marine miles from the coast; or is there any room left for the supposition that in the renunciation, which applied only to matters in controversy and only to the waters within the maritime jurisdiction of Great Britain, the word "bays" meant anything except the bays that were within that maritime jurisdiction and were a part of the subject-matter of controversy?

THE PRESIDENT: In this supposition, have the words "bays, creeks, or harbors" any distinct meaning or are they superfluous?

SENATOR ROOT: They have the same meaning that they had in the treaty.

THE PRESIDENT: Yes, I mean in the treaty. Have the words "bays, creeks, or harbors" in the renunciatory clause any distinct meaning within this supposition, or are they superfluous? If the words had been left out, would the sense have been different?

SENATOR ROOT: They are an enumeration of the different elements of the total coast — the coasts, the bays, the creeks, the harbors. There are two principles under which these words can be classified. There is a series of words which are used to designate the physical conformation of water — gulfs, bays, coves, creeks, inlets. These all relate to the physical conformation. There is another series of words which relate to the use to which they can be put by mankind — harbors, roads or roadsteads, havens, ports. Now, a harbor may be a bay, or it may be the particular kind of bay that is called a cove, a very small one, or it may be the particular kind which is called a creek, which, in common usage, is a long, narrow, winding indentation in the land, and which, in America by what is purely an Americanism, has come to be extended to the running stream which may come down into this inlet from the sea. When you use the term " bays and harbors " you are using alternative expression for very much the same thing, looking at it, in one way, as to its physical conformation, and, in the other, as to the uses to which it may be put. So, it is an enumeration of the elements going to make up the total coast, going to make up that thing which was granted to the French upon Newfoundland and which was granted to us upon Newfoundland, within limits. Here they go into an enumeration of the elements — coasts, bays, harbors, creeks.

THE PRESIDENT: This enumeration would not have been necessary to express the idea ?

SENATOR ROOT: I think the same idea could have been expressed without it perfectly well.

THE PRESIDENT: If the word " coast " had stood alone it might have expressed the same idea, according to your view of the renunciatory clause ?

SENATOR ROOT: I should think it would have, although it is a little difficult to put oneself in the position of those gentlemen there. I think they were looking at this question from the fisherman's point of view. Naturally, the fisherman looks at things in detail and at short range, rather than from a distance. But we are precluded absolutely from assigning to the words that were used in this article any meaning to apply to bays or creeks or harbors that will put them outside of the jurisdiction of the maritime league from the coasts.

SIR CHARLES FITZPATRICK: They are mere words of description, Mr. Root, I suppose ?

SENATOR ROOT: I think so, sir.

SIR CHARLES FITZPATRICK: If the negotiators of the treaty had intended to exclude citizens of the United States from the coasts and the geographical bays what words would they have used ?

SENATOR ROOT: You mean from the great bays ?

SIR CHARLES FITZPATRICK: Yes; what words would they have used ?

SENATOR ROOT: I think they would have used the words " chambers between headlands."

SIR CHARLES FITZPATRICK: Why ?

SENATOR ROOT: Because those were the words which were appropriate to discriminate between these interior bays and the greater, outside bays, and they were the words which they had been using in the negotiations of 1806 and the words which they used in their own proposal for this very treaty regarding the maritime jurisdiction.

SIR CHARLES FITZPATRICK: Were those bays described anywhere at that time as chambers between headlands ?

SENATOR ROOT: Undoubtedly — including Mr. Madison's proposal for the treaty of 1806 and this proposal relating to maritime jurisdiction in 1818.

SIR CHARLES FITZPATRICK: So you think that " chambers between headlands " would have been a more accurate geographical description of these bodies of water than the term " bays " ?

SENATOR ROOT: I think it would have been a more discriminating description of them.

THE PRESIDENT: Would the term " chambers within headlands " express what is meant by the term " bays " ? Does it not signify something much larger than bays ? For instance, are the celebrated King's Chambers bays ?

SENATOR ROOT: King's Chambers are partly narrow seas and partly chambers between headlands.

THE PRESIDENT: But not bays ?

SENATOR ROOT: Yes, chambers between headlands are bays. "Chambers between headlands" was an expression in customary use and was used by these very people to refer to bays, or to indentations in the coast which were larger than the ordinary interior bay that came within the territorial zone measured from the shore.

THE PRESIDENT: For instance, was the place where the "Argus" was seized a chamber within headlands, or was the place where the "Washington" was seized — the Bay of Fundy — a chamber between headlands?

SENATOR ROOT: The place where the "Washington" was seized was a chamber between headlands.

THE PRESIDENT: Would you make no distinction between the place where the "Argus" was seized and the place where the "Washington" was seized?

SENATOR ROOT: There is no distinction between the two places except that the width of the chamber between headlands in the "Argus" case was much greater than the width of the chamber between headlands in the "Washington" case. The "Washington" was seized between headlands in the Bay of Fundy and the "Argus" was seized up here (indicating on map) in an indentation between Cape North and some other point.

THE PRESIDENT: Would the place where the "Argus" was seized, in the geographical sense, be called a bay?

SENATOR ROOT: I could not say whether it would or not. It might as well be called a bay as the Gulf of Lyons or the Gulf of Genoa might be called gulfs. Many quite shallow indentations in the shore are called bays.

JUDGE GRAY: There is Egmont Bay, a very shallow bay on Prince Edward Island, a mere little cove or horseshoe, and yet it is called a bay.

THE PRESIDENT: Mitchell's map does not call it a bay, but Jefferys' does call it a bay, if I am not mistaken.

SENATOR ROOT: I think it is probable that the use of the words "chambers between headlands" is appropriate to describe bays and perhaps indentations so shallow that they might not be ordinarily called bays, but it is a very comprehensive term and it certainly would include all the bays along these coasts.

It would have included Massachusetts Bay, it would have included Cape Cod Bay — many bays along the coast of the United States to which the United States has never claimed jurisdiction, any more than Great Britain ever claimed jurisdiction to these bays here (indicating on map).

Of course, this term, used in this letter to Baker, which limits the maritime jurisdiction of Great Britain to the maritime league, plainly uses the word "coasts" as identical with the word "shores." That had been the general usage of the parties. I will again call the attention of the Tribunal to these two papers of later date, the letter of the Earl of Kimberley to Lord Lisgar, and the memorandum of the Foreign Office which used the term "three marine miles from the coast" as equivalent to "three marine miles from the shore." The Tribunal will remember that the term was used in the treaty of 1806 "five marine miles from the shore", and an interior line was spoken of as "three marine miles from the coast." Plainly, they were using the two terms convertibly. The Tribunal will remember also that in the report of the American negotiators, which is in the American Appendix at p. 307, they use the term "three miles from the shore" as convertible with "three miles from the coast." On p. 307 the report of Messrs. Gallatin and Rush to Mr. Adams, 20th October, 1818, contains this language, in the second paragraph on the page:

> It will also be perceived —

they are speaking of the treaty which they transmitted, just signed on that same day —

that we insisted on the clause by which the United States renounce their right to the fisheries relinquished by the convention, that clause having been omitted in the first British counter-project. We insisted on it with the view — 1st: Of preventing any implication that the fisheries secured to us were a new grant, and of placing the permanence of the rights secured and of those renounced precisely on the same footing. 2d: Of its being expressly stated that our renunciation extended only to the distance of three miles from the coasts.

And the Tribunal will perceive that they had been taking the British Government at its word. They had there this letter of Lord Bathurst to Mr. Baker; both sides had it. And the Tribunal has here the evidence that the American commissioners understood it as I have been presenting it to the Tribunal, of its being expressly stated that our renunciation extended only to the distance of three miles from the coast:

This last point was the more important, as, with the exception of the fishery in open boats within certain harbors, it appeared, from the communications above mentioned, that the fishing-ground, on the whole coast of Nova Scotia, is more than three miles from the shores; whilst, on the contrary, it is almost universally close to the shore on the coasts of Labrador.

There the Tribunal will see they use the word "coasts" and "shores" convertibly, and they understand the declaration of the Government of Great Britain to Mr. Baker, which draws the line between the first and the second parts of the treaty of 1783, the line between the rights that continued and the rights that ended, to be drawing the line at three marine miles from the coast, using that as equivalent to three marine miles from the shore.

We are now in a position to understand that there was no inconsistency at all in what Lord Bathurst told Mr. Adams about the Baker letter. The first interpretation of the Baker letter that we have is in Mr. Adams's report of his conversation with Lord Bathurst immediately after the letter was written. It is to be found in the United States Appendix, at p. 265. Mr. Adams is writing to his chief, Mr. Monroe, the secretary of state, under date of the 19th September, 1815. Of course Mr. Adams had made the complaint about the "Jaseur" incident, and he was anxious to know what the British Government had done about it, and he went to Lord Bathurst to learn, and was told that Lord Bathurst had sent an instruction to the British representative in Washington, Mr. Baker, and he asked him what it was. I read from about two-thirds down the p. 265:

> I asked him if he could, without inconvenience, state the substance of the answer that had been sent. He said, certainly: it had been that as, on the one hand, Great Britain could not permit the vessels of the United States to fish within the creeks and close upon the shores of the British territories, so, on the other hand, it was by no means her intention to interrupt them in fishing anywhere in the open sea, or without the territorial jurisdiction, a marine league from the shore.

The Tribunal will perceive that Lord Bathurst is there stating the vital feature of the letter to Baker, using the word "shore" as the equivalent of the word "coast" which occurs in the Baker letter. He instructed Mr. Baker to say to the American Government in behalf of the Government of Great Britain, that Great Britain did not propose to interfere with the fishing anywhere without the maritime jurisdiction of three miles from the coast. And when Mr. Adams asked him what he had written, he said that he had written that it was by no means the intention of Great Britain to interrupt fishing without the territorial jurisdiction a marine league from the shore — precisely answering to what he had directed Mr. Baker to say, substituting the word "shore" for the word "coast". Of course, if you ignore that line that is drawn in the Baker letter and give the British sense to the word "bays" in the Baker letter, you have a frightful inconsistency here. You have Lord Bathurst, who was conducting the foreign affairs of a great empire, either willfully deceiving Mr. Adams or not knowing the meaning or purport of an important letter that he had just written himself, an important instruction that he had just given himself. As I have shown the true meaning, the consistency is perfect.

Mr. Adams, to have no misunderstanding about what the position of Great Britain really was, in writing to Lord Bathurst shortly after, a few days after, on the subject, recites to Lord Bathurst what Lord Bathurst had told him on this subject.

The Tribunal will perceive that Mr. Adams was not at all grateful for liberty to fish outside the maritime jurisdiction of three leagues. What he wanted to do was to combat the determination to exclude us within the three marine miles from the shore. He had girded his loins, and set to work to combat that, in this long and elaborate argument of the 25th September, 1815. And in laying down the lines for his argument he states the position which he is combating, and states it to Lord Bathurst, as being the position that Lord Bathurst had stated to him, a matter about which an experienced man, entering upon an argument, would, of course, be careful and distinct. The statement which he made to Lord Bathurst, of his understanding of Lord Bathurst's communication to him, is just above the middle of p. 269 of the American Appendix. It is the second paragraph on that page. Mr. Adams said:

> But, in disavowing the particular act of the officer who had presumed to forbid American fishing-vessels from approaching within sixty miles of the American coast, and in assuring me that it had been the intention of this Government, and the instructions given by your Lordship, not even to deprive the American fishermen of any of their accustomed liberties during the present year, your Lordship did also express it as the intention of the British Government to exclude the fishing-vessels of the United States, hereafter, from the liberty of fishing within one marine league of the shores of all the British territories in North America, and from that of drying and curing their fish on the unsettled parts of those territories.

If there was any uncertainty about that, any mistake, any misunderstanding, there was a challenge to Lord Bathurst to state it. But Lord Bathurst acknowledges the receipt of that letter — Dr. Lohman has already called attention to that fact — on the 30th October, and the acknowledgment and answer appear at p. 273 of the American Appendix, near the foot of the page. I will read the first paragraph of Lord Bathurst's letter:

> The undersigned, one of His Majesty's principal Secretaries of State, had the honor of receiving the letter of the minister of the United States, dated the 25th ultimo, containing the grounds upon which the United States conceive themselves, at the present time, entitled to prosecute their fisheries within the limits of the British sovereignty, and to use British territories for purposes connected with the fisheries.

And then he proceeds to attempt to confute the arguments of Mr. Adams in respect of the proposal of Lord Bathurst which Mr. Adams had quoted to him in the letter that he is acknowledging. I do not see how you can have any statement of the position of a government more clear and distinct than we have it here; and I need not cite to the Tribunal the record to show that these papers were in the hands of the negotiators of 1818 on both sides. Both the instructions sent by the State Department of the United States to Mr. Gallatin and Mr. Rush referred them to these papers, and the instructions sent to Messrs. Robinson and Goulburn by the British Foreign Office referred them to these papers. They say: "You have them." And they did have them, and their understanding from them was necessarily complete and distinct as to what Great Britain's claim to the extent of her maritime jurisdiction was; that jurisdiction, within which the renunciation clause must be limited, and within which must have been all the coasts, bays, harbors, and inlets, mentioned in that renunciation clause.

That leads us to a conclusion regarding the meaning of the word "bays" in the renunciation clause that agrees perfectly with a variety of circumstances tending in the same direction. In the first place it agrees with what we would naturally suppose was meant by the use of the word in the class of places in which we find the word " bays "; " coasts " in the distributive sense, bays, creeks, and harbors. On the principle *ejusdem generis*, the kind of bays they were talking about were the kind of bays that could be classified properly with creeks and harbors — not these great stretches of sea belonging to a different classification, and which must be considered with a different set of ideas altogether. It agrees with the inference we would naturally draw from the fact that these men who were making this treaty were treating of bays as places for shelter, and for repairs, and for obtaining wood and water. It is probable that men who were thinking about bays as places for shelter and for repairs and for obtaining wood and water should, when they used the word " bays", use it with reference to that kind of a bay. It agrees with the inference we would naturally draw from the use of the word by men —

SIR CHARLES FITZPATRICK: Pardon me a moment, Mr. Root. You say " that kind of a bay." That would be a bay which would form part of a coast; that is to say, a bay less than six miles wide ?

SENATOR ROOT: It would be a bay where people could find shelter; where they could —

SIR CHARLES FITZPATRICK: You say " such bays " would mean the bays referred to above, which bays would be, on your construction, bays less than six miles wide ?

SENATOR ROOT: Precisely. And there let me make a remark about an argument that has been made on the other side that that would exclude all bays larger than six miles from the liberty of access for shelter, and so on. No! Because they can go for shelter wherever they find a harbor.

SIR CHARLES FITZPATRICK: That is not under the treaty ?

SENATOR ROOT: Under the treaty. They can go for shelter or for repairs or for wood and water wherever they find a harbor: " Provided, however, that the American fishermen shall be permitted to enter all such bays or harbors "; and there is a harbor wherever you find a shore under the lee of which you can come to and keep from being blown out of water. But that is incidental.

The conclusion to which these facts have brought us, or have brought me, and I hope have brought the Tribunal, agrees with the inference you would naturally draw from the fact that these men were talking about drying and curing fish on bays, and would naturally have in mind the kind of bays in which you can dry and cure fish. They would naturally have in mind the kind of bays which could be settled. They were not talking about settling the Bay of Fundy. People settle the little places where there are little strips of arable land running in from the sea, a little beach, or place where a fisherman's hut could go, or where there may be a place for a farmer, like places in the little valleys among the hills. They agree with the inference that you would naturally draw from the fact that this term " coast " was used distributively: " On or within three marine miles of any of the coasts " — looking at it as a fisherman would look at it, going along the coast, one coast on the starboard and another to port. And they answer to the requirement which was fundamental in this whole business, that they should draw a line that a fisherman could find. I do not care so much whether you can find a line with the help of all of these gentlemen here. The treaty was not made for you and me. It was not made for gentlemen to find a line by poring over a chart. It was made for fishermen, going out on to the sea with their small boats, to navigate in fair weather and in storm, by daylight and in the dark, in clear weather and in fog; and when the treaty makers were laying down a line, they were bound to lay down a line, and we are bound to assume that they were laying down a line that a fisherman could find. What fisherman could find a line three miles outside of a line sixty miles in length drawn from Grand Manan to the headland here (indicating on the map), not clear across the bay; that would be more than one hundred miles; but a line from the headland of Nova Scotia to the nearest point of British land on the other side of the Grand Manan, or Mur Ledge, which I think sticks up out of the water, is a full sixty miles in length! What fisherman could, on peril of the seizure and forfeiture of his vessel, be expected to find that line? It would be wholly impracticable. That is not the method by which international law proceeds to construe instruments. There is a basis for that talk in these letters here, that old idea about being able to see from headland to headland, taking in what comes within a line of sight. It is because the rules of international law are made, and treaties are construed for the practical use of mankind. You do not give a book on navigation to an unlettered fisherman who is to sail along the coast and find his way to the place where he earns his daily bread. You give him a rule of thumb; you give him something he can see and guide himself by. And the conclusion to which we have come here, upon these plain declarations of Great Britain as to what the limits of her territorial sovereignty, of her maritime jurisdiction were, is in agreement with the requirements of the making of this treaty — to lay down a line that fishermen shall not transgress, that it is possible for a fisherman to find.

THE PRESIDENT: If you please, Mr. Senator Root, is the word "any" in the renunciatory clause in no connection with the word "bays," or is it to be considered as having relation to the word "bays"?

On or within three marine miles of *any* of the coasts, bays, creeks, or harbors.

SENATOR ROOT: I should think that that qualified the whole.

THE PRESIDENT: The whole?

SENATOR ROOT: I should think so.

THE PRESIDENT: Then it refers also to "bays"?

SENATOR ROOT: Yes; any of the coasts, bays, creeks, or harbors.

THE PRESIDENT: Then it would be the same if it said "of any of the coasts, any of the bays, creeks, or harbors", if it refers to the whole? One could repeat before every one of those words?

SIR CHARLES FITZPATRICK: It must be repeated, under grammatical construction.

SENATOR ROOT: It would not give the same force of classification as where they are grouped in under the same words. "Any of the coasts, bays, creeks, or harbors" carries the idea of a combination of coasts, bays, creeks, or harbors; and any of those combinations of coasts, bays, creeks, or harbors is the idea carried in this form of words.

SIR CHARLES FITZPATRICK: If you were parsing that sentence, would you not say "of any of the coasts, of any of the bays, of any of the creeks, or of any of the harbors"?

SENATOR ROOT: I should say "any" qualified all those words. In connection with this suggestion, I think the distributive use of the word "coasts" occurred in the treaty of 1783, as well as in the treaty of 1818, and I think that it had its origin in one of the British proposals, which appears at p. 96 of the British Counter-Case Appendix. This paper in which this occurs is a draft of the preliminary articles sent by Mr. Townshend to Mr. Strachey, and the whole thing consists of proposals made by the British at a meeting which, I think, was on the 25th November, between the negotiators in 1782. That proposal I will read, from about the middle of the page:

The citizens of the United States shall have the liberty of taking fish of every kind on all the banks of Newfoundland, and also in the Gulf of

St. Lawrence, and also to dry and cure their fish on the shores of the Isle of Sables, and on the shores of any of the unsettled bays, harbors, and creeks of the Magdalen Islands in the Gulf of St. Lawrence, so long as such bays, harbors, and creeks shall continue and remain unsettled. On condition that the citizens of the said United States do not exercise the said fishery, but at the distance of Three leagues from all the coasts belonging to Great Britain, as well those of the continent, as those of the islands situated in the Gulf of St. Lawrence. And as to what relates to the fishery on the coasts of the island of Cape Breton out of the said gulf, the citizens of the said United States shall not be permitted to exercise the said fishery, but at the distance of fifteen leagues from the coasts of the island of Cape Breton.

That is treating these coasts distributively and separately. It is not treating of a great coast as a whole, as we shall think of it when we sail back to America. It is treating specifically of the shores and of the unsettled bays, harbors, and creeks of the Magdalen Islands, and of the coasts " as well those of the continent as those of the islands, and the coasts of the island of Cape Breton." When they came to agree upon an article, they rejected the quite narrow specification of limits within which the Americans might fish, and they put in " any of the coasts."

THE PRESIDENT: But is the " any " also in the grant, or is it only in the renunciation? I think it is not in the grant. It is only in the renunciation. In the treaty it reads:

> And also on the coasts, bays, harbors, and creeks, from Mount Joli, on the southern coast of Labrador,

and, in the first part:

> on that part of the southern coast of Newfoundland, etc.

There is no " any." As to the drying and curing —

SENATOR ROOT: In the treaty of 1818?

SIR CHARLES FITZPATRICK: No, 1783.

THE PRESIDENT: Ah! In the treaty of 1783, you mean?

SENATOR ROOT: Yes.

THE PRESIDENT: Oh! I beg pardon. Well, I do not believe it is there, either.

SENATOR ROOT: They have a number of forms of this third article of the treaty of 1783. The first one —

THE PRESIDENT: As to the drying and curing, the word " any " is in, but not as to the right of fishing.

SENATOR ROOT: The first form that they agreed upon for the treaty of 1783 gave general reciprocal fishing rights both to the United States and Great Britain on all places where they had been accustomed to fish. The second form contained some limitations, not very great; and the third form was this which I have been reading. That was not agreed to, but instead of agreeing to it, that was made the basis of a modification, and the next form was what came out finally as the treaty. Instead of talking about the shores of the Isle of Sables, and the " shores of the unsettled bays, harbors, and creeks of the Magdalen Islands", and the coasts of the continent, and the coasts of the islands and the coasts of Great Britain, they said:

the people of the United States shall continue to enjoy unmolested the right to take fish of every kind on the Grand Bank . . . and also that the inhabitants of the United States shall have liberty to take fish of every kind on such part of the coast of Newfoundland, as British fishermen shall use, . . . and also on the coasts, bays, and creeks of all other of His Britannic Majesty's dominions in America, and that the American fishermen shall have liberty to dry and cure fish in any of the unsettled bays, harbors, and creeks of Nova Scotia, Magdalen Islands, etc.

The distributive idea which is carried in this proposal, by the specification of particular coasts, particular places, is carried in the final form which grew out of this in the difference which the president has already called attention to, between the singular use of the word " coast " and the plural " the coasts, bays, and creeks of all other of His Britannic Majesty's dominions."

THE PRESIDENT: That was a great success of the American negotiators, that they obtained all — the whole coast.

SENATOR ROOT: Yes; it certainly was.

The President: But I thought, Mr. Senator Root, that you were referring to this passage as explaining the word "any" in the treaty of 1818; and I found —

Senator Root: No; I was referring to the treaty of 1783.

The President: Yes.

Senator Root: I think the use of the word "any" carries the distributive idea, shows that they were thinking of these things not *en bloc*, but as separate elements of consideration, and that it also carries the idea of the completeness of the renunciation. After reciting that differences had arisen, and after providing that the inhabitants of the United States shall have liberty to take fish within certain specified limits, then the purpose of the renunciation was to cover everything else, and to make it a complete renunciation. They must either say: "The United States renounces the liberty heretofore enjoyed or claimed to take, dry, or cure fish on or within three marine miles of *all* the coasts, bays, creeks, and harbors of His Britannic Majesty's dominions not included within the above-mentioned limits", or they must say: "Renounces the liberty to take, dry, or cure fish on or within three marine miles of *any* of", etc. Either use of words serves to accomplish the effect of completeness of the renunciation. To use the word *all* would have carried the idea that they were looking at them *en bloc*. To use the word *any* accomplishes the completeness of the renunciation equally, but carries the idea that they were looking at them as separate elements.

I wish here to make a few further remarks. If the Tribunal will give me a very few minutes more I can complete what I have to say on this subject today.

Something has been said here about the relaxation of the British position regarding the Bay of Fundy in 1844 constituting an arrangement between the two countries. That is negatived positively by Lord Malmesbury in a letter to Mr.

Crampton, the British minister at Washington, on the 10th August, 1852, which appears in the American Appendix at p. 518, where he says that everything but the Bay of Fundy was left for further negotiation.

Quite an argument has been made here to the effect that the French order ordering the American fishermen off the coast of Nova Scotia in 1820 and 1821, and which was the subject of diplomatic remonstrance on the part of the United States, carried an inference that the United States recognized the right of Great Britain to control the waters of St. George's Bay in Newfoundland. The fact is that it appears with the greatest fullness in these affidavits that the French cruisers ordered these American fishing vessels off the coast; they forbade them to fish anywhere on the coast; and there is not a bay on that coast that is more than six miles wide at the mouth except St. George's Bay; and the bulk of the vessels were not at St. George's Bay. They were up in the Bay of Islands, and along there. Of course nothing was ever said about the fact that there was a part of St. George's Bay that they were entitled to fish in. That was of no consequence. They could not accomplish anything by fishing in the open portion of that one little bay. They were not permitted to come within the limits of the three-mile zone, or into any bay or creek or inlet or harbor on that coast unless they did it at the peril of seizure by the French cruiser. That was the subject-matter of the controversy. Of course it carried no inference whatever regarding the use of the water outside of that which the Americans claimed under their treaty, and which they went there to enjoy. An inference has been drawn from the fact that there was a resolution of the American Congress in 1789 in which the words, " coasts, bays, and banks " were used; and that is in the British Counter-Case Appendix at p. 13, a little below the middle of the page. A substitute was moved by Mr. Morris, in the words following:

That an acknowledgment be made by Great Britain of a common right in these states to fish on the coasts, bays, and banks of Nova Scotia, the banks of Newfoundland and Gulf of St. Lawrence, etc.

And the inference drawn was that the American Congress considered "bays" as a different thing from "coasts and banks"; and having said "coasts" they must also say "bays." It is not of much consequence, but if you will turn over to the next page, p. 14, you will see that that resolution was finally adopted with the omission of the word "bays." Just above the middle of the page is the resolution as finally adopted:

That the right of fishing on the coasts and banks of North America be reserved to the United States as fully as they enjoyed the same, etc.

THE PRESIDENT: But, by the words "as fully as they enjoyed the same when subject to the King of Great Britain", — by the use of these words, is not "bays" included?

SENATOR ROOT: Certainly.

THE PRESIDENT: Therefore it was not necessary to mention bays specifically?

SENATOR ROOT: Certainly, it was not necessary to mention bays specifically. The argument of the Attorney-General was that the mention of them indicated that we thought it was necessary to mention them. The first form of the resolution mentioned coasts, bays, and banks; and my learned friend founded an argument on the fact that "bays" were specially mentioned.

THE PRESIDENT: Might it not be said that in the first form the mentioning of bays was necessary, because there could be some doubt whether "coasts" embraced bays; whereas, in the second form, where it is said "as fully as they enjoyed the same when subject to the King of Great Britain" there could arise no doubt that the word "coasts" embraced in this connection also the bays, because there is no doubt that when they were subjects of the king of Great Britain they had also the right to fish in the bays?

SENATOR ROOT: Well, perhaps that may be said. But my particular object here is to destroy the argument of the Attorney-General, which, certainly, is destroyed if you find that the word on which the argument is based was not included in the final form of the resolution.

The Attorney-General has founded an argument here upon the use of the term " bays " in some of the old treaties, the treaty of 1686, between Great Britain and Spain, I think it was, and the treaty of 1778 between the United States and France. The phrase used in both was " havens, bays, creeks, roads, shoals, and places." There are two things that are said about that by the other side: one is that it shows that " bays " were considered of very great importance. It does not show that they were considered of any more importance than " havens, creeks, roads, shoals, and places." In the time when the subject of jurisdiction and right of control over the sea was very unsettled, people making treaties about portions of the sea next to the land used to put in everything they could think of to describe those portions, because they had not any definite line of jurisdiction to appeal to; and that is what was done here. It does not show any importance, particularly, given to bays, and you can draw no inference from it about the meaning of bays without putting that meaning into it. If you assume that " bays " here mean what Great Britain says " bays " mean in the treaty, then you have something in which " bays " will be of some help to them, because they would say: " Here is a treaty in which ' bays ' is used with this meaning." But you have to put the meaning into it in order to get it there; and there is nothing in the treaty which shows what kind of bays they are talking about. If there is any inference to be drawn from the occurrence of the word in this connection, it is the inference that people had been in the habit of using the word as designating something quite close to the shore, and something in the way of interior waters. If it ever is permissible to say *noscitur a sociis*, you can say it here. The bays here are the bays that associate with havens, creeks, roads, shoals, and places. The word " places " is quite general, of course, but all the other things are things quite close to the shore; so that if there is any inference from those treaties, it is an inference that is quite favorable to the United States.

I shall not take the time to go into an examination of the local statutes in regard to the bays of Chaleur and Miramichi further than to say that the statute about Chaleur applied only to the beaches, the shores, and did not relate to the general surface of the bay. Chaleur lies between the old province of Lower Canada and New Brunswick, and the line of Lower Canada ran along the north shore of the Bay of Chaleur, while New Brunswick was bounded by the bay on the north. These statutes were statutes which related to the use of the north shore of the bay in Lower Canada, and her jurisdiction was bounded, not by the bay, but by the north shore; and an examination of the statutes will show that they had no relation to the general body of water at all. Perhaps they may have had a relation to the water in connection with the shore, but nothing which could run out anywhere in the neighborhood of the three-mile line.

SIR CHARLES FITZPATRICK: Is that the statute that provides for the boundary between Old Canada and New Brunswick?

SENATOR ROOT: That is a different statute. I stated what I understood to be the fact, and which I believe would be found in that statute to which you referred, Sir Charles, but the statute I am now referring to was one in 1785, to be found in the British Appendix at p. 554.

SIR CHARLES FITZPATRICK: That is the old statute that provides for fishery regulations made by the coroner or the justice of the peace.

SENATOR ROOT: That is another one, that I referred to the other day. Then, there is another statute of 1788, to be found in the British Appendix at p. 592.

JUDGE GRAY: Where in the British Appendix is the first, the statute of 1785 ?

SENATOR ROOT: The statute of 1785 is in the British Appendix at p. 554; the statute of 1788 is in the British Appendix at p. 592.

Along down in 1887, during the discussion of the Bayard-Chamberlain Treaty, Lord Salisbury makes a note, upon one of the American projects, with regard to Chaleur, in which he refers to a subsequent statute as amounting to a claim to have territorial jurisdiction over it. That was a statute passed in 1851, which is not in the Appendix, and does not appear except that Lord Salisbury refers to it.

Then, with regard to Miramichi, there was the statute of 1799, which appears in the British Appendix at p. 597, and one of 1810, which appears in the British Appendix at p. 603. I think those were the only ones counted upon. The first, of 1799, was chiefly a shore statute, but I think it prohibits the casting of gurry for several leagues out from the shore, and so far as to be plainly applicable only to citizens of New Brunswick. And the one of 1810 provides for placing buoys in Miramichi, and for the imposition of dues upon vessels coming into the bay.

THE PRESIDENT: The statute of 1799, concerning Miramichi, in section 2 refers also to the placing of seines, or nets, in the bay or river Miramichi or its branches except as therein before provided for, except at the places admitted by section 1.

SENATOR ROOT: Yes.

THE ATTORNEY-GENERAL: This statute for settling the boundaries is on p. 572.

SENATOR ROOT: Yes; Mr. Anderson has just called my attention to that. That statute carries the boundary of New Brunswick down through the middle of the Bay of Chaleur to the Gulf of St. Lawrence, and that is the statute of 1851 that Lord Salisbury refers to.

I shall take up no more time with these statutes, further than to say that, in our view, they do not constitute such a claim to territorial jurisdiction over the waters of these bays as to have any effect internationally; and of course they were never referred to in any way whatever or made any ground of prescription, or definition of maritime jurisdiction of Great Britain before or at the time of the negotiations of 1818.

One other subject I ought to speak of, and that is what the Attorney-General said about the renunciation clause. He says there were two renunciation clauses: one by the British and one by the Americans. The difference between them is that one was a renunciation clause and the other was not. The American proposal was the renunciation clause with which we are familiar. The British proposal was contained in Article A, presented by the British, to be found on p. 312 of the American Appendix. That article begins by saying that the " inhabitants of the United States shall have liberty to take fish " on such and such coasts. Then follows a regulation regarding the rivers, and then follows this, which is the British substitute for the renunciation clause as we now have it:

His Britannic Majesty further agrees that the vessels of the United States, *bona fide* engaged in such fishery, shall have liberty to enter the bays and harbors of any of His Britannic Majesty's dominions in North America, for the purpose of shelter, or of repairing damages therein, and of purchasing wood and obtaining water, and for no other purpose; and

all vessels so resorting to the said bays, and harbors shall be under such restrictions as may be necessary to prevent their taking, drying, or curing fish therein.

That is not a renunciation clause. That is a grant. That is a grant from Great Britain. And the difference between the two is that the clause proposed by the Americans renounced the right of taking and drying and curing of fish, and, by necessary implication, asserted that the Americans had the right that they were renouncing; while the clause proposed by the British granted a right for specific purposes, and, by necessary implication, asserted that the British had the right that they were granting. The two are world-wide apart. One is a renunciation and the other is not. Of course the Americans were abandoning their claim of right to all the coasts, that they did not expressly get granted to them in this article. They were abandoning it. They could no longer have it when the settlement had been made upon the basis of their having a right to fish only on such and such coasts. But the American renunciation was an abandonment by their renouncing what they had, what they still asserted was theirs, while the British proposal was that the abandonment should be accomplished by being silent, assuming that they had nothing except what the British chose to grant in making an express grant for that purpose.

There is only one other subject to which I feel bound to refer, and that is the Webster circular, or the Webster pronunciamento or proclamation. That paper appears in the British Appendix, p. 152, and it is the contention of Great Britain that that paper was a surrender by the United States, or an admission by the United States, that the treaty did give to the renunciation clause the effect of covering these great bays. It is an extraordinary statement — extraordinary in every feature; and it is especially extraordinary in the fact that it says, at the same time, that

It would appear that, by a strict and rigid construction of this article, fishing vessels of the United States are precluded from entering into the bays or harbors of the British provinces

and that it was an oversight in the negotiators of the treaty to make so large a concession to England, and that Mr. Webster does not agree with the construction put upon the treaty which makes it a concession. A most amazing paper, by the secretary of state of the United States, charged with the conduct of her foreign affairs. The lines were drawn, and had for years been drawn, between the two countries in direct opposition upon the construction of this treaty; and he issues this public proclamation, which he publishes in a newspaper. It is quite inexplicable upon any ordinary grounds, in any ordinary way. Mr. Everett says, in a letter which appears at p. 543 of the American Appendix, that Lord Malmesbury ascribed the extraordinary nature of the paper to two causes: one "the influences which periodical events exercised in those localities might perhaps be able to account for," that is to say, political exigencies; and the other that the preparation of the notice was to be ascribed "to the excitement induced by the disease, whose fatal termination he handsomely laments." I would rather that he had given only the latter explanation. I think it was the true explanation. Within a few weeks after the publication of this extraordinary document, Mr. Webster died. He was a very great man — one of those rare men of power and genius, surpassing ordinary men, who come in a century or two in a country. He was an advocate of such power and cogency of reasoning that now, almost a century after they were delivered, his arguments are cited at the bar, as are the decisions of the great judges before whom he practiced. He was a diplomatist of great wisdom and courage. It was he who made with Lord Ashburton the most important treaty that has ever been made to preserve peace between Great Britain and the

United States, in settling the boundaries, the Webster-Ashburton Treaty of 1842. He was a statesman of commanding influence in his country, and it was his voice more than any other, more than all others together, that built up in the people of the United States that sentiment of loyalty, of union, and of love for freedom that in the great Civil War enabled the North to determine, by the issue of the sword, that our country should be free. His influence over his country passed beyond that of any man, unless it be the influence of Washington and of Lincoln. The boys of America have all been thrilled with a kindlier feeling and a quicker pride in the ties of blood to the great empire that Webster described to them — the empire "whose morning drum-beat, following the sun and keeping company with the hours, encircles the earth with one unbroken strain of the martial airs of England." Altogether he was the man of his time, from whom was to be especially expected wisdom, judgment, cogency of reasoning, and effectiveness in maintaining the part of his country in a discussion of this kind. Yet look at this paper! We must conclude that the fatal disease that took him from earth within but a few short weeks was the origin of such an incoherent and insensible document.

I am indebted to this case for a kindlier feeling toward President Fillmore, because of the kindly way in which he performed his duty of instantly setting right the erroneous impressions that might be derived from this public document. It appears in the record that Mr. Fillmore, on the day after the paper was published, had an interview with the British minister in which he stated authoritatively what the position of the United States was, and that on the same day he wrote a letter to Mr. Webster. The paper was published on the 19th July, and on the 20th July there was an interview between Mr. Fillmore and Mr. Crampton that appears in the British Appendix at p. 154. Mr. Crampton is reporting that interview to the Earl of Malmesbury, and in that letter the Tribunal will see that Mr. Fillmore distinctly stated what his view was. In the last paragraph on p. 155, Mr. Fillmore said to Mr. Crampton:

> What he would propose was that Mr. Webster and myself should make some temporary arrangement of the matter until the true sense of the treaty should be determined by the two governments between themselves, or, if necessary, be referred to the decision of some friendly power.

And in the paragraph before, he stated his view; he said:

> We had been examining the Convention of 1818, and although he contested the construction put by the British Law Officers upon the clause regarding the limits assigned, within which American fishermen could not legally carry on their operations, he nevertheless admitted that the wording of the passage, which he thought somewhat obscure, countenanced to a certain degree that construction. With regard to the opinion of the Law Officers of the Crown by which this construction was maintained, he remarked, however, that it seemed to him singular that they adverted to expressions as being used in the Treaty which were nowhere to be found in it: he alluded to that part of the opinion where it is said, "as we are of opinion that the term headland *is used in the Treaty* to express the part of the land we have before mentioned including the interior of the bays and indents of the coast." Now, said Mr. Fillmore, there is no such term as headland in the Treaty at all, which would look as if the opinion had been drawn up without reference being made to the text of the Convention of 1818. He also remarked that as well as he had been able to ascertain the fact, the Government of the United States had, on various previous occasions, contested the construction maintained by the opinion in question.

And the interview closed by his saying:

> while the United States Government, on the other hand, should take every means in their power to prevent their own citizens from fishing within the prescribed distance as understood by the British construction, until such time as the question as to which construction ought to prevail, should be determined on, or until the question should be otherwise disposed of by treaty or mutual legislation.

And on the same day, in Mr. Fillmore's letter to Mr. Webster, not criticizing him, or finding any fault with what Mr. Webster had done, but in the most kindly and respectful way, he suggests to him that he and Mr. Crampton should concur in a statement as to the position of both countries upon this question; and here is the way in which Mr. Fillmore wished it stated:

but as for those waters in the several bays and harbors which are more than three marine miles from the shore of such bay or harbor upon either side, and within three marine miles of a straight line drawn from one headland to the other of such bay or harbor, that you as the Representative of the United States conceived that our fishermen have the right under the Treaty to fish therein, but the British Government having held that by a true construction of the Treaty such right belonged exclusively to British subjects; and as those waters were thus in dispute between the two nations, you respectively advised the citizens and subjects of both countries not to attempt to exercise any right that either claimed within the disputed waters until this disputed right could be adjusted by amicable negotiation.

That is the disposition of the subject made by Mr. Webster's superior in office, Mr. Fillmore, immediately upon the publication of this paper of Mr. Webster's; and the substance of the same thing was communicated to the British ambassador. And so the Webster paper must go for naught as any expression of the position of the Government of the United States, or as affecting in any way the opinion of Great Britain regarding the position of the United States; and we must deem it as one of those mistakes for which the great are to be forgiven when they are gone.

That brings me to the end of what I have to say on the Fifth Question, and I shall very easily conclude what I have to say during the day tomorrow, and perhaps before the conclusion of the time tomorrow.

Sir Charles Fitzpatrick: Mr. Root, if you will kindly pardon me for a moment, may I ask you to revert again to the Bathurst letter on p. 64 of the British Appendix? I would like you to say whether I have understood your argument based upon that letter correctly. I understand your argument to be that the bays from which Lord Bathurst says it is the intention to exclude United States fishermen are not the bays of all His Majesty's possessions, but only such of those bays as are within the jurisdiction of a maritime league ?

SENATOR ROOT: I do not say they are not the bays of all His Majesty's possessions. I say that they are only the bays that are within the jurisdiction of the maritime league.

SIR CHARLES FITZPATRICK: You say the bays of His Majesty's possessions are those which are within the maritime league ?

SENATOR ROOT: Yes.

SIR CHARLES FITZPATRICK: In the sense of that letter ?

SENATOR ROOT: Yes.[1]

THE PRESIDENT: Will you kindly continue, Mr. Senator Root ?[2]

SENATOR ROOT: As to Question Two:

> Have the inhabitants of the United States, while exercising the liberties referred to in said Article, the right to employ as members of the fishing crews of their vessels persons not inhabitants of the United States ?

As to the scope of the question: In the view of the United States, if the Tribunal said that the inhabitants exercising the liberties referred to have or have not a right to employ any person who is not an inhabitant of the United States, the question is answered; and to undertake to say that they have or have not a right to employ all persons in the world who are not inhabitants of the United States would be wholly unnecessary to a resolution of the question, and wholly impossible for any tribunal to undertake.

The question points directly and solely to the competency of the inhabitants of the United States who exercise the liberty to employ. It is a question of the employer's right, and it

[1] Thereupon, at 4.35 o'clock P.M., the Tribunal adjourned until Friday, 12th August, 1910, at 10 o'clock A.M.

[2] Friday, August 12, 1910. The Tribunal met at 10 o'clock A.M.

points to inhabitancy or non-inhabitancy of the employé as the sole test of the employer's right to make the contract of employment, nothing else. Have I, an inhabitant of the United States, purposing to exercise the treaty right, the right to make a contract of employment with a person who is not an inhabitant of the United States? That is the question.

Upon the other side, a multitude of quite different questions might arise, regarding the right of this, that, or the other, or any number of persons to accept employment. Those questions must be resolved not by treaty between Great Britain and the United States, but by those laws which govern the persons who are contemplating acceptance of the employment. If a Frenchman is offered employment by an inhabitant of the United States for the purpose of this industry, he must regulate his conduct by the laws of his country. If a British subject is offered employment, he must regulate his conduct by the laws of his country, and so through the whole range of non-inhabitants. The two questions are quite distinct. The question of what right we, of the United States, have under this treaty to employ non-inhabitants, and the infinite number of possible questions which there may be as to the right of other people of the earth under their laws to accept such an employment.

There is a rather leading case in the United States, which Mr. Justice Gray will recall, the Terre Haute Railroad case, which illustrates this. Two railroad companies had made a contract of lease. The question as to the validity of the lease went up to the Supreme Court of the United States, and the Supreme Court held that one of those companies had, under its charter, corporate power to make such a contract. It held, however, that the other of the companies had not under its charter the corporate right to make such a contract, and declared it invalid. There were two quite separate and distinct questions, which illustrate this question here — the two entirely separate and distinct classes of question which may arise regarding the making of a contract of employment by an inhabitant of the United States with a non-inhabitant in respect of taking part in this fishing industry. This question relates solely to the right under the treaty of the inhabitants of the United States to make a contract with one who is not an inhabitant.

THE PRESIDENT: If you please, Mr. Senator Root, what was the consequence of this decision ? Was the right of one of these companies limited by the absence of the right of the other company or was the absence of the right of one of these companies supplemented by the right of the other ?

SENATOR ROOT: In the contract the two rights must necessarily exist to support the contract.

THE PRESIDENT: Yes.

SENATOR ROOT: The right of the company which was acting within its corporate power was full and complete.

THE PRESIDENT: Yes; but could it exercise its right in relation to the other company whose right was defective ?

SENATOR ROOT: No.

THE PRESIDENT: No; it could not.

SENATOR ROOT: Not in relation to the other company, but not through any defect of its right.

THE PRESIDENT: Not through the defect of its right, but through the defect of the right of the other.

SENATOR ROOT: It could not make a contract with the other company any more than it could make a contract with a person under the lawful age of contracting, or any one not *sui juris*. The defect, however, was not a defect of the right. No invalidity was imported into the right of the company which was keeping within its corporate powers.

The practical bearing of this question, — it is a mistake to suppose that it relates practically to any prohibition upon the citizens of Newfoundland. There is no such prohibition. It is true that in the recent correspondence Sir Edward Grey made an observation to the effect that he did not suppose that the United States would contend that it had a right to withdraw the citizens of Newfoundland from obedience to their own laws. That was not answered. There was no occasion to answer it, because no such situation arose. No such situation existed, and none has ever existed. Newfoundland never has prohibited her citizens as Newfoundlanders from taking employment upon vessels of the United States. It is curious that the one thing that our friends upon the other side say the Tribunal ought to decide as incident to the decision of this Question 2 is the one thing that never has arisen to be decided.

Newfoundland has done these things: In the first place (British Appendix, pp. 757 and 758, American Appendix, pp. 197 and 199) she has forbidden any person whatever, of whatever nationality or race, to engage in the crew of any foreign fishing vessels in the waters of Newfoundland; and on p. 197 of the American Appendix, towards the latter part of the first article, will be found the provisions to which I specifically refer. You see that does not apply to Newfoundlanders specifically. If any person is engaged within that jurisdiction, the vessel is forfeited; and that really was the pivot upon which the subject revolved. The United States vessels had been in the habit of supplementing their crews in order to enable them to take their fish more expeditiously. They had been in the habit of supplementing the crews by picking up men from Nova Scotia. North Sydney was the great shipping place. They also employed these men up on the Newfoundland coast. This statute forbade the shipment on the Newfoundland coast, in Newfoundland waters, of anybody, it made no difference who, and that forced the United States vessels back to these ports in Nova Scotia to supplement their crews. That was, of course, much less expensive than to bring people clear up from the Massachusetts coast, and pay them and feed them during the long voyage up and back. Then Newfoundland put in a provision forbidding any Newfoundlander to leave the colony for the purpose of engaging in foreign fishing vessels, " which are fishing or intend to fish in the waters of the colony." That is the seventh article of the Act of 1906. That was to prevent their going over to North Sydney and forming a part of the material from which the supplement to the crews was obtained. Still there was no prohibition against the Newfoundlander shipping in an American crew. There was the specific prohibition against his leaving the colony for the purpose of doing it. Any Newfoundlander who had left the colony for any other purpose was entirely at liberty to do it; but for the fact that he would run against another provision, which was not directed against Newfoundlanders, but against British subjects generally.

JUDGE GRAY: I beg pardon, Mr. Root; would you mind repeating that ? I did not catch it.

SENATOR ROOT: I say any Newfoundlander was at liberty to ship in an American crew unless he had left the colony for the express purpose of doing it; but for the fact that he would run against another provision of law which was directed against British subjects generally. That is Article 6 of the Act of 1906:

> No person, being a British subject, shall fish in, from or for a foreign vessel in the waters of this Colony.

That is not a prohibition against Newfoundlanders. It is a prohibition against all British subjects.

JUDGE GRAY: Then Question 2 would seem to have been framed with reference to the provisions of sections 5 and 6 specially ?

SENATOR ROOT: No; it was framed for the purpose of meeting a fundamental question, the decision of which would be beneficial in dealing with all these various provisions. Article 6, you see, relates to a general prohibition against British fisheries.

JUDGE GRAY: But not Article 5?

SENATOR ROOT: Article 5 relates to a general prohibition against aliens; that is, aliens to Newfoundland, aliens from the Newfoundland point of view. That would take in all Germans, Dutch, French, Portuguese, Italians — everybody in the world except Americans and British subjects; and the provision of Article 6 covers British subjects; and the provision to which I referred before, relating solely to the waters of Newfoundland, to shipment in the waters of Newfoundland, covers all the world — everybody.

The only way in which Newfoundlanders are involved in these, apart from that specific provision against leaving the country for the purpose, is by being included in the general category "British subjects."

In dealing with all these various provisions, and in dealing with any number of future provisions which the ingenuity of Newfoundland legislation might devise, and which it would be impossible to forecast, it was manifest, as a preliminary to an intelligent discussion, that we must ascertain whether, quite independently of all these laws, under the treaty the United States vessel owner was at liberty to employ anybody who was not an inhabitant of the United States; because if he is not at liberty to employ anybody who is not an inhabitant of the United States, then we cannot object to any of these things. We cannot discuss them. That lies at the threshold of the discussion of any of these statutes. We cannot call Great Britain to account for making a statute prohibiting British subjects from going into our crews, or fishing from our ships, unless the treaty right includes employing non-inhabitants. We cannot call her to account for prohibiting Germans and French and Dutch from fishing from our ships unless, under the treaty, we can employ non-inhabitants. If, under the treaty, we cannot employ a non-inhabitant, we are cut off from discussing any of these questions. And therefore we have put here this preliminary question, asking you to decide it for us, and all these other questions we shall have to take care of, and there will be no serious difficulty about taking care of them, when we come to consider them with Great Britain in the light of whatever your award may be upon the question that is now asked here. And if there is any danger that your answer to this question may conclude either country upon any one of these other questions, this other great and indefinite range of possible questions relating to the effect of statutes and the right of people to accept employment, why it is perfectly simple, and the only practical way is to say that your award upon this question does not pass upon the effect of any statutes regarding the subjects of any country. That, certainly, is a much more practical way of disposing of the subject than it is to try to decide all these questions, the material for deciding which is not before you, and the reasons for deciding which one way or another have not been argued before you.

Let us pass to the question as we take it to be.

Sir Charles Fitzpatrick: Before you leave that, may I ask you a question? I understand you to say that it was not the intention to submit that aspect of the question, that is to say, the aspect with reference to the engagement of Newfoundland fishermen, to this Tribunal?

Senator Root: Yes.

Sir Charles Fitzpatrick: May I ask you, in the light of that statement, to refer to Mr. Whitelaw Reid's letter, on p. 506 of the British Appendix, with respect to the *modus vivendi*, second paragraph:

My Government understand by this that the use of purse seines by American fishermen is not to be interfered with, and the shipment of

Newfoundlanders by American fishermen outside the three-mile limit is not to be made the basis of interference or to be penalized.

Then, again, on p. 509, in a letter of the 12th July, 1907, he says:

> Without dwelling on minor points, on which we would certainly make every effort to meet your views, I may briefly say that in our opinion, sustained by the observations of those best qualified to judge, the surrender of the right to hire local fishermen, who eagerly seek to have us employ them, and the surrender at the same time of the use of purse seines and of fishing on Sunday would, under existing circumstances, render the Treaty stipulation worthless to us.

Do you think that these paragraphs have any bearing upon your submission?

SENATOR ROOT: I think they are very relevant indeed. They relate, however, to this statute to which I have referred, which forbade Newfoundlanders to go out of the jurisdiction for the purpose of engaging —

SIR CHARLES FITZPATRICK: I do not think my reference is quite sufficiently complete, perhaps.

The first letter of the 6th October, 1906, refers to the Foreign Fishing Vessels Act, 1906, which contains the provision that Newfoundlanders shall not fish in or from an American fishing-boat.

SENATOR ROOT: That Newfoundlanders shall not?

SIR CHARLES FITZPATRICK: Yes; that British subjects shall not.

SENATOR ROOT: Oh! British subjects.

SIR CHARLES FITZPATRICK: They are Newfoundlanders. Newfoundlanders are British subjects.

SENATOR ROOT: Newfoundlanders are British subjects, but —

JUDGE GRAY: But all British subjects are not Newfoundlanders.

SENATOR ROOT: No. You will see this first reference is a reference to the violations of the statute prohibiting Newfoundlanders to leave the jurisdiction for the purpose of engaging in fishing. These fishermen were dependent upon the prosecution of this American fishing enterprise for their livelihood; and they were cut off from engaging, within the territorial jurisdiction, in common with everybody else in the world; and accordingly they rowed out, by the hundreds, in boats, across the three-mile limit, to engage with the American fishermen outside of the jurisdiction. Then this statute is put in, penalizing their going out for the purpose of making that engagement. That is what this refers to. And the second reference —

SIR CHARLES FITZPATRICK: So that, in your construction, in that letter it is asked that the Foreign Fishing Vessels Act should be suspended for the protection of Newfoundlanders, and not for the protection of American fishermen.

SENATOR ROOT: It is to be suspended, certainly, for the advantage of American fishermen. It was to relieve American fishermen from the very great disadvantage which was imposed upon them by the fact that the men whom they wanted to employ would be punished if they accepted employment within the jurisdiction of their country, and would be punished if they left the country for the purpose of accepting such employment.

THE PRESIDENT: Was it understood, Mr. Root, by both parties, that Question 2, as it is now framed, excluded the consideration of the right of Americans to employ Newfoundlanders in their fishing industry, and of the right of Newfoundland to prohibit Newfoundlanders to enter that service?

SENATOR ROOT: I would not say so. I think the understanding of the question — I am a little embarrassed in answering this, because I cannot answer it as counsel. My own past relation to it is such that I, perhaps, ought to have Mr. Bryce here to join with me in answering it; but I will go so far as this: I do not think it entered into the mind of any one that the answer to this question disposed of any question relating to the acceptance of employment by Newfoundlanders or by British subjects, or by people of any other nation dependent upon the statute of any other countries; that it related solely to the competency of the American making his side of the contract under the treaty.

Sir Charles Fitzpatrick: What would be the meaning of the words used by Mr. Reid in his letter of the 12th July, 1907, "that the surrender of the right to hire local fishermen . . . would, under existing circumstances, render the treaty stipulation worthless to us"?

On the face of that letter, does it not rather imply an intention to make that a condition of the reference?

Senator Root: Will your honor give me the page?

Sir Charles Fitzpatrick: Page 509 of the British Appendix. In the very next paragraph he goes on to say:

> My Government holds this opinion so strongly that the task of reconciling it with the positions maintained in your letter of June 20th seems hopeless.

Senator Root: May I call your attention to another feature of the fourth paragraph? What Mr. Reid says is:

> in our opinion, sustained by the observations of those best qualified to judge, the surrender of the right to hire local fishermen, who eagerly seek to have us employ them, and the surrender at the same time of the use of purse seines and of fishing on Sunday would, under existing circumstances, render the Treaty stipulation worthless to us.

Sir Charles Fitzpatrick: He put the three things together there.

Senator Root: The prohibition against the use of that kind of implement which was appropriate to the vessel fishery, and could be used by the crews without having a great number of supplementary men; and, at the same time, the prohibition of the employment of these supplementary local fishermen, whether Newfoundlanders or not, amounted to a foreclosing of them from the profitable exercise of that industry. But that does not import into this Question 2 any questions regarding any of the obstacles that had been introduced to prevent local fishermen from engaging with us.

As to that part of the question which both sides agree is here: Whether it is competent under the treaty for an American prosecuting this fishing enterprise to employ and send to the waters of the treaty coasts as parts of the fishing crew persons who are not inhabitants of the United States; and laying entirely aside, not undertaking to consider, whether the persons are unwilling or unable to accept the employment, but assuming a willing and a competent contractor on the other side, is the American owner of the fishing enterprise competent under the treaty to make the contract on his side ?

SIR CHARLES FITZPATRICK: Perhaps you will allow me to say there would be no personal disqualification, except the fact that he is not an inhabitant.

SENATOR ROOT: Exactly; there would be no personal disqualification, except the fact that he is not an inhabitant — that being a qualification arising or not arising under the treaty.

SIR CHARLES FITZPATRICK: Under the treaty.

SENATOR ROOT: And therefore something going to the employer's right.

We are all agreed that this is an industrial enterprise, I think. There certainly cannot be any question about it, in view of that fundamental British statute of 1699 (British Case Appendix, p. 525), which opens its provisions by reciting:

> Whereas the trade of and fishing at Newfoundland is a beneficial trade to this kingdom, not only in the employing great numbers of seamen and ships, and exporting and consuming great quantities of provisions and manufactures of this realm, whereby many tradesmen and poor artificers are kept at work, but also in bringing into this nation, by returns of the

effects of the said fishery from other countries, great quantities of wine, oil, plate, iron, wool, and sundry other useful commodities, to the increase of His Majesty's revenue, and the encouragement of trade and navigation; Be it enacted by the King's most excellent Majesty, by and with the advice and consent of the Lords spiritual and temporal, and Commons, in this present Parliament assembled, and by the authority of the same, That from henceforth it shall and may be lawful for all His Majesty's subjects residing within this his realm of England, or the dominions thereunto belonging, trading or that shall trade to Newfoundland, and the seas, rivers, lakes, creeks, harbors in or about Newfoundland, or any of the islands adjoining or adjacent thereunto, to have, use, and enjoy the free trade and traffic, and art of merchandise and fishery, to and from Newfoundland, etc.

There is an industrial enterprise vastly important to the country, to the nation which is authorizing its subjects to engage in it.

In the second place, it appears beyond dispute that it was the universal custom to employ aliens as well as citizens of the country in which the vessel was owned in such enterprises. That cannot well be disputed, in view of the other British statutes which are here. For example, the British statute of 1663, which is in the British Counter-Case Appendix, at p. 213 and which provides, in Article 16:

And for the Encouragement of the Herring and North-Sea Island, and Westmoney Fisheries, (2) be it enacted, and it is hereby enacted by the Authority aforesaid, That from and after the first Day of August which shall be in the Year of our Lord one thousand six hundred sixty and four, no Fresh Herring, Fresh Cod or Haddock, Coal-fish or Gull-fish, shall be imported into England, Wales, or the Town of Berwick, but in English-built Ships or Vessels, or in Ships or Vessels *bona fide* belonging to England, Wales, or the Town of Berwick, and having such Certificate thereof as is above-said, and whereof the Master and three Fourths at the least of the Mariners are English, and which hath been fished, caught and taken in such Ships or Vessels.

And the Act of 1775, in the British Appendix at p. 543, provides in the first article for the payment of bounties to vessels which shall appear by their register to be British built, and owned by His Majesty's subjects residing in Great Britain or Ireland, or the islands of Guernsey, Jersey, or Man; and be of the burthen of fifty tons or upwards, and navigated with not less than fifteen men each, three-fourths of whom, besides the master, shall be His Majesty's subjects.

You see the stress is laid upon the ownership of the vessel and the construction of the vessel. It must be British built and owned by His Majesty's subjects. But the crew are required to be three-fourths subjects of His Majesty; of course, permitting one-fourth not to be, and showing quite clearly the custom which made it necessary to put such a restriction upon them, the custom which might have made a far greater proportion of the crew composed of aliens to Great Britain but for the restriction.

The Attorney-General quite frankly concedes the custom, and he says they have to do it; that the conditions of the British marine all over the world make it necessary. They have to employ lascars and so on. That but sustains our position. Of course there are reasons; there are always reasons; there were reasons here that must have been in the contemplation of the people who made the treaty of 1783 and those who made the treaty of 1818, that this kind of an enterprise, pursued and carried on by means of vessels fitted out and sent from a great distance would be carried on through the employment not merely of natives of the country from which the vessels came, but the employment of crews in the ordinary way, which took in these sailors who are floating all over the world, and the men who can be collected in the port from which the vessel comes and the ports at which the vessel touches. The ordinary, universal usage must be supposed to have been in the minds of the parties making the conventions, and the terms of the conventions must be read with reference to the existence of such a usage. Indeed, there is quite a distinct admission by Sir Edward Grey that, so far as crews are concerned, it is not contended by Great Britain that the crews of the vessels may not be partly aliens. But they make the distinction that a man shall not pull a fish out of the water, and shall not take hold of a net. There is no basis for the distinction. These industrial enterprises were carried on by the servants who were partly English and partly aliens. As my learned friend the Attorney-General says [p. 1058, *supra*]:

> We do not forbid the employment of foreigners, because that would be in particular cases to handicap an industry.

He thinks Newfoundland may employ foreigners.

THE ATTORNEY-GENERAL: I hope my learned friend will not put that as a statement of mine. I said we did not forbid the employment of foreigners, but I was speaking of the commerce of Great Britain generally. I distinguished between these statutes that dealt with our general commerce and statutes which, like those referring to Newfoundland, are dealing with a particular trade, in which only a particular class of foreigners is entitled to be engaged. The learned senator is putting what he calls my admission to a purpose to which never applied it. I drew a distinction between the general trade of shipping over the whole world and the particular industrial right exercised in this particular part of the world, which is not an industry at all, but a mere right in an industry.

SENATOR ROOT: I quite agree with the Attorney-General in the limitation which he has stated. I am talking about the same thing he was talking about. I am talking about the general right of employment. I shall speak hereafter as to the question whether there is any particular ground of exception from that general right. I hope the Attorney-General will realize that I was not intending to impute to him any observation regarding this particular instance. I was establishing the existence of the general practice of employing foreigners.

The Attorney-General says [p. 1058, *supra*]:

He (Mr. Elder) wants to show, of course, that in 1818, when there is a right given to take fish, that according to the custom of that time that right was exercised, not by Britons for themselves alone, but by Britons employing foreigners. Well, he does not show it. He does show this, that according to the law in Asia and in Africa and in different parts of the world, Britons were allowed to employ on their ships a certain proportion of foreigners.

That is the proposition to which I refer. And he says:

I am afraid, in those days, when maritime troubles or naval wars came on, we were not very particular about the nationality of those whom we impressed, but still we did not want those, of course, who could not be trusted to fight in our interests, so we did not discourage the system of foreign seamen in England, if it was found convenient for their employment. So that you see here where we say three-fourths of them must be British subjects, we did not say the other fourth may be foreigners. We do not forbid the employment of foreigners, because that would be in particular cases to handicap an industry. But, we say each vessel must be fitted out at a British port, and you are not likely at a British port to get any foreigners, except those who are inhabitants or domiciled in England.

I make this observation upon that: that we have just as much right to say that you cannot take this industry out of the general and universal practice and make it an exception for the purpose of handicapping it, as the Attorney-General has to explain that they do not prohibit the employment of foreigners in other particular cases because that would be to handicap an industry. It is very well to refrain from handicapping British industries by not making them exceptions to the general rule. But we object to their handicapping our industry by making it an exception to the general rule.

The next proposition is that, in the conduct of an enterprise for profit, servants and agents may be employed to act with and for the proprietors, owners of the enterprise. That is the lesson taught by this statute of 1699, which is at p. 525 of the British Case Appendix, and which provides in the first article that it may be lawful for all His Majesty's subjects residing within this his realm of England, or the dominions thereunto belonging, trading or that shall trade to Newfoundland, and the seas, rivers, lakes, creeks, harbors in or about Newfoundland, or any of the islands adjoining or adjacent thereunto, to have, use, and enjoy the free trade and traffic, and art of merchandise and fishery, to and from Newfoundland, and peaceably to have, use, and enjoy, the freedom of taking bait and fishing in any of the rivers, lakes, creeks, harbors, or roads, in or about Newfoundland, and the said seas, or any of the islands adjacent thereunto, and liberty to go on shore on any part of Newfoundland, or any of the said islands for the curing, salting, drying, and husbanding of their fish, and for making of oil and to cut down woods and trees there for building and making or repairing of stages, ship-rooms, train-vats, hurdles, ships, boats, and other necessaries for themselves and their servants, seamen, and fishermen, and all other things which may be useful or advantageous to their fishing trade.

Here is a law which limits the privilege of fishing in Newfoundland waters to "His Majesty's subjects residing within this, his realm of England, or the domains thereunto belonging." The right is limited to them. The right is to be exercised through the use of vessels and implements which, according to universal custom, may be handled by servants, seamen, and fishermen, and part of whom are not subjects of the realm of England, and who, therefore, have themselves no right under the treaty; and this statute makes express provision for the going ashore and engaging in this business of fishery by servants, seamen, and fishermen.

Manifestly, there, the servants, seamen, and fishermen are not going under their own right. They are going under the right of the vessel owner, the liberty of the class to whom the right is given. No rights are given to the servants, seamen, and fishermen, and when they are permitted to engage, as they are permitted by this statute, in the fishery business, they are not exercising any right of theirs; they are acting as the hand of the British subject who has the right to carry on the fishing industry. It is quite independent of any right of their own. They would need no right of their own. It is his right that qualifies them to be there.

A similar result follows from the statute of 1775 relating to a different kind of fishing or quasi fishing industry. That is at p. 543 of the British Appendix. If the Tribunal will turn to Articles 10 and 11, on p. 545, the following will be observed:

> And it is hereby further enacted by the Authority aforesaid, That from and after the first Day of September, one thousand seven hundred and seventy-five, it shall and may be lawful for any Person or Persons to import into this Kingdom any raw and undressed Seal Skins taken and caught by the Crews of Vessels belonging to and fitted out either from Great Britain, Ireland, or the Islands of Guernsey, Jersey, or Man respectively, and whereof the Captain or Master and Three-fourths at the least of the Mariners are his Majesty's Subjects, or by Persons employed by the Masters or Owners of such Vessels, without paying any Custom, Subsidy, or other Duty, for the same, any Law or Usage to the contrary notwithstanding.

The Tribunal will see that contemplates the employment of persons who, themselves, have no right granted to them. Then, Article 11 reads:

> Provided always, That nothing in this Act shall extend, or be construed to extend, to give Liberty of importing any such Seal Skins Duty-free, unless the Captain or Person having the Charge or Command of such Ship or Vessel importing the same shall make Oath before the Collector or other Principal Officer of the Customs at the Port of Importation (who is hereby authorized and required to administer such Oath), that all the Skins imported in such Ship or Vessel were really and *bona fide* the Skins of Seals taken and caught by the Crews thereof, or by Persons employed by the Master or Owner of such Ship or Vessel, or of some other Ship or Vessel qualified as aforesaid.

It is the qualification of the vessel, and the privilege is given quite irrespective of the nationality of the persons employed, except that it is required that three-fourths of the crew, three-fourths of the mariners, shall be English. One-fourth may be aliens to England. And the qualified vessels, qualified by having three-fourths of their mariners English, and by belonging to or being fitted out in Great Britain, carry along with them the right of having the benefits of the act, though the taking is done by a crew one-fourth of which may be aliens, or done by anybody who comes in the class of persons employed by the master or owner of such ship or vessel. And this is a great fishing statute, this Act of 1775. This is the same statute the seventh article of which relieves all vessels fitted and cleared out as fishing ships to be employed in the Newfoundland fishery from any restraint or regulation with respect to days or hours of working.

Now, to the same effect were these cases which were cited, the Duchess of Norfolk case, and Wickham *vs.* Hawker, in 7 Meason and Welsby Reports.

There the question was regarding a right granted to Lord Seymour in one case and to one of the parties in Wickham *vs.* Hawker in the other, a right granted for hunting for profit — whether persons who had not the right could come in and take part as servants of those who had the right; that is, persons not sailing under their own flag, sailing under the flag of the grantee of the right, but who were not qualified themselves personally. The decisions settled the law of England that they could.

My friends on the other side, in their argument, quite covered up the real point of these decisions, and the real point to which those statutes are cited, which is, that while the right is granted to one class of persons it may be exercised for them by employees who themselves have no right whatever, but who are coming in and acting under the right of their employer.

The president called attention to a similar characteristic in a Delaware statute or a Maryland statute which was referred to some time ago. There was a prohibition against fishing, except by citizens of the state. When somebody came with a vessel to fish, the requirement was that the master should make an affidavit, and what he had to swear to was that the vessel was fishing in the interests of the citizens of the state. He did not have to swear that the men who were doing the fishing were citizens of the state, but that the vessel was fishing in the interest of the citizens of the state. It carries that same idea, you see.

My learned friend, the Attorney-General, has exhibited great disquietude lest we should flood the coasts of Newfoundland with Orientals. He apprehends that the United States fishing vessels will stop in the various Oriental countries that intervene between Passamaquoddy Bay and Newfoundland and will collect great hordes of Mongols and, to use his own words, will inundate the waters of Newfoundland with them. He fears that we will make of the treaty waters " multitudinous seas incarnadine " with Chinamen. Perhaps his view is that these fishing ships, these little bits of fifty or sixty, or one-hundred-ton boats may sail away ten thousand miles to the other side of the globe and collect Asiatics to come and fish on the coast of Newfoundland.

I cannot really think he was serious about it, but sometimes, particularly when treating of Far-Eastern matters, we are apt to fail to appreciate the true effect of what may be said. Yet I prefer to believe that my learned friend, who has a very pretty wit, was really playing with us a little about the danger of inundation by Orientals, particularly in view of the fact that he contended that it was all right for the Newfoundlanders to employ them themselves — no objection to that seems to exist. They may be allowed to come ashore and enter into the life of the country and mingle with the people of the country, but, when there is a possibility of our bringing some unfortunate Chinese laundryman there on a fishing vessel, we are to be regarded as making a sort of gurry ground of the coastal waters for the disposal of Mongols.

There is only one further subject regarding Question 2 that I care to speak of:

Something was said about the presentation of a certificate by anybody coming there to exercise this right, saying he is an inhabitant of the United States. That occurred during the course of the discussion by Mr. Elder upon the kind of papers which a vessel should produce.

I merely wish to guard against its being taken to apply to individuals, as distinct from people coming upon vessels, and exhibiting the documents of the vessels.

Of course when any right, any general right is granted to a country to have its subjects or citizens or inhabitants have rights or privileges in another country, the presumption always is that any of the class specified as the class for the benefit of which the right is granted are entitled to exercise it. If there is to be a prohibition or limitation, why that must be stated, and in the absence of any express prohibition or limitation upon the part of the country to which the class belongs, the intent of the grantee of the right must be presumed to be that all of the class shall exercise it.

I will pass to Question 3.

> Can the exercise by the inhabitants of the United States of the liberties referred to in the said article be subjected, without the consent of the United States, to the requirements of entry or report at custom-houses, or the payment of light, or harbor, or other dues, or to any other similar requirement, or condition, or exaction ?

First, as to the requirement of entry or report at custom-house. Those are two very different things. The Attorney-General was not inaccurate in stating that the paper to be signed would not differ very much in one case from the paper which might well be signed in the other case, but " entry " and " report " are two quite distinct things.

I think it is quite appropriate that a vessel going upon the treaty coast, and intending to claim the treaty right, should declare herself; that if the place where she purposes to exercise the right is a place where there is a custom-house, or any officer qualified to receive a report, she should make it; or if, without interfering with the exercise of the right, passing a custom-house or a place where there is an official, she can make the report, that she should make it. That is quite reasonable. I should take very kindly to a class of regulations such as we have illustrated under the British treaty with France of 1839. If I remember correctly, there were a series of regulations prepared a few years after that treaty. Under the North Sea Convention of 1882, and many other conventions, vessels are obliged to carry numbers plainly displayed. You can see the numbers up here in the fishing port of Scheveningen. I believe they have a sort of special flag or vane that they carry, something to identify them. I quite agree that it is a reasonable, sensible thing that vessels going to the coast of another country to exercise a right under a treaty should identify themselves in some appropriate way, and indicate in an appropriate way to the authorities of the country who they are, and what they are, and what they are there for, and what the rights are that they propose to exercise. We will not quarrel about that. I do not think there is really much difference between the counsel on the two sides in this respect.

But I want to emphasize the distinction between " report " and " entry ", because a failure to observe that might lead to unintended results.

The entry of a vessel is the transaction, the process by which a vessel carries itself and its merchandise across the line of exclusion of a country; quite a different thing from a report. It is the process by which it acquires a right to have the merchandise, the goods that it brings, enter into the general stock of merchandise of the country, upon payment of whatever dues and exactions the laws may impose.

The laws relating to entry in Newfoundland, in Canada, all the laws all over the world, relating to the entry of vessels, are designed to regulate that process, and they are not applicable to vessels that do not go through the process. These vessels never really do get into the country at all. These fishing vessels never get into Newfoundland. They never pass that invisible line which makes the distinction between what is in Newfoundland and what is out of Newfoundland, what can be dealt with as being part of the general stock of property of Newfoundland, and what cannot be. And imposing upon our fishing vessels the steps of that process is quite unnecessary, quite inappropriate, and might lead to consequences that nobody has ever contended for at all. It is agreed and expressly conceded that there is no right to impose duty upon articles which may be upon these fishing vessels. Subjecting them to entry would carry an implication that the articles that they had on board, being carried across that line, became subject to duty. I especially ask the attention of the Tribunal to guard against making any award under this question which might possibly give rise to an idea on the part of any one hereafter that the process that has taken place justifies the exaction of duties, and might lead to the exaction of duties upon the material or articles upon these vessels.

Sir Charles Fitzpatrick: A vessel that calls at a port for orders, as I understand it, Mr. Root, merely reports; it makes no entry ?

Senator Root: I understand so.

Sir Charles Fitzpatrick: It simply reports its presence there.

Senator Root: Clearly that is all. We have here an illustration. Under this so-called *modus* with Canada of 1888, the *modus* which has worked so well that we have gone on under it for twenty years without trouble, provides that no entry or clearance shall be required of any fishing vessel which enters Canadian ports for shelter, repairs, wood, or water, if the vessel does not remain more than twenty-four hours, provided they do not communicate with shore. There is a practical illustration of the distinction which is made.

THE PRESIDENT: Do I understand well, Mr. Root, that " report " is something like the delivering of a statement for the identification of the vessel, and its loading, whereas making an entry is applying for admission for intercourse ?

SENATOR ROOT: That I understand to be the distinction.

SIR CHARLES FITZPATRICK: The president said " report the loading."

THE PRESIDENT: What she had on board.

SIR CHARLES FITZPATRICK: Does not " report " mean merely reporting the fact of the presence of the ship in the port, pure and simple ?

SENATOR ROOT: That is the ordinary scope of " report." I should think that the kind of report which ought to be made here would be to report the presence of the ship, and American fishermen on the ship to exercise the treaty right under the treaty, and having on board articles appropriate to the exercise of the right.

JUDGE GRAY: And no other; to identify her as not a trading vessel.

SENATOR ROOT: Precisely. I do not want any inferences to be drawn, however, that will affect Question 7.

THE PRESIDENT: And " entry " has to do with the admission into intercourse on the land ?

SENATOR ROOT: Precisely. You see, if " entry " means anything more than " report " it is quite unnecessary, for " report " does everything that is requisite.

Now the second question under that head: Can an American fishing vessel be subjected, without the consent of the United States, to the payment of light, harbor, or other dues ?

First let me ask your attention to the question of strict right. What is the justification for the exaction of light or harbor or other similar dues from any vessel that comes into the territorial waters of a country? What is the basis of right? There must be some basis of right creating an obligation, of course. Civilized countries do not take property away from aliens who come. If they require aliens to hand over their money when they come into the territory, in these civilized days, they do it upon the theory that there is an obligation on the part of the alien, that he owes the money, always. It must be so, otherwise we go back to the dark ages.

Now, what is the basis of obligation upon which anywhere ever a country requires an alien coming with his ship into the territory of the country to pay money under the name of light dues or harbor dues? Why, it can be only that the requirement is a condition upon the exercise of the privilege.

SIR CHARLES FITZPATRICK: Not exclusively; the result of a creation of a convenience, for instance?

SENATOR ROOT: But that is involved. I mean to include that.

SIR CHARLES FITZPATRICK: Yes.

SENATOR ROOT: That is in the privilege. The obligation arises from the fact that the ship has come there to enjoy the privilege. It arises from the voluntary act of the ship coming to enjoy the privilege. But when a ship comes into the waters of a country other than its own to exercise a liberty that generations ago was granted to its country, and paid for by its country, the other country cannot exact a second time a payment for the enjoyment of the privilege. That ship is not beholden to the country into whose waters it goes for the enjoyment of any of the privileges there. It takes the right to enjoy the privilege there from its own country under the right that its country long before acquired, and paid for, in the consideration of the treaty which granted it. And you cannot predicate any obligation upon that ship under those circumstances.

As Mr. Lansing suggested the other day, when we were speaking of this subject, it is as if one man were to grant to another a right of way over his land, and then were to put up a toll-gate and charge him toll for passing over the way; and do it upon the excuse or for the alleged reason that he had improved the road. It is a privilege of the man who has the right to pass over the way to say whether the way shall be improved at his expense or not, and a new charge for the privilege of using the way already granted cannot be imposed upon him without his consent.

Now, all these statutes cited by Great Britain are merely statutes which fix, determine, what the obligation of vessels coming in to exercise the privilege shall be. They determine the exaction that shall be made. They are merely the merchant fixing the price of the goods on his shelves which shall be charged to the customers that come in. They have no relation at all to determining whether ships that are not subject to any obligation shall be subjected to it. They have no bearing at all upon the question whether a vessel coming in for the exercise of a right already granted to its country shall be required to pay again for the exercise of the right. They tell what the vessel shall pay if it is bound to pay. They regulate the exactions, but that is all that there is to them. Of course they are couched in general terms because the legislatures of these states and colonies in passing their laws and fixing their light dues, and so on, are not studying the treaty of 1818.

I have been considering this as if there were no question of discrimination. I do not think there is any strict right — any lawful right to exact against our will these dues from us, whether there be discrimination or not; but, I have one observation to make upon the position taken by my learned friends on the other side, as to discrimination.

Their view is that although the statutes of Newfoundland do not impose these light dues upon their own fishing vessels, nevertheless that is not a discrimination, because they say all citizens of Newfoundland have paid taxes. Newfoundland is supported, they say, by a system of indirect taxation, and every citizen of Newfoundland pays his share.

Now, what does happen when light dues are imposed by legislation? Why, either the legislature making the law fixes a scale of dues sufficient to pay the whole expense, or it apportions the expense in a way which it deems to be equitable and reasonable between the country at large and the owners of the ships, so that that part of the burden shall be borne by the country which is proportionate to the benefit the country gets to its commerce, its prosperity, and wealth, and that part of the burden shall be borne by the ship-owners which is appropriate to the special benefit the ship-owners get, and the two are quite distinct things.

Many countries take the entire burden. Canada, for example, takes the entire burden. She charges no light dues. She goes so far as this: that among the lighthouses along this rocky coast about the Straits of Belle Isle, Canada, on Newfoundland's territory, maintains, I think it is seven, of the lighthouses at her own expense for the benefit of her transatlantic steamship service. There the benefit to the country is deemed so great that she maintains her own lighthouses without charging the vessels anything, and even maintains lighthouses on the shores of the other colony.

Now, when there is an apportionment of the burden, the citizen of Newfoundland who pays through this system of indirect taxation by paying a little higher price for the things that he uses, who pays his share of the burden that is covered by general taxation, is not paying any share of the other burden that it casts specially upon the ships. They are two quite different things, and when he is exempted from his share of the burden that ought appropriately to be defrayed by the ships, he is exempted from something that is not made up for by his having to pay his share of the burden commensurate with the benefit which his country gets and which he gets as a citizen of the country. One man lives in Gloucester, Massachusetts, and owns a fishing vessel that comes to the Newfoundland coast; another man lives in St. John's, Newfoundland, and owns a fishing vessel that comes to the same coast; if one of them is exempted and the other is charged, there is a discrimination that is not made up by the fact that the Newfoundland man has paid his share of the benefit that his country gets. The Gloucester man has not got any part of the benefit, and therefore he has paid no part of it; but the Gloucester man and the St. John's man both get a special benefit for their vessels, and if the St. John's man is exempted from it there is a discrimination in his favor and against the Gloucester man.

Now, that leads me naturally to the further question, not of strict right, but whether it is quite reasonable for us to insist on our right not to pay for these privileges. Upon that the fact that the fishing vessels of Newfoundland are exempted and that under this old British statute fishing vessels were exempted is very cogent. The fact is that these little fishing vessels ought not to have to pay for the burden created for the benefit of commerce. They feel along the coasts, they know the ground, they have but little use for lighthouses, they have no use for port privileges, and this provision of the statute of Newfoundland which exempts her fishing vessels and coasting vessels is an expression of the real common sense of things, and our position, quite apart from the strict, technical, legal right, is that common sense ought to be exercised for our benefit, as well as for the benefit of her own vessels.

Passing to Question 4, it is as follows:

> Under the provision of the said Article that the American fishermen shall be admitted to enter certain bays or harbors for shelter, repairs, wood, or water, and for no other purpose whatever, but that they shall be under such restrictions as may be necessary to prevent their taking, drying, or curing fish therein or in any other manner whatever abusing the privileges thereby reserved to them, is it permissible to impose restrictions making the exercise of such privileges conditional upon the payment of light or harbor, or other dues, or entering or reporting at custom-houses or any similar conditions ?

You will perceive that that is a much narrower question. It relates solely to the right, under the treaty, to impose such restrictions as may be necessary to prevent the taking, drying, or curing of fish, or in any other manner whatever abusing the privileges reserved. It does not trench upon this ground that I have been discussing under Question 3. It does not involve, or relate, in any manner whatever, to any general rights to impose light or harbor dues. It relates solely to the exercise of the power to impose restrictions necessary to prevent the taking, drying, or curing of fish, or other abuse of the privilege of entry.

What I have said about the reasonableness of a vessel declaring itself, reporting where there is somebody to report to, and about such regulations as those regarding a special flag, or bearing a number, things designed to prevent concealment or evasion, applies here to restrictions necessary to prevent drying, taking, and curing fish, and to prevent abuse. What I have said about entry applies also.

SIR CHARLES FITZPATRICK: Do you think so ?

SENATOR ROOT: I should think so.

SIR CHARLES FITZPATRICK: You are in touch with the land here. You are constantly going to and from your ship to the land.

SENATOR ROOT: I quite agree that special regulations are appropriate to govern that intercourse with the land.

SIR CHARLES FITZPATRICK: Repairs involve a great deal.

SENATOR ROOT: I do not think that the way to deal with it is to apply these statutes that are meant to apply to an entirely different thing. It is like a man trying to lend somebody else his clothes, and they do not fit.

SIR CHARLES FITZPATRICK: A smuggler wears a great many different garments.

SENATOR ROOT: Quite different statutes are intended to deal with smugglers from those intended to deal with vessels that come to the custom-house and make entry. They are statutes relating to a lawful proceeding, while your smuggling statutes are quite different. I quite agree that there are many provisions of smuggling statutes — statutes that are intended to be side-lines, to prevent ships from straying off, from wandering over the pasture, and to make them come into the custom-house if they are going to bring any goods in — that furnish illustrations of regulations which would be quite appropriate, and the provision of the 1888 *modus* in Canada, which I have just referred to, indicates that. That is that they need not enter or clear.

SIR CHARLES FITZPATRICK: That is where they come in for shelter. But my difficulty has reference to their conduct when they come in for repairs. Repairs involve close contact with the land.

SENATOR ROOT: They do not involve taking anything into the country; they involve getting something out.

SIR CHARLES FITZPATRICK: Not always.

SENATOR ROOT: And they call for quite a different set of regulations. At all events, I am not disputing that —

SIR CHARLES FITZPATRICK: There will be some different provision required in this case.

SENATOR ROOT: I quite agree to that. I do not for a moment want to have a conclusion which will enable Americans to go up there and really abuse the privilege, as I have no doubt that sometimes they do.

Sir Charles Fitzpatrick: You see St. Pierre, Miquelon, is so convenient.

Senator Root: Yes, undoubtedly, but I will leave the British Government to deal with its French ally on that subject.

Now, on the subject of light and harbor dues, these are no restrictions at all. It is perfectly plain that they cannot be imposed under this question, because they do not come within the purview of this renunciation clause. There is nothing in requiring a man to pay light, or harbor, or any other kind of dues, which tends in any way to restrict the taking, drying, or curing of fish, or to prevent the abuse of privileges; unless it be upon the theory, which sometimes happens in domestic affairs, that by taking a man's money away from him you may keep him from going off and getting into trouble. There is no other conceivable way in which the exaction of this money from the master of an American fishing vessel can be deemed to come within the terms of the treaty which provides for making him subject to "such restrictions as may be necessary to prevent their taking, drying, or curing fish therein, or in any other manner whatever, abusing the privileges thereby reserved to them."

I wish to make one observation about both Questions 3 and 4. Whatever may be required in the way of report, declaration, identification, or, on the non-treaty coast, regulation of intercourse with the shore, should be, of course, of such a character as not to prevent the exercise of the treaty right. We made very serious objection to some provisions of this Act of 1905 of Newfoundland, objections to which the British Government gave their practical assent. The provisions objected to in form were directly solely to the prevention of something which, very likely, they had a right to prevent; that is, certain trade transactions, the purchase of fish, or the purchase of nets and implements of fishing which, I say, very likely, they had a right to prevent. I put in " very likely " because it might depend upon your decision under Question 1, and I do not want to ignore that. But those provisions to which I refer in the Act of 1905, while directed only to the prevention of certain trade, authorized the local officer to go on board of any fishing vessel, take it into port, take it away from the fishing ground, subject the master to examination and the vessel to search for the purpose of ascertaining whether he had on board any fish, or fishing gear, the purchase of which was prohibited, and whether he had purchased any fish or fishing gear, and provided that the presence of any fish or fishing gear on board should be *prima facie* evidence that he had purchased it. Those provisions, though directed to the enforcement of a statute which I am not now contesting the right of Newfoundland to make, were provisions which plainly interfered with and prevented the exercise of the fishing right, because they took the ship away and put it in a position where it might be impossible to prevent it from being condemned, and made the mere presence upon the ship of the very things which the ship was entitled to have on board as a result of its fishing enterprise, the implements which it was entitled to have to carry on its enterprise, a condemnatory fact. Anything of that kind should be avoided in any provision relating to the conduct of these vessels under Question 3 or Question 4.

SIR CHARLES FITZPATRICK: Have you looked at the regulations applicable to the North Sea fisheries ?

SENATOR ROOT: I have run my eye over them.

SIR CHARLES FITZPATRICK: Can you not find something there which would be useful ?

SENATOR ROOT: It is quite probable, and you will remember that there was not any real difficulty in settling upon those regulations with Canada, and unless some disputed question of the basis of right comes in I should think there would be no difficulty.

Sir Charles Fitzpatrick: You see Newfoundland has a pretty extended coast line to look after.

Senator Root: Undoubtedly, and I do not blame them for wanting to be pretty careful.

Sir Charles Fitzpatrick: Do you think there is any very serious objection to applying the same liberal spirit that you have manifested in connection with Questions 3 and 4 to No. 2? Is there anything to be gained by leaving this question of the employment of Newfoundland fishermen to uncertainty?

Senator Root: Sir Charles, my difficulty about that is that when you come to pass on the question of the effect of these statutes, you have to consider them in reference not to the question in No. 2, that may be a necessary preliminary to the consideration of them; but you have to consider them specifically in reference to the question in No. 1.

Sir Charles Fitzpatrick: I am presupposing that is out of the way.

Senator Root: We have not presented that aspect of these statutes. We have not presented these statutes at all. We have not presented the relation between these statutes and the principles that will be involved in your award undoubtedly under Question No. 1. We have not argued them, or put them in our case, or our counter-case, or our written argument.

Sir Charles Fitzpatrick: It is exactly my embarrassment that you have submitted all the statutes except the statute of 1906, so that that question might arise hereafter. That is where the difficulty is.

Senator Root: That was omitted from the enumeration of the statutes because its effect has been suspended.

Sir Charles Fitzpatrick: When it comes into force the question arises: What advantage is there to be derived from keeping open that difficulty when we want to settle all the difficulties ?

Senator Root: I know. It is merely that we did not intend to submit any question arising from the effect of these Newfoundland statutes on the persons at whom they were directed, and we did not present the material for it in the case, in the counter-case, or in the printed argument. We have not argued it here, and the questions that will arise when we have disposed of this question of inhabitancy may be very serious questions, dependent upon what your award is under No. 1; and they ought to be studied, the material relevant to them ought to be presented if they are to be decided, and they ought to be argued if they are to be decided. Counsel occupy a little different position from the head of a Foreign Office dealing with this subject. Our warrant here is only to present these questions. We are here not to present new questions, but we are here with authority only to make oral argument before this Tribunal within the limits of the questions that were stated. I think that perhaps if we were now to go back again to the making of the special agreement, we might possibly make some sort of an agreement classifying these statutes, and submitting an eighth, or another, question in relation to the effect of local statutes upon the citizens of the British Empire, or of the locality, and present it, with the material relating to it, and argue it. But, as it is, our warrant is to argue these questions, and of course, the jurisdiction of the Tribunal is to decide these questions, and I do not think we can go beyond it.

Sir Charles Fitzpatrick: When will the statute that has been suspended because of this reference go into effect ?

Senator Root: That is a question that I cannot answer.

SIR CHARLES FITZPATRICK: You understand the spirit in which I put these questions to you?

SENATOR ROOT: Certainly I do, and that is why I said that perhaps if we were meeting together now and making a new agreement we might devise some form classifying the various questions liable to arise on the other side of the shield relating to the effect upon citizens of other countries of the statutes of their own countries. If we had done so we would have presented a question relating to it, would have presented the material bearing upon it, and would have argued it; but we did not.

THE PRESIDENT: Is not Question 2 framed in quite a general way, so that we are asked whether the inhabitants of the United States have a right to employ as members of the fishing crews of their vessels every kind of persons not inhabitants of the United States?

SENATOR ROOT: I think not. I think it is the right to employ any persons.

THE PRESIDENT: It is persons not inhabitants of the United States. Is not that to be understood as every kind of persons? There is no distinction between the different categories of non-inhabitants.

SENATOR ROOT: I think the limitation comes from two things: the fact that the question relates to the competency of the employer solely, and to the existence or non-existence of the status of inhabitancy. That is all the question relates to and it excludes other causes which might prevent the contemplated employee from accepting employment and prevent the making of a contract.

SIR CHARLES FITZPATRICK: It would not, I suppose, be assumed that if a foreigner — without mentioning any particular nationality — were prohibited from entering the country, such foreigner could be employed by an inhabitant of the United States in connection with this industry?

SENATOR ROOT: Well, there is another question which is not here.

SIR CHARLES FITZPATRICK: Is it not impliedly here? He would not be an inhabitant of the United States?

SENATOR ROOT: No; but it would not be his non-inhabitancy of the United States, which is all that this question involves, that would prevent his being taken in. It would be the existence of a law that excluded that particular class of aliens.

SIR CHARLES FITZPATRICK: It would be by reason of some personal disqualification?

SENATOR ROOT: Yes, of a law prohibiting criminals to be brought in. I should not say that you are called upon, in passing upon this question, which specifies the right of the employer and the criterion of inhabitancy, to pass upon the question whether they would be entitled to take habitual criminals in, or people who are of immoral character, or people who are diseased, or people specially excluded for any particular cause. The range of the questions is too vast to regard them as being included within this question, which simply points to inhabitancy as affecting the right of the employer.

THE PRESIDENT: You consider the question as if it were put in these terms: Is non-inhabitancy a reason for preventing the United States from employing certain persons in their crews on fishing vessels?

SENATOR ROOT: Yes, from employing such persons.

THE PRESIDENT: Is non-inhabitancy a reason for preventing them?

SENATOR ROOT: Yes.

THE PRESIDENT: But the question is not framed in that way. It is framed in a more objective way:

> Have the inhabitants of the United States, . . . a right to employ as members of the fishing crews of their vessels persons not inhabitants?

We are asked whether the United States are entitled to employ these persons, and we are not asked whether the United States are prevented, by reason of non-inhabitancy, from employing certain categories of persons. It may be that the question has this meaning, but it seems not to be clearly expressed.

SENATOR ROOT: That may be. Perhaps after ascertaining what doubts arise upon the form of the question in any case, a question might be usefully reframed for the purpose of meeting the doubts. But I do not see how it is possible for you to decide upon anything but the effect of the habitancy or non-inhabitancy upon the right of the employer, for that is all there is in the question, and, as to the incidental effect of the legislation, I do not see how it is possible for you to limit that by going on and deciding a lot of other possible questions, rather than by a safeguarding phrase in your award showing that you do not decide them.

SIR CHARLES FITZPATRICK: But this question calls for "yes" or "no" for an answer. If we say "yes", what is the result?

SENATOR ROOT: Of course, it will be competent for you to say that you do not pass upon any question relating to the right of any non-inhabitant to accept employment.

SIR CHARLES FITZPATRICK: That means that our answer "yes" is not sufficient, but that it must be qualified.

JUDGE GRAY: It must be qualified in view of the fact that counsel for Great Britain in this case distinctly raised that question, and we cannot avoid qualifying it in order to make it effective if the answer should be one way.

SENATOR ROOT: If the answer should be "no" then, of course, that excludes the United States from the employment of non-inhabitants, and these statutes are of no consequence at all.

The President: But the difficulty arises if the answer should be "yes."

Dr. Drago: I understood Senator Turner to say that in such a case we would make the reservation that nothing had been decided about this.

The President: Mr. Root says the same thing now.

Senator Root: Yes, my intention was to repeat the suggestion of Senator Turner.

Sir Charles Fitzpatrick: Yes, but that would not meet the difficulty. If it is necessary to make a reservation, is it not because there is something more involved in the question than appears on the surface of it?

Senator Root: I should not say so, your honor. I should say that it is necessary because counsel for Great Britain have insisted that there is something more in it, and it is reasonable to guard against people making your award the basis of dispute and controversy by inferring that you meant to do something more, and did it.

The President: Perhaps it is convenient to adjourn now and continue at two o'clock. The court adjourns until two o'clock.[1]

The President: Will you kindly continue, Mr. Senator Root?[2]

Senator Root: As to Question 6:

> Have the inhabitants of the United States the liberty under the said Article or otherwise to take fish in the bays, harbors, and creeks on that part of the southern coast of Newfoundland which extends from Cape Ray to Rameau Islands, or on the western and northern coasts of Newfoundland from Cape Ray to Quirpon Islands, or on the Magdalen Islands?

I wish merely to point out the historical origin of the use of the word "coasts" in the treaty of 1783 to describe

[1] Thereupon, at 12 o'clock, the Tribunal took a recess until 2 o'clock P.M.

[2] Friday, August 12, 1910, 2 P.M.

the fishing right granted by that treaty to inhabitants of the United States.

As I have suggested in the argument upon another question, the preliminary articles of peace agreed upon by the British and American negotiators in 1782 were made subject to and not to take effect until the conclusion of the treaty of peace between Great Britain and France, the ally of the United States in the then existing war; the definitive treaties of peace between Great Britain and the United States and between Great Britain and France were parts in effect of the same transaction, the treaty between Great Britain and the United States being limited according to the recital of its preamble to the conclusion of the French treaty.

I have already pointed out that both the treaty of the 3d September, 1783, with the United States, and the treaty of the same day and forming part of the same general settlement between Great Britain and France, treated of the fishery rights upon this same coast; and the treaty dealing with those rights granted to Americans naturally employed the same words, the same forms of expression, which were found in the preëxisting treaty between Great Britain and France granting the same rights upon the same coast, and said the inhabitants of the United States should have liberty to take fish on the coast of Newfoundland, as that preexisting treaty said the subjects of the French king should have the liberty to take fish on the coast of Newfoundland, and the words, the form of expression, must be deemed to have the same meaning in the grant of that right on that coast to the two different Powers who were concerned in that transaction.

While Mr. Turner was making his argument, the court called for or expressed a wish to have the proceedings of the Halifax Commission, and Mr. Turner said that he would procure them for the court, and I now have the honor to hand them up. Both sides, of course, are in possession of them. In doing so I beg to call the attention of the Tribunal to the second map which is enclosed in this volume of proceedings. That is the same map which is referred to in the copy of the proceedings of the Halifax Commission, or that part of the copy of the proceedings of the Halifax Commission printed in the American Counter-Case Appendix, at p. 547. In the next to the last paragraph on that page occurs this statement:

> A reference to the accompanying map will show that the coast, the entire freedom for which for fishing purposes has thus been acquired, etc.

The map which is now before the president, in that volume which I have handed up, is a copy of the map here referred to. I ask the Tribunal to observe that in that map, which is the British map used in the Halifax proceeding, there is a legend which states that part of the coast colored red is the part not within the limits of the grant of 1818, but carried by the new grant of 1871, while the part colored blue is the part within the limits of the treaty of 1818, and to observe that the blue line which marks the limits of 1818 takes in all the bays and harbors, showing that at that time Great Britain quite well understood that all the bays and harbors that were included within that blue line were within the grant of 1818.

We have a provision in the New York code of procedure, a code prepared by Mr. David Dudley Field, the same gentleman whose international code the Tribunal is familiar with, to the effect that —

THE PRESIDENT: May I interrupt you a moment, Mr. Senator Root? Of course this map, as being in the British Blue Book, is familiar to the British counsel?

THE ATTORNEY-GENERAL: I cannot say that we are familiar with the whole of the proceedings in the Halifax Commission. I was just consulting my friend Sir Robert Finlay about it. It comes upon us as somewhat of a surprise, but I do not want to interrupt my learned friend, Senator Root. We will look at this map, and we will see whether we have any observations to make upon it. I am sure each side only desires to act fairly by the other, and if any observations occur to us, I am sure Senator Root would not mind our sending a memorandum —

SENATOR ROOT: I certainly should.

THE ATTORNEY-GENERAL: You say you would mind ?

SENATOR ROOT: Yes; certainly. I think any observations to be made must be made now.

THE ATTORNEY-GENERAL: Then I am sure I must object to the evidence. How can I make observations now, in the middle of a speech ?

SENATOR ROOT: I do not think my learned friend will insist upon his objection in view of the fact that this is the very volume from which Mr. Ewart read.

THE ATTORNEY-GENERAL: Certainly I have no objection whatever to the admission of any evidence which has been already put before the Tribunal, and which both sides have had an opportunity of considering. Of course, my friend Mr. Root is putting in various documents which we have not had an opportunity of considering. Some of these documents I can deal with in a few minutes at the end of his speech, in accordance with the understanding that when any new points are raised in the last speech there shall be permission to the other party to deal with them. But a matter of this kind, which involves the examination of the maps and of a very lengthy record, is not a matter with which I can deal immediately upon the termination of Mr. Root's speech. We have not seen it, and I do not even know to what he is referring.

Of course, the final speech is intended to be a speech dealing finally with the evidence before the Tribunal, and is not intended to be a speech in which new evidence may be put in. There are many passages of different documents of a bulky character which have been put in evidence. That does not mean that the whole document is treated as being part of the evidence. I have no objection to anything being done which may facilitate the case for the United States on the point, but one must have the means of dealing with them one's self in some fair and rational way.

Senator Root: Of course, there is not the slightest objection to the Attorney-General calling attention to any matter which he thinks worthy of attention in regard to this book which I have handed to the Tribunal. I am merely calling attention to the very book, portions of which were printed in the American Counter-Case, and from which the British counsel have read. Surely I am entitled when this book has been produced here, and the attention of the Tribunal called to certain features of the proceedings, to call the attention of the Tribunal to other features of the same proceedings in the same book.

The Attorney-General: By all means, provided of course that the passages to which my learned friend refers are passages which he proposes to put in as evidence, and which, therefore, are material; but I must have the opportunity of considering them.

Senator Root: I am not putting in any new evidence whatever. The map was distinctly referred to in the Counter-Case Appendix of the United States, and this map was referred to in the Counter-Case of the United States at p. 101:

> A reference to the accompanying map will show that the coast, the entire freedom of which for fishing purposes has thus been acquired by the United States, etc.

The Attorney-General: That does not put in the map. It refers to the map, but the map has not been one of the documents put in.

It is unnecessary to trouble over a matter which may turn out to be quite unimportant. I have not seen the map, and it may be that there is nothing at all to which I object in it. I do not anticipate that there will be. I am only suggesting that if it should turn out, upon a careful examination, that there is any observation which might properly be made about this map, I should be at liberty to make it, to send it afterwards to Mr. Root and let him see what is said about it, and then forward it with his own observations to the Tribunal. I thought that was a simple way of dealing with it. I dare say there will be no observations to make at all.

Senator Root: It is too simple. There must be an end some time to argument. Any observation that the learned counsel sees fit to make regarding this map, which has been the subject of repeated reference, which was referred to in our Counter-Case and referred to in our Counter-Case Appendix, and which is in a volume from which both parties have printed, and which was in the volume that British counsel a month ago used in his argument to the Tribunal — any observation the learned counsel chooses to make regarding that, before the conclusion of this oral argument, of course is entirely beyond objection. But there must be an end some time to the argument of this case. Personally I am about to leave the city, when the argument of the case is completed, and the other American counsel are in the same situation. We cannot remain here for the purpose of receiving and examining, and perhaps answering briefs or further printed arguments put in after the conclusion of the oral argument. I think in that respect we must stand upon the treaty, which is that cases shall be exchanged within a fixed time, and that counter-cases shall be exchanged within a fixed time, that printed arguments shall be exchanged within a fixed time, and shall be delivered to the Tribunal within a fixed time, and that then there shall be oral argument, the oral argument to end the proceedings so far as the presentation of the case is concerned.

I have made no objection, and shall make no objection, in view of the fact that my argument is the concluding one, to any observation or correction on the part of the Attorney-General of my manifold shortcomings and inaccuracies. But I think that the proceedings should close with the oral argument today, and that we should not be subject to remain here for a further course of proceeding after the conclusion of it.

The Attorney-General: I can assure my learned friend that I am not suggesting that we should remain here. That is the very last alternative that I desire to submit to the Tribunal. I understood my friend was putting in all the proceedings. If he is simply putting in this map I dare say we may look at the map and find there is nothing objectionable in it; but if he is putting in the whole volume of proceedings it is rather a different matter.

Senator Root: I am putting in nothing. I am responding to a promise made by Mr. Turner in response to a question and the expression of a wish by the Tribunal to have the proceedings of the Halifax Commission, which had been the subject of repeated reference and the basis of extensive argument. The court asked if they could have access to that proceeding, and Mr. Turner said he would get it for the court, and I am handing it to them.

The Attorney-General: If it is the desire of the court, of course, that it should see the volume, then I make no objection. But my learned friend has put in several pieces of fresh evidence, and, really, that is a procedure which is covered by the statement he has just made. He says the treaty stipulates that the evidence should be delivered within a certain time, and then it shall be met by a counter-case and by other evidence, and that the parties are concluded when that is done, and that they are not able to put in further evidence. I was only objecting to having a great mass of evidence put before the Tribunal at the very last moment, when it is impossible for any one to deal with it effectively; but as far as the map itself is concerned, if I may see a copy of it, then those who instruct me and advise me will be able to judge whether there is any objection to it, or any observation to make upon it, and I may deal with it at once. At present I have not even seen a copy. I do not know what is being referred to.

THE PRESIDENT: The court will consider the point. Perhaps Mr. Root will continue his speech, and we will consider this point at the end of it.

THE ATTORNEY-GENERAL: In the meantime we might see the map.

SENATOR ROOT: There have been a number of papers produced in response to expressions from the Tribunal, and there have been some expressions regarding papers which have not been produced. I have understood that that was all in accordance with Article 68 of the General Hague Convention:

> The Tribunal is free to take into consideration new papers or documents to which its attention may be drawn by the agents or counsel of the parties.
>
> In this case, the Tribunal has the right to require the production of these papers or documents, but is obliged to make them known to the opposite party.

I was about to say that we have, in Mr. Field's code of procedure, in the state of New York, a provision that a plaintiff or complainant who conceives that the answer of the defendant is frivolous may move to strike out the answer; and if it is stricken out, the result is that he is entitled to take his judgment *pro confesso*. I remember many years ago a motion being made of that character before a very experienced judge, and counsel making the motion began to argue upon the frivolousness of the answer. The judge stopped him and said: " If this requires argument, the answer is not frivolous, and your motion is denied." With that view I shall say nothing more whatever about Question 6.

As to Question 7:

> Are the inhabitants of the United States whose vessels resort to the treaty coasts for the purpose of exercising the liberties referred to in Article I of the treaty of 1818 entitled to have for those vessels, when duly authorized by the United States in that behalf, the commercial privileges on the treaty coasts accorded by agreement or otherwise to United States trading vessels generally ?

I quite agree with an observation made the other day from the bench that these questions are all questions of both parties. Both parties have united in framing them, and presenting them to the court, and both parties are responsible for them. Nevertheless, when a difference arises as to the construction in two ways of a question, it may be of some advantage to the Tribunal, in endeavoring to put itself in the attitude of the parties who framed the question, at the time when they framed it, to know what the origin of the question was, from what element of controversy the question came. For that purpose, as an aid to the construction of the question by the Tribunal, I advert to the fact that this question, like Question 6, had its origin in Newfoundland. It was a Newfoundland question, not a United States question or a British question. The United States was not particularly concerned about it. We find on p. 1014 of the United States Appendix a letter from Governor MacGregor to Lord Elgin of the 14th September, 1907, and the paragraph of that letter numbered 2 touches this subject. Said Governor MacGregor:

> It may be presumed that neither His Majesty's Government nor that of the United States would desire to withhold any part of the case from consideration, a complete and full representation of which is clearly necessary and desirable in order to arrive at finality, and to save future mis-

understanding. Your Lordship is, for example, aware that my Prime Minister has consistently disputed the right of American fishermen to fish or trade in the bays, harbors, and creeks of the West Coast, a point of great importance on which special stress is laid in the letter, copy of which is enclosed.

On the preceding page, p. 1013 of the same Appendix, is a telegram from Governor MacGregor to Lord Elgin, in the third paragraph of which he said:

> My Ministers, however, still desire to aid His Majesty's Government as far as possible consistently with their duty to this Colony, and the preservation of its rights; they will therefore grant permission to the fishermen of the Treaty Coast to sell to Americans during the coming season on the receipt of an assurance from His Majesty's Government that the terms of reference to the Hague Tribunal shall include the question of the right of American vessels to fish or trade in any of the bays, harbors, or creeks of that portion of Newfoundland Coast between Cape Ray and Quirpon Islands, together with all other questions that may be raised under the Treaty.

And on p. 1014 again, we find the telegram from Lord Elgin to Governor MacGregor, dated the 2d September, 1907, saying:

> Your telegram, 1st September. It will be necessary to refer to United States Government the question of the terms of arbitration; but provided that your Government now accept proposed *modus vivendi*, His Majesty's Government would favorably consider the reference to arbitration of question of bays.

And from that grew these two questions, Question 6 and Question 7: the question of the right to fish and the question of the right to trade. Of course, the question being framed, it becomes our question and Great Britain's question. It was rather a surprise to us, because the diplomatic correspondence between the two countries, the United States and Great Britain, indicated an entire agreement upon this trading matter.

The American secretary of state, in his letter to the British minister at Washington, on the 19th October, 1905, which appears in the American Appendix at p. 966, had referred to certain dispatches which had been received from masters of American vessels in Newfoundland waters, in these words:

> These dispatches agree in the statement that vessels of American registry are forbidden to fish on the Treaty Coast. One captain says that he was informed that he could not fish by the Inspector of the Revenue Protection Service of Newfoundland, and several of them that they had been ordered not to take herring by the Collector of Customs at Bonne Bay, Newfoundland.
>
> It would seem that the Newfoundland officials are making a distinction between two classes of American vessels. We have vessels which are registered, and vessels which are licensed to fish and not registered. The license carries a narrow and restricted authority; the registry carries the broadest and most unrestricted authority. The vessel with a license can fish, but cannot trade; the registered vessels can lawfully both fish and trade. The distinction between the two classes in the action of the Newfoundland authorities would seem to have been implied in the dispatch from Senator Lodge which I quoted in my letter of the 12th, and the imputation of the prohibition of the Minister of Marine and Fisheries may perhaps have come from the port officers, in conversation with the masters of American vessels, giving him as their authority for their prohibitions.

And the same letter further said:

> far the greater part of the fleet now in northern waters consists of registered vessels. The prohibition against fishing under an American register substantially bars the fleet from fishing.

To those representations the reply was received from the British ambassador, which appears in the American Counter-Case Appendix, at p. 633, saying:

> His Excellency —

the governor of Newfoundland —

> telegraphs that no Newfoundland officer is preventing American vessels from fishing on the treaty coast, and that no distinction is being drawn between registered vessels and licensed vessels.

And Sir Edward Grey, treating of the same subject, said in a memorandum, a rather formal and maturely prepared memorandum transmitted by him on the 2d February,

1906, to the American ambassador at London, some things about this treatment of American registered vessels, that is, American vessels which are authorized by their own Government both to trade and fish. The letter of Sir Edward Grey enclosing the memorandum is at p. 971 of the American Appendix. The memorandum is found beginning on p. 972, and on p. 974 of the memorandum occurs this statement, in the last paragraph on that page:

> It is admitted that the majority of the American vessels lately engaged in the fishery on the western coast of the colony were registered vessels, as opposed to licensed fishing vessels, and as such were at liberty both to trade and to fish.

And at p. 976, the same memorandum says, in the next to the last paragraph on that page:

> The distinction between United States registration and the possession of a United States fishing license is, however, of some importance, inasmuch as a vessel which, so far as the United States Government are concerned, is at liberty both to trade and to fish naturally calls for a greater measure of supervision by the Colonial Government than a vessel fitted out only for fishing and debarred by the United States Government from trading; and information has been furnished to His Majesty's Government by the Colonial Government which shows that the proceedings of American fishing vessels in Newfoundland waters have in the past been of such a character as to make it impossible from the point of view of the protection of the Colonial revenue, to exempt such vessels from the supervision authorized by the Colonial Customs Law.

That was the occasion of no controversy whatever between the Government of the United States and that of Great Britain. The question of supervision is certainly one about which there could be no controversy. If an American vessel seeks to trade with Newfoundland, whether she is a fishing vessel or not, she must be subjected to the kind of supervision which is appropriate to a trading vessel. What my learned friend said about hovering is covered by that perfectly. A vessel going to the coast to trade cannot hover. If she is going to trade, she must clear from her home port for a specified port. Every one of these registered vessels has to do that. She must clear for a specified port, she must not deviate from her voyage, she must go to that port, and go directly to the port. She cannot stop, she cannot hover, she must go to the port and she must make entry, and she must subject herself to those regulations and provisions of law which are appropriate to the supervision of trading vessels. The real question is whether, when the vessel has discharged her function as a trading vessel, and is completely through, she can then abandon her trading function and take a cargo for the return voyage by catching fish.

That is what the practical question comes down to. There is no question about the mingling of the two at the same time. And I repeat that it was a matter of considerable surprise that Great Britain should have wished to include this question in the list that was submitted to the Tribunal. It is explained by these letters and telegrams passing between the Government of Newfoundland and the Government of Great Britain, to which I have now referred, but which, at the time, we did not know of.

JUDGE GRAY: It does not give the trading vessel, does it, Mr. Root, the right to buy bait if there is a statute forbidding the sale of bait to any foreign vessels, registered or fishing?

SENATOR ROOT: Certainly not. No such question is raised here. I wish again to put in a guard against waiving or giving up any possible consequences of your agreeing with the British theory of our rights, as a result of your decision on Question 1. It is possible, if you go with the British view under Question 1 and say that our exercise of the right is a matter so common with the exercise of the right of the Newfoundlanders that we must be subject to the same right of restriction and modification that they are subject to, you must also say that we must have, as we insist, all the privileges and opportunities that are connoted by the obligation.

SIR CHARLES FITZPATRICK: That does not arise here.

SENATOR ROOT: I wish always, in what I say about the effect of this question, to file a caveat against being understood as saying or implying that that may not be a consequence of your award under Question 1. But this question does not in any degree whatever touch the question whether Newfoundland can be compelled to trade with us, or whether Newfoundland is not perfectly at liberty to prohibit the export of any particular article or prohibit the sale of any particular article. It merely goes to the question as to whether a vessel of the United States which is authorized to trade is, by virtue of that fact, excluded from the fishing privileges or whether a vessel which is there to fish is thereby excluded from the trading privileges, whatever they are, that have been accorded to trading vessels generally. What the extent of the trading may be is not involved at all, and it raises no question whatever as to what the provisions against trade, the provisions against the export of anything, or against the dealing in anything, or trading in anything, of the Newfoundland Government may be, or what the effect of them may be. Nor, may I say here, is it really a question of the purchase of bait. The real question of the purchase of bait, the great, the substantial one, arises when American vessels bound for the banks wish to buy bait in Newfoundland for the purpose of taking it down to the banks and using it there. The Tribunal will perceive that those vessels are not exercising the treaty right at all. They do not come under this question. This question is not framed to cover them in any way whatever. Perhaps if the United States had been exercised about this, and had been getting up questions, if the origin had come from us, we would have been concerned about that, which is really a very serious question — that is the question as to whether we can get bait for use on the banks. But this question does not touch it. The question is limited strictly to the vessels that go there for the purpose of exercising the liberty under Article 1 of the treaty:

> Are the inhabitants of the United States whose vessels resort to the treaty coasts for the purpose of exercising the liberties referred to in Article One of the Treaty of 1818 entitled to have for those vessels . . . the commercial privileges, etc.

That does not touch at all that great bait procurement question in which we are so vitally interested.

JUDGE GRAY: The question would have been, of course, easy to answer if it had been:

> Are the inhabitants of the United States resorting to these coasts for the purpose of exercising their treaty rights as fishing vessels disentitled thereby to exercise the privileges generally accorded to trading vessels if they are properly registered ?

But this is put the other way.

SENATOR ROOT: I know; but if you answer that they are not entitled, you say that they are disentitled; you must; that is, that must be the effect of your answer, because the postulate of the question is that commercial privileges are accorded to the United States trading vessels generally. The Tribunal, of course, is not at liberty to say they are not; and the question is entirely irrespective of what they are. The question also assumes that the United States has authorized or may authorize particular vessels to exercise the privileges of trading vessels; that is to say, that the United States makes particular vessels of its own its trading vessels. The question is: is a vessel which, for convenience, we may as well call what it is — a registered vessel — going to the treaty coast purposing to exercise the treaty right, belonging to the general class to which by the postulate of the question trading privileges are accorded, entitled when it gets there to those trading privileges ? If not, it must be because there is something in the treaty which excludes it from those privileges. If not, it must be because there is something in the treaty which authorized the Government of Newfoundland to discriminate against that vessel. If there is anything in the treaty which justifies the discrimination against that vessel, which justifies taking it out of its class and excluding it from the privileges of its class, why, then, the Tribunal will have to say that such a vessel is not entitled. If there is nothing in the treaty which justifies making a discrimination against that vessel, making it an exception to the class to which it belongs, to which has been accorded or may hereafter be accorded trading privileges, the Tribunal will, I submit, have to say that the vessel is entitled. The true answer, I submit, is that the treaty neither entitles nor disentitles any American trading vessel to use the privileges accorded to its class. The treaty does not affect the subject at all. My learned friends say these privileges may be withdrawn. Of course they may be withdrawn; but the postulate of the question is their existence, and their existence is protected by far wider interests than the particular question Sir Robert Bond was so much interested in: the trade between two great nations, affecting many, many millions of people, the relations of kindly feeling, the enormous benefits received by both nations from their intercourse in commerce — those are the considerations which preserve the trading privileges accorded by each nation to the vessels of the other, and we are not concerned about there being a cessation of commercial intercourse between the United States and Great Britain. The only thing we are concerned with here is whether there is anything in this treaty which entitles the Government of Newfoundland to say: "These particular vessels, belonging to the class to which has been accorded trading privileges, certified by their government as belonging to that class, are to be discriminated against and excepted from the class."

THE PRESIDENT: What is the basis, Mr. Senator Root, on which we have to decide this Question 7 ? Where have we to take our answer to Question 7 ?

SENATOR ROOT: I think the basis is the consideration of the terms of the treaty.

THE PRESIDENT: The consideration of the terms of the treaty ?

SENATOR ROOT: As to whether there is anything in the terms of the treaty which affects or changes any commercial privileges accorded to the class of trading vessels.

DR. DRAGO: The commercial privileges are not given in virtue of the treaty ?

SENATOR ROOT: Not at all. They are entirely outside of the treaty. The question is whether there is anything in the treaty that takes them away.

THE PRESIDENT: But the question is not put in that way, as was mentioned by Mr. Justice Gray. The question is put in the affirmative form, and not in the negative form.

SENATOR ROOT: I do not think it matters much, Mr. President, whether it is put in the affirmative or the negative. Your answer has to be affirmative or negative.

SIR CHARLES FITZPATRICK: That is the difficulty.

SENATOR ROOT: You say they are entitled, or they are not entitled. Your answer relates to the treaty. They are entitled, if at all, not by virtue of the treaty, but by virtue of these privileges having been accorded to the class which is the postulate. Of course, they had those unless there is something in the treaty to lead you to answer this question in the negative. You cannot find a negative to this question unless you find the ground for it in the treaty. That is the position.

SIR CHARLES FITZPATRICK: What would be the effect, now, if this question were put in the way you suggested at the beginning, so as to cover the case of a trading vessel going direct from an American port to a Newfoundland port, discharging her cargo and then proceeding to fish? I think there is only one answer possible to it. Any inhabitant of the United States may fish from a trading vessel under those circumstances; he may fish from a raft or from a balloon, or any other means of conveyance he may have. But let us look at the question. If that question is answered in the affirmative, what would be the result? The result would be that this Tribunal would declare that the inhabitants of the United States whose vessels resort to the treaty coast for the purpose of exercising the liberties referred to in Article 1 of the treaty of 1818 are entitled to have for those vessels when duly authorized by the United States in that behalf the commercial privileges on the treaty coasts accorded by agreement or otherwise to United States trading vessels generally. That would be the result. In my opinion that would mean that a fishing vessel, licensed to fish, could go up there and exercise her fishing right, and then, if authorized by the United States, would be entitled to supplement her action as a fishing vessel and become a trading vessel; and in the interval, of course, the Hovering Acts and all these other acts would not apply to her, so long as she remained a fishing vessel. Putting the case the other way about, instead of sending your trading vessels direct to Newfoundland and then afterwards having them act as fishing vessels, this question here, in my judgment, as I see it now, presupposes the action of the fishing vessel coming up to Newfoundland and then afterwards being converted into a trading vessel.

SENATOR ROOT: Of course, trading privileges are subject to the regulations appropriate to secure the proper conduct and the proper exercise of the trading privileges. There can be no claim of a right to trade on the part of a vessel which does not conform to those regulations; and the regulation against hovering, the regulation which requires a trading vessel to come directly into the port in which it is to trade would apply equally to any vessel that seeks the privilege of trading which has also purposed to fish, as to any vessel which has not. It is perfectly within the competency of Newfoundland to say to any vessel which has not come direct from port to port that it cannot trade. The moment the vessel applies for the trading privilege, it subjects itself to all the limitations upon that privilege; and it must not have disqualified itself by any conduct which is in contravention of those regulations.

This concludes the argument which I had in mind to make, and I beg to express, on behalf of the counsel and the agent of the United States, our very high appreciation of the attentiveness and consideration and courtesy with which we have been received and heard by the Tribunal.

THE NORRIS PE

WASHINGTON, D. C.

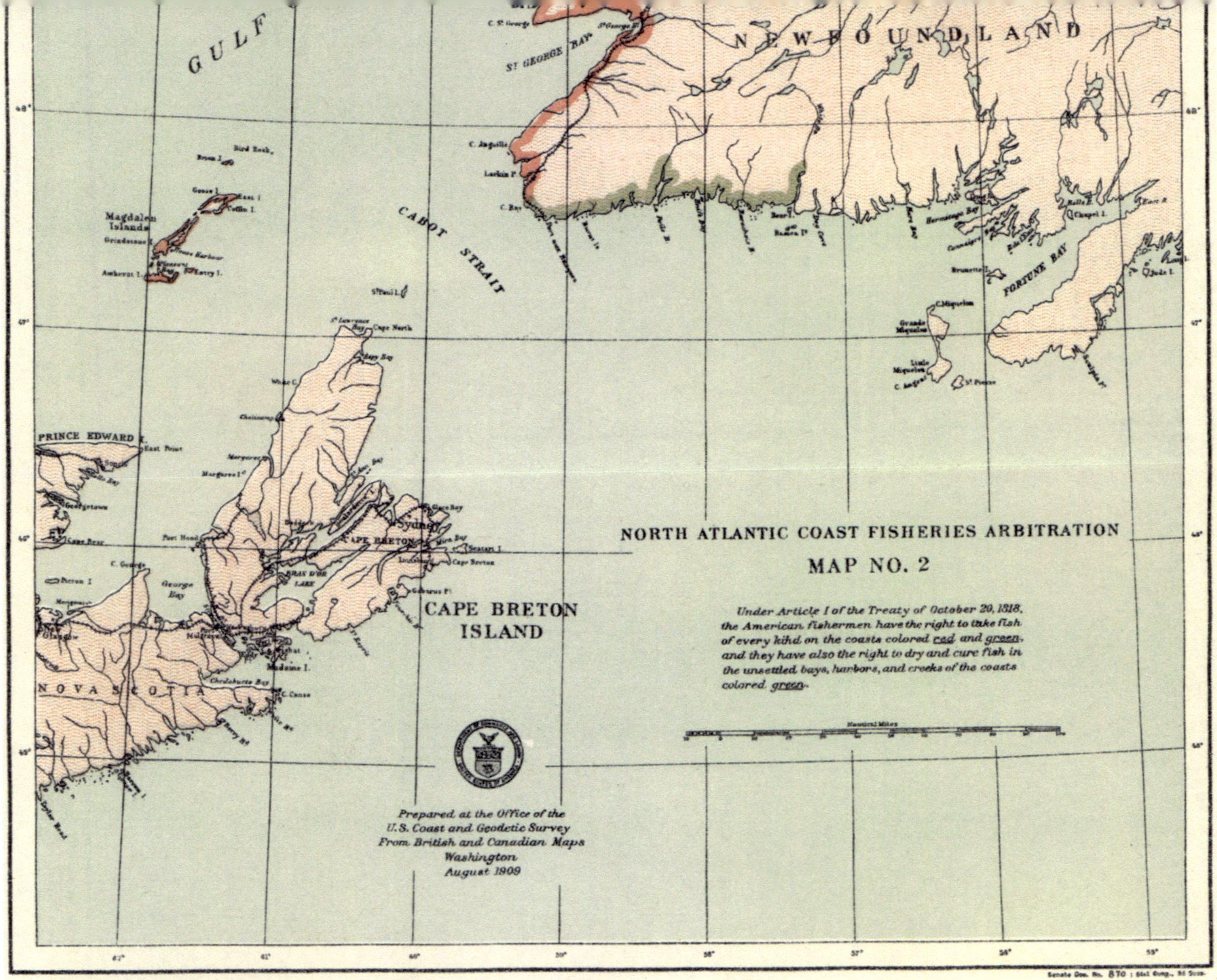

Senate Doc. No. 870 : 61st Cong., 3d Sess.

THE NORRIS PETERS CO., WASHINGTON, D. C.

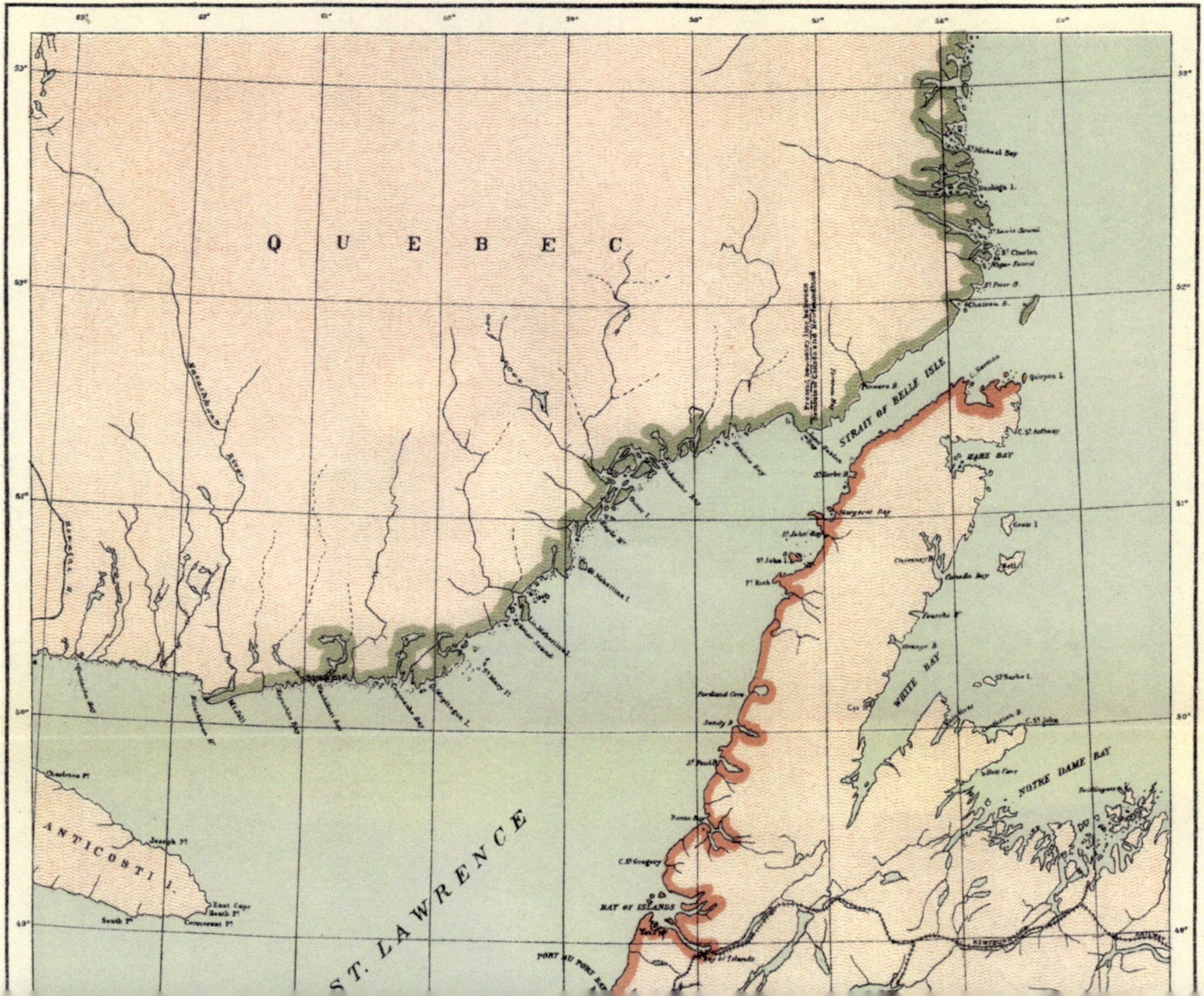
QUEBEC
ANTICOSTI I.
ST. LAWRENCE
STRAIT OF BELLE ISLE
WHITE BAY
NOTRE DAME BAY
HARE BAY
BAY OF ISLANDS
Present boundary line between Dominion of Canada and Newfoundland
St. Michael Bay
St. Lewis Sound
C. St. Charles
Chateau B.
C. Norman
Quirpon I.
C. St. Anthony
St. Barbe B.
St. Margaret Bay
St. John B.
St. John I.
Pt. Rich
Canada Bay
Groix I.
Bell I.
Portland Cove
Sandy B.
St. Paul's B.
C. St. Gregory
C. St. John
St. Barbe I.
East Cape
Heath Pt.
South Pt.
Cormorant Pt.
Joseph Pt.
Charleton Pt.

INDEX

INDEX

PRINTED AT
THE HARVARD UNIVERSITY PRESS
CAMBRIDGE, MASS., U.S.A.

Bei Fragen zur Produktsicherheit wenden Sie sich bitte an:
If you have any questions regarding product safety,
please contact:

Walter de Gruyter GmbH
Genthiner Straße 13
10785 Berlin
productsafety@degruyterbrill.com